Past Lives
Future Choices

PAST LIVES
FUTURE CHOICES

THE ASTROLOGY OF REINCARNATION

MARITHA POTTENGER

International Standard Book Number 0-935127-54-2

Cover design by Daryl Fuller

Published by ACS Publications
5521 Ruffin Road
San Diego, CA 92123-1314

First Printing, August 1997
Second Printing, January 1998

TABLE OF CONTENTS

CHAPTER TEN
PAST LIFE SCENARIOS: PLUTO

CHAPTER ELEVEN
SATURN: MAJOR KARMIC KEY

CHAPTER TWELVE
PAST LIFE SCENARIOS: SATURN

**Dedicated
to
Marc
with Love —**

for all we've done together in the past
and all we'll do together in the future.

CHAPTER ONE

BACKGROUND ON REINCARNATION

For many people, the idea that we have lived before (and will live again) makes sense. It helps to explain why some people come into life as child prodigies. (They have practiced their talents before and honed their skills to great heights.) Reincarnation is one possible explanation for *deja vu*: "This feels familiar. I know this place/these people, yet I've never been here/met them in this life-time." Past lives seem to offer insight into deeply ingrained psychological patterns with which people deal. Some individuals have mastered phobias or difficult emotional blockages by making connections to events and experiences in previous lifetimes.

Reincarnation Research

Reincarnation is not something that can be "proved" (or disproved) in the strict scientific sense. (Alternate hypotheses are possible: telepathy, racial memory, etc.) Nonetheless, some dedicated scientists are investigating the field. The most impressive anecdotal evidence comes from researchers who have studied the spontaneous memories of young children. Ian Stevenson has looked at instances when young children can lead researchers to and through villages those children never saw before in the current lifetime. The children recognize and call by name people whom they have known "before."

In one case, a young girl recognized her best friend from the previous life and called that friend by a **secret, pet name known only to the two of them** (in that previous life). In another case, a child led the investigators to a stash of valuables which he had hidden in the previous life (and no one in the family had been able to find). In some cases in India, the memories are threatening to the family of this lifetime as the child who is recalling a past life may be more emotionally attached to that former family than the family of this lifetime!

Trends Suggested by Studies of Spontaneous Recall

There are a few trends suggested by cases of spontaneous childhood memories.

(1) There is **no universal pattern or "rule" about how long between incarnations**. There is, however a tendency. The younger a person dies, the sooner that person tends to return to another life—often within a few months or years.

(2) Souls appear to "hang out" together. People often (**not** always!) will come back to a **similar cultural group**, often to the **same geographic area** as the last time around. It seems somewhat common for individuals to return to the **same family** (albeit in different roles each time).

One case which is suggestive of reincarnation involved a young girl who, as soon as she could toddle, would go around the house grabbing certain knickknacks and saying, "Mine!" The knickknacks the young girl grabbed all had been inherited from a great aunt of the mother's. The mother noticed the behavior, but never said anything to the little girl. A bit later, the girl was listening as her older brother had a geography lesson. The mother was pointing on a map to a city in southern California, telling the boy that he had been born there. The little girl came up and said, "Where me born?" The mother replied: "Oh, you were born here also," pointing to that same city. "No!" declared the little girl. "Me not born there." So, the mother asked: "Well, where were you born?" The little girl took her finger across the map diagonally into New England, where the great aunt had been born, and said: "Me born there!"

Another case involved a young American woman who was almost diagnosed as retarded because she had such trouble learning how to speak. She was a so-so students for many years. Then, in high school, she took French, and learned it almost instantly. She also showed great facility for French cooking and French dressmaking. Again, no absolute proof exists, but we suspect that particular soul incarnated in France last time and found America a tough adjustment in the beginning!

(3) **There is no pattern in regard to gender across lifetimes**. Each person has his/her own individual pattern. Gender, like culture, often has a strong degree of continuity. One researcher told me that cases in the U.S., for example, seem to show about a 10% gender cross-over. So, we could say "on average" people do about 9 lifetimes with one sex before switching over to the other sex for a time. However, this is only an "average" with lots of individual variation. Furthermore, this changes from culture to culture. Certain cultures (Arabic) report **no** gender crossover. This is probably a combination: low levels of crossover with huge cultural pressure **not** to report any actual cases of cross-

over. Other cultures (Polynesian) report a **high** level of gender crossover. People are willing to flip from female to male and back to female without much concern.

Physical Evidence

One of the more impressive forms of "evidence" that comes close to pleasing a materialistic scientist comes through the connection of **marks on the body in this lifetime with traumas from the past**. Investigators are discovering that the emotional trauma of the past and will often carry "forward" into the present and people will be born with moles, birthmarks, or some kind of physical indication of where they suffered great bodily injury in the past. Someone who dies from a blade through the heart, for example, is born again with a birthmark in the exact spot the sword entered. Someone who is hanged is born with interlocking marks on the neck. This kind of example is not conclusive, but again, makes us think (or makes the shivers go up our spines).

Some therapists have been successful in treating chronic physical ailments by looking backward. Neckaches, for example, may relate to memories of hanging or strangling. A man with chronic back pain was helped considerably by remembering a life when he was run over by a wagon and suffered an agonizing death from a broken back. After "reliving" a previous death at age seven, beaten over the head with an iron bar by her father, a woman found her chronic migraines of this life disappeared. Stomach problems may relate to incredible terror from the past, or lives of dying from dysentery, poison, or starvation. Some individuals remember repeated wounds (over several lives) to the same area of the body which is "weak" in this lifetime.

Other Methods for Looking Back

Hypnosis, regression techniques, and imagery have been used to seek past-life memories. Astrology, too, has its traditions in regard to which factors might be indicative of former lifetimes. Dreams, movement, or highly emotional experiences have triggered what some people feel are "bleedthroughs" or "flashes" of a previous life.

There is a fair amount of literature already on the use of hypnosis to explore past lives. We also know that the hypnotist must strive for total objectivity. All of us have our own biases and can unconsciously affect the people with whom we interact. We know, for example, that people working with Freudian therapists tend to dream in with lots of Freudian symbolism, while individuals working with Jungian therapists have dreams full of archetypes and classic Jungian themes. A hypnotherapist or anyone doing past life regression could unconsciously (or consciously) sway the client. Yet there are also a number of cases of individuals who feel they have been greatly helped by the past-life memories which emerged through hypnosis or regression.

One case was a woman who had struggled for many, many years with overweight. During a regression, she recalled being trapped in a cave and starving to death. It was a major turning point for her in regard to her lifetime pattern of overweight.

"Flashbacks" or "bleedthroughs" can come in almost any setting. They may be quite brief (just a quick image) or rather emotionally elaborate. One woman had a flashback when she was doing yoga. She made a certain movement and, all of a sudden, she looked down and "saw" ragged clothes on an old man pushing a chair. She "knew" she was that old man and had the impression that he was in Russia, probably in a prison camp. That was the extent of her impression, but it was extremely vivid, and she believes she was that old man in another life.

A more dramatic case involves a woman who has been unable to wear necklaces of any sort all this lifetime. If she tried to wear necklaces or turtlenecks, her skin would break out in a rash. As an adult, this woman was having an argument with her spouse and he began to shake her and grabbed her throat. She had an immediate flashback to a previous life. What was eerie is that the flashback involved not only the same circumstances (a love triangle), but the same souls! The three people involved (the woman, her husband, the man with whom she was having an affair) were the same in this life as the life before. The time before, however, the woman's husband strangled her and threw her body in a lake. This time, she divorced him. So, we do see **some** progress!

Some people connect with possible past-life memories through dreams, visions, journaling or other forms of accessing the subconscious. If one accepts the theory that **all** memories do reside in our unconscious, then any method which opens the channel could lead to past-life remembrances. Of course, the experience of *deja vu* ("recognizing" someone you have never met; knowing a place you've never been) is often a clue to a past life experience. One case involves a woman pilot. She was flying in the Pacific, in an area in which she had never before flown, and told one of her mates (they were flying in a formation) that she felt she knew where the airport was. She pinpointed exactly an old runway which had been used during World War II. The woman believes she was a pilot in the Second World War and was shot down. She came back again, determined to be a pilot once more, but in a female body this time having to break more barriers to achieve her goal.

Another case involved an American who went to Italy to study art. One day he was visiting an Italian villa for the first time, and he began "freaking out" (along with his hosts) because the American art student "knew" the villa. He could identify rooms he'd never seen before, and "knew" that the garden had a very unusual door, and all sorts of details which he "couldn't" have known. Again, we could argue racial memory, or some unusual emotional residue in the walls of the villa itself, but reincarnation seems a more tidy explanation!

Astrology and Reincarnation

Astrology is another possible tool for looking backward. Certain astrological traditions associate parts of the horoscope with the past, including past lifetimes. Naturally, this is very speculative. As is usual with reincarnation, nothing can be "proved." However, I have had occasion to discuss certain astrological patterns with some of my clients who feel they have had past-life memories or bleedthroughs. Some of the parallels to astrological tradition are quite striking. One example was a woman whose chart suggested a great deal of artistic talent, but the likelihood of some issues around creativity. She had some placements which suggested the danger of blocking or devaluing her creativity, of feeling what she made was not good enough—even if others admired her creations. After the consultation, she told me that she had past life recall of two lifetimes as males in which she had the talent and ability to be a painter, but was afraid to take the risk. She chose to enter the "safe" family business even though she yearned to travel the path of an artist. In both those earlier lives, she worried that she would not be "good enough" to make it as a painter. Her horoscope reflected that issue very clearly.

All theories and approaches, however, are speculative. Since there is no way to "prove" reincarnation in a scientific fashion, to believe (or disbelieve) in other lives comes down to faith and assumptions. The material in this book is written from the assumption that reincarnation happens. The phrasing assumes that you have had past lives (and will have future ones). **The contents are therefore all theoretical**. In some cases you may identify literally with possibilities which are given. In other cases, you may relate more to a lifetime on a metaphorical level. Some sections may "resonate" more for you than others. I hope that you will use this material in the ways which suit you.

The speculations within this work are based on astrological traditions. Among the astrological traditions included here are:

(1) an examination of Saturn and the Moon's Nodes (considered "karmic" factors by most astrologers) in regard to major life lessons and ingrained psychological patterns [chapters 11, 12 and 13];

(2) an explanation of talents signified by stellia and other repeated themes in the chart [chapters 13 and 15];

(3) a discussion of each planet in sign with extra weight given to planets in and ruling the 4th, 8th, and 12th houses (considered keys to one's past lives) [chapters 2 -10 and 12];

(4) a look at potential karmic debts and karmic gifts (earned in past lifetimes) signified by aspects to karmic factors, intercepted, and retrograde planets [chapters 14 and 15].

It is my hope that illuminating your possible pasts will help you to cope better, choose more wisely, grow more rapidly, and enjoy yourself more fully in this lifetime!

of **continuity** (along with much continuity of culture as discussed in Chapter 1). People who are abused this lifetime usually have previous lives of being abused. Their karma is emotional residues (habit patterns) which incline them toward giving away their own power, not being sure of themselves, being too vulnerable to other people. They have **not** done anything bad for which they are being punished. They are merely reaping the consequences of a habit of victimhood! When we change our habit patterns (or ingrained ways of feeling and acting), we change our karma — and we alter our future as well.

People will often discuss "good karma" and "bad karma." Talents and abilities are usually "good karma." We come into a lifetime already skilled in certain respects because we've had lots of practice in the past. "Bad karma" is a matter of a dysfunctional behavior pattern; it is **not** a matter of guilt or punishment. I've heard some people make statements such as "You owe it to your alcoholic spouse to stay with him because last time you were the alcoholic and he stayed." I don't think that is true. Most of the time, people keep on doing the same thing as they've done before. If you are entangled in an alcoholic's life this time, the odds are that you were entangled in previous lives as well. The only "debt" you have is to recognize the pattern—and change it for the better. I've seen a number of relationships where the only real karmic lesson was learning how to **leave** (both emotionally and physically).

Some people experience a sense of a "karmic debt," that they feel drawn to go "above and beyond" for certain people. Although the occasional client remembers an actual debt of one sort or another, the feeling of indebtedness usually has more to do with the debtor's own nature. Many people who feel strongly indebted are caretaker types who have a series of lifetimes of carrying more than their fair share of the load. Rather than taking on more, they need to learn to share the burdens of life, to let other people have some responsibility.

What my experience shows me is a loving universe, one which offers us a multitude of tools for awareness and transformation. Suffering is **not** necessary. The more deeply, fully, and completely we come to understand ourselves, including submerged emotional reactions, the more fulfilling and happy our lives become.

Why Bother Looking Back?

As the proverb says: "Those who do not remember their history are doomed to repeat it." It is amazing to me how often people recreate the same scenarios— often with the same exact souls—over and over again. We see the cycles of loyalty and betrayal countless times. We see the cycles of the homebody and the explorer tearing each other's hearts repeatedly. We see a pattern over many lives of blocked creativity, or of endless intellectual curiosity, or of rebellion and becoming the outcast.

A number of issues appear to repeat for people:

Phobias: past-life memories have been linked to fear of animals, knives, hanging, drowning, fire, water, storms, volcanoes, people in uniform, etc. People remember burning, freezing, being buried alive, choking, etc.

Eating disorders or poverty scripts: past-life recollections of starvation, inescapable poverty, economic catastrophes, being put out to die in famine conditions, etc., may relate to current eating disorders or financial difficulties.

Family dynamics: past-life connections often shed light on current feelings of rivalry, Oedipal issues, fights about inheritance, favoritism, abuse, abandonment, betrayal, and so on. Marital strife may relate to inequities of the past— being of a different class as one's mate, or involvements of owner/slave or master/concubine spilling over from the past.

Sexual blockages: memories of celibacy or sexual abuse or torture (forced abortion, mutilation, human or child sacrifice, rape and other horrifying practices) often lurk in the past.

Depression: may be related to old memories of losing a loved one, of suicide, of disruptions through war, "ethnic cleansing", massacres and similar dislocations.

Excessive guilt: often connects to a sense of "I deserve this suffering" due to recollections of killing loved ones or feeling responsible for the deaths of others (e.g., the chief who fails to lead his people to freedom; human sacrifice; the military leader, the matriarch who cannot save everyone, etc.).

Violence: seems connected to our violent past. Many people remember lives as warriors or other adventurous, brutal, power-hungry activities.

Setting a Script: some people die with a certain thought/feeling in high focus. They appear to make that emotion/thought central in their next lives. For example, someone dying slowly due to an avalanche, quicksand, or a falling tree might come in with an attitude of: "I'll never make it. I'm stuck." An individual tortured to death as a witch remembers thinking: "What you say doesn't matter. No one will listen." and spends this lifetime with major blocks in terms of expression. People who lost their parents young in previous lives may enter with a script of: "I'm alone; I have to make it on my own." People who suffered from the betrayal of a loved one may enact a conviction that "You cannot trust men/women." People who had great physical pain, including torture, in the past may cut themselves off from sensation as much as possible: "I don't want to be in my body."

Looking back offers us the opportunity to understand the past, and to accept it and move on — releasing and letting go of old patterns. Then we have the hope of creating a better future!

Indeed, even if one does not accept the theory of reincarnation, reading about possible past lives can be helpful. It's a bit easier to identify with issues when they are "less personalized." And reading a story about some other time and place is just distant enough to make it easier for some clients to face certain challenges or acknowledge strengths. Thus, the material in this book can also be read on a metaphorical level, to help people cope better in this lifetime.

Psychology is just coming to terms with how much of our everyday life is run by our emotional habits, including unconscious ones. And those emotional residues have their roots in our past—including past lives. The better we understand ourselves, the more we can transform ourselves and create new habit patterns. The goal is growth, letting go of negative patterns and strengthening positive ones.

With that in mind, let's take a look at some of the habit patterns depicted by your horoscope!

CHAPTER TWO
PAST LIFE SCENARIOS: SUN

I have discussed past lives in the chart with a number of clients and students, particularly in cases when people do have recall—either spontaneously or through regression or other techniques. The interpretations here are based on the feedback I have gotten. The exact details of place or time may or may not be true, but the themes implied within the horoscope seem to resonate strongly for people. Naturally, the scenarios set here are speculative, but if they suggest more positive ways to direct your future, they have served their purpose! Read the section in this chapter which relates to the sign occupied by your Sun.

January 21	-	February 19	**Aquarius**	♒
February 20	-	March 20	**Pisces**	♓
March 21	-	April 20	**Aries**	♈
April 21	-	May 20	**Taurus**	♉
May 21	-	June 21	**Gemini**	♊
June 22	-	July 22	**Cancer**	♋
July 23	-	August 23	**Leo**	♌
August 24	-	September 23	**Virgo**	♍
September 24	-	October 23	**Libra**	♎
October 24	-	November 23	**Scorpio**	♏
November 23	-	December 22	**Sagittarius**	♐
December 22	-	January 20	**Capricorn**	♑

Remember, depending upon leap years and the time you were born, your Sun Sign may not be what appears in this table. If you were born two days before or after any of the dates in this table, it is best to have your actual horoscope calculated. (See back of book to get a FREE horoscope.)

Some people resonate with several karmic issues, as if they came in to work on many challenges this lifetime. Although one past-life description is usually more significant than the others, you are not limited to just one. You may have come in with a dual (or even a triple) focus. Trust what feels familiar to you. The scenarios that feel like memories pinpoint issues of importance to you.

In astrological tradition, the element of water (which is associated with emotions, depth of perception, the subconscious, sensitivity, and loss of boundaries) is a key to the past. Particularly the water houses of the horoscope—the 4th, 8th, and 12th—are considered keys to past lives. Tradition has it that your 12th house (planets in it and rulers of the 12th) depicts your most recent past life or lives. The 8th and 4th houses are traditionally associated with the "more distant" past. Some people believe the 8th house is the furthest back, while others say the 4th house represents our most distant past lives. As a result of my work with clients, I would say that "most recent" should be read as "most relevant to your current life." That is, 12th-house indicators speak to a past life (or lives) which involved themes and issues still impacting your current life. The 4th-house and 8th-house indicators are sometimes not as significant for you at this time.

Scenarios in this chapter would be extra relevant for you if you have the Sun occupying your 4th, 8th, or 12th house or if you have Leo on the cusp or intercepted in any of those houses. (If your Sun conjuncts a ruler of the 4th, 8th, or 12th, I would also count that as a "hit.") However, people who do not have the Sun occupying or ruling one of the water houses have found these descriptions meaningful. So, **read all the scenarios which apply to the sign of your Sun.**

☉ Sun in Aries ♈

Rough and Ready

You were a real risk-taker. As a youth, you went "where angels fear to tread." You enjoyed pushing the limits — especially physically. You had many more than your share of scrapes, bruises and broken bones. You got a thrill out of taking chances. In fights, you didn't care if your opponent was bigger; you couldn't resist a challenge. When you were old enough, you went off to war and became a hero. Your reckless ways earned you medals, but wreaked havoc with your body. Some of your wounds led to actual physical impairment. You demanded the impossible of yourself and eventually paid the price, dying on the battlefield.

Dangerous Questions

You served the Spanish king well in the Army and earned a reputation for great cunning in addition to bravery in battles against the Moors. Your quick wits saved your troops on several occasions. Eager to learn, you talked to everyone you could in an effort to expand your knowledge. Posted to Madrid, your duties came to include escorting heretics to the stake to be burned. You were troubled and began to ask questions. Because of your excellent military record, some leeway was given, but eventually the Inquisition caught you in its toils as well. You perished for the crime of wanting to know more.

Parental Surrogate

Your parents were carried away by the plague when you were only 7. You went to work doing whatever odd jobs you could, and farmed your three younger siblings out to different aunts and uncles. You lived on the streets—barely surviving. Then fortune came your way. An old man-at-arms adopted you and trained you for service with a great lord. You continued to feel responsible for your two sisters and brother, and helped them out financially as much as you could. Distinguishing yourself with great bravery, you earned cash bonuses and prize money which went almost entirely to your family. Even after your sisters married and your brother was of age, you helped to support them, never taking a wife or starting your own family. Everything you did was oriented toward protecting your siblings from life's harsh realities.

What Price Heroism?

You grew up as a pretty, sociable, fun-loving young lady. As was expected, you married and had three children. One day, while you and your family were having a picnic, a bull which had escaped a neighboring farm charged your youngest child who had wandered off a bit. Your husband was paralyzed with horror, but you were able to act. Running all out, you managed to snatch your child out of harm's way, but were struck a glancing blow by one of the bull's hooves. The neighbor saw everything from too far away to help, but managed to reach you in time to distract and eventually capture the bull. The neighbor told everyone around how brave you were. Your husband brooded over what happened and began to put you down more and more. He couldn't stand being married to a "heroine." Nothing you could do was right. Eventually, your marriage degenerated to a state of siege. You stayed because of the children, but dreamt of freedom.

Never Enough for Dad

Born into a military family and being a dutiful son, you naturally followed tradition and joined the Army.(With your father of that time, any other course would have been unthinkable.) Physically gifted, you did well in your training and maneuvers. When a conflict boiled up in the south of China, you volunteered for hazardous duty. In battle, you covered yourself with distinction. You came home to find your father could not be satisfied. He picked at everything you did. No matter how well you performed your duties, he focused on something you could have done better. Regardless of the tremendous respect you earned from your peers and superiors, your father proclaimed loudly and often that you weren't "good enough." Although you tried not to let it bother you, his fessed minister. He played on your sympathies and you gave large amounts of money to him, thinking it was going to charity. When you found out the truth—that he was keeping almost all of it, your disillusionment felt crushing. You died shortly thereafter.

☉ Sun in Gemini ♊

Denied Dependency

A curious and courageous young woman, you took one of the few professional paths available and became a schoolteacher in the unsettled West. In one of the frontier mining towns, you met and married a local businessman. Although the town did not fully approve of a married school teacher, they had no one else, so let you keep the job. The next 10 years included six miscarriages. You were anguished, really wanting a baby, and became convinced that something was wrong with the town water—perhaps due to the nearby mines. Before you could persuade your husband to consider a move, he was accidentally shot by a drunken prospector. You moved away, but avoided close relationships. You continued to teach, but did not get as close to your students as before. Ties hurt too much when broken.

A Challenging Choice

As a young child, you were forever bringing home wounded birds, hurt dogs and cats—all the forsaken animals in the neighborhood. Your parents encouraged your solicitude. You trained as a teacher and took a position in an institution dealing with deaf, dumb, and blind children. The salary was pitiful, but you had amazing successes with the children and grew to love many of them very deeply. While working there, you met an interesting, ambitious young man. He was working his way up in business and planning to move further West where development was occurring at a rapid pace. You two fell in love and he asked you to marry him and move West. (The institution's rules forbade married women to work there.) Although you loved your young man, you felt you could not leave "your" children so you stayed—forever.

Shared Satire

Blessed with an observant eye and a satirical wit, you were quite an entertaining child. When you grew old enough to draw, you became skilled at dashing off caricatures and other quick sketches to illustrate people's foibles and prick their pomposities. Your parents were sympathetic, but warned against revealing your talents to the outside world where such "unladylike" behavior would be condemned. Nonetheless, you successfully submitted some cartoons to local newspapers (under a pseudonym). You fell madly in love with, and soon married, a political columnist. Although he'd seemed to admire your abilities while courting, once you were married everything changed. He became critical. He would find flaws in everything you did. Several times you noticed in his column insights which you had brought to his attention. Supporting his career was OK; supporting yours was not. Feeling trapped, you went underground with your skills and hid them from your husband.

Woman of Wisdom

You were one of the local wise women during the "burning times." Skilled with herbs, midwifery, and a worship of nature, you were a teacher to young women. Full of wonder for the beauty of nature, you loved conveying the excitement of learning to the maidens you taught. Ever curious, you sought out strangers, and anyone and everyone who could teach you something. Expansion of your knowledge was a constant goal. You also dabbled in white magic—or the use of directed will and intent to achieve constructive results. But this was a time when women of wisdom were often viewed with suspicion. When a nearby farmer's cattle started dying—for no apparent reason—the cry of "witch" was soon raised. You refused to flee, holding firm to your innocence, but dying within the flames.

Kindling Knowledge

Born with a hunger for information, you pursued knowledge throughout your life. After training, you became a tutor. Your final position was tutor to the youngest son of the local king. You were very conscientious and strove to instill ethical and moral principles, a conscience, and empathy as well as facts and figures. You became very close to your charge. Then, disaster struck! The king and his two older sons perished in a shipwreck. Your young charge was king now (with a regent until he came of age). He wanted you around, but the people of power in the court were opposed to your influence. You were offered a considerable bribe to depart, but you felt you owed your allegiance to the young king-to-be (and his subjects), so you stayed. So, the nobles threatened by your impact on the young man had you assassinated.

Thirst for Knowledge

As a child, your first impulse was to take things apart. You dismembered flowers and pried all manner of objects into little pieces. Oddly enough, you respected animal life. You never tried to figure out the components of a dog or any other beasts. You devoured books and you grew, and asked many questions of everyone you met. You elected tutoring as a profession, which left you time to devote to your true love: invention. Your neighbors viewed you as quite eccentric. You voiced ideas they considered quite strange. The two explosions in your workshop didn't help matters. (Fortunately no one was hurt.) People began to avoid you, and you didn't get any new students. Although you made barely enough money to survive, you continued seeking your breakthrough in terms of human flight.

you conducted several secret affairs. The women were kept cloistered until it was determined they were not pregnant, and then sent off to another country. You knew then that you would never have children of your own and felt a failure to yourself, your parents, and your country.

Disabled Distinction

Born into a minor royal family in India, you were raised to be a beautiful wife. Despite your longings to create, to achieve, to shine in the world, you were taught to be in the background, promoting your husband. You had, of course, no choice in the selection of your spouse. The marriage was based on politics and the division of power and property. Your husband was not a cruel man, but neither was he kind. He was actually a rather weak individual who would have been better suited to a life of contemplation. His favorite pursuit of poring over old manuscripts. You wielded some influence, but not enough. Despite the pampered life you had, you were frustrated. With your ambition, you could have accomplished a great deal, but that path was denied to you as a woman.

Restricted Ruler

In the ancient times of matriarchy in Mesopotamia, you were a priestess/queen. Your kingdom was peaceful, with much commerce and material prosperity. You helped to support the arts and literature and even turned your own hand to poetry on occasion. Alas, barbarian warriors from the north invaded your realm. Your people were more traders, business people, and farmers than warriors, and were no match for the fierce Aryan nomad warriors. You were taken prisoner and forcibly wed and raped by the leader of the invaders. In chains, you were presented to your people as the queen, with the invader pronounced king in the eyes of all.

Conflicts and Changes

Raised to be an African chief, your father prepared you well for your role. He taught you to listen to everyone, but make up your own mind. Your mother taught you to pay attention to your heart and to look to the least among your people for the state of your rule. Your father had a heart attack when you were only 22, so you became chief. But the tribal elders had much control within your realm. You were young and impatient, eager to make changes. You envisioned more diverse representation on the tribal councils. You wanted to get younger people more involved. Of course, the old guard resisted your desires. Your life became a constant struggle to bring more openness and freedom into the government. You lost many battles, but won a few.

Martyred Monarch

Although of royal blood, you felt the call of the Spirit from a young age. As soon as you could, you took your vows to the Church and entered a monastery. There you spent 20 years in seclusion, worshipping nature and the other glories of God. With a knack for herbs and medicines, you advanced the knowledge of that time. Alas, in the outer world warfare had decimated the royal house and you were left the closest descendant to the throne. A collection of nobles convinced your abbots you must serve as king and then descending upon you in the monastery. Although you shrank from the task, you felt constrained to do what you could to help heal the wounded land and try to bring peace to your subjects. The reality of what you could accomplish fell far short of your dreams, but you continued trying—even though you missed your life of quite contemplation to your dying day.

☉ Sun in Virgo ♍

Suffering Sibling

The eldest of 8 children, you were expected to supervise your younger siblings from a fairly early age. When your parents were working in the fields, it was up to you to ride herd on all the children. Several of your siblings were rambunctious and delighted in making life difficult for you. One day, a younger brother snuck away to play in the nearby river. The other kids milled around enough to cover his absence for a time. When you discovered what had happened, you couldn't leave to go after him as that would mean deserting the other six children. Worried, you eventually asked your next-oldest sister to watch over the other five children. When you got to the river, you discovered your younger brother had waded too far, and drowned. Grief-stricken and guilty, you never recovered from the loss. To the end of your days, you felt you owed something to your parents, your other siblings and the brother that died.

Punitive Parents

You were a dutiful child who loved to be of service. Your parents reacted by putting you to work young. Many were the tasks you were expected to accomplish. As bosses, your parents were impossible to satisfy. No matter how hard you tried, they found some flaw in your performance. They criticized everything you did. Although you worked very hard, their attitude toward you was grudging. You felt they only kept you around because you were useful. Their harshness affected your self-esteem. You started to feel worthless and insignificant. The more they put your down, the more convinced you became that you were an incompetent individual. You became more and more depressed, believing no one cared if you lived or died. At the instant of your passing (due to a farm accident), the thought flashed through your head: "I don't really matter."

Fatal Attraction

Born a serf, you labored in the fields from an early age. Close to the earth, you had a special affinity for green, growing things. Plants flourished around you—even when the soil was poor. Eventually even the master noticed a difference between the lands where you toiled and the areas tilled by other serfs. He put you to work longer hours, and the greening of his lands increased. On one of your forays, you noticed an attractive young woman, and snatched a few moments of conversation each time you saw her. She seemed to respond well to you. Eventually, you worked up your courage to ask your lord if you could take her to wife. His first query was how having a family would affect your work. You assured him all would be well and he eventually gave his permission. But when you went to look for your love, she had disappeared. Suspecting foul play, but powerless to object, you resolved never to look at another woman.

Steadfast Service

A humble servant, you felt strongly the glory of God. You tithed faithfully to your Church and often gave extra which you could ill afford. Some of your friends pointed out the less-than-priestly manner of some of the Church's representatives, but you wanted dearly to believe the best in your spiritual advisors. When you were exhorted to contribute more to charity, you did. Whatever the priests requested, you gave. Even though it meant you sometimes suffered dearly with inadequate heat, clothing (and sometimes food), your faith was so strong, you could not imagine keeping for yourself what went to the glory of God. You continued, lifelong, to deny yourself basic necessities in order to contribute to your Church.

Serve and Suffer

Eager to prove your worth, you joined a sect which promoted suffering as a path to God. You and a small group of fellows ate a diet barely adequate to sustain life, labored long hours in fields, gardens, masonry, barrel making and other arduous activities. You slept at night with hair shirts. Poverty and self-denial were a way of life. The more you could do without, the more spiritual you were assumed to be. Physically, you suffered greatly. Emotionally, you felt an incredible sense of accomplishment. Even when you became very ill, you continued your demanding regime. Eventually, the stress was just too much for your body, and you perished at a young age.

Intuitive Overload

Even as a child, you were sensitive to the suffering of people around you. Although herbs were primarily "women's work," you learned their properties in order to assist people who were in pain. You considered training as a physician, but felt it wasn't really possible financially. Instead, you became a nurse and served during the Crimean War. The carnage was awful—far worse than anything you'd imagined. You were overwhelmed and could barely cope. After a few weeks, you had to escape. You were so open to everything around you, it seemed you were absorbing the pains of all the wounded. You returned home, retreated to the country, and avoided taking care of any but the most minor of ailments or injuries.

☉ Sun in Libra ♎

Beauty's Burden

You were an actress admired for her beauty as well as talent. Because actresses were equated with prostitutes, you could not just follow your muse. You were constantly subjected to demands from male theater goers, owners, and patrons. Having very little power, you mostly gritted your teeth and hid your anger. Much of the time, you were furious that you were not allowed to just be yourself and pursue your abilities. The world discounted your talent because you were female, seeing you as just another "pretty face." You knocked yourself out seeking professional respect, but the doors of the world were closed.

A Bursting Nest

Following in the footsteps of your father, you became a silver smith. You loved working with the beauty of the metal and creating lovely tea services and other objects of great worth and splendor. Making attractive pieces moved you greatly. Marrying young, you and your wife proceeded to raise a family. Your wife proved exceptionally fertile, and your family grew larger and larger. As your number of progeny increased, you feelings of pressure did as well. You could envision how to provide for 20 children! You did your best, but resources were limited. Feeling guilty, you tried to meet all the needs of your family, but it was simply impossible. In the end, you had to send some of your children to be fostered by other relatives. You never got over the guilt.

Creative Block

Born into a family of artists, you showed an eye for color at a young age. Your interests drew you to dress designer and you became quite popular among the nobles of the court. Although your work was very demanding, you also managed to marry. Despite everything you and your husband could do, however, you did not conceive. As the years rolled by, you became more and more depressed, blaming yourself for the lack of children. You felt like a failure. Eventually, even your artistic ability dried up. You withdrew, unable to create anything, spending your days sunk in doldrums, hardly moving.

Excluding Intimacy

Your parents had a miserable marriage—full of abuse, fights, and much destructiveness. You spent as much time as possible away from home. At one point of your wanderings, you came across a glass blower, and were enchanted. The delicate beauty of his creations appealed greatly to you, so you apprenticed to him. Eventually, you were capable of making very lovely objects as well. Fanciful figures were a favorite with you, although goblets and such were the bread-and-butter portion of your business. You avoided marriage. Despite feeling lonely and wishing for a family, you were convinced a happy marriage would not be possible for you, so refused to try.

Rules and Restrictions

You struggled against the limits from the day you were born. When swaddled into the boards on which you were carried as an infant, you protested loudly. You wanted to run before you could walk. The expectations of your tribe were very confining. Everything in which you expressed interest, it seemed, was not done! Drawn to pottery, you were told that pottery and weaving were women's work, and unsuitable for a young boy's interest. Spending all day observing the behavior of a colony of ants was considered a waste of time. Your father worked very hard at redirecting your curiosity toward approved channels. You eventually learned not to do what you wanted, but to fit in. As a result, you were a very disciplined, self-restraining adult. You came to expect that if you wanted something, you probably couldn't have it.

Fatal Faith

Drawn to beauty, you explored many different aesthetic pathways. Eventually, you settled on singing. Your voice had exceptional clarity and range, and many came to hear you perform. Likened to an angel, you had a strong attraction to religious selections. One night, you dreamt that an angel of the lord came to you. He "told" you that you were ready to rise above your physical existence and become an angel yourself—that you could leave the flesh behind and join the spirit. You took that to mean you should stop eating—and did. Slowly, you wasted away. The remonstrations of others did not move you. Convinced your destiny awaited, you perished.

☉ Sun in Scorpio ♏

Basic Blocks

You were a Greek courtesan, renowned for your sharp wit as well as sultry seductiveness. You held court regularly, impressing your admirers with your depth of insight. Yet you were female and society had a very narrow niche for you. Frustration dogged your heels because many things which you wished to do were forbidden by virtue of your gender. You fought against the prevailing views by being brilliant, intuitive and impressive. But you knew always it was a losing battle.

Sensual Satisfaction

You were a priestess at Dodona. You read the rustling of the leaves of the oaks to peer into the future and answer questions posed by the faithful. Surrounded by the beauty of nature, your work involved a feast of the senses. Appetite control was vital for your intuitive insights, but what you ate was only the best—the most satisfying and highest quality of food and drink. You wore beautiful robes which caressed your body sensually. You often slept under the stars at night, enjoying the connection to nature.

Selfless Service

You were a priestess in the temple of Hestia, charged with helping to keep the hearth fires burning. Cleanliness was essential and you labored long to keep the temple scrupulously clear of dirt or imperfection. Eager to be of service to people, you often went above and beyond the call of duty in your efforts to answer people's questions and concerns. Very humble and self-effacing, you kept yourself in the background and worked hard.

Irresistible Attraction

You were a priestess in the temple of Isis who became obsessed with one of the pharaoh's advisers. You dreamt of the man night and day, and were consumed by the desire to get close to him. He was promised to another, but you felt compelled to seek him out. When he proved impervious to your charms, you turned to witchcraft and black magic. You researched love potions and sought out incantations to weave a spell of attraction. One of your subordinates realized what was going on and reported you to the authorities. You were convicted of sorcery based on your activities and sentenced to death.

Twisted Truths

You were a priest who followed the teachings of Paul of Damascus. With fervor, you preached the dangers of women, and the necessity of the man remaining the head of the household. You traveled about, spreading the gospel. Although some people questioned your beliefs and values, you remained convinced that you knew the truth. Everywhere you insisted that women were weak-willed, less intelligent, childlike individuals who needed to molded and guided by men.

Women's Welfare

A priestess in service to The Great Mother, you were particularly dedicated to serving women. As a midwife, you helped women prepare for and undergo childbirth. As an herbalist, you saved the lives of women and children. As a counselor, you helped people to make choices. You lived in unstable times. Although yours were the ways of peace, your land was invaded by men whose ways were the ways of war. They brought fire, rape, and pillage. You perished trying to save one of the children you had delivered from a burning hut.

☉ **Sun in Sagittarius** ♐

Relative Rivalry

Born into a minor principality in Central Asia, you became a ruler fairly young when your father died. You had a number of younger siblings, who spent much time conspiring against you. Dynastic in-fighting became quite intense. You cared about your siblings, but were worried about your crown. You consulted with many wise advisors, had your priests read the omens, and prayed for strong. You found yourself torn between science and religion. Searching and seeking, you could not decide who to believe. You very much wanted to know the structure of the universe, and the meaning of life. Different world views pulled at you, but you could not decide what to follow. You remained torn, tasting and trying on many different beliefs, but never quite finding a faith that felt satisfactory to you.

Bad Company

Born into the French nobility, you were educated to become a conformable wife—all that was expected of women of your class. Although you had a talent for a witty phrase and wicked caricatures, your function was to make a good alliance and bear sons to your husband. In due course, you went with your husband to court. Although you were somewhat perturbed by rumblings in the country, your husband pooh-poohed your worries. The two of you were imprisoned with many other members of the French court and ended up perishing at the hands of Madame Guillotine.

Dream Life

Born into the Chinese upper class, you led a sheltered life. Education and ample material goods were at your fingertips. Due to your family's position, you rarely saw true poverty and imagined that it was a rare occurrence. You developed an idealized view of your society, thinking that rationality and fairness were widespread. Unable to cope with "real life," you withdrew more and more, staying in the world of books and fantasy. Refusing to see the ugliness that existed, you insisted on believing in a land of beauty, truth, and justice.

☉   Sun in Aquarius   ♒

Shut Out

Born dumb into a family that did not understand, you were dismissed as stupid for many years. Although you eventually grasped the language of the people around you, the ability to form intelligible words was beyond you. So, no one ever heard anything you had to say. You felt extremely cut-off and isolated from everyone. Although some interchange was possible with gestures, it was quite limited. You went through life feeling as though you had no real connection to the world around you.

Denying Dependency

Your mother became quite ill when you were ten, so you took on the burdens of the family. Becoming surrogate mother to your four younger siblings, you also nursed your mother for 16 years until she died. Your father depended upon you to manage all matters of the household. Your brothers and sisters looked to you as the strong, capable person. Having lost your childhood young, you developed a pattern of avoiding dependency. Refusing to lean on anyone else, you were comfortable only when independent or in the role of caretaker.

Without Wedding

Born female in a time when husbands had absolute sway over wives, you saw your father totally dominate your mother. She had to ask permission to do anything and was totally squelched. Despite pressures to conform and become a biddable young woman, you were determined not to marry. You scouted out the possibilities before you decided housekeeping was your best bet. Your family had trained you well (for "marriage") in that regard. By dint of careful suggestions, your father decided that having you work for a time as a housekeeper might be preferable to paying out a dowry to a man who would wed you. The position you obtained was not ideal, but you felt it was better than staying at home or being forced to marry.

Executed Explorer

Born female, you had a lust for adventure. Although your family tried to suppress it, your drive to explored could not be destroyed. As a young teen-ager, you took to the road. Cutting your hair short, you passed yourself off as a boy and began wandering the world. Dissatisfied with the culture in which you were raised, you visited many other lands, paying particular attention to their beliefs and values. You knew you were looking for something, but you were not sure quite what. In one rough and ready frontier, your sex was discovered. The men reacted with outrage to your invasion of their territory and you were raped and killed.

Rash and Rebellious

As a youth, questioning authority just came naturally. To you, the old ways seemed hidebound and inefficient. Whatever exciting new ideas were around, you were in favor. Tribal elders counseled more wisdom, caution, and moving slowly into change, but you were impatient. You would rush in—sometimes endangering others as well as yourself. Eager to alter, ready to rebel, you kept on pushing and pushing. After many warnings, you were banished — rejected by your people for your unwillingness to conform.

Illusive Ideals

You fell in love with an ideal. The philosophy of Rousseau had a great appeal to you. Enamored with the idea of a "natural man," you sought far and wide for the innate perfection in which you believed. But what you observed was tremendous imperfection. Even young children did not inevitably exhibit truth, love, and beauty. You continued to write essays and promote the ideas, but began to question your dreams. The older you got, the more you wondered if your entire lifework was built on shifting, unstable sands.

CHAPTER THREE
PAST LIFE SCENARIOS: MOON

The format of this chapter follows the format of Chapter Two. Read all the possibilities for your Moon sign, but give most weight to those which seem familiar to you. (If you don't know your Moon sign, send for the free chart from Astro which will tell you.)

☽ Moon in Aries ♈

Financial Frustration

You worked very hard as a laundress. Your duties were very physically demanding with hot water, strong soaps, and lots of back-breaking rubbing as well as lifting heavy pots of slippery water. You were paid little for your efforts, but not much else was available to women in the way of work. (You were unwilling to consider prostitution as a career path.) You felt guilty that you could not provide more for your family, but your financial circumstances were just too limited.

Severed Self-Esteem

Trapped in an unhappy marriage (arranged by your parents), you longed for a child whom you could love. After many years of trying, a son was born. He, however, was quite an independent tike. Even as a baby, he loved to explore. The older he became, the more wanted to wander off and do things by himself. You were hurt, feeling he didn't really love or care for you. The more self-reliant he became, the more your self-esteem plummeted. You saw yourself as a failure as a wife and as a mother and didn't believe that anyone truly loved you.

Perennial Prison

Born female, you did not fit in well. Independent, even as a youngster, you didn't do the acceptable feminine things. You enjoyed taking objects apart (and putting them together) rather than playing with dolls. You liked being alone. Your father tried to "beat some sense into you," but you wouldn't change. Although you hoped for marriage to someone more tolerant, the only "suitable" men (in your parents eyes) were cut from the same cloth. The man you ended up finally marrying was initially OK, but became less tolerant with pressure from his family and friends. Eventually he began beating you, but not as often as your father had. You decided that marriage was a prison, but one you had to cope with as best as possible.

Homeless

Your parents weren't bad parents, but they weren't good ones either. In many ways, you had to raise yourself. Without a sense of "home" anywhere, you took off to see the world. Your wanderings entailed a fair degree of hardship, but you felt driven to continue exploring. You were searching for something—but not sure quite what it was. You dreamt of finding a place and people with whom you would feel safe and familiar. But it never happened. Each new land was just a foreign arena. You were left with a nagging lack of place, lack of roots, and lack of purpose.

Unacknowledged

Even as a child, you felt your parents didn't really care about you. Largely ignored, you would sometimes go hungry unless you could fend for yourself. Although you learned to look after your own needs, you developed a sense of unworthiness. Inside, you felt you must not be very good if your own parents didn't care about you. You looked for other people who would respond. Because you could be fiery and emotional, people did take note, but not always in a positive way. Your life fell into a pattern of you pushing at authorities to acknowledge your existence and the powers-that-be responding by punishing you which just fed your inner inadequacy.

Imprisoned by Prejudice

A resolute youngster, you grew into a strong-minded young woman. After your father's death, you had some financial independence. A distant cousin, however, wanted to get his hands on the money. When you would not agree to marriage, he took his case to the authorities. Witnesses were called regarding your "abnormal, unwomanly attempts at independence." You suspected that your cousin was not above bribery of the court either. Your own lawyer did not appreciate your directness. The court found you incompetent to handle your affairs, consigned you to an insane asylum and gave your cousin custody of the funds.

☽ Moon in Taurus ♉

Going "Away"

You were born to European nobility and an arranged marriage. Although you sought to be yourself, first your father and then your husband squashed any attempts at independence. The slightest move on your part toward expressing yourself led to brutal suppression. Physical beatings as well as emotional abuse were common. You learned to develop a sweet smile and a soft, off-focus look in your eyes. When you appeared to be "not there" emotionally, the men in your life left you alone more.

Parental Pressures

Easygoing and sensual, you were a relaxed infant. Your family, however, belonged to the intelligentsia and they all prided themselves upon their verbal skills and breadth of knowledge. As you grew older, you preferred to learn slowly and easily, but family pressures pushed for speed. Your performance was always compared (unfavorably) with your siblings. School became more and more painful as familial expectations increased. You want to mull things over before reaching decisions and stating your mind. They demanded instant, articulate, brilliant deductions. You felt intellectually inferior and withdrew as much as possible.

Burdens and Bother

A pleasant and placid baby, you grew into an easygoing young woman. People felt relaxed around you and you enjoyed seeing to everyone's comfort. As a consequence, more and more responsibilities were laid in your lap. Slow to anger, you seldom spoke up, continuing to cope with increasing burdens. Soon, the lion's share of family duties were on your shoulders, but you just hung in there and continued to cope. Unwilling to be unpleasant, you did what you felt you had to do. Your endurance and patience were tried, but you managed. And the more you managed, the more people added to your pile of tasks.

Progeny Pressure

Raised to be a good Catholic, you married young and proceeded to get pregnant. Your first child was a joy; you felt the awe of creating new life. Shortly, you were once again with child—and pregnancy began to roll around regularly every year! You felt overwhelmed—lacking the time and energy to deal with all those children. You spoke with your priest, but he advised abstinence which was not possible with your husband. You began to dread pregnancy. Each new child felt like an additional burden and you prayed for your womb to shrivel up and become infertile.

Steadfast

Your mother was a patient woman and taught you her stillness and silence as well. Close to nature, you would go work with the earth when feeling frustrated.

Like most of your peers, you followed the obligatory path for young women of marriage and children. Your husband was a good fellow, but very careless and forgetful. It was left for you to keep track of everything. The burdens of the family fell on your shoulders. Soon, you were keeping the books for the business, organizing the household, doing all the chores and still waiting on your husband. It never occurred to you to try a different way, to see if you could change anything.

Pressures of Power

Born to a position of power, your marriage solidified your position within society. Although your husband was the major authority, you were expected to take on the mantle of ruler in his absence. When he was suddenly assassinated, the kingdom was in a crisis. A neighboring land was ready to invade, and immediate decisions by you were essential. You preferred time to mull things over, to gather all your facts, to be really sure. That was not an option. You were forced to make many rapid decisions, knowing that people would die as a result. That time and the rest of that life solidified your feeling that responsibility for others was too great a burden to bear.

☽ **Moon in Gemini** ♊

Ends of Education

A cheerful and stimulating child, you showed much intellectual promise. But there was no avenue for a girl to excel in regard to education, so you were given the minimal training for your sex: needlework, housekeeping, decorum, etc. You were taught to read which became your greatest pleasure in life. In due course, your family married you off to a man they judged appropriate for husband material. He was not interested in a wife who loved to read, and controlled your literary habit. He kept the keys to the library and would not allow you access until you had satisfied his demands about the household. You were totally in his power financially and otherwise, so had no recourse.

Soul Recovery

Born a twin, you were extremely close to your sister. You shared everything and often huddled together under the covers at night whispering secrets to one another. When you were eleven, a freak accident killed your twin. Devastated, you took years to return to normal. At last, you met a man you could love and married him. When your first child arrived, you looked into her eyes and felt your twin had returned! It was eerie, but you were convinced her soul was back with you. You began to neglect your husband, spending all your time with the child. Your marital relationship got worse and worse as you wound your whole world about this baby girl.

Limiting Learning

Bitten by the curiosity bug at an early age, you were insatiable in the quest for information. Once you learned to read, you devoured every book you could. Your parents were alarmed as authorities were convinced that too much study by young women led to brain fever. They forbade you to read more than a few pages a day. You never got brain fever, but you did damage to your eyes from straining to read at night with a candle when you were supposed to be in bed, asleep.

Intellectual Inequities

Chatty as a child, you continued to enjoy the world of the mind and communication as an adult. You were attracted to your husband because he was a professor and you thought you could learn from him. After the marriage, he informed you that women were not really capable of rational thought, and you should confine your discussions to household matters. Shortly after that, you avoided speaking with him as much as possible. Judging your marriage a failure, you sought out friends who could enjoy stimulating conversations, books, and questions.

Dangerous Domains

Born in what is now Latvia, you were a curious child. Bits and pieces of conversations you heard piqued your interest and you ended up getting to know the local wise woman. She taught you much about herbs, potions, candle magic, and the cycles of the earth and stars. The more you learned, the more you wanted to know. Although she warned you not to reveal your association, the secret was impossible to keep in your small community. At the first hint of trouble, you two were the targets for scapegoating. When a blight hit the potato fields, you were both denounced as having cast an "evil eye" and died at the hands of a mob.

Outsider

An alert and peripatetic child, you got into anything and everything. As you grew, you channeled most of your restlessness toward learning as much as possible. You became a voracious consumer of the news and would talk with anyone, seeking to gain as much information from they as you could. When a Chinese family moved into town, you were eager to meet them. You became good friends with the daughter of the family who was around your age. The rest of the community was horrified by this fraternization. "Normal" (white) folks weren't supposed to hang around with the Chinese—who were only allowed the most menial of jobs. Your refusal to give up your friendship meant being an outcast at school. The other kids avoided you because their families disapproved. You learned to expect nonacceptance.

Pride through Progeny

Born a girl child, you learned early that your worth was not equal to your brothers. They were valued as potential powers in the world. You were just to be married off. Following the course of duty, you were wed to a man your parents selected. However, you achieved recognition for you produced the first son! Your son—the first grandson of your parents—appeared before either of your brother's wives produced a baby. You basked in the reflected glory. At last, your parents noticed you and praised you for such speedy, excellent work.

Marital Metamorphosis

Born with brilliant copper hair, you turned people's heads even as a child. With a knack for drama, you learned how to keep center stage. Dramatic license and exaggerated emotional responses allowed you to get attention just about when-ever you wanted it. As a debutante, you capitalized on your flamboyant appear-ance and had droves of men waiting to dance with you, talk with you, or take you for a walk in the park. You married one of your admirers and he promptly turned into a husband. He wanted you to subdue your "wild" hair, to start wearing demure clothes, and to cease flirting with all his friends! Everything he had been in transports over when you were a young, unmarried woman, he now deemed totally unsuitable within a wife! The more you tried to be yourself, the more he demanded someone entirely different.

No Life Without Love

A warm and loving child, you adored playing with dolls and baby animals. As you grew, you would look after babies, enjoying nurturing and caring for them. Wanting more than anything else to become a wife and mother, you carefully observed the men in the neighborhood. Then, a visitor to the area caught your eye. He was dashing, exciting, and magnetic. You felt vital and alive when you were with him. After a whirlwind romance, you were married. He became your whole world. Your husband was your meaning for existence, along with your young son (born after 10 months of marriage). When a freak accident took them both, you couldn't believe it. You raged against God. You refused to believe this tragedy had occurred. When forced to acknowledge reality, you went into a decline, unable to live without your loves, and died.

Imaginary Existence

When still quite young, you attended the opera — and knew what you wanted to do. Your parents were horrified at the idea of you becoming an opera singer. It was not appropriate for a woman of good family, and they were not about to allow it. They unbent sufficiently for you to continue music lessons (a necessity for a well-bred young woman), but forbade you to see or speak about the opera. You yearned in silence, going through many imaginary plots in your head. Fantasies of running away occurred, but you knew you had no means for surviving. So, you lost yourself in dreams of what your life could have been life—if only things had been different!

☽ Moon in Virgo ♍

Blocks and Barricades

You were a homesteader in the American West. You put in long hours of arduous labor to work your land which was not very fertile. Life was a constant struggle, and you never seemed to get ahead. An unseasonable hailstorm ruined your crops one year. During a two-year drought, hardly anything survived. Just when it seemed a harvest might be reasonable, or some livestock were beginning to flourish, terrible weather or some disease would wipe out your gains. You felt as if nothing you could do would win over the environment. Like Sisyphus trying to roll the huge boulder up the hill, you kept on getting defeated.

Competitive Comparisons

The youngest of four siblings, you ended up following the footsteps of your brothers and sisters in almost everything. This was very hard on you because they were all older and better at almost anything. Your oldest brother was a great scholar and you suffered in comparison. Your second brother had an amazing memory, and you didn't have his prowess. Your sister was an incredible musician and gifted speaker. You fell into a great deal of self-criticism—too hard on yourself because you felt you couldn't be as good as they were. You teachers admired your discipline and sense of order, but you felt dumb compared to the rest of your family, and continued life-long to doubt your intellectual capacities.

Maternal Misfortune

Quiet and shy as a child, you grew into a reserved young woman. With marriage, you knew part of your duty was to produce children. You suffered repeated miscarriages for several years. The doctor warned you that your health was at risk, but you saw being a mother as part of your duty. Also, your husband was not about to give up his spousal rights and you didn't see much choice for yourself. Reliable birth control was not available. You continued to try to bear a full-term baby. Eventually, the stress was just too much and you perished.

Economic Exigencies

Raised to be a lady of leisure, you were trained in needlework, sketching, menu selection, and similar pursuits. When you came of age, you were duly presented to society. An agreeable young man asked for your hand. Suddenly, however, your father died, leaving huge gambling debts outstanding. There was no money left for your maintenance or dowry. The young man made it clear his interest had waned. You were unwilling to hold him to a contract that no longer appealed, so you buried any thoughts of marriage and found employment as a governess.

Heedless Healer

When still a tiny tot, you would bring home wounded animals and try to fix them. After making the acquaintance of the town doctor, you knew that repairing bodies was what you wanted to do. Your parents, and society, were horrified. Woman could not be doctors. That was simply not done. Your parents couldn't even imagine "wasting" the money on a female child to teach her to do a career such as teaching or (horrors!) nursing. Everyone "knew" you would just grow up and get married anyway. Although you begged and pleaded for more schooling, it was to no avail. You had a number of fights with your parents, but they were adamant. Eventually you got some nursing training and went to work with the poor—horrifying your family.

Precise Perfection

Helpful and eager to be of service, you were a valued member of your family. Once you were married and had children of your own, everyone noticed your dedication and focus on doing things well. Your conscientiousness was extreme. You had an artistic eye and expressed in your quilt making. A perfectionist, you would rip out and redo seams if they were not quite correct. Often frustrated, you complained that reality never quite matched the vision in your head. Although other people admired your work and were awed by its precision and beauty, you always wanted it just a little more ideal!

☽ Moon in Libra ♎

Unhealthy Helpfulness

You ran a taverna, a restaurant in a busy part of Athens. It was your legacy to your family. You were an ever smiling host, kind to everyone. You took everyone's troubles on your shoulders and tried to help. Ever ready to loan a sympathetic ear—or a few coins—you were a "soft touch." Whatever your family wanted, you tried to get for them. Your daughter had the wedding of her dreams. You purchased the expensive commission in an elite army corps which your son wanted. Your siblings were paid salaries in the business, but didn't do much. People took advantage of your sympathy. You ended up feeling drained and frustrated, surrounded by takers with no one willing to give to you.

Compliant and Conforming

A kind-hearted person, you were the peacemaker in the family. You spent all your early years trying to build bridges between warring factions within your household. Strife upset you, but those around you seemed to delight in quarreling. When you married, you set out to create a lovely and loving home, doing everything possible to avoid contention. As a result, you gave in repeatedly to your husband and indulged your children considerably. Too late, you realized that your desire to keep things nice had encouraged your children to believe they had a right to whatever they wanted.

Docile Dependency

Your mother was revered by all as a true lady. She never raised her voice, was always immaculate and devoted her life to your father's happiness. You adopted her as your role model and honed the womanly skills of compromise, sweetness, and docility. You could not make up your mind among the young men asking for your hand, so allowed your parents to choose for you. Your husband seemed a reasonable sort in the beginning. As your marriage went on, you discovered that the more you gave, the more he took. You felt as though you were shrinking away and he was getting bigger and bigger. (You did stay petite and he put on weight as you catered to all his menu requests.) But you didn't know how to do anything other than follow your mother's example.

Power Players

When you were quite young, you were introduced to your family's secret: your mother was a witch! When you demonstrated an aptitude, she provided you with training in herbs, in concentration, in directed will, in methods of contraception, and techniques for enhancing sexual desire and pleasure. When you were eighteen and dedicated to the Goddess, your mother showed you her files. She had notes on every important person in your town! "Never forget," she told you, "that we remain alive on sufferance and because people know that we can be a threat. The power players in this town will kill you unless you make it very clear that they would also suffer from your death!" And so you learned to be vigilant, to collect information, and to deal in intimidation and threatened blackmail if necessary.

Social Status

Brought up to "fit in" and "do the right thing," you learned to socialize with the "best" group of people. You became adept at lovely dinner parties with beautiful furnishings, perfectly matched china, and refined, polite conversation. You worked hard at creating an attractive and elegant home for your husband and children. Occasionally, someone would question the underpinnings of your life ("Why do all the 'right' people have to have a maid? Why is that maid always poorly educated—and given no chance to better herself?") Such occurrences disturbed you and you quickly sought out your familiar friends who assured you that you all had the best of lives and your group was the one which really mattered.

Impossible Dream

Born with an ear for music, your parents encouraged you with lessons and opportunities to perform. Several of your teachers said that you could be a great concert pianist—if only you were female. Minor artistic forms of expression were available to you, but the upper echelons were simply out of reach. "Now, if you had been a singer," one sighed, "That would be acceptable." Although you continued to dream for a few years, eventually you just gave up. When you finally decided it was hopeless, you married a man who did not like music and did not have a piano in the house.

☽ Moon in Scorpio ♏

Inner Integrity

You were a nurse who was considered "uppity" by the doctors. Although your work was excellent, authorities in the hospital put blocks in your way. You were labeled a trouble-maker and had to really struggle to continue in your chosen career. Just the smallest bit of self-assertion on your part was viewed very negatively by those around you. Your main problem was that you often saw or sensed problems in people and had a tendency to disagree with the doctor's diagnosis or treatment in such cases. Even though your intuitive sense proved correct in almost every case, your "arrogance" was considered shameful in a woman.

Birthing Battles

Born in the Middle East, your family arranged a political marriage. Although you were the first wife, your husband took several more (and concubines) after you. Understanding the importance of an heir, you were overjoyed to discover you were pregnant with what you were sure would be the first son. However, you soon heard that wife #3 was also pregnant and the race was on. You knew that bearing the eldest son would be your best chance for achieving any power, so when you heard that wife #3 was apparently very near her time, you insisted your serving ladies take measures to stimulate your delivery. You almost died in the process, but felt the danger was worthwhile when you delivered a boy (before wife #3).

Secret Suffering

As a young child, you were very reserved. Your feelings were quite strong, but you did not know how to direct them and were taught that women should be smiling and sweet. You had a rich inner life, but no one to share secrets or thoughts with. As was expected, you eventually married. You husband had no great interest in how you felt, but you had not expected him to be and did your best in looking after the household and being an obedient wife. You had only one child — a daughter and thought of your family as perfectly normal. When she was ten, your daughter told you that her father was having sex with her. Appalled, you did not know what to do. You thought about killing your husband, but eventually decided to run away. Even though you could not imagine how your daughter and you would survive, you could not bear for her to be in the house one minute longer.

Alone Together

Your parents told you that you were born with "invisible antennae." As a young child, you knew when someone was lying to you. As you became older, however, so many people did not tell the truth that your system apparently got overloaded and shorted out. It was a relief at the time. As most young women of your age and time, you found a young man and got married. Your "invisible antennae" abruptly resurfaced. You could tell even when he was evading, avoiding, or stretching the truth just a bit. Your insights were not at all welcome, and he soon began to avoid you. After a short period, you were essentially a hermit—with you and your husband leading totally separate lives.

Consuming Curiosity

Despite being born female in a time when education of girls was not done, you hungered for knowledge. With a little help from a sympathetic brother (too young to know better), you learned to read. Thereafter, you sought knowledge in secret. You would read at night when no one knew you were up. You would casually talk to people, picking up information about how they worked and what they knew. You would remain just within earshot of the men (but out of sight) whenever possible and eavesdrop on their conversations. A few beatings merely intensified your desire not to get caught. You did not know WHY you had to know and could not see any particular application to what you were learning, but your driving inner demand for knowledge would not cease.

Painful Present

Raised within a noble family, you knew that your fate would be a political marriage. When you were old enough, an alliance was struck and you wed an older gentleman with considerable lands and authority in the Far East. He was erratically cruel. The doctor who served your household prescribed opium for your pain. Soon, you became dependent on the drug in order to escape your everyday existence. When you had ingested enough opium, nothing mattered. You felt as if you were in a different, better world. Eventually, you were barely aware of the outer world more than an hour or so each day.

☽ Moon in Sagittarius ♐

Unattached

Your family never really understood you. Tied to home and hearth, you wandered even as a small child. You would venture quite far afield before returning. At a young age, you took to the road. The life of a traveler suited you. Although pleasures were very spartan and you owned almost nothing, you were content to see nature and visit many different places. You learned to make do with few possessions and little money. The material felt unimportant; your intellectual and spiritual sides were strongly stimulated.

Education Eliminated

As a child, you had a lot of freedom to roam about and ask questions. As a youngster, you were pressured to turn into a "young lady." You desperately wanted to read everything and be tutored in some of the topics offered to your brothers, but that was not considered suitable. Any requests for additional education were met with the statement that you had no need for such as a female. You felt extremely frustrated that your hunger for knowledge was denied and fantasies about traveling to a faraway land, but could not discover any other country that would treat women better.

Evading Encumbrances

When you were four, you mother deserted the family, leaving a note which stated that she was feeling utterly trapped and had to get away. An aunt came to help your father with you and your five siblings. When you were ten, your aunt found religion and started spending most of her waking hours in church, Sunday school, choir practice, Bible study, or similar activities. You learned that being a child meant being vulnerable to the eccentricities of your caretakers. You resolved never to depend upon anyone else again.

"Bad Blood"

When you were 10, your mother ran off with the local curate. It was a major scandal! As you grew older, everyone was watching you, waiting for the smallest slip. Any misbehavior was taken as a sign that you might follow your mother's path. When you came of age, all the young men were warned against your "bad blood." Eventually, you realized there was no chance for a decent marriage in your town, and you emigrated to Australia.

Completely Committed

An idealist, you became drawn to the early women's movement. You helped to promote the idea that women should be able to vote. At the time, the concept was a radical one. Your political activism meant that you had to face threats, intimidation, and physical violence. Some men were fanatically opposed to even letting women speak in subject about the topic of women voting. You were called crazy, extremist, man-hater, and a lot of other names. Several of the women who pushed for equality with you also opposed alcohol (because so many husbands drank away their wages and then beat their wives). Although what you did was very challenging, you were determined not to give up.

Religious Rules

Moral principles were very emphasized in your home and you developed a strong ethical sense. You were very drawn to the church, spending much time with prayer meetings, services, and classes. At age 12, you had a vision and announced that God wanted you to become a priest. This created quite an uproar. Your family believed you were telling the truth because you had always been an incredibly honest child, but explained to you that you simply could **not** become a priest because you were female. You insisted that God wanted you to serve him, to train in a seminary and work for a parish. Your confessor tried to explain the limits to you, but you kept insisting that the priesthood was where you belonged. Finally, with everyone pushing you toward a convent, you gave in and began training to become a nun. But you knew you'd be taking the wrong vows.

☽ **Moon in Capricorn** ♑

Material Mastery

Growing up in a slum, your life was difficult. Your mother died young because the family could not afford any medicine when she became ill. You swore that you would be rich when you got older. You labored long hours at whatever you could master and began saving your pennies. Every bit of money that wasn't saved was invested toward other business ventures. Your commercial base grew and you began to wield some power. You became obsessed about getting more money. It was your primary emotional drive—as if to make up for the deprivations of your childhood. No matter how much you accumulated, you never felt it was enough.

Lifelong Labor

Born in a small African village, you learned women's work early. You had to carry heavy jugs a mile to fill them at a stream for drinking water. You went foraging with your mother for firewood. All the cooking, cleaning and washing (back to the river) for a family of six was done by the two of you. When you married and had you own family, the back-breaking labor continued. You worked from dawn til past dusk. You also tilled the small field you family had. Life was one never-ending cycle of effort.

Maternal Malice

Your mother labored long and hard with your delivery, almost dying. As you grew older, you realized that she held it against you. Nothing you could do was right. From your earliest memories, she was hard on you. As a small child, you believed she would not care if you died—and might even hasten the event! You grew up quite guarded. As an adult, you avoided depending on anyone else. It was much too dangerous. You became practically a hermit as a self-protective measure.

Murdered Mate

A quiet and serious child, you grew into a conscientious young woman. When your family arranged a marriage, you did as you were told. No better (nor worse) than most marriages, yours with your spouse rolled along for about ten years until his death. Your dead husbands relatives all demanded that you join the suttee (the funereal pyre). You appealed to your family, but were a liability for them and they suggested you follow custom as well. Although you did not want to die, you felt you had no real choice or power.

Hardly There

Your mother took pride in what a "good" child you were—well behaved, clean, quiet, and obedient. You learned early on that there was no room in your family for individuality or uniqueness. Although you often felt stifled, choking with a need for freedom, you did not see any way to express it. So, you continued to act as expected. As you suppressed more and more of your inner self, you became less and less concerned with the outer world—and more docile. Finally, you felt you were little more than a doll—going through the motions of an "appropriate" life with no real feeling.

Handicapped by Hurt

Your childhood was very difficult. Since your mother died in birthing you, your father blamed you for her death. You were a frequent target for his rage. With no place else to go, you stuck it out til around age eight and then ran away from home. Barely surviving the next few years, you eventually found your way to a spiritual master who lived out in the country. You studied with him and decided to devote your life to contemplation and meditation. He told you stories warning of false spiritual paths, of choosing the hermit lifestyle as a retreat from the world, but your were adamant. Although your spiritual hunger was strong, part of the reason you were drawn to withdraw from the world is you could not imagine enjoying it.

☽ Moon in Aquarius ♒

Intermittent Attachments

Your mother claimed that you were an erratic nurser—totally involved one minute and distant and disinterested the next. As you grew, you attitude toward possessions seemed similar. You would collect things and seem very sentimentally attached—and then throw them all out, give them all away, or change to some completely different interest. You would enjoy old, familiar things—and then demand something totally new, individualistic and one-of-a-kind. You never quite figured out the pattern, but grew to expect the unexpected in your relationship to money and objects.

Spousal Separation

Born near the ocean, you loved the sound of the surf. Although you would have liked to sail the seas yourself, you settled for marrying a ship's captain. It was an odd union. He was away for months at a time, on board his vessel. During those times, you had to be extremely independent and manage everything on your own. Upon his return, however, he expected instant obedience (as if you were one of his crew he could have whipped). He became enraged if you acted without consulting him and expected you to be available to him whenever and however he wanted you. Shortly, you grew to detest his times ashore and pray for storms to delay his homecomings when he was at sea.

Inferences and Innuendoes

Born into the Japanese nobility, you learned young that power was a vital commodity. The art of gaining (and the fear of losing) face was drummed into you. Although you had relatively little power as a female, you were expected to listen, to plot, to scheme, and maneuver in order to help advance your family's agenda. Although you detested the dishonesty, you became quite skilled at reading hints and innuendoes—and puzzling together tiny bits of information, factoring what was NOT said along with what was said. It became a challenging game for you, but you hated the whole process when people were hurt or killed.

Essential Education

Born at a time when women were barely educated, you received only the rudiments of reading and writing. After that, your "education" consisted of training in cooking, sewing, candle making, and other "womanly" arts. But you hungered for knowledge. You begged and borrowed books to improve your reading skills. You practiced making letters in the dirt to enhance your writing. You broached the idea of further schooling to your parents who derided the idea as a complete waste of money for a female. Having no funds of your own, you looked around for a husband who might support (or at least accept) your quest for knowledge. You could not discover such a man. Eventually, you taught yourself enough to get a job as a schoolteacher out west. You left, vowing to teach as many young women as you could.

Erratic Eccentricity

Your childhood was not exactly normal. Orphaned, you were raised by two aunts. They loved you, but were a bit eccentric. Thus, the training you got was erratic and many of the rules and conventions which other children learned naturally, you just never absorbed. Consequently, your peers found you odd as well. You remained ambivalent about your position all your life. Sometimes, you longed to become a part of a group, to blend in with everybody else. Other times, you rejoiced in being different. You bounced back and forth between making gestures to fit in, and being adamant in your independence.

Child Martyr

Your parents were not very warm, and left your raising mainly to an older sister. When you were nine, your sister died of a fever. You heard about the children's crusade and decided this was something you wanted to do. Your parents seemed just as happy to see the back of you. The travel toward the Holy Land was extremely difficult. Many children perished — from thirst, hunger, disease, abuse. Most were sold into slavery by ship owners who promised them safe passage. You never made it to the Middle East and died a martyr to the holy cause of Rome.

☽ Moon in Pisces ♓

Beauty's Blessings

From the earliest days, you were drawn to beauty. Seeking serenity, you would go outside and discover the wonders of nature. When family tiffs arose, you were the one attempting to smooth things over and make everyone happy, sometimes at the expense of your needs. Pursuing grace was your paramount desire. You were not terribly realistic about money and tended to lose track of your possessions as you were often in another world, caught up in some artistic vision. Your material foundation was very tenuous, but you were very committed to the world of the ideal.

Right-Brained

As a child, your feelings were easily hurt, Quite sensitive, you sometimes felt the pain of others as well as your own suffering. School was not easy for you. You tended to learn through absorption. You picked up images, whole patterns. The step-by-step, piece-by-piece approaches of your teachers was not suited for your brain. As a result, you began to believe that you were "confused" and "not very bright" as they said. You retreated more into the world of emotions since the world of the mind seemed too uncomfortable.

Poisonous Possessiveness

Blessed with lovely auburn hair and beautiful brown eyes, you had quite a few suitors. The man you chose was well-off, seemed pleasant and was quite handsome with his dark brown hair and eyes. After the marriage, things went reasonably well although he wouldn't let you go much of any place without him and acted jealous if you were just friendly to men in a social setting. Then, your daughter was born—with her lovely blond hair and blue eyes. Your husband went crazy, accusing you of being unfaithful, declaring she couldn't be his. You swore your innocence and the servants all testified that you had no moments away in which to be unfaithful. He decided to keep you, but refused to have anything to do with his daughter.

Endlessly Idealistic

Raised by idealistic parents, you accepted the then new ideas of Rousseau— that humans are not born with original sin, but are innately good. From childhood onward, you trusted people and believed they had your best interests at heart. When you were in your late teens, your parents perished in an epidemic. You became involved with a traveling evangelist. He was preaching a new sort of gospel and urging people to join him in a journey to the promised land. You became inspired by the idea of an intentional community out west, in the wilderness. Selling your parents home and farm, you joined the caravan. Despite signs and clues that this guru was not as holy as he seemed, you continued to believe. Even when some people talked of misappropriated funds, you trusted him. Even when people left the community, complaining of abuse, you wanted to believe in goodness and you continued to deny the possibility of any wrongdoing.

Special Sensitivities

When you were little, you spoke of the pretty colors you saw around people, and your grandmother told you that you were crazy. When you felt ill and woozy as your little brother was fighting a fever, you father beat you for "pretending." When you told your mother that you felt one of the hens was doing poorly, she asked you how you could tell and berated you when you said you just "felt" something was wrong. (She spanked you the next day when the hen died, saying you must have damaged it.) Eventually, you stopped saying much of anything. Convinced that anything you experienced was unacceptable, you withdrew more and more from the world.

Refuge

A foundling, you were left on the steps of a nunnery. The mother superior elected to take you in, and you became the child of the entire community. Raised by 50 mothers, you were loved, but sometimes overwhelmed. The chapel with its beautiful stained glass windows became your place of retreat. Oddly enough, you showed no interest in the outside world. In fact, when you were urged to visit outside the walls, you were afraid. The mother superior decided that your earlier childhood had been quite traumatic and did not force you, but worried that you would have no life beyond the community. You insisted that was enough and took your vows as soon as possible.

CHAPTER FOUR
PAST LIFE SCENARIOS: MERCURY

If you do not know the sign of your Mercury, check the tables in the Appendix (pages 284 - 290). Read all Mercury scenarios for your sign.

☿ Mercury in Aries ♈

Dangerously Direct

A quick, alert, curious child, you were trained for service as was the rest of your family. You became a footman to a Prussian aristocrat. Because you spoke your mind and were quite direct, some of the other servants did not like you. You coped, however, until you were rash enough to question one of your "master's" orders. He had you severely beaten. Without references, and physically weakened, you could not continue in domestic service. You did not want to be a burden upon your family, so took some foolish, heroic risks and ended up perishing in a fire.

Surrender to Silence

Incredibly shy as a child, you avoided people and conversation. With several siblings, there was no lack of people to speak for you. Eventually, it became a habit to let others do your communicating. When you were old enough to learn a trade, you apprenticed to a paper maker. Although you eschewed the spoken word, you adored reading and writing. You could lose yourself for hours in books. You felt incredibly lucky to be working in a field contributing to the production of something you loved. Yet your phobia about speech increasingly impeded your social life. After a time, you could barely bear to speak to anyone—even your family members. You retreated into silence.

Performance Pressure

A quick and agile child, you developed an interest in and talent for juggling while still quite young. Your parents decided this was adorable and would schedule performances by you when people visited. What had been fun became a major pressure. You came to dread the appearance of people at the door because you knew you'd be expected to juggle and your parent would be terribly disappointed if you made any mistakes. As a result of the family pressures, you never volunteered for anything at school and tried to be invisible.

Ceaseless Seeking

When you were 10, your local priest could not satisfactorily answer your questions, so you left the Orthodox Church. (Your parents were appalled, but could not sway you.) As you grew older, you questioned everyone, from every faith, whom you met. You wanted to understand people's concepts of God, of life's meaning, of faith, of truth. Searching for answers, you hunted through books, went to many services and rituals, and sought a connection to the Ineffable. Although you enjoyed your discussions and quests, you never satisfied that inner hunger for Ultimate Understanding.

Odd Outcast

Somewhat impulsive in speech, you tended to ask questions that proved awkward for the people around you. Many of your "why's were unanswerable. "Why can't I go adventuring with my brothers?" fetched "Because you're a girl." "Why can't a girl do that?" brought back "Because it's not done." "Why not?" led to irritation and admonitions not to bother the person. You never fit in. You wanted to do the unusual, non-normal, non-standard activities. You didn't follow the rules. Both your parents and your society worked hard at convincing you that something was wrong with you. Sometimes you believed them—and sometimes you felt they were the crazy ones!

Savoring Seclusion

From an early age, you discovered a good degree of dexterity. As a youth, you dabbled with magic shows and learned to do rope tricks. Alert and flexible, you could adapt to most circumstances. People, however, disappointed you. Expecting them to be better than they were, you were often let down. Disillusioned with city life, you traveled west and got work on a cattle ranch as a hand. You thrived on long periods of solitude, riding the range, fixing miles of fencing, looking for strays. Sometimes you wondered if you were avoiding people too much, but you felt much better off with nature and yourself.

☿ Mercury in Taurus ♉

Deprivation
You were a bank clerk who labored long hours in poorly ventilated, poorly lit rooms. Your employer took advantage of the tough economic times to get as much out effort as possible out of his workers—for as little money as he could pay. You felt like no matter how hard you worked, you just wouldn't ever get ahead. Any sign of slackening just a little brought a strong reprimand and the threat of dismissal. You knew times were tough and didn't dare leave, but you felt your joyless life was hardly worth it. You had almost no time to relax, enjoy the beauty of nature, or gratify your senses.

Spirit Sisters
You were exceedingly close to a younger sister. Very frail and delicate, she was susceptible to a number of childhood ailments. But you told each other stories, shared secrets, and were best friends. As she grew older, the doctors diagnosed consumption—with no real cure. You both knew she would not be able to marry and have children. Some of her life experience was gained through you. Unwilling to concede to death, the two of you continued to confide in one another. She enriched your life. Everything you saw and did was more vital and vibrant because you wanted to share it with her later. Particularly once she was bedridden near the end, you were her window to the world. When she passed on, you swore you'd be together again soon.

Material Memories
As a child, you sought familiarity. Repetitive rituals soothed you. You liked hearing your favorite stories over and over and over again. When disruptions occurred, you sought safety by returning to the known. If a parent exploded, you'd seek out a corner of the house where you had been happy recently and return there. When the family had to move, you hung on to possessions, reluctant to let them go. You found your security in the things around you and resisted any attempts to change that.

Lost Art
As a young child, you had a strong feeling for design, form, and color. Your teacher was very impressed with your creations and called your parents in for a conference. She wanted you to have extra training in sketching and painting, feeling you had real talent. Your parents insisted that your scribbling were useless and certainly would not support you as an adult. They wanted you to focus solely on the three R's forget this "artsy nonsense." Although you missed drawing terribly, you followed your parents wishes.

Business Burden

Born into a merchant family, you developed a talent for commerce. Your ability to select items that would prove popular and sell quickly was highly prized by your family. Your heart, however, was drawn to music. Drawn to the harpsichord, you would have gladly spent many hours a day practicing, playing, and composing. It was forbidden by your family. You could have tried to blackmail your business services for time with your music, but you didn't want to engage in acrimonious exchanges. You gave up your music (except in your head) and devoted yourself to the family business.

Ties over Talent

Born into the middle class, you saw the business world as you best opportunity for advancement. You found, however, that who you knew was more important than what you did. Roadblocks were put in your way—which you overcame only with very great effort. People with less talent—and who labored less—were promoted over you because they had "connections." It became clear that the powers that be had their own agenda and doing good work wouldn't necessarily mean you'd get to the top in your profession. Nonetheless, you continued to work hard, strive mightily, and do your best to overcome each of the barriers in your way.

☿ Mercury in Gemini ♊

Speak Up!

You were born into an intellectual family and grew up with a lively, inquiring mind. In due course, you gravitated toward newspaper work as it gave you an opportunity to indulge your curiosity and meet many people. However, the political regime in power at the time was not very open. Many of your stories were censored or deemed unsuitable. Eventually, you fell badly afoul of the authorities and were sent away to a prison camp. You spent many years shut away from society, unable to communicate with friends and family. Along with missing loved ones, your greatest regret was the loss of literature. Books were almost non-existent at the camp. (Discussions with fellow prisoners were also discouraged.) So, you tried to keep your mind active by writing on any scraps you could and by composing endless stories and reports in your head.

Eliminating Emotion

Your parents were fairly inadequate and overwhelmed by their circumstances, so you spent a lot of your early life on the streets. A good observer of people, you learned the value of picking up quickly on gossip or stories in the neighborhood. As soon as you could, you got a job as a newspaper reporter. You viewed yourself as a citizen of the world and avoided family ties of any sort. Dependency, in your mind, was just a trap, an emotional morass from which people had a hard time escaping. You put your security in your mind, your objectivity, and your ability to know what was going on. Safety involved eschewing ties to other people, staying in the role of observer.

Missing Marriage
Born into poverty, you had a burning curiosity, but little education. You asked questions incessantly, learning as much as you could from the people around you. Flexible, you developed some athletic skills and got hired on as an acrobat in a traveling circus. This allowed you to broaden your horizons and meet even more people. Yet you never met that special someone and wondered if you would grow old alone. You were able to chat with almost anyone, but had no burning attractions. Someone would seem interesting, but would be too old. Another would be too young. Another had unappealing personal habits, and so on. You decided that partnership was just not your lot in life.

Faraway Fantasies
Solidly middle class, you had a normal, rather bland childhood. The only unusual occurrence was that you would periodically dream of faraway lands where you observed people with a different color skin speaking a different language (which you understood in your dreams). Occasionally you would voice the idea of going to look for those people and your family always laughed at the notion. In due time, you entered the family business: a merchandiser of woolens. Once in a while, you would go down to the wharf to meet a ship coming in and talk with the sailors about the exotic places they had been. You fantasies about sailing 'round the world, but never left the town in which you were born.

Real Restrictions
Your father was a tutor and your mother quite well educated for women of the day, so they encouraged you to learn. You took eagerly to the world of books, loving to read. With the fullness of time, you found occupation as a librarian and cataloguer of wealthy people's literary collections. In order to remain gainfully employed, you had to follow societal expectations. You were expected to be quiet, humble, and self-effacing. You could never show that your knowledge was much greater than that of the people who employed you. Working conditions were often inadequate in poorly lit, poorly ventilated, illy maintained, cold rooms, but you were expected to show gratitude for the opportunity to labor. Everything had to be done exactly as the noble families who employed you demanded (even if it was bad for the books).

Severely Sensitive
Born near the shore, you felt a connection to the ocean. As a small child, you would walk on the beach and feel a part of the ocean waves. As you aged, you discovered that being around people was very painful. You absorbed the ailments and ill moods of the people in your environment and that was very difficult to deal with. Eventually, you became quite solitary. You earned a living

family was quite dysfunctional. Dad was volatile with a dangerously unpredictable temper. Mom was alternately smothering and withdrawn. Lacking security at home, you sought out other people, believing that they might take care of you if they liked you. You developed a life-long pattern of pleasing people—or making them laugh—as a self-protective measure.

Risky Business

Your family emigrated to the U.S. in one of the early waves from Ireland. Prejudice was widespread and a number of businesses posted signs: "Irish need not apply." As a youth, you were quite athletic, so you started earning money as a daredevil. You would go over waterfalls in a barrel, ride a bicycle on a tightrope, leap from great heights, and other risky ventures. Your family begged you not to take such chances, but you were determined to contribute. A fatal fall ended your career (and life).

Restricted Relationship

You grew up in a large Southern family in the late 1800's, much loved, but expected to be sweet, kind, and pretty. Although you played the role of a biddable female, you definitely had some ideas of your own. You trained as a teacher while you were waiting for Mr. Right to show up. Dedicated to your children, you often worked after hours on projects. You got to know the school janitor, sometimes having long, fascinating discussions into the evening. He was incredibly bright, but only self-educated because he was Black. The two of you had to be very cautious in your interactions because he risked being lynched just from speaking with you. Although you were attracted to him, you knew that marriage was totally impossible.

Way Out There

Full of excitement and vitality, you loved life—from the instant you arrived on Earth. Your parents insisted that "gusto" was your middle name. You sought out adventures and thrived on thrills, chills, and the rush of adrenaline. Stability was anathema. Variety and new challenges were essential. Society's conventional element found you shocking and outrageous, but you did not care. You were eager to blaze a path into the unknown, to explore new vistas, to do things which had not yet been done. You believed going too far was better than stopping short.

Forsaking Fantasy

Eager and enthusiastic, you dived full tilt into life as a child. Seeking experience, you tried many different things. Others discovered an attractive charisma within you and flocked about. You also uncovered a talent for drama and had quite a following for your amateur theatrical productions. The stage called you strongly, but you knew it was a profession with little recompense. So, you closed your eyes to your dream, ignored your great creative abilities and entered the family business.

☿ **Mercury in Virgo** ♍

Not Yourself

You were born to a poor family that had just enough to send you to a boarding school. You were abused and mistreated by the teachers in the name of training and education. (Almost all of the students were beaten.) Because you loved learning, you became a tutor. You served several noble families, having to completely suppress your personality and desires in order to fit the model of a tutor. As long as you showed no signs of independence, your behavior was approved. You presented yourself as a nonentity so long, it was hard to reclaim yourself during your rare, "off-duty" hours.

Creative Criticism

A painstaking observer, you were a rather quiet child. Drawn to nature, you could spend hours watching butterflies gather nectar, or birds build a nest. Soon, you were moved to sketch some of what you saw. Your drawings were extremely realistic, carefully detailed, and quite elegant. Although other people greatly admired your work, you were critical toward it, always focusing on the nuance you missed, the angle that was wrong, etc. Even after a naturalist insisted that your sketches were essential in his book, you did not believe you had any singular talent or ability.

Productive and Practical

Your parents raised you to believe in a strong work ethic. From an early age, you were expected to contribute to the household. When you discovered a patient talent for numbers, you ended up becoming an accounting clerk. Dedicated, you put in long hours and even worked overtime whenever asked. You didn't let anything interfere with your job and your social life was practically nonexistent. Even on Sundays (the one day of rest), you often honed your skills. Although you took great pride in your productivity, you sometimes wondered if something was lacking in your life.

Missed Marriage

Your parents were quite poor, but wanted you to make something of your life, so saved and scraped in order for you to have a good education. Fortunately, you loved school and did well. Words, particularly, fascinated you. Whenever possible, you would read. Thus you were drawn to become a librarian—and caretaker to the tomes which provided so much pleasure to you. Due to your work, you rarely met any men, and most were intimidated by your learning. As a "bluestocking," you were not considered appealing wife material. You often longed for a partner, but were unable to find a man who could accept you.

Careful Control

A cautious child, you tested life before entering it. Your mother used to say you took twice as long to arrive as her other children! Quite bright, you did well in school and chose to study law. A superb researcher, you spent many happy hours in the library, tracking down briefs. As a lawyer, however, you were compulsive. You'd spend excessive hours in combing through background cases. You'd go over details again and again. You became obsessed with a case while on it and could think of nothing else. Your desire to get things JUST RIGHT was overpowering. You tried to control everything in which you were involved as a way to feel safe.

Consummate Craftsman

You worked in wood, creating lovely cabinets and furniture for prosperous families in northern Italy. The textures, colors, grain, and shadings were all blended beautifully in your creations. Although you made a reasonable living selling what you made, you were never satisfied. The visions in your head never matched the physical objects you cut, wedged, and sanded into being. In your mind, what you did never really measured up. You were seeking a degree of perfection which was impossible to reach. No matter how spectacular your woodworking was, you wanted it to be more ideal.

☿ Mercury in Libra ♎

Almost Absent

You were a chambermaid in eastern Europe, expected to keep everything lovely and comfortable for hotel guests. Your job was to be as pleasant and attractive as possible, but self-effacing. You could never express your personal desires or put yourself forward in any way or it would be grounds for dismissal. You were expected to do your job, but not be noticed. If anyone demanded anything, you were to take care of it, regardless of what it meant for you. You fought against constant messages that you didn't matter and were of no importance.

Limited Luxury

You were a sales clerk in an English emporium. Wages were very low and working conditions very demanding. You had to share lodgings with other clerks and could only afford the poorest quality of food. Nevertheless, you appreciated the beauty of every sunset. You savored what material gratifications were available. You enjoyed the feel of fabrics which you sold. The luxury of a rare, truly hot bath refreshed you. The indulgence of an expensive — but oh, so gratifying — chocolate was a once-a-year treat. Generally, you remained overworked and underpaid.

People Pleaser

Born into a Turkish family of artisans, you too developed an eye for beauty. Working with precious gems and metals became your forte. As a jewelry designer, you created some truly lovely items. Your work began to become quite popular, when something interfered. Eager to please everyone, you listened to suggestions from your family members and your friends. Soon, you were overwhelmed with different (and conflicting) ideas and suggestions. You began to lose your own style because you were so swayed by others. You creativity drained away as you tried to include everyone else's thinking.

Used

Born into poverty, you were orphaned early. As a young child, you desperately sought love, but no one adopted you. As soon as you were old enough, you were put to work in a mill. An agreeable young woman, you wanted everyone to like you and would often help out the other girls. You would work parts of their shifts or help them clean their quarters in the women's dormitories. Eventually you realized that a number of the women were taking advantage of your good nature. They were slacking off with you there to do the extra work. You were grinding away with no real payment for it. You felt stuck in the situation, knowing they were using you, but wanting terribly to be liked.

Accommodating

Quite a lovely child, you could have modeled for baby food pictures. Your parents doted on your appearance and encouraged you to always look as lovely as possible. Naturally sweet, you were trained to be considerate, polite, and always consider the needs of the other person. When you married a man (who was attractive, polite, and seemed suitable to your friends and family), you continued to put his needs first. The more you gave, the more he took. You became more and more unhappy—feeling worse and worse about yourself—but did not know what to do. Being the loving, giving, sacrificing female was all you knew how to do.

Uncertain and Unsure

Born into an artistic family, you showed early promise as a singer. Although you loved music and adored your family, you were reluctant to follow the muse. Unsure whether you were truly good enough, you felt it might be better to give up early before trying so hard and being disappointed. You spent many years vacillating about your talents. When other people reassured you, your belief soared. When you were on your own again, the fears and anxieties returned. You struggled with the search for faith in yourself and your abilities for a long time.

☿ Mercury in Scorpio   ♏

Personal Peril

As a child, you asked many questions. You developed a keen sense for hypocrisy and lies, so tended to make many of the adults around you quite uncomfortable. Insatiably curious, once you wanted to know something, you would not give up until you found it out. Your skills led you to become an insurance investigator in the 1800's. Methods of covering up were quite rough and ready, so you faced actual physical danger in your work. You learned to be quite defensive, to expect an attack at any time. Your suspiciousness was honed to new heights in order for you to survive!

Safety in Silence

Even as a child, your mind was sharp and incisive. It was not, however, necessarily welcome. Your questions tended to embarrass adults: "Mommy, why does Uncle Ferdinand hit Aunt Maria and then say he loves her?" or "Father, why are you always too sick when we're ready for a picnic?" You family punished your utterances. You began to associate speaking up (particularly speaking the "unspeakable") with pain. Silence became your escape. You withdrew more and more inside, determining safety required not revealing what you thought, saw, or felt.

Neglected Nurture

Your mother died when you were three. Your foster mother (an aunt) died when you were seven and you were passed on to a distant cousin. Things didn't quite work out (her husband liked young children) and you were shuffled off to another relative. By the time you were of age, you had known almost no security. Wherever you went, a sense of angst accompanied you. Plagued by nightmares, you dreamt of a loving mother from whose arms you were torn by monsters, flood, fire, and other disasters.

Lasting Love

When you were 10, you fell madly in love with a young Scottish warrior. You decided he would be your husband in two years (when you reached a marriageable age). He was killed before you reached twelve, and you continued to mourn him. Refusing other offers for your hand, you remained unwed. Although you very much wanted children and a family, you could not imagine having any husband but your first and only love. Throughout your long life, you gave your heart to no other.

Putting Off Partnership

Quite an inquisitive child, you managed to secret yourself in many unnoticed corners. As a result, you heard a number of conversations not meant for your ears. You also saw a few shocking incidents—including the rape of a servant girl by a palace official—not meant for your eyes. The result was that you ended up not very suited for marriage. The thought of the power your husband would have over you terrified you and you put off the dreaded deed as long as possible. When forced by your parents to marry someone, you settled on an old, old man whom you hoped would die soon and leave you alone.

Eccentric Experimenter

A natural scholar, you began trying to figure the world out from an early age. With supportive parents, you had ample opportunities to study and experiment. You became fascinated by hypnosis, hysteria, psychokinesis, and other facets of the human intellect. Most scientist were outraged. Your work was viewed as crazy and unscientific. With dogged determination, you continued to plumb the depths of the unknown potentials in human perception. Although you missed the camaraderie of a support group, you were unwilling to give up your unpopular views. You continued as an outcast to the end of your days.

☿ Mercury in Sagittarius ♐

Censored Speech

As a child, you were bright, gregarious, and somewhat amusing with your naive comments. However, your honesty was not appreciated by many of the adults in your family. "Mommy, why did you tell Mrs. Hansen that Daddy was ill when he's been drinking all day?" Cuffs and curses eventually taught you to be less spontaneous in your utterances. Eventually, you learned to say what people wanted to hear. You developed quite a talent for sales after your mastered the art of disguising the truth to make it palatable, but you never felt comfortable again just chatting with someone.

Creative Conflicts

From your first babbled word, to your last bon mot on your death bed, language was a source of play for you. You kept a diary from an early age, and eventually became a published author. You were extremely torn. Half of you wanted to write a great, literary masterpiece and the other half wanted to write something that everybody would read. The novels you created were—in your eyes— reasonably good, but you were never satisfied. They were neither great contributions to literature nor widely popular best-sellers, but somewhere in between. Consequently, you always felt a bit lacking.

Out of Balance

An outgoing and attractive child, you became more vivacious, witty, and charismatic with age. An older gentleman became very interested in you. He assured you that you could have a life of fun and playfulness with him. He liked your youthful spirit. Although you had some reservations, you accepted the proposal. It was true that you didn't have to work and he took care of you, but you felt a lack of equality in the marriage. It seemed your husband knew no other role than the kindly (but firm) father. As long as you kept him entertained, all was well. If you attempted to be serious, or convinced him you were an equal adult, he became threatened and dictatorial.

Continual Questions

When you were five years old, you asked your mother, "What is God?" After that, you kept on asking everyone else. When you became old enough, you visited different churches, temples, mosques, rituals, and religious ceremonies of all kinds. You searched far and wide, talked to many learned people and many people respected as holy. Some of your meetings and experiences were inspirational, but none provided a sense of Final Truth. Your inner hunger for meaning continued, and your quest for answers remained through the end of that lifetime.

Beyond Boundaries

Born blind, you were restricted as a child "for your own protection." When given any opportunity, you proved yourself capable of much more independence than people were willing to grant. Inclined to question, you often made your parents uncomfortable. Although your siblings were relatively obedient, you always wanted to know "why" you had to do something. Many times the reasons given seemed insufficient, so you asked more questions. Despite being punished for this behavior, you felt an urgent need to know. You continued to be the odd one out with your curiosity and resistance to authority.

Wishful Wanderer

A restless, curious child, you became addicted to reading at a young ago. When you were old enough, you took up employment as a traveling bookseller. Moving from town to town suited you and selling your beloved books was very rewarding. An idealist, you wanted to believe that everyone was good. Consequently, you often gave people credit, and sometimes they took advantage of you. Your finances suffered because you would take almost anything in trade, wanting people to be able to read—but chickens and knitted caps didn't pay your bills. Although your life was more difficult that way, you refused to relinquish your rose-colored glasses.

☿ Mercury in Capricorn ♑

Subjugating Self

You were a butler at a "Great House" in Prague. You were expected to be stone faced at all times. Showing any spark of anger or excitement was particularly forbidden. You learned to always think before speaking. You were selected partly because you had a very deep, resonant, impressive voice which did well announcing the notables. The hierarchy within the servants was very rigid, and you often felt constrained. Life was serious and earnest and personal desires seemed to have no place. What you wanted was immaterial. Following the rules was everything.

Identified with Ownership

You were a letter carrier in Switzerland. Storms and bad weather added to demands of your job. Some people looked down upon you for your work. Your salary was low, but you were reluctant to leave the security of the known. Your inability to buy much contributed to your sense of inadequacy. You started to doubt your own worth because many people had more than you did. The more you measured yourself in terms of possessions, the worse you felt. Eventually, you started neglecting yourself physically which exacerbated the downward spiral.

Hard Labor

Born into poverty, you learned to work young—simply to survive. Your life involved a great deal of physical labor. Because you had limited education and no powerful connections, employers took advantage and worked you very hard. Although you recognized the strain you were under, you felt you had to continue just to survive. Life became one long grind, with very little break. Recreation was rare; relaxation even more uncommon. Most of your waking hours were spent on the job.

Pestering Partner

Although you had good managerial skills, marriage was the only acceptable avenue for a woman of your time and class. Your family was ordinary and your dowry limited. Not a raving beauty, you had some trouble locating a potential spouse. You accepted your first proposal, afraid you might not get another. After the wedding, you found that your husband was extremely critical. He would find flaws in everything you did. No matter how hard you tried, he was impossible to please. You avoided interaction as much as possible, but the negativity still affected you and your spirits and health sunk lower and lower.

Physical Handicap

Born nearsighted in a culture that did not yet include glasses, you gained a reputation as a clumsy youth. Hunting (the job of men and boys) was clearly beyond your skills, so you were grudgingly taught to gather (the job of women and girls). Although this allowed you to contribute to the tribe, you were almost an outcast since you did not fit into traditional roles. Other youths would pick on you, tripping you if you didn't pay close attention, and moving items just out of your reach and sight. Life became a constant struggle. Everything was more difficult for you than most people, and many paths were blocked due to your handicap.

Uneasy Imagery

Raised to believe that man should "tame" and "conquer" nature, you became one of the developers of the American Old West. Yet you would find yourself moved by the vastness of the desert, inspired by the beauty of a sunset, chilled by the mournful howl of a coyote. As you mapped out roads and railroads, and envisioned concrete covering the creosote bushes, a part of your wondered if this was all a mistake. Yet you couldn't really afford to listen to that still, small voice. So, you continued your practical course with the occasional strange yearning or restless dream.

☿ Mercury in Aquarius ♒

First and Foremost
Eager to explore new territory, you went west as soon as you could. Interested in progress, the cutting edge, and communication, you became involved with the telegraph, enduring great physical hardship. Excited by new technology, you eagerly followed the lines as soon as they were built. You suffered through drought, Indian attacks, blazing heat, runaway horses and worse. You were determined to be first in your work. Despite the danger, you responded to the thrill of breaking new ground, of expanding people's opportunities to talk to one another.

Unconventional Utterances
Your mind did not follow the usual channels. Even when quite young, you thought for yourself and questioned authorities. Naturally, people bigger than you tried to suppress it. You were ridiculed, criticized, and punished for taking contrary positions. Your unconventional thinking and speech were attacked, but you could not completely subdue your inner rebel. Although you went into hiding for a time, underneath, you were silently contemplating a different approach. As a result, simple conversation became a challenge because you were always struggling between a conventional and unconventional attitude, unsure how much to do of each style.

Tender Trap
A bright and expressive child, you enjoyed learning and exploring your world. When you came of age, however, it became clear that marriage was your only real option. You delayed as long as possible, but eventually had to take the plunge. Your husband was a product of the times and really not bad, but expected you to be obedient to him. You felt utterly trapped and rebellious. You didn't have the words (and the concepts weren't yet invented) to describe your need for freedom and equality, but you started feeling stifled. You'd wake up at night from dreams of choking and suffocating. With each child you had, the dreams got worse, but you saw no way out.

Constant Queries
Even as a small child, you had many questions. Particularly in regard to life's meaning, a truth which came down from "on high" was unacceptable to you. Somehow, you wanted a more personal experience that being told an authority figure had revealed all. Your skepticism toward familiar ways and paths was not

a popular position. Indeed, the faith in which you were raised was sufficiently outraged to cast you out. Your quest for more personal inspiration became a life-long search. Although you had flashes of insight and special mystical moments, you never felt you found what you were seeking.

Resisting Rules

Your parents used to tell you that you were born backwards and had been contrary ever since. As soon as you could talk, you asked questions. As soon as you could question, you challenged authorities. You fought with your father. You argued with the priest. You talked back to employers. You had little respect for authority and none for tradition and custom. As a result, much of your life was harder than it had to be. People would give you the toughest tasks because they felt you had a "smart mouth." Authorities put roadblocks in your way because you were a "trouble-maker."

Inner Idealism

An independent thinker, you parents encouraged you to ask questions. Your streak of nonconformity led you into some unusual situations. If people assumed something was true, you were likely to test it. In that way, you eliminated many stereotypes from your life. Your penchant for getting involved with the downtrodden in society was sometimes dangerous to your health. You associated with tuberculosis patients and other very ill people as you didn't believe their disease was sufficient to isolate them. A natural humanitarian, you wanted to make a difference. In the end, however, you caught a fever from one of the ill people you visited—and you perished.

☿ Mercury in Pisces ♓

Special Strain

You were a clerk in a hospital who was extremely conscientious. You always went above and beyond the call of duty, convinced that your little contributions helped make the world better. You sometimes felt overwhelmed by the immensity of ways in which the world needed improvement, and were inclined to try to rescue and save too many people. The physical demands were more than you could handle. You often ended up frustrated, trying to do the impossible. Yet your idealism would not let you rest; you felt you must do SOMETHING.

Living with Less

You worked as a mason in Greece, creating majestic stonework. Although you enjoyed the beauty of what you did, business was poor. You barely made enough to survive and could not afford a family. You considered trying other lines of work, but the economy was bad everywhere around. So, you hunkered down and just "got by"—not expecting much of life and not getting much pleasure from it. You didn't feel able to change anything, so you settled for much less and tried not to think about what could have been. You did without often.

"Don't Tell"

You were quite an intuitive and imaginative child, but out of place in your family. Very earthy types, they did not appreciate your imaginary friend and ridiculed the idea that you might have contact with fairies or elemental creatures. Your fantasies and the wonderful stories you made up in your head were viewed as lies and punished harshly. As a result, you learned to reveal as little as possible. Even when you knew certain things were going to happen, you did not dare mention them because earlier prophecies had terrified your family and brought much wrath on your head as an "unnatural" child. You became quite a silent, inward person, afraid to share with the world.

Deadly Dependency

You didn't know what happened to your parents, although you assumed they perished. You wanted to believe they had died rather than selling you to your master (as some of the other children were). Small for your age, you were one of the more adept beggars. You learned the art of limping, of making yourself appear disfigured. Your secret terror was that your master might permanently disable you in one of his fits of rage. He had beaten other children so badly that they lost a limb or an eye (and thus were extra pitiful as beggars), and you lived in fear that you might be next. Dependent upon him for the little bit of shelter and food that kept you alive, you saw no way out.

Favoring Fantasy

An imaginative and sensitive child, you developed a romantic disposition. Fairy tales suited your fancy. As a young woman, you fell madly in love. The object of your affections was of suitable age and class, so you were married. Disillusionment soon set in. You discovered that you had idolized your husband, seeing what you wanted to see, rather than what was there. Reality came as a shock. You kept on trying to reclaim your dreams, to put him back on a pedestal, but it was hopeless. Since your Prince Charming of real life turned out to be imperfect, you returned to the world of literature for satisfaction. As often as possible, you entered a fantasy and avoided reality in regard to relationships.

Otherworldly

Your parents swore that you were conceived inside a fairy ring, and that's when it all began. As a child, you were sweet and loving, but very inwardly focused. You would occasionally speak about incredibly beautiful visions and otherworldly vistas. Other people didn't understand, but those images were very real for you. Your parents tried to ground you in the "real world," but it had no particular appeal. You spent us much time as possible out with nature, drifting, dreaming, communing. The more they tried to make you stay with the physical plane, the more you retreated within and sought out your inspirational moments when space and time dissolved.

CHAPTER FIVE
PAST LIFE SCENARIOS: VENUS

If youo do not know the zodiac sign of your Venus, check the tables in the Appendix (pages 291 - 296).

♀ Venus in Aries ♈

Making Music

You were a minstrel and acrobat in medieval times, playing your lute and wandering about to various festivals. You enjoyed the freedom of travel and the creating of new songs and lyrics to commemorate various deeds or occasions. You got in trouble with a number of authorities when the tales you told did not feature glory to the "right" side. You had a habit of being direct and forthright in your stories, rather than praising whoever was in power. You often ended up hungry or physically suffering. If you had compromised, you might have found the security of a court position, but you were too independent to do so.

Limited Learning

You grew up the youngest girl in a large Welsh family. Since your father was quite wealthy, you were trained to be a wife. As part of your accomplishments, you learned to play the harp. Strumming your instrument brought you a great deal of pleasure. You enjoyed your ability to create music with your hands. Your other schooling—like that of most women—was minimal. You often felt stupid compared to you older siblings, particularly your brothers. There was so much that they knew—Latin, math, science—of which you had no inkling. But your pleas to study more were rejected on the ground that too much mental effort would strain the brain of a young woman.

Pricey Partnership

Even as a young child, you had an instinct for beauty and harmony. Following family tradition, you became trained as a potter and designer of fine china. You loved working with colors and figuring out the most aesthetically pleasing appearance for a plate, a cup, a bowl, etc. The owner of the shop where you worked became attracted to you. He made it clear that your job depended on marrying him. Although he was much older, you accepted his "proposal." It seemed the safest way to secure your job. (If he had dismissed you, finding other work without references would have been difficult.) He proved to a jealous, controlling husband and you had to work apart from everyone else thereafter. Your art was your solace in an unrewarding relationship.

Dangerous Desires

Born into poverty, few options existed for you. Through an acquaintance and your natural grace, you managed to get a small position in the Folies Bergere. With time and effort, your dancing improved and you were given more demanding parts. The pay, however, was not very much. Most dancers supplemented their income by taking on wealthy "protectors." You were quite pretty and got your share of offers, but did not want to become anyone's mistress. But you were also aware that in a few years you would be too old to dance and too old to attract someone's prurient interest. Finally, in desperation, you forced yourself to become the mistress to an admirer in an effort to save a little money toward the hard times ahead. The man proved to be insanely jealous and one evening, in a fit of rage, he strangled you.

Ambitious Arbiters

Born into the nobility, your life revolved around court activities. As you grew, your sense of color, design, and harmony led to your appearance being universally admired. You became quite an arbiter of fashion. Your gowns and accessories were widely copied. If you made a change, others rapidly followed. Your husband was quite pleased to have a wife who set the trends; it added to your status. You felt the pressure of your position. Other people also competed to set the standards of taste, and you knew your reign could not last forever. You worked very hard at maintaining your looks and your position. At times, parties seemed like a tremendous burden because you couldn't just relax and enjoy. You had to be on display, with everyone cataloging your appearance and deciding whether to still follow your lead.

Virtuous Victim

As a young child, the interplay of light and shadow fascinated you. Once exposed to the art of stained glass design, you rapidly became obsessed by it. After serving an apprenticeship, you sought opportunities to ply your art. At that time, the major market for stained glass was in the great cathedrals of the day. With a mystical turn of mind, you were very motivated to symbolize the beauty and wonder of God within your work. A less than scrupulous church official took advantage of your idealism. You worked for a number of years at a near-starvation wage. The cold winds of winter took their toll each season as well. Eventually, your body succumbed to malnutrition and pneumonia.

♀ Venus in Taurus ♉

Last in Line

You were the owner of a candy store and provided materially for many in your family. You felt they did not value you as a person. They only cared about what you could give them. You overindulged in your candy as a solace for a lack of love in your life and ended up quite overweight and critical of yourself. Your self-devaluation along with the uncaring of your family contributed to you feeling quite worthless. Unwilling to assert yourself or put yourself first, you continued to suffer.

Insisting On Independence

Abandoned at birth, you grew up in an orphanage. Knowing you had been abandoned, left you feeling as though you had some fatal, inner flaw. What could be wrong with you that your parents didn't want you? As you grew older and stronger, you became determined to be independent—to never need anyone again. Your rich, mellow voice let you to a career as a singer. You specialized in songs of love and loss. However, you continued to avoid any emotional connections and refused to let anyone close enough to risk hurt again.

Sold to Suitors

Born in Sumatra to a poor family, you had the misfortune of being incredibly attractive as a child and quite lovely as a young woman. Your family sought out the richest men around and offered you up for sale. Several of the men were willing to forgo the usual dowry to be paid by your family. Instead, they would pay to get you as a wife. Your family selected one of the oldest and wealthiest of your "suitors." Ironically, you ended up in a celibate marriage as your husband wanted you to show off to other men, but did not exercise his marital rights. However, he died of a heart attack after only two years of marriage. His will left everything to his children from his first marriage, so your parents took you back to go through the whole degrading process again.

Dangerous Deals

You served in a European court as a pastry chef and were quite proud of your skills. Even the king and queen admired the lightness and beauty of your creations. Politics, however, abounded everywhere. Every few days, people would invade your kitchen seeking to persuade you to slip a "love potion" into this or that person's tart or savory. Sometimes the "love potions" were exactly that. More often, they were noxious mixtures designed to sicken or even kill a competing courtier. A hotbed of gossip, people sought out any damaging information about other members of the court. The longer you stayed, the more your repugnance grew, yet you were also fascinated to be in the power center.

Negating the New

Following the footsteps of your father, you designed furniture in Serbia. Many of your early clients had worked with your father and expected you to follow his patterns. At first you did, but then you began to visualize very different designs. You sketched some radical chairs and tables, but the response was quite cool. Giving up on your new approach, you continued in your traditional path. But you regularly dreamed of clean, fresh lines and controversial, unusual shapes for furniture. You kept your innovations to yourself, afraid of risking them in the outer world.

Flights of Fancy

After a period of apprenticeship, you became a wig maker in Europe. Life was harsh and demanding, but inside the shop, you could lose yourself in your work. You spent hours daydreaming, while assembling a wig. You'd imagine a more ideal world where no one went hungry and people were never ill. In your imagination, you'd replace the squalor of the street outside with lovely boulevards — lean and full of flowers and happy, smiling people. Coming back to reality was a crash. Your work was artistically gratifying, but did not pay much. Your world was narrow and ugly, but you could escape in your fantasies to a world of beauty, grace, and happiness.

♀ Venus in Gemini ♊

Repressed Rage

You sold cosmetics and were expected to always be friendly and smiling. People would only purchase if they felt you appeared attractive. Being constantly ingratiating was a strain. You held in lots of anger and trained yourself to act as if life were always pleasant. Although you put a good face on everything, you had tremendous rage inside. Sometimes you felt as if it would just burst out, but it never did. You submerged it all and got periodic migraine headaches.

Poor Poet

You were a poet in Denmark. Never highly recognized, you just scraped by selling an occasional poem and doing odd jobs here and there. Unwilling to be anything other than an artist, you lived a life of poverty. With almost no possessions and sometimes going hungry, you remained faithful to your inner inspiration. You continued to write poetry, to produce, even though you received no material rewards for your efforts.

Inadequate Esteem

You worked as a seamstress in Argentina. You spent what little time you were not working designing beautiful dresses in your head. Occasionally, you would sew one of your creations for yourself or a friend. Everyone raved about your designs, but you felt they were not good enough. Although others urged you to break out and sell your own designs, you were afraid. You did not believe your talent was strong enough to support you. Although your inner muse compelled you to continue creating, you never did try to sell what you saw in your mind's eye.

Worked to Death

Born into a large Finnish family, you had to go to work young. Starting out as a scullery maid, you eventually became a barmaid. The job was difficult. You slept in a tiny chamber at the top of the tavern: freezing in the winter and unbearably hot in the summer. Of quite a petite build, you sometimes had trouble carrying the trays of food and heavy tankards of ale. Patrons would grab you as you passed, making your work more difficult. Although you detested the job, you made enough to survive on, and had no training for anything else. But it took its toll on your health. When you became ill, your employer warned you that he wouldn't support a "layabout." But your weakened body succumbed to pneumonia. As you were drawing your last breaths, you felt tremendous relief that you could leave that terrible job behind.

Pampered Partners

Born into poverty in rural Japan, your parents sold you to a woman who trained geishas. The costs of your training were added to your debt. Matters were arranged to that it was almost impossible for you to earn enough to pay off your debts. Inwardly quite resentful, circumstances required that you be graceful, charming, and diplomatic almost all the time. Although you met many men in your profession, naturally none of them would consider you as a potential spouse. They were all intent on being soothed, pampered, and having you cater to them. As a result, you came to view men as self-centered, demanding, and immature.

Ethical Issues

Raised among the German intelligentsia, you developed an ironic style at a young age. Inclined toward cynicism, you became interested in the politics of the day. Satires, political cartoons, and caricatures emerged as your tools of the trade. Particularly enraged by hypocrisy, you symbolically skewered all who engaged in double-speak and obvious lies. People nicknamed you Diogenes—on a quest for an honest man. Although your opinions were often strong, you also felt great doubt and searching. Unsure about life's meaning, you kept asking questions, pushing other people to clarify their values, and generally seeking an experience that would make you feel your life had a definite purpose.

♀ **Venus in Cancer** ♋

Saving for Security

You worked as a cook for an aristocratic Scottish family. You were able to indulge in the finest of cuisine and put on quite a bit of weight sampling your creations. Life was comfortable. You lived at the manor and had quite a luxurious room. You kept a collection of beautiful Christmas ornaments which you would bring out every season. Except for your artistic hobby, you saved every penny you made. You were terrified about losing your security in your old age, and determined to provide for yourself. Despite your concerns, you had a comfortable old age as you were pensioned off in addition to your savings.

Burdened by Brother

Born into "genteel poverty," you knew you'd have to make your own way in the world. Your mother perished with the birth of your brother, when you were 10. He was retarded and could never learn very much. Your father trained you to believe that you had to support and care for your brother as long as he lived. When you came of age, you accepted your first position as a governess, taking your brother with you. Because your employers agreed to feed and house your brother as well, they paid you almost no salary. Each next position was harder and harder, but you refused to turn your brother over to the parish. He was your burden, but one you would not surrender.

Family Fatality

Growing up in a large family, you had lots of brothers and sisters to play with. Even when quite young, you enjoyed taking on the role of "mother" to your younger siblings. You'd feed them, change them, entertain them. You married young, eager to start a family. Three miscarriages left you with a tremendous feeling of loss and worry. You were able to carry your fourth pregnancy to term, but the birth was very difficult. Your child was born with a club foot, but you were just thankful he was alive. Your next pregnancy produced a baby girl, but you almost died. The doctor warned you that you would be highly at risk should you try for another child. Determined on a large family, you ignored the doctor. You perished during the childbirth of your second son.

Partnership Prevented

You worked as a lady's maid, and were particularly skilled at hairdressing. Your abilities gained you a comfortable position in a noble house for a lovely young countess who had a very active social life. Also in the house was a very handsome young footman. You and he would trade glances when your paths crossed and walked together to church on Sundays. Gradually, you fell in love. But your employers were opposed to servants marrying. They felt it would disrupt productivity (particularly if pregnancy ensued). The lady you served threatened to turn you off with a "bad character" charge which would make subsequent employment nearly impossible. Rather than risk starvation, you and your young man decided to part. He was transferred to a remote holding and you never saw him again.

Positive Parent

As a youngster, you nurtured all the farm animals. You were fascinated by baby animals and loved cuddling and taking care of them. As soon as you were old enough, you married the boy from the farm down the road and started out to have a LARGE family. Your farm was small, and as the children mounted up, people warned that you and your husband would not be able to take care of all of them—but you paid them no heed. You and your husband ended up with 15 children. You were all quite poor, and worked very, very hard, but you felt it was worth it. Even though the weight of responsibility was immense, your nurturing side was satisfied.

Fading Away

You communed with the spirits of the Earth. As a young child, you could make friends with almost any animal and you often felt the trees were talking to you. As you grew older, your closeness to nature transformed to a religious calling. You wanted to enter a convent, feeling your place was as the bride of Christ. Your family, however, had come upon hard times and your dowry—if you married well—could be their salvation. They refused to let you train to take vows. Instead, they battered you mentally and emotionally until you agreed to marry. Although your marriage filled your family's coffers, you went into a decline. The doctors could not find what was wrong. You just became weaker and weaker until you died.

♀ Venus in Leo ♌

Minimal Material

You were a composer in Europe. Although some of your creations were well received, you did not make enough money to do much. You lacked a wealthy patron to ease your way. Your life was hard because your resources were so limited. Despite the material restrictions, you were dedicated to your art and refused to consider doing anything else. So you lived with hardly any material possessions, but much wealth of spirit and creativity. Yet, sometimes, you wondered if you had made the right choice.

Family Focus

Born into a large family with ties to the theater, you were the eldest. Your education was erratic, but you developed a strong sense of commitment to family. A skilled seamstress, you worked as a costume designer in the theater. Pay was low—but regular. You also took in piece work on the side, to bring in a bit more income. Several of your more flamboyant siblings elected to work in front of the footlights as actors and actresses. Their finances were often worse than yours, and they depended upon you for a helping hand. You often felt more like a mother than a sister to your brothers and sisters. You knew you could never have children of your own because your family of origin needed you too much.

Crushed Creativity

From an early age, you felt the rhythm of life. You danced your way through meadows as a child. You skipped down dirt lanes and swayed around trees. The tinkle of a brook was your orchestra. The lowing of cows provided harmony. Born into a family of farmers, they could not understand your need for graceful movement. The idea of becoming a professional dancer was utterly foreign to their thinking and values. Although you thought about running away, you knew from the little that you heard, you were already probably too old to become a truly top-notch dancer. Besides, you didn't really trust your ability. Your family also looked down upon you. So, you buried your dream, married another farmer and only danced occasionally alone in the moonlight when no one else was there.

Perpetual Practice

Before you were fully walking, you were trying to dance. Your parents were very poor, but like so many Russians, understand the glory of the ballet. You began training at age 3. Life was very harsh and difficult. Your food was limited and not always of the best qualities. Your teachers pushed you and the other students unmercifully. You practiced hours and hours. Over time, you broke toes, developed back problems and were often cold and sometimes hungry. But you couldn't imagine doing anything else. Your art was your life. Regardless of the impact upon your health and body, you were determined to dance, to fly on the wings of imagination.

Nature's Grandeur

Although your family was rather ordinary, you knew from an early age that you were different. The beauty of nature often moved you—sometimes to tears. You were obsessed with exploring new areas, seeing new places. While still in your teens, you ran away from home—to see the world. Disguising yourself as a man, you worked your way from country to country—driven by your need to explore. In each new land, you would seek out the hidden waterfalls, the special gardens, the inspiring mountains. You took many physical risks in your quest. Life was harsh and demanding, but you felt the grandeur that you experienced made everything worthwhile. You perished on a slippery slope in Tibet.

Severe Suffering

Apprenticed at an early age, you became a seamstress. Conditions were very harsh at that time. You and your fellow workers were paid a pittance, laboring long hours to create tiny stitches in garments for the nobility and upper class. The rooms where you worked were poorly lit and usually quite cold. Illnesses were common. Food was inadequate because your wage was minimal. You enjoyed the beauty of your creations, but were trapped in a demanding spiral of overwork. You felt powerless to change your conditions and would not even consider looking for a different employer. You were convinced all people in power were equally harsh and inhumane.

♀ Venus in Virgo ♍

Stuffing Self

The daughter of impoverished "gentle folk," you had little choice but to become a governess and chaperone to a young woman. Your hours were long and you were socially cut off. Your position was above most other servants, but well below family members. Generally, you were expected to be seen when necessary and not heard at any time. Your wages were minimal, but you had few options. The family which employed you did not believe in "coddling" servants so your tiny room had no amenities. You roasted during the summers and froze during the winters. Because food was almost your only source of pleasure, you ended up overindulging in it and gained a great deal of weight. Meals and snacks were your sole solace.

Captive Communicator

Born in India to British parents, you were to go home to England at age 12, to be "finished" at a proper school for young ladies. The ship on which you were traveling was captured. Most of the other passengers and crew were killed. You survived, along with a few women, but were sold into slavery. With an aptitude for languages, you quickly picked up the basics of your captors' tongue. Luckily for you, the women of the household in which you were bound were endlessly curious about both India and England. You spent long hours improving your verbal skills by entertaining them with stories about India and anything you could remember your parents telling you about England. Sometimes, when you were at a loss, you made something up. Your mind and communication skills became your major source of protection.

No Notice

Shy as a child, you were fascinated by the different colors and textures of wood. You would seek out different woods, examining their grains, the way they were cut, how well they worked for constructing different items. Although it was not considered appropriately "feminine," you badgered your family until they let you apprentice with a furniture maker. He was quite skilled, and you enhanced your good eye working for him. He offered you a position in his shop, but you had to keep your sex a secret. You worked in the back, hidden away from customers. Eventually, you got to design some of the furniture on which you worked, but you never got the credit. Your employer insisted no one would purchase your work if they knew a woman had created it, so he told everyone he was the sole designer. You labored long hours, for little pay, and no recognition, but felt being able to create the beauty you did was enough.

Helpful Herbalism

As a child, you were fascinated by flowers. You would collect all kinds. A natural scientist, you began rubbing herbs and flowers on cuts or burns to see what would help. You ate tiny amounts of various plants to test their effects. When you were old enough, you haunted the footsteps of the local wise woman. After her passing, you became the herbalist, midwife, and source of medical assistance for your village. People looked to you to help with their aches, pains, injuries, birth and death. You were fascinated by the human body and sought endlessly more avenues to repair, enhance, and improve people's physical functioning. When one of the "burning times" swept the land, you were called "witch" and put to death.

Endless Education

Raised by indulgent parents, you were permitted much more leeway than most young women. When you wanted to learn, they allowed you to be tutored with your brothers. When you became fascinated by science, they permitted you to study it—even the shocking anatomical texts of early medicine. You desperately wanted to be a doctor, but that was totally impossible for any woman— much less a young woman of "good family." However, your "excessive" education meant that most men would not consider you for a wife. Your parents had enough money so you would not have to work, and were able to pursue your quest for knowledge. You never married, feeling what you learned from books was adequate recompense.

Structured Service

Your parents were in service, and you naturally followed the same route. You became a downstairs maid in one of the "big houses." Conscientious and hardworking, you did your very best. You found, however, that others would take advantage of your dedication. More and more tasks were piled upon you, allowing the servants above you to slack off a bit. Since you were on the bottom of the totem pole, you did not feel you could complain. You attempted to handle everything you were assigned, but it was often too much. You felt guilty for not being able to cope better, but felt trapped in a position where you wouldn't be able to progress. You realized that as long as you worked as hard as you did, no one would encourage you to move up the servant hierarchy. They liked having you available at the bottom.

♀ Venus in Libra ♎

Simple Silence

The last child of a large and boisterous family, you were often overlooked in family gatherings. Everyone else was so loud and expressive, you hardly got a work in. You became used to being "invisible"—unseen and unheard. Indeed, after a time, you felt you had nothing of any worth to say, and didn't even try to have any input. Although quite silent, you had a wonderful eye for color and design. You ended up working for a decorator. Your skills at window displays were particularly valuable. You created some absolutely beautiful environments, but were never comfortable enough to talk to customers. You let your work and your boss speak for you, even though you could have made more money had you gotten over your social discomfort.

Emotional Isolation
While your parents were alive, they received just enough income to support the three of you (barely). After their death in a carriage accident, you had to seek employment. The local vicar found you an initial position as a paid companion to an elderly woman. After she died, you went to another household. The woman you served was quite crotchety. Because positions were hard to find, you did not dare leave. She kept few servants, expecting you to wait on her as a servant as well as a companion. Your room was tiny and freezing most of the time. Your food was barely adequate. Usually critical, your employer was a difficult companion. Pets were absolutely forbidden to you, and you hungered for some loving contact. Eventually, you made friends with a mouse sharing your quarters. Your adopted mouse became your sole connection with emotional warmth and attachment.

Sweetly Serving
Incredibly beautiful as a child, you were sold to the owner of a Hong Kong brothel. Very warm and loving, despite your mistreatment, you made good friends with the other girls and women at the brothel. You became interested in acupressure and learned a little of the art which you would use to help ease the aches and pains of your fellow workers. Because you were so eager to help everyone else and be pleasant, you were often taken advantage of. Your health suffered from the people with whom you had to deal. You ended up dying at a young age, much missed by the women you left behind in the brothel.

Muse or Marriage?
From the earliest age, you were driven to sketch. Eventually, you began to paint. Although your society did not accept the idea of women as creative artists, you continued to paint, feeling you had no choice. Your art left you no real room for relationships. Although a few man asked for your hand in marriage, each one expected that you would stop painting upon marriage—and you could not accept that. Given a choice between a relationship and your creation of beauty, you stayed loyal to your muse.

Addictive Art, Addictive Affair
Blessed with extraordinary talent, you found your medium in sculpture. Your statues were intense, emotionally moving pieces. While still quite young, you

fell in love with an older artist—well established as a sculptor—and an already married man. Your passions became equally divided between an affair with him and your inner burning need to create. A few people felt your abilities surpassed your mentor's, but most dismissed you as "only a woman." Even your family, who loved you very much, could not understand that art was as essential as air to you. Obsessed with your lover, you became more difficult for people to deal with. Finally, the people around you had you committed to an insane asylum.

Pursuing Purity

You believed in beauty, in truth, in love. You practiced charity toward all, but sometimes lacked common sense. As a consequence, you were victimized by people less ethical than you. Despite repeated disillusionment, you refused to take steps to protect yourself. You continued to act as if everyone had your highest good on their minds. Your artistic style was one of lovely, ideal vistas occasionally people by incredibly beautiful beings of light. People did not understand you; they accused you of being possessed and crazy. Because you kept on turning the other cheek, many people became even more cruel, trying to teach you "realism." You never learned.

♀ Venus in Scorpio ♏

Closed Channel

Born mute into a large family, you were an outsider from an early age. Your family was too busy to try to master other forms of communication, so they pushed and shoved when they wanted you to move and otherwise treated you much like a "dumb animal." Other people did not know how to cope with you, so they often ignored you. As a result, you often felt invisible and insignificant. Although you were quite bright, the barriers to communication frustrated you greatly. You developed rough a rough sign language, but most people around you had no interest in adapting to your system. Since you couldn't speak their language, they dismissed you. By the end of this lifetime, you had a raging, insatiable need to talk!

Chancy Childbirth

Born into the upper classes of Europe, you married well. Your husband expected an heir to carry on the family line. Pregnancy was extremely difficult for you. Severe morning sickness plagued you. Time after time, you miscarried. The doctors worried about your health, but the demands of "heritage" kept you trying. As much as you yearned for a son, you grew to detest being pregnant. You felt trapped and knew that the repeated pregnancies were threatening your life. After twelve years of suffering, you carried a baby to term. Fortunately, it was a boy. Your husband, however, believed in "an heir and a spare," so you were expecting again a year later. That time, you died in childbirth, swearing to yourself that family and vulnerability were to be avoided at all costs.

Unhealthy Habits

An early student of medicine, you were also artistically talented. Your skills were called upon to create a textbook of anatomy. The State disapproved of such studies and all subjects for your sketching were cadavers obtained through questionable means. Due to the limited understanding of the times, you were often exposed to dangerous diseases. You suffered through many serious illnesses, managing to pull through each time, but getting progressively weaker. Your friends begged you to give up medicine, feeling you were risking your life, but you felt a drive to be of service. Eventually, your overworked, over stressed body gave out.

Miserly Mate

Although your family was well off, everything you owned became your husband's upon marriage. Unlike some spouses, he did not beat you. But he was incredibly miserly. He doled out barely enough money to purchase food in the market. He threw a fit if the household did not use up the last little smidgen of every candle. He expected all linens to be repeatedly mended and reused, even when everything was in tatters. Even the smallest bit of "pin" (personal) money was denied you. He maintained absolute control over everything. You lived with tremendous resentment at the unfairness of it all. You dreamed of the day when he would die and you would have some financial say in your life. He lived many years and continued to deny, deprive, and dictate to you that entire period.

Puritan "Prison"

You were blessed with a highly sensual nature. From a young age, you savored life's sensations. You sought out every kind of physical contact because you found it highly pleasurable and stimulating. When you discovered sexuality, it was a wondrous time! Your peers, however, were of a Puritan persuasion. Your behavior was viewed as scandalous, perhaps even the work of the devil. Nothing you could say swayed their beliefs. You were ostracized, barely tolerated in the village. Although your outsider status saddened you, and made mutually gratifying sexual encounters more difficult, you sought refuge in nature. Unwilling to adjust to the group, you continued your own way, spending many lonely hours in the woods or by the sea.

Ecstatic Enlightenment

From an early age, you yearned for a connection. Inside, you knew that you were meant to merge; you just weren't sure how or in what circumstances. You tried many mystical paths and did enjoy the Oneness of the ocean and the mountains, but you wanted more. You also experimented with some drugs, but rejected them as ultimately unsatisfying. Then you met someone who introduced you to selected Tantric practices. This became your path to ecstasy. You became obsessed with prolonging sexual bliss. Your body, and your partner's body, became temples. You developed an incredible, acute awareness of even minute sensations within your body. You raised the intensity of your orgasms to amazing heights. This part of your life became so important that everything paled in comparison. You neglected family, work, friends, and hobbies to pursue enlightenment through sexual ecstasy.

♀ Venus in Sagittarius ♐

Personal Pressure

You were an artisan who wandered from one craft fair to another. Your family constantly complained about the level of support you provided, about the travel, about everything. You felt like no matter what you did, it was never enough to satisfy them. You knocked yourself out trying to please them, but they just demanded more. Although you enjoyed the freedom and open air of the fairs, you felt guilty for being away from your family. You tried to make it up when you were home, and pushed yourself much too hard, trying to satisfy your loved ones. You felt you could never do enough.

Small Pleasures

You were a seamstress. Although your work was excellent, the pay was terrible. You shared housing with other seamstresses, and just barely got by materially. Your employer and society in general treated you as insignificant. You felt almost guilty about wanting more out of life. Hard work was not enough to get ahead. Your life was limited, yet you savored the moments of beauty which you could find. A sunset, flowers in the park—small, fleeting experiences brought you much gratification. Despite the harshness of life in general, you pursued goodness and beauty.

Diverse Directions

Multi-talented, you had many interests as a child. As an adult, you pursued art. You began as a painter, then switched to sculpting. After a stint with clay, you turned to pottery. Then you became inspired to work with stained glass for a time. In each fields, your teachers and peers were impressed with your potential. But you never stayed long with anything. Your restless curiosity would pull you in another direction. Even when you had excellent patrons and good prospects for success, you felt an irresistible urge to try something new. Although you lived a rich and varied life, you often wondered if you should have focused on one or two areas instead of pursuing so many different directions.

Domestic Demands

Eldest in a family of 10 children, your parents perished in an accident when you were only 14. Feeling responsible, you scattered your siblings among other relatives and kept the three oldest (13, 12 and 10) with you. Finding work in a kitchen as a candy-maker, your wages allowed only bare survival for you and your brothers and sisters. Your 13-year old sister began doing piece work as a seamstress. Your 12-year old brother ran errands and got little tasks from neighboring businesses when he could. Although you tried hard to maintain family feelings, life was too tough to do much other than get to work, labor, go home and eat and go to bed. As much as you loved your family, you felt burdened by their care. You dreamed of a time when you could be independent—not emotionally tied to anyone.

Avoiding Applause

From an early age, you thought in poetic phrases. Metaphors and imagery came naturally to you. Blessed with a talent for rhythm, you instinctively worked with rhyme. Your parents however, had little respect for poetry—particularly when written by a female. They derided your efforts. Your inner compulsion to create was too great to deny, so you stole paper whenever and wherever you could. You wrote in private, late into the night, and hid away your poetry. Although you yearned to share your work with the world, you feared rejection, so continued to avoid public exposure. Even after your parents died and your spouse admired your work, you were too terrified of negative feedback to risk submitting your work for publication.

Miserable Marriage

As a child, you loved learning and sought out opportunities to expand your knowledge. Your family, however, felt that education was wasted on a girl. You were told to focus on household matters and not pine after learning to read or other "nonwomanly," intellectual pursuits. At a young age, your parents had you married to a much older man. They thought he would be a stabilizing influence. You felt trapped throughout that marriage. Your husband controlled everything you did. You couldn't do anything without letting him know. You barely had any time to yourself. You had no money of your own and he demanded an accounting of all household expenditures. You swore to yourself that once he died, you would never marry again.

Innocent Idealism

You were an midwife in the "burning times." You lived close to nature and loved wandering the fields and forests collecting your bounteous herbs and plants. Sickness struck the land, and people wanted a scapegoat. You were denounced as a witch. A friend warned you, and urged you to flee. You declared your innocence, however, and believed (naively) that God and the people you had served would protect you. A mob frenzy developed, and no one would witness for you, or contradict your accusers. You died, still unwilling to accept that people would do such wrong in the name of religious beliefs.

♀ Venus in Capricorn ♑

Self Stress

You were a carpenter who labored very hard his whole life. You supported all your siblings for many years, and carried the burdens of your own spouse and children as well. You took responsibility for everything. All the people around you relied upon you. Emotionally, the weight of the world rested upon your shoulders. As a result, you developed back problems. Life became more and more of a burden, and you couldn't see any way out. You were unwilling to release any of your responsibilities, so became more and more stressed.

Lost Learning

Because of family pressures, you left school at a young age. Agile, quick, alert, and observant, you got hired to help in a neighborhood store. By working hard, you eventually got to the point where you could invest in a store of your own. You build yourself up to considerable success. However, you always felt your lack of schooling keenly. You hated for anyone to know how difficult it was for you to read. You thought often about going back to school, but never seemed to have time and felt you were "too old" to be taking basic classes. You compared yourself a lot to people who were very articulate or well-read and felt inadequate in comparison. Despite your considerable material successes, you continued to feel your mind was not as good as the people around you.

Concealed Creativity

From a young age, you showed talent in design. You had a way of putting together bits of this and that to create a harmonious room. You sketched clothing and designed jewelry. Although your family enjoyed your efforts, they did not view what you did as significant. They felt more practical skills (such as cooking, taking care of livestock and gardening) were much more valuable. However, some of your sketches were noticed by the town jeweler and he took you under his wing. He began creating some of your designs —and selling them for a good price. He gave you only a pittance, saying it was his materials and time to make the jewelry that mattered most. Although you wanted more respect for your creativity, you did not know how to achieve it, so continued to create with no real credit. Many times, the people who purchased "your" jewelry were not even told who the designer was.

Ill-Used

Born into poverty, you were "fortunate" to be apprenticed to a milliner at an early age. The wage was substandard, so your body became malnourished. Working hours were long, in dark, poorly lit back rooms. Any damage to fragile materials, such as feathers, was subtracted from your inadequate salary. You felt unable to go anywhere else. Your family could not help; you had no spouse. Each winter, your cough became worse. Your health steadily declined, but you continued to do your job the best you could. Eventually, when you were too sick to carry out your duties, your employer simply put you out. With no savings or safety net, you ended up perishing on the streets shortly thereafter.

Married to a Mercantile Man

Your family trained you to be a "good wife." In due time, you married the proprietor of a dry goods store. It was considered a fortunate alliance, as your husband's business insured a good income to your family, but you actually fell in love with your husband. The hours of running the store, however, were very long. You hardly saw him. Almost all his waking hours were spent supervising employees, doing the books, ordering materials, or looking after other store matters. You suggested helping out in the store, but he wouldn't hear of it. He insisted you be a "lady of leisure." The more time passed, the more you resented the store, feeling your marriage competed with the business—and the business was winning.

Consolidating Connections

As a child, you enjoyed observing people working together. You were fascinated by shared efforts, people who combined forces to get what they wanted. Your family was very disconnected. No one seemed to care much about anyone else. None of your siblings were close to you. Your parents did the minimum in terms of raising you and then invited you to leave. As an adult, you became a matchmaker. Although you knew many people, you were not close to any of them. Your objectivity and detachment was an asset in making judgments regarding putting people together. You worked very logically and found great success. But your skill in bringing other people together could not bring any emotional closeness into your life. You remained the outsider, not knowing how to get in.

♀ Venus in Aquarius ♒

Material Misery

You were an opera singer, eager to share your gift with the world. Competition was fierce, and although your voice was excellent, other women had truly superb voices. You ended up having only small, insignificant roles. The pay was also minuscule. As a result, you could barely buy enough food and shelter. Materially, you were almost totally destitute, yet you continued to strive to get larger roles. You did your best to exist on beauty alone.

Power Puzzles

Born into an aristocratic Persian family, you were taught superiority from a young age. Servants were hardly to be seen or heard, and your wants were paramount. As you grew older, you enjoyed the attention, but a part of you wondered. You were not sure you deserved this "special" place. As you read,

few forbidden books. You began to investigate the occult, to experiment with tarot cards, tea leaves, and other tools of divination. Your community discovered your studies and was horrified. In their eyes, you were consorting with the Devil. They decided banishment was necessary and you were forbidden to talk with anyone—even your family—ever again. You were dead to them all.

Vivid Visions

Water fascinated you. Growing up by the sea, you learned to swim and felt at peace when in the ocean. As you grew older, you learned canoeing and spent much time exploring nearby rivers and waterways. But art as well as nature drew you. After much experimentation, you settled upon watercolors as a medium. But the normal soft pastels were not for you. Vivid, strong colors inflamed your palette. Potential buyers were put off by your unusual style, but you were unwilling to compromise. Ready to change the world of art, you took on the role of visionary outlaw—proclaiming a new message through this unusual medium. Society, however, turned its back. You had gone outside acceptable boundaries, and they would not let you back in.

Spiritual Crisis

Raised in an orphanage run by a nunnery, it was natural for you to turn to the Holy Orders when you came of age. Interested in herbs and healing, you trained as an apothecary. Your skills were particularly needed because the Alsace region you inhabited—between modern Germany and France—was the setting of much warfare. You and your fellow brothers often tended the wounded of both sides. It was this constant carnage that created your life crisis. One day, in the midst of the bloodshed, you started to question God. You asked for a sign, a reason for all the destruction—and received no response or omen. So, you faith began to diminish. With each day, your belief in God lessened, and your anxiety and insecurity increased. Life became more painful and threatening as the underpinnings of your life had shifted, and you felt no real purpose, meaning, or understanding any more.

CHAPTER SIX
PAST LIFE SCENARIOS: MARS

If you do not know the zodiac sign of your Mars, check the tables in the Appendix (pages 297 - 300).

♂ Mars in Aries ♈

Scant Survival

You were a fierce Zulu warrior who was captured by an enemy tribe while still only in your twenties. You spent 10 years fighting your captivity, being beaten, and barely staying alive. Two times, the leader of the tribe put on a show where you were humiliated so that he would look good. Sheer will power kept you alive despite poor nutrition and physical abuse. By chance, you learned you were finally to be sacrificed to the gods of your captors. You managed to escape, but were so physically worn down that you did not survive the attempt to return to your home.

Frozen Feelings

You were a knight who joined the First Crusade. You saw so much cruelty — from others in your group and by the "infidels" — that you strove to cut off your feelings. You felt you could only be effective in war if you denied your compassion and vulnerability. When you finally returned home, you did not know how to reconnect to your emotions. You remained cut off, afraid to care, afraid to let others care.

Diligent

You were a foundry worker who labored hard and long. Your health suffered under the harsh working conditions. But you felt an obligation to do your best and refused to look elsewhere for work. Plus, you doubted that your skills were sufficient to get you a better position elsewhere. If others were critical of what you did, you accepted their judgment, because no one was as demanding of you as you were of yourself. You often pushed yourself very hard physically. You ended up doing great damage to your health.

Political Perils

You were a guard outside a sultan's harem, and were a eunuch. You learned to totally deny even faintly sexual feelings. You sublimated all your sensual needs into wonderful massages and collected many different kinds of oils. You had excellent intuition and used it to keep your feet within the complicated machinations that went on at court. Each wife and concubine had her political ambitions and the older children were involved as well. Your skills at political game-playing were kept at high pitch as it was sometimes a life-or-death decision.

Battling Beliefs

You were a Berber warrior who was captured and had to become a gladiator in ancient Rome. You enjoyed the thrills of the arena, the challenge of putting your life on the line. At one point, you were exposed to some of the early Christians. You ended up having long discussions with them about the meaning and purpose of life. Your beliefs and ethics began to shift. Then, you were assigned to "battle" (slaughter) some of those early Christians. You decided you could no longer kill. You were executed for your beliefs.

Wishing and Wanting

You worked as a lumberjack, enjoying being outdoors. At times, the immensity and beauty of the woods would sweep you into an altered state of consciousness. You felt a mystical connection to life and groped toward spiritual understandings. Your brief glimpses of another dimension led you to investigate areas other people overlooked and to seek out individuals who shared your transcendent leanings. You got involved with a charlatan who pretended to be a psychic. He ended up making a fool of your in front of your friends and you were mortally embarrassed and disillusioned.

♂ Mars in Taurus ♉

Simply Surviving

You were a shepherd in what is now Greece when invaders from the north captured the area in which you lived. You attempted to stay in the wild and survive. The beauty of your world was destroyed as they burned some areas, cleared others, and altered all. Living off the land was difficult, especially in winter, and you often went hungry. You looked all over for other herders or people from your village who might have reacted as you did, but found no one. You felt the constant pressure of time and survival needs. You moved almost constantly, changing directions erratically and often lest you establish a pattern the invaders could spot. Despite all your efforts, you were eventually hunted down for sport by the barbarians.

Learning Loss

You were a serf in Bohemia. You had a thirst for learning and wanted to enter into the Church was the only path for someone of your background to escape your birth. However, your father died and you had five younger siblings and you were forced to remain on your lord's estate in order to provide for your family. Although you did your duty, you often thought longingly of the life you could not enter. When you went to church, you kept all senses alert for picking up more information or understanding. Once you were able to touch an illuminating manuscript and you almost wept for its beauty and the knowledge you knew lay within, beyond your reach.

Leaving Love

You were a Flemish bodyguard assigned to protect a small group of noblewomen on a pilgrimage to Rome. You found yourself falling in love with one of the young women and you were led to believe that she felt the same way about you. However, given the differences in status between you two, you knew that the chances of marriage were impossible. After successfully escorting the women to Rome, you found them another bodyguard and regretfully left their employ, resigned to never seeing your love again.

Mystical Mountains

You were a fur trapper in the American West. For awhile you trapped beaver ("brown gold") until you could not find anymore. For awhile, you trapped red wolves until you couldn't find anymore. Although you had been raised in a traditional Christian background, you experienced many mystical moments when alone in the woods. You began to wonder if perhaps the disappearance of the beaver, the disappearance of the red wolf, had some deeper, underlying meaning. You gave up trapping for profit and became a hermit, living off the land, taking no more than what you needed.

Subsistence

You were a settler in the Plains of the Midwest, but the site you chose was rocky and difficult to farm. Developing your place meant years and years of backbreaking labor. Winters were particularly difficult and life was harsh. Although you had a small family, you struggled constantly to provide for them. Although you did everything possible, you were haunted by guilt, feeling that somehow you should have been able to overcome all the obstacles.

Cosmic Connections

You were an Eskimo hunter, artist and mystic. You found periods alone on the ice soothing and often entered an altered state of consciousness. When you had time, you would carve beautiful figurines out of bone. You spoke with the spirits of the animals you hunted, asking their forgiveness and telling them of the uses to which you would put their meat, fur, and bones. Although your life was physically harsh, you felt a strong spiritual connection to the world around you.

♂ Mars in Gemini ♊

Curtailed Caresses

You worked as a village blacksmith in the Bible Belt. You labored fiercely long hours. At home, frivolity was forbidden. You practiced extreme self-discipline in regard to food and drink. Dancing, card playing, and drinking were prohibited. Too many possessions were seen as detracting one's attention from the glory of God. Your physical pleasures were extremely limited. You enjoyed the sensual contact of stroking horses when you fixed their shoes, but even felt slightly guilty about that.

Lots of Languages

You were born a member of the Crow Nation. Eager to avenge the deaths of your two older brothers (slain by the Lakota Sioux, your people's traditional enemy), you joined the U.S. cavalry as a scout. Although you helped them find and kill many of the Sioux, you also felt frustrated because they could not really understand why you would help them (white men) against other Indians. To them, all Indians were the same. The soldiers also belittled your eagerness to learn many languages and to read everything you came across. Although you doubted your abilities at times, you did not give up your endless curiosity.

Doubts and Denial

You were a stage coach driver in England. One day, in driving rain, your reins got tangled and you had an accident. Some of the horses and a couple passengers were injured. Horrified and guilty, you quite your job and emigrated to the United States. You did a number of odd jobs, but were afraid to use your driving skills again. After several years, however, you were riding on a stagecoach between Yuma and Tucson when the driver became seriously ill. You took over and did marvelously. At the end of the line, the company representative talked you into hiring on as a driver for them and you spent many happy years plying your trade before retiring.

Undercover Underground

You were a union organizer in the coal mines of West Virginia. Of course this had to be a secret activity, because if you were discovered, the mine bosses would fire you. One day, company thugs came to your house, beat you up, and told you to leave town. While you were waiting at the railroad station, a friend came up and told you that your girlfriend had informed on you for the reward the company offered. You spent the rest of your life as an organizer, but traveled from town to town and never formed a close, intimate connection again.

Reason and Religion

You were raised in a highly religious family which had done very well in the livery stable business. Your parents sent you to college because it was considered a mark of distinction for the family. What you learned in college clashed with some of the religious precepts with which you had been raised. You started asking some embarrassing questions of the church elders, but none of the answers you received satisfied you. Neither were you fully satisfied by the responses of your professors. You ended up reading, wondering, and seeking throughout your life for a way to bring together faith and scientific reasoning.

Outside the Norm

As a youth, you enjoyed sports of many kinds, but took significant chances. Although other kids admired your courage, they considered you a bit crazy. You never quite fit in because the kinds of things you did well were less socially acceptable. You tried for a few years to "settle down" and handle an ordinary job, but you just couldn't. So, you went off to the circus and got a position as an acrobat. You grew very fond of the camaraderie of the circus because everyone was eccentric in one way or another.

♂ Mars in Cancer ♋

Stranded and Starving

You were trained as a Viking warrior, well tested to endure ice, snow and constant physical demands. Hardship was common during winter months, especially if supplies had been damaged or inadequately stockpiled. On one foray, your ship was damaged in a storm. You managed to make it ashore to a rocky island, but were stranded there. With no game available, you could not catch enough fish to survive and eventually starved to death.

Scarcity

You were born into severe poverty in a family of 10 children. Several of your siblings perished from childhood diseases worsened by poor health and inadequate nutrition. Although both your parents tried hard to eke out a living, they worked as sharecroppers and could never get ahead. The hardship and heavy responsibilities led to their deaths at an early age. You had no real option but to continue the life you knew and refused to marry or have children because you did not want to prolong the cycle of deprivation.

Unobtrusive

You worked as a servant in a "great house" in England. There were separate, narrow, dimly wit passageways for the servant. You were expected to be "invisible." If a guest happened to enter a room in which you were working and you could not make an unobtrusive exit, your job required you to freeze and remain silent. The people employing you treated you as if you were barely human. Conditions in the servants' quarters were quite bleak. Years of this existence battered your spirit and made you wonder if you deserved anything better.

Critical Couple

You were born into a Japanese fishing family in which your parents constantly found fault with one another. Although they were relatively loving toward you, they constantly criticized each other. Each tried to control the other. It was apparent to you that both your mother and father were very hurt by their relationship, but they appeared unable to find a way out. You chose fishing as your livelihood as well, but made a deliberate choice not to marry. You feared to end up as your parents.

Idealistic Images

You were raised in a family of ship-builders in New England. Dreamy and imaginative, you spent a lot of time visualizing exploring going all over the world in your vessels. You tended to idealize adventurers and people who traveled long distances. An idealist, you preferred to believe that all people were good. Several times, con artists took advantage of your good nature to persuade you to invest in an exciting "import" plan—with your money disappearing and no goods to show for it. Although your friends remonstrated with you about your gullibility, you were unable to give up your optimism and belief that people meant well.

Patient Practice

You grew up wanting to go to sea, but lacked the connections to become an officer. Aware of the awful conditions under which the average sailor labored, you refused to consider that route. So, you worked your way up instead to be a barge captain —piloting down rivers, transporting goods to markets. Although you felt sometimes you were accomplishing less than you were capable of, you enjoyed your limited authority. You worked hard to hone your skills to higher and higher levels of expertise.

♂ Mars in Leo ♌

Haves and Have Nots

You were the only child of well-off parents who achieved considerable recognition as an athlete. Your early life centered around your physical prowess and you took great pleasure in your success. As you grew older, you became aware of the large numbers of people suffering poverty and great deprivation. Although strongly motivated to help, you could only do so much. You grew more and more frustrated with the gaps between rich and poor. Once your parents were gone, you gave all your possessions to charitable organizations and ended as penniless as those you were striving to assist.

Sharing the Scepter

You were a minor rajah in the region of Punjab (India). You lived many years as an honored and respected ruler of your small state. As you got older, it became increasingly difficult for your to administer. But you were reluctant to hand over the reins of government to your oldest son. You took great pride in what you had accomplished and were unsure your son could rule wisely. You saw him as rash and immature—as you had been at that age. Finally, more in sorrow than in anger, he deposed you and you spent the remainder of your life in a small villa away from the palace.

Slight Sharing

You were born to an aristocrat family in what is now a part of Denmark. As a daughter, you were raised to make a political alliance. At the appropriate time, you were married off to a neighboring lord. He was enamored of another and made no attempt to hide it. Although you made the appropriate ceremonial appearances, you had no real closeness, no real relationship. You consoled yourself with incredible tapestries. You and your ladies-in-waiting created some gorgeous wall hangings in your hours away from your husband. Although you enjoyed the company of women and were very moved by working with beauty, a part of you always yearned for a close connection with a man. You felt you had something—you couldn't quite identify—that you needed to share.

Sensual Seesaw

You were a coach at an exclusive boy's school. The directors of the institution felt the example you set was very important. You were expected to remain celibate and eschew alcohol and tobacco. Your sensual nature was very strong, and you resisted giving up your pleasures. You would spend most of the week denying yourself and then "binge" on your half-day away from the job. You traveled to another town to make it less likely you would be recognized. The extreme of over-indulgence and then total denial were hard to deal with. You often felt off balance.

Conscientious Concubine

You were the lover to the monarch of small area now part of Thailand. He governed with quite a firm arm, so people often came to you, hoping you would intercede on their behalf, or soften a decision. You felt a tremendous weight of responsibility from your position. You truly wanted to do the right thing and often agonized over matters brought to your attention. You suffered great pangs of guilt when you were not successful to turning the wrath of the ruler aside. You kept on trying, but were always aware that the power you wielded was very limited and likely to run out some time (when you would be replaced).

Western Ways

You were an Apache warrior during the period when the Apache were confronting the white man's advance across the continent. The elders of the tribe were totally set on following the traditional ways. You and a few other young men suggesting learning the ways of the whites in order to fight them more effectively. The chiefs refused to listen to your radical approach. They insisted that the old ways be respected. They demanded that you follow the paths of your ancestors. Although you felt change was necessary, you bowed to their authority.

♂ Mars in Virgo ♍

Stoking Steam Engines

You were born into a large family which could barely feed all its members. Hunger stalked the household throughout your childhood. As soon as you were big enough to work, you left home, to make your way in the world. After a number of odd jobs (mostly involving physical labor), you became a stoker on a steamboat. You fed the coal into the engine, often getting blasted by hot air. At the end of each day, you were filthy and exhausted. Your wage was just enough to survive, but allowed no luxuries. Life, for you, was harsh with no ease and little beauty.

No Nurturing

You were born into poverty, with your mother dying when you were young. With no education, you found employment as a scullery maid. The hours were long and arduous, but you actually liked being involved with the kitchen and feeding people. Eventually you married another servant. Your hopes for a family were dashed, however, as you experienced one miscarriage after another. Eventually, even the thought of getting pregnant was too painful. You tried to tell yourself that any baby was better off not coming into your harsh world, but you yearned for one to nurture.

Deadly Dedication

You were a poor, struggling medical student in Rome. Eager to learn more about the functioning of the human body, you took advantage of any opportunity to observe illness, disease, or accidents. Because you were exposed to many germs, you ended up suffering through a number of illnesses yourself. Your workload as a student was also massive. The students were expected to perform long hours of medical work, so you were usually exhausted. One day, while you were observing the anatomy of laborers at a warehouse, there was an accident and you ended up being crushed to death by collapsing crates of merchandise.

Regular Raids

You were a raider in Scotland. Winters were harsh and most clans found raiding richer agricultural areas a way to survive. Alliances came and went with various marriages and clashes of arms. A trusted comrade from another clan could become a deadly enemy. Who owned what was often unclear. A man might steal a horse or sheep from a neighbor only to have it stolen in turn by a third party. Although you accepted your way of life as natural, a part of you always wondered why people couldn't all just ban together and help each other out.

Elusive Illumination

You were a laborer who sought out projects near some of the great churches of Europe. You traveled farther than most of your contemporaries, under great hardship, because you felt a need to observe these incredible cathedrals. You were inspired by the story of Jesus, but yearned to learn more. You would seek out priests to ask questions, but their answers did not satisfy your inner burning desire to understand. You did not know what you were looking for, but you felt that life had something grand and ultimate waiting for you to find it.

Skilled Sherpa

You grew up in the shadow of Mount Everest. A Sherpa, you often operated as a guide to individuals who came to climb the mountains of your homeland. The snow-swept peaks were harsh and unforgiving of mistakes. Only your arduous training and careful, conscientious following of safety procedures saved you and your party many times. Each trip was a new challenge. Regardless of how many times you survived, each new journey required tremendous effort. Your self-discipline was immense and you actually enjoyed pitting your skills against the Himalayas.

♂ Mars in Libra ♎

Hearth Hunger

Born into a reasonably well-off family, you were fostered out, as was the custom, to another family, to learn the skills of becoming a squire and then a knight. Although your foster family was not cruel, they were not particularly warm. You felt a lack of love from an early age. Their focus was upon teaching you to fight, and to preserve the honor of your lord. Winning in battle was valued highly. You learned to suppress any feelings of vulnerability. You developed considerable ability and ended up with a great public appeal at many jousting tournaments. But the applause and recognition never satisfied your inner hunger for warmth, a home, and a family connection.

In Name Only

You were the daughter of a count. Your father married you off to a neighboring lord. While he was not unpleasant, he was inept. Within a few short years, and after providing him an heir, you became the governor in all but name of the now well-managed vast estate. Although you took pride in your accomplishments, a part of you was always bothered by the fact that your achievements were not openly recognized because of your gender.

Pining for a Partner

You were trained as a warrior and were often chosen to be the King's Champion. Rather than risking the king himself, you would battle another warrior in an attempt to prove the right of your side. Whoever won was assumed to have God on his side. You survived many bouts on behalf of your liege lord. Although you would have liked to take a wife, you did not. You felt it would not be fair to start a family when you might perish at any time. You had a long-term affair with an older widow, but continued to regret and pine for a committed partnership.

Initiating Inquiries

You were a strongly religious metal worker who created beautiful objects for the churches of Europe. Your creations were a form of worship for you. Even a simple gold candlestick became your homage to the Lord. You fell into the company of a young man who had been exposed to concepts of scientific proof and testing. Discussions with him led you to question some of your beliefs. When you went to the priests, the answers you received were not satisfactory. Yet you could not leave the service of the church, because you yearned for a sense of Higher Meaning. You spent the rest of your life torn between Science and Religion, feeling neither one gave you the Truth you sought.

Philistine Parent

You were an Eskimo artist who carved beautiful objects out of bones. But you came of age in a very poor family, during a time when hunting was sparse. Your father was particularly harsh in his attitudes toward you. He felt you "wasted" time doing your art, when your efforts at finding food were essential to the family's survival as well. You certainly did your share of stalking seals and other game, but he begrudged every moment you spent creating beauty. "But you cannot eat that!" was one of his favorite phrases. Although life was difficult and demanding, with mere survival a challenge, you refused to give up your art.

Insidious Individuality

You were an extremely graceful child who took training to become a flamenco dancer. Although the beauty in motion called to you, difficulties remained. You wanted to spend time with your friends. You wanted to play rather than follow the discipline of training. You felt like an outsider because none of your childhood friends had your talent. They were interested in more mundane forms of collecting money or settling in with a home and family. Although a part of you wanted to pursue your special gifts, another part was terrified of remaining separate—of not ever really fitting in with everyone else. Despite your promising beginning, you chose to marry and forsake your career. Although your individuality fought to emerge, you spent the rest of your life trying to be like your peers.

♂ Mars in Scorpio ♏

A Knack for Knowledge

You were born into a poor family and became laborer at the docks like your father before you. Although the work was difficult, you loved hanging around the sailors. You'd listen to their stories of faraway people and places for yours. Endlessly curious, you talked to anyone and everyone. Although you could not read and write (the family was too poor), you learned from each person you met. You thought of yourself as stupid and uneducated, but you actually gathered more information and knowledge than most people. Your life was filled with constant learning.

Continual Caretaker

You were born into a large Irish family—the oldest of 10 children. Your father died at a young age, but you followed his footsteps to become a police officer. You continued to live at home and helped your mother with all your younger siblings. You worked to get them all to gain some schooling and eventually become independent. Even after several brothers and sisters gained spouses and children of their own, you continued to be the wonderful, dependable uncle who would be there when needed. You were the rock on which the family rested, but had no idea how to get any nurturing from them. You suppressed any needy feelings and continued to do everything possible for your family.

Total Transformation

You were trained as a ninja in Japan. As a follower of the dark path, your skills were available for intimidation. If it served your master, you would threaten—and abuse—people. Debts which were owing would be collected by you—in money or in flesh. Able in the art of surveillance, you also served as a spy, uncovering important information. You explored occult ideas and magic, seeking additional powers. One day, a woman you knew introduced you to the concept of reincarnation. It rang true for you. Concerned about the karma you were creating, you disappeared. Moving far away from your master, you became a poor, humble digger of drainage ditches.

Safe and Structured

Born into poverty, you trained to become a soldier in the armies of the Tsar. Extremely conscientious, you memorized all the rules and regulations. You followed the letter of the laws exactly—both in your own behavior and in executing the law upon others. Justice was not tempered by mercy—but neither was it vengeful. The structure of the army made you feel safe; you had escaped the chaos of your childhood. As a result, you could be quite rigid. Your world was black-and-white with clear demarcations between right and wrong.

Student of Science

You were a scientist at a time when religion held more sway in people's lives. Although you had enough inherited wealth to not have to work for a living, your neighbors viewed you askance. They did not approve of your attitudes and saw you as close to a heretic. Despite general ostracism, you were wrapped up in your investigations, plumbing the workings of the material world. In later life, you became interested in explosive substances and experimented with a number of mixtures. Unfortunately, an unexpected combination and a stray spark resulted in your demise.

Everyday Escapes

You worked as a guard at the docks of New York. Many of your hours were spent day dreaming about other places and better times. You imagined many different scenarios for your life: as a ruler, as an explorer, as a perpetual hedonist. You visualized yourself adventuring in faraway lands, meeting fascinating people. You fantasized about meeting an ideal woman and sweeping her off her feet. In reality, you did not do anything to change your life, merely using your wonderful creative imagination as an escape from your boring, everyday reality.

♂ Mars in Sagittarius ♐

Detached and Disconnected

The youngest in a family of five, you often felt lacking in comparison to your older brothers and sisters. As you grew, you tended to doubt your mental abilities because the people around you knew things sooner than you did. You develop an odd quality of detachment, often feeling as if you were watching your family—but not really in it. At a young age, you left Europe to explore the New World. You became a trader, wandering from one rare white settlement to another and trapping in between. You also met many of the friendly Indian tribes and learned their languages. Your life was full of learning and new experiences, but you continued to feel more like an observer than a participant.

Rootless

You never knew your father and your mother drank herself to death on your tenth birthday. You took to the sea. Fortunately, you were strong enough to survive the abuses of starting out as a cabin boy and eventually ended up as a sailor on a ship with a fair—but not harsh—captain. You eschewed the alcoholic excesses that were common at sea, due to the example of your mother. You were soothed by the rocking motion of the waves and never got seasick. Driven by your inner (unconscious) sense of abandonment, you left your home as far behind as possible. At one point, you were involved with Admiral Perry's mission to open up Japan to the Western World. You never risked a home of your own—declaring the sea was your mother, father, mistress, wife, and child.

Marital Mirage?

You were raised in a family in which your father beat your mother. As you grew older, you lost any respect for him, seeing him as a bully. You spent as little time as possible at home, going away to school early and losing yourself in your studies. As you grew older, you watched your friends seek out women. Although they seemed satisfied to have purely physical relationships with some women, that was not enough for you. Unsure what you wanted, you continued to avoid relationships. You poured yourself into a quest to understand the world better. You joined an expedition to help identify and map the West Indies. As the years went by, your friends mostly married, but you stayed single. They teased you for being an idealist, but you were sure the marriage you wanted was not possible.

Quests and Questions

Born with a yen for adventure, you "ran away from home" often when young. Although your schooling was erratic, you made sure to learn about mapping, tracking, and living off the land. As soon as you could, you got involved with expeditions to explore faraway places. You spent quite a bit of time wandering the Himalayas. Their grandeur and majesty aroused feelings of awe in you. Being with nature helped you feel a connection to the cosmos, but much of your seeking a searching was a personal searching for answers about life's meaning. You questioned everyone you met. At special moments, you felt you understood, but those satori moments were few and fleeting. You traveled til the end of your life, each time hoping that you'd find more meaning or truth "over the next hill."

Command Central

You were born with itchy feet into a well-off family. When it became clear that your heart lay in exploring the world, your family encouraged you and helped to fund several expeditions. You hired people and took off to see the world. You were particularly active in investigating the interior of Africa. Because you dealt with physically dangerous circumstances and had to interact with different cultures, you felt the pressures of leadership very strongly. Your responsibilities lay heavily upon you. If one of the bearer fell ill or was hurt by a wild animal, you felt guilty. You tried to control and manage everything—to look after everyone. Inevitably you were frustrated as certain matters lay beyond your personal control. You pushed yourself unmercifully and periodically got ill from the stress. You established a lifetime pattern of feeling you had to be in charge and take care of everything. Life was often burdensome. (Yet exploring continued to excite and revitalize you.)

Massacred Martyrs

You were an early rancher in the American west. An idealist, you were convinced that if people would just communicate with one another, they could get along. You learned several Indian language and had a number of fascinating discussions, particularly with certain shaman, regarding life, God, and the purpose of humankind. Most other settlers and military folk hated Indians. While you were still rather young, a "massacre" of a near-by homestead occurred. It appeared to be the work of Indians, although a few people (including you) thought renegade whites could have done it as easily. You rode hard to reach the Indian camp nearby, trying to prevent bloodshed. But the military leaders had decided to take action and—when you refused to step aside, convinced from your discussions your Indian friends were innocent—you perished with them.

♂ Mars in Capricorn ♑

Physical Fitness

You were an American engineer who worked overseas. A foreign power accused you of being a spy and kept you imprisoned for many years. Although strong self-discipline kept you alive, your health suffered due to the conditions imposed on you. When you were finally released, your physical strength and stamina had decreased tremendously. You continued to do what you could, but had to work within very narrow limits.

Malnourished

Born into tremendous poverty, your mother's milk dried soon after your birth, due to inadequate nutrition. Although your parents tried to provide for you, hunger was often your lot. When you were only six, a "nobleman" out hunting and drinking wounded your father by accident. Infection set in and he died a painful death. You worked as a serf in the fields, beside your mother. Two years later, she was taken away "for sport" by a group of well-off young men. You never saw her again. A neighbor told you she had died; you were too young to fully comprehend the circumstances. You were not quite old enough or strong enough to get enough food, so you gradually starved to death.

Family First

You were a father who was ordnance commander (in charge of cannons) during Civil War. Although offered on numerous occasions a chance to command a battery in the field, you always declined, preferring to stay in the rear and be a supply master. This was not from a fear of battle, but because you had six motherless children that were being taken care of by your sister. You were highly motivated to return home to them. Called a coward by some of your fellow soldiers, you nonetheless remained true to your family. You survived and managed to raise them all to adulthood.

Abandoned Art

You grew up in the midst of poverty. Although you had strong artistic leanings, you knew life as an artist would not be possible. So you put aside your sketches, and became a solider of fortune. You worked your way up to captain of a mercenary unit. Occasionally you would sketch late at night by the campfire, but usually you were too exhausted. One winter, when you were out looking for employment, you noticed a young woman of good family painting. It felt like love at first sight. Her family was totally opposed to your background, and you felt she deserved a better life than the struggle she would have has your wife. You left her, and continued to regret the loss of your love and your art until perishing in battle a few years later.

Constrictive Conscience

You were an extremely conscientious prison warden. Although punitive approaches were the order of the day, you tried to always be fair. Your rules were clear, and transgressors suffered the consequences, but people who helped to keep order were allowed minimal privileges. You felt the weight of your responsibilities very heavily. You took your job personally, believing you were supposed to mold the criminals you oversaw into model citizens. You drove yourself unmercifully, looking for ways to have more of an impact. Guilt rode on your shoulder daily as you put so much pressure on yourself to achieve results. No matter how much you did accomplish, you felt you ought to have done more.

Mandating Materialism

Born into a family with a very controlling father, you were raised within a very restrictive religious viewpoint. Working hard, you put yourself through college, earning several degrees and an excellent scientific background. Eventually, you became a geologist and delighted in citing the evidence for the age of the Earth to people who believed in the literal word of *The Bible*. You placed your faith in material reality and had little patience for people who looked for a Higher Source in regard to creation. You wrote a number of papers defending materialism, and declaring that religion was dead (or unnecessary in the "modern" world). You enjoyed proving your father wrong.

♂ Mars in Aquarius ♒

Frustrated Freedom

You were an agitator during the long period before independence in India. You encouraged people to attack the "foreign devils" and throw out the English Raj. You refused to recognize any authorities and fought against the power structure at all times. At times, your very life was in danger due to your positions. Courageous, sometimes to the point of being foolhardy, you refused to back down. Chronic frustration became a way of life as the English remained in power throughout this lifetime.

Hidden Influence

You lived in the period prior to (and during) the American Revolutionary War. Active as a writer, you penned many popular pamphlets and broadsides in support of American Independence. All them, however, were published under a male pseudonym as a woman would not be taken seriously. Even members of your own family did not know of your literary/political influence. You were in the odd position of having your writing well-known, but your person totally obscure.

Harsh and Hard

You were born into a family of servants and naturally followed the pattern of working on one of the estates of the aristocracy. Life was very demanding. You labored long hours for little reward. Nutrition was poor and your health was not very robust. Ignorance of medical and lifestyle facts contributed to your many illnesses and physical problems. With the rise of the French Revolution, you became excited by the idea of equality and justice. At great personal risk, you traveled to Paris to be a part of these exciting developments, only to perish from the hardships of living on the streets.

Dutiful Daughter?

You were born into an Argentinean family with considerable wealth and were allowed some latitude. Although female, you were extremely active, athletic, and encouraged to learn. In many ways, your parents treated you more like a son than a daughter—until you hit puberty. Then they bundled you into skirts and demanded propriety and the development of ladylike skills in preparation for matrimony. You fought against your loss of freedom, but had no real options. As you were coming of age, Some Argentineans spoke of fighting for independence from Spain. You had hopes that the new republic would allow more independence on the part of women, but your hopes for equality were dashed. In the end, you were forced into marriage with a husband of your parents' choosing.

Testing Times

Your life was a series of test. Born the youngest of four brothers, your early years were full of challenges. Each sibling would demand that you "prove" you could measure up to his standards. As you were younger, you were often not as strong, or swift, or as capable. You learned to carefully assess your prospects before tackling a task. At maturity, you joined the military and underwent many more tests in order to move up through the ranks. You became involved with Poland's struggle to separate from Germany and took arduous training to serve as a spy and scout. Although you gave your utmost, you felt often that people less dedicated and capable than you achieved more recognition and power.

Resistance by Retreat

Much attached to your land, you had a mystical sense of connection to the spirits of the earth. You tried many art forms when young to convey the beauty and inspiration which you say in your dreams, but you were never satisfied with your results. You trained briefly as a healer, but decided that path was not for you. When white men came to your land (which they called New Zealand), you urged resistance. But you saw your folk seduced by beads and gauds and falling prey to the alcohol of the invaders, becoming passive. You sought guidance from the gods of the mountain top, but your impressions were unclear. In the end, you decided the whites were unstoppable, and so you retreated further inland to avoid them as long as possible.

♂ Mars in Pisces ♓

Minimal Metabolizing

You were a pioneer in Iceland who struggled greatly just to stay alive. You were constantly fighting the elements. Keeping warm was a major challenge. Hunger was often your companion. You experienced life as a constant battle. Taking care of your minimal, basic needs required great effort. At times, you thought it was all too much. Your burdens felt overwhelming. Although the stark beauty of the land appealed to you, the physical demands of your existence were unceasing.

Softness Suppressed

Your mother died when you were two, so your father became particularly active in your upbringing. Although aunts were in the picture, you tended to reject would-be maternal influences. From a young age, you felt if you couldn't have your "real" mother, you didn't want anyone. You took to warrior training with alacrity and did your best to eradicate tenderness, sympathy, or any softer traits from your character. Despite pressure on successful braves to marry and raise families, you resisted. Your inner fear of being vulnerable was too great. You decided you'd rather avoid the whole issue than risk the deep hurt of losing a loved one.

Conception Curtailed

You were one of the first Dutch settlers in Cape Town, South Africa. You and your husband were able to establish a large and successful farm. You were particularly proud of the orchards you had established from seedlings carried a thousand sea miles from Holland to Africa. However, your talent for being fruitful ended when it came to children. You and your husband were unable to have children. You both had great disappointment at not having a direct descendant who could inherit the fruits of your labors.

Missed Out on Matrimony

You traveled with your family to pioneer in the Louisiana bayous. You came to love to subtle beauty of the shifting mists, Spanish moss, and wild birds. You learned your way about the channels of swamp and water. When you matured, there was hardly anyone else around near your age. Your family was far from civilization, and the few other families nearby also happened to have boys. The few females available were either very young, or quite a bit older than you were. You were idealistic about marriage and very much wanted a wife who would be your equal, and near your age. Although you made a few trips to other areas to be introduced to women, nothing clicked. You ended your days alone rather than settle for a relationship you felt would not be what you wanted.

Career Commitment?

You were an adventurer in the South Pacific, wandering from place to place. You rarely stayed anywhere for long. At various times, you made your living as a guard, tinker, soldier, etc. You couldn't seem to settle into anything. Your conscience nagged you constantly. Part of you felt you should be committing yourself to a career, making some kind of contribution to society. The larger part of you was happy exploring, traveling, and meeting many different people. Although guilt remained a constant shadow, you continued your unstructured, open lifestyle.

Other Options

You were a dreamy youth who imagined fantastic vistas and other worlds. Yet you worked for a living in a fish cannery in Baja California. Your co-workers made fun of you because you sometimes missed an important detail on the job, dreaming about the universe. You'd stand under the canopy of stars at night and wonder if people lived in the far reaches of space, and if we'd ever meet them. Your peers viewed you as very odd, and you were never really accepted. No one wanted to associate with you as they felt you were a bit "loco" (crazy).

CHAPTER SEVEN
PAST LIFE SCENARIOS: JUPITER

The table below provides dates when Jupiter enters each sign of the zodiac. Jupiter remains in each sign until the next date in this table. Identify your Jupiter sign and then read the appropriate scenarios.

Year	Mon	Day	Time	Sign		Year	Mon	Day	Time	Sign
1930	Jun	26	10:42 pm	Cancer		1948	Nov	15	10:38 am	Capricorn
1931	Jul	17	7:52 am	Leo		1949	Apr	12	7:18 pm	Aquarius
1932	Aug	11	7:16 am	Virgo			Jun	27	6:30 pm	Capricorn
1933	Sep	10	5:11 am	Libra			Nov	30	8:08 pm	Aquarius
1934	Oct	11	4:55 am	Scorpio		1950	Apr	15	8:59 am	Pisces
1935	Nov	9	2:56 am	Sagittarius			Sep	15	2:23 am	Aquarius
1936	Dec	2	8:39 am	Capricorn			Dec	1	7:57 pm	Pisces
1937	Dec	20	4:06 am	Aquarius		1951	Apr	21	2:57 pm	Aries
1938	May	14	7:47 am	Pisces		1952	Apr	28	8:51 pm	Taurus
	Jul	30	3:02 am	Aquarius		1953	May	9	3:34 pm	Gemini
	Dec	29	6:35 pm	Pisces		1954	May	24	4:44 am	Cancer
1939	May	11	2:09 pm	Aries		1955	Jun	13	0:07 am	Leo
	Oct	30	0:45 am	Pisces			Nov	17	3:59 am	Virgo
	Dec	20	5:03 pm	Aries		1956	Jan	18	2:05 am	Leo
1940	May	16	7:55 am	Taurus			Jul	7	7:02 pm	Virgo
1941	May	26	12:48 pm	Gemini			Dec	13	2:17 am	Libra
1942	Jun	10	10:36 am	Cancer		1957	Feb	19	3:38 pm	Virgo
1943	Jun	30	9:46 pm	Leo			Aug	7	2:11 am	Libra
1944	Jul	26	1:04 am	Virgo		1958	Jan	13	12:52 pm	Scorpio
1945	Aug	25	6:06 am	Libra			Mar	20	7:14 pm	Libra
1946	Sep	25	10:19 am	Scorpio			Sep	7	8:52 am	Scorpio
1947	Oct	24	3:00 am	Sagittarius		1959	Feb	10	1:46 pm	Sagittarius

Table continues on next page.

	Apr	24	2:11 pm	Scorpio		1976	Mar	26	10:25 am	Taurus
	Oct	5	2:40 pm	Sagittarius			Aug	23	10:25 am	Gemini
1960	Mar	1	1:10 pm	Capricorn			Oct	16	8:25 pm	Taurus
	Jun	10	1:53 am	Sagittarius		1977	Apr	3	3:43 pm	Gemini
	Oct	26	3:01 am	Capricorn			Aug	20	12:43 pm	Cancer
1961	Mar	15	8:02 am	Aquarius			Dec	30	11:51 pm	Gemini
	Aug	12	8:55 am	Capricorn		1978	Apr	12	0:12 am	Cancer
	Nov	4	2:49 am	Aquarius			Sep	5	8:31 am	Leo
1962	Mar	25	10:08 pm	Pisces		1979	Feb	28	11:36 pm	Cancer
1963	Apr	4	3:20 am	Aries			Apr	20	8:30 am	Leo
1964	Apr	12	6:53 am	Taurus			Sep	29	10:24 am	Virgo
1965	Apr	22	2:33 pm	Gemini		1980	Oct	27	10:11 am	Libra
	Sep	21	4:40 am	Cancer		1981	Nov	27	2:20 am	Scorpio
	Nov	17	3:09 am	Gemini		1982	Dec	26	1:58 am	Sagittarius
1966	May	5	2:52 pm	Cancer		1984	Jan	19	3:05 pm	Capricorn
	Sep	27	1:20 am	Leo		1985	Feb	6	3:36 pm	Aquarius
1967	Jan	16	3:50 am	Cancer		1986	Feb	20	4:06 pm	Pisces
	May	23	8:21 am	Leo		1987	Mar	2	6:42 pm	Aries
	Oct	19	10:52 am	Virgo		1988	Mar	8	3:45 pm	Taurus
1968	Feb	27	3:34 am	Leo			Jul	22	0:00 am	Gemini
	Jun	15	2:44 pm	Virgo			Nov	30	8:55 pm	Taurus
	Nov	15	10:44 pm	Libra		1989	Mar	11	3:27 am	Gemini
1969	Mar	30	9:37 pm	Virgo			Jul	30	11:51 pm	Cancer
	Jul	15	1:30 pm	Libra		1990	Aug	18	7:31 am	Leo
	Dec	16	3:56 pm	Scorpio		1991	Sep	12	6:01 am	Virgo
1970	Apr	30	6:45 am	Libra		1992	Oct	10	1:27 pm	Libra
	Aug	15	5:58 pm	Scorpio		1993	Nov	10	8:16 am	Scorpio
1971	Jan	14	8:50 am	Sagittarius		1994	Dec	9	10:55 am	Sagittarius
	Jun	5	2:13 am	Scorpio		1996	Jan	3	7:23 am	Capricorn
	Sep	11	3:33 pm	Sagittarius		1997	Jan	21	3:14 pm	Aquarius
1972	Feb	6	7:37 pm	Capricorn		1998	Feb	4	10:53 am	Pisces
	Jul	24	4:43 pm	Sagittarius		1999	Feb	13	1:23 am	Aries
	Sep	25	6:20 pm	Capricorn			Jun	28	9:30 am	Taurus
1973	Feb	23	9:28 am	Aquarius			Oct	23	5:50 am	Aries
1974	Mar	8	11:12 am	Pisces		2000	Feb	14	9:40 pm	Taurus
1975	Mar	18	4:48 pm	Aries			Jun	30	7:36 am	Gemini

Example: If you were born in 1969, after March 30 but before July 15, your Jupiter is in Virgo. If you were born in 1969 after July 15 but before December 16, your Jupiter is in Libra.

♃ Jupiter in Aries ♈

No Nest

Your parents never understood you. From a young age, you were restless and needed to explore. Your mother became perturbed when you wandered far afield. Your father expected you to settle down and be quiet even when you were quite small. The older you grew, the more it seemed you could never satisfy them. At age 12, you hopped aboard a freighter and took off to see the world. You never went back to your family and never got married or had children of your own. To you, a home was a prison, and you liked having the whole world to explore.

Faraway Fever

Born in a seaport village, you yearned for faraway places. Had you been a male, travel would have been possible, but as a female, it was "inappropriate." Despite your dreams, you ended up marrying one of the young men in your village. Although you tried to be a good wife and mother, you often felt trapped. When your husband had a few opportunities to travel for business, you asked to accompany him, but he insisted your place was at home. You became more and more resentful and withdrew emotionally from the relationship. You promised yourself you would leave your husband the instant your youngest child left home.

Hints and Hazards

A very direct and forthright individual, you practiced honesty and expected it in return. Due to your family's position, you had to be somewhat involved with the politics of the time. You could never quite master the art of innuendo. Many times you were embarrassed because other people were engaging in secret or underhanded communications. You overlooked danger because you expected people to tell the truth. Susceptible to manipulation, you tended to find out about people's hidden agendas too late.

Crazy Confidence

As a youth, you were a daredevil. You loved taking chances. Quite athletic, you would risk your live trying dangerous stunts. The kids around you growing up were in awe of you. None of them had the raw courage (or foolishness) that you did. Your parents worried that you wouldn't survive to adulthood. Foolhardy, you had too much faith and confidence that you could handle anything. The more exciting the activity, the more attracted you became. After a number of close calls, you met your death taking a barrel over a waterfall.

Family Failure

Born into a "good Roman family," you were expected to measure up to a certain standard. From an early age, you learned that you had to be "better" than anyone else—because your blood demanded it. Life became quite a burden. Doing well was not quite good enough; you could have done superlatively! You became accustomed to repeated judgments of "still not perfect" and felt like a failure due to your inability to meet those inhuman standards. Although you never stopped trying, you never succeeded in accomplishing on a level that would get the kudos and satisfaction from your family.

Nature Nurture

Born into urban life, you knew it was not for you. Even as a tiny child, you felt stifled and confined. As soon as you discovered the country, you knew your path. You left the city and became a hermit. Close to nature, you felt close to God. Being on your own was easier than dealing with people. Although you felt guilty sometimes for avoiding people and running away from the city, you were not sure you could survive urban interactions. So, you had a very solitary, very quiet, introspective life.

♃ Jupiter in Taurus ♉

Possessions or Principles?

While still young, you discovered you had a talent for making money. Eventually you focused on the stock market and developed into quite a tycoon. You bought beautiful things and amassed quite a bit of property. Then, one of the Panics of the late 1800's hit Wall Street. Your portfolio was devastated, and you began to question your values. Although you still really wanted to enjoy the material (and sensual) world, you began to ask yourself if you should be pursuing other goals. You died without resolving your questions.

At Home in the World

You felt you had been born in "the best of times." The world was expanding. Trade routes were opening up to China, the Americas and other exotic ports. You were excited by all the opportunities and got into the import/export business at a young age. Quickly you built a name for yourself with a reputation for honest dealing and an excellent eye for merchandise which would prove popular. You loved traveling to choose new and unusual items. Married, with four children, you also adored your family, but often felt trapped by them. They could not understand why you needed to leave home so much. They wanted more of your company, but you felt the lure of other lands. Guilt was a constant companion for many years—until your children had grown and left home. Then you persuaded your wife to go sailing into the sunset with you.

Plenitude of Progeny

Born in Ireland, you were raised to be a good Catholic. As was expected, you married a local young man and started having children—just about one child every year. After the first six children, you became worried. The farm you and your husband had could not support that many people. You spoke with your priest who told you abstinence was the only possible path, but neither you nor your husband had any interest in that. You had two more children, feeling terribly guilty because you resented the pregnancies and did not love those two as much as the earlier ones. At that point, you sought—in great secrecy—a local midwife whose products to prevent pregnancy helped you slow your rate of production to only two more in the next ten years. But you felt great guilt and had tremendously conflicted feelings about sex, children, and love due to your experiences.

Never Enough

Born on the edge of poverty, you had a great deal of material ambition. By dint of much hard work, you built up an excellent business. Inside, however, you still felt inadequate. What you had gained never felt like enough. You worried that failure was just around the corner. Instead of enjoying some of the fruits of your labors, you continued to put in 14 and 16-hour days, working yourself much too hard. Periodic physical breakdowns were not enough warning. You kept slaving away until your death—convinced you had to achieve more.

Agricultural Advances

Born into a farming community, you felt extremely close to the earth. You love the feel and smell of rich soil. All aspects of planting, protecting, weeding, harvesting, and sowing again appealed to you. Drawn toward the future, you read widely on agricultural topics. The farm, however, belonged to your father who was quite traditional. He refused to try any of the "new-fangled" ideas which interested you. He insisted on following the old ways. You could have left and struck out on your own, but felt very connected to the actual land of your birth. So, you struggled for many years, trying to bring about progress without any real success.

Special Sphere

Your family was moderately wealthy and you were raised to be a "lady of leisure." Protected from misfortune, you had very little understanding of the real world. You lived almost a cloistered life, within the family estate. Seen as "delicate" by your parents, you lived with them until their deaths and then your older brother took you under his wing. You spent much time reading, fantasizing, and sleeping. Sometime you wondered about the outer world, but your family had convinced you that it was much too threatening for you to venture forth. So, you continued to exist in a private sphere for the rest of your days.

♃ Jupiter in Gemini ♊

Freedom of Information

You were a journalist who was drawn to danger. You put yourself at risk physically for stories. You faced imprisonment, physical hardship, and great stress in order to pursue the news. You fought with politicians, world leaders, and important citizens in your quest to gain information. You refused to recognize any limits to "free press" and suffered greatly at times from your assertiveness. You died young, at the hands of a foreign dictator who did not appreciate your efforts to reveal what was happening in his country.

Scholastic Suffering

Born into poverty, you were an extremely bright child. The local vicar was impressed with your intelligence and brought you to the attention of a neighboring earl. He arranged for a scholarship for your studies. Although you were enthralled by all you learned at the university, living conditions were horrific. Scholarship students were thrown together with no real discipline. The older and larger preyed upon the smaller and weaker. Food was inadequate and beatings were common. Although you learned much intellectually, your strongest conviction upon leaving school was that you would make sure you never went hungry again.

Paramount Passion

As was customary for young English women of your time, you were raised to make a "good" marriage with a respectable man. Having no particularly strong feelings for anyone, you accepted a man deemed as suitable by your parents. Although the marriage was not particularly rewarding, you and your husband did create a daughter whom you loved with all of your heart. Although it was unfashionable, you spent lots of time with her, adoring each step she took, each advance she made. Walking in the park with your daughter, you got to know a widower who took his son to play there. You soon fell deeply in love. Divorce, however, was unheard of—and would definitely mean you would lose your daughter to your husband. In terrible pain, you felt you had to choose between the love of your life and your daughter. You chose your daughter, refusing to ever see your beloved again, and wondering ever after if your choice had been wrong.

Extensive Exploration

Restless and twitchy, you needed much movement as a child. You ran away from home several times, eager to see the world. The final departure occurred at age 12. From then on, you refused to return to your place of birth. You wandered the earth, particularly drawn to wild, faraway places. Many of your travels were physically dangerous, but that fed your sense of adventure and urge to go beyond usual boundaries. You developed quite a flair for languages and became used to talking yourself out of many a tight spot. Eventually, however, you luck ran out. You tried to explore an area many had told you was forbidden to foreigners and the inhabitants slew you as an affront to their religious beliefs.

Prim and Proper

Light-hearted and lively, you grew into the role of family clown. People could depend upon you to crack jokes, act out, and generally entertain people. You often counted your blessings that you had escaped the "eldest son" pressures which lay upon your older brother. Everyone loved you, but no one—including yourself—took you seriously. Then your brother was killed in an accident. All the family pressures descended upon you. Your relatives expected you to learn the family business, dress soberly, marry the "right" spouse and live a "proper" life. The thought terrified you. The burdens and responsibilities felt overwhelming. You didn't believe you could measure up to what was necessary, so you ran away.

Forbidden Facts

As a young child, you were fascinated by the natural world. You would study bees and ants and anything which caught your fancy. Your parents grew weary of your questions, although they tried their best to answer. As you grew older, you decided to pursue a career in science. The Church, however, was quite powerful. Studying the natural world and staying within the approved limits of what God (in the eyes of the Church) permitted was very difficult. You ran afoul of the authorities several times and came close to losing your life. You struggled between a desire to stay alive and a burning need to break the rules and study whatever and however you wished!

♃ Jupiter in Cancer ♋

Pale Presence

Born into a very large family, you were overwhelmed as a child. Everyone else was so busy jockeying for attention, you developed a habit of fading into the background. After a bit, everyone seemed to forget you were there. Your parents often forgot your name, calling you by a sibling's name half the time. Since no one ever asked your opinion, or paid any real attention to you, a feeling of inadequacy surfaced. You doubted your own thoughts and feelings. You decided your perceptions were useless as no one was interested in them. You became like a ghost—drifting through life, but barely involved.

Excessive Eating

Raised by a family which believed fat babies were healthy babies, you learned at a young age to consume lots of food. As an adult, you were particularly fond of rich foods, but your society encouraged consumption and overdoing. Having multiple courses in a meal was considered a mark of social and material success. You developed gout and other problems at an early age, but the doctors of that time did not really understand all the dietary connections. Your lifestyle left you with damaged health, but you really did not know any better, or what to fix!

Hazardous Hobby

Fascinated by secrets, you turned to the study of witchcraft in your youth. Soon, magical implements and rituals were a part of your life. The politics of the time necessitated some self-defensive measures. Much of your occult knowledge had to be hidden. Had people known what you did, you might have been killed. Consequently, you had very few people you could trust fully. That made for a difficult life. At one point you let your guard down with a lover and he betrayed you to the authorities. You barely escaped with your life, so you eschewed relationships thereafter.

Perennially Peripatetic

An active, curious child, you decided early on that you wanted to travel the Earth. You were one of the very first Europeans to venture all the way to China and back. Your life consisted of one trip after another. Avoiding family and close friendships, you kept yourself packed and ready to take off on a moment's notice. Yet an inner hunger remained. You were searching for something; you weren't sure what it was. You never found the inner peace and meaning you needed in any of the faraway places you explored.

Heavy Heritage

Your father was a Japanese diplomat and your mother was also from the upper classes. From a young age, you were trained to live up to high expectations. Family pressures went back generations; you "owed" it to your heritage to do something extraordinary. The times in which you lived did not seem to offer much scope for heroism or some outstanding accomplishment. Consequently, you lived with a feeling of failure. In your eyes, you had let down a long line of special people. Your guilt was tremendous. Nothing you did seemed enough for your family history.

Defending the Downtrodden

You were an unusual child. Willing to share as a youngster, you had no great attachment to property or personal possessions. As you grew older, your outlook broadened. You became involved with idealistic causes. If an underdog existed, you fought for that underdog. Zealous on behalf of the downtrodden and less fortunate, you put all your efforts into improving the world. Some of your actions were far from popular. Certain groups were demonized by other people. The well-off wanted to blame poor widows and orphans for their plight. The comfortably middle class could not imagine the pressures which drove a young woman into selling her body on the streets. Many times, you were physically threatened because of the people you served. In the end, you died trying to rescue several refugees from a sinking ship.

♃ **Jupiter in Leo** ♌

Too Far, Too Fast

An impetuous, eager child, you were somewhat accident-prone. Inclined to rush into situations, you ended up getting hurt rather often. Full of faith and trust in people, you didn't adequately watch out for yourself. Susceptible to dares, you ended up proving yourself by taking lots of chances. As an adult you continued your high-risk behavior. You risked yourself physically, emotionally, and financially. Eventually, you pushed the limits just a bit too much and ended up perishing in one of your rather foolhardy stunts.

Financial Flyers

As soon as you learned the concept of gambling, you would bet pennies with neighborhood children. You felt enamored of any number of "sure things" in your life. Speculating on the Stock Exchange was another favored activity—

whenever you had a bit of cash. A natural promoter, you made most of your money by getting people excited about something and persuading them to fund it. Financially, your world was a roller-coaster ride. You had times of great wealth and times of great poverty, but throughout you retained your confidence that taking risks was the way to go!

Wheeler-Dealer

Confident and expressive, your skills inclined you toward fields of sales, promotion, and persuasion. Your dreams were huge. What most excited you was the prospect of some large-scale projects. You loved the idea of bringing water to the desert, of building huge cities where none had been, or constructing major bridges. With a tendency to overextend yourself and to overreach, you had to give up on many possibilities, but a few of your huge ambitions did come to pass. The questions of how far to reach, how high to aim, and how much to hope for pervaded your entire existence.

Really Responsible

You were an English aristocrat born to a fine estate. You felt the burden of your responsibilities tremendously, and tried to help all your tenant farmers and the families dependent upon you. Although you had an overseer, you were very active on your lands wanting hands-on knowledge of the planting and harvest. Because it was tough economic times, everyone was suffering, but you felt terribly guilty because you were "in charge." Although many envied your position, you felt the strain of trying to look after others and provide opportunity for all.

Fascinating Future

The future beckoned to you. As a child, you were fascinated by scientific discoveries. As an adult, you wanted to become an agent of change. You were eager to sell people on the latest technology, the newest idea, and the most modern gadgets. You had mixed success. Although you had good promotional skills, the resistance people have to what is new astonished you. When you met someone with a determination to preserve traditions, to do what had always been done before, you couldn't really understand them. To you, moving toward the future made sense; clinging to the past did not. So, you lost sales whenever you had to deal with someone who was frightened by the prospect of change— or viewed it as an affront to the "old ways."

Proselytizer

Your beliefs were central to your life. Blessed with a firm faith and confidence in a Higher Power, you did your best to promulgate your values to others. Missionary activities, outreach, and just talking with anyone and everyone about your religion was natural for you. Although you had ample charisma, some people were resistant. Acquaintances withdrew. People avoided you. Your enthusiasm about faith was not contagious for everyone. Some individuals felt you lacked sensitivity and were invasive in your need to loudly praise the Lord. Too firm in your convictions to be shaken by the misgivings and evasions of others, you continued to forcefully put your beliefs forward forcefully.

♃ Jupiter in Virgo ♍

Admonished Assertion
You were a teacher in what is now Rumania. Some of your beliefs were seen as politically incorrect. When you attempted to assert yourself, you were imprisoned for years. Although you continued to educate other prisoners when you had the opportunity, you grew weary of the hardship of that life. Eventually, you recanted and were allowed to teach in the outer world again. However, you had to constantly hold yourself back and monitor what you said. You knew that the smallest sign of assertion or independence on your part would bring the wrath of the authorities upon your head.

Ambushed Ambitions
Your father was an extremely cruel man. He delighted in encouraging you to plan for some grand accomplishment. He would egg you on, push you to try for something spectacular, and let you get almost within reach of your goal. Then he would pull his support, take away what you wanted, or in some way prevent you from attaining your dream. Usually his method included some harsh judgments regarding your capability. When your mother protested, he insisted he was teaching you to "cope with reality." As a result, you became afraid to pursue goals, unwilling to risk, convinced that any speculation would lead to a very unhappy ending.

Rheumatic Researcher
When you were young, your best friend perished from rheumatic fever. Devastated, you decided to dedicate your life to pursuing disease. You became a voracious researcher, trying to identify the patterns of illnesses. Although you had some mild successes, you experienced much frustration. You never managed to get the final answers regarding any of the ailments you pursued. Full understanding—much less eradication—of rheumatic fever just was not possible. Yet you kept on striving, pushing yourself harder and harder in the lab, determined to reach your dream, unwilling to admit you were aiming for something beyond your skills.

Couple of Convenience
The oldest girl in a family of merchants, you learned the family business. Your father had no son to carry on the line, and you showed considerable commercial expertise. With an excellent grasp of financial matters, shrewd merchandising instincts, and a feeling for sales, you helped expand your father's business empire. In due course, however, you were expected to marry. Concerned about the impact on your business, you chose a mild-mannered artist who had no

interest in what you were accomplishing, and no inclination to interfere in your life. The marriage was one of convenience rather than sentiment. You provided a stable financial base for him to ply his art and he provided a husband so that you were socially approved and could continue to run your company from behind the scenes.

Radical Reforms

Coming of age during the Protestant Reformation, you became quite caught up in the religious fervor of the times. Change, you believed was inevitable. At first you stayed within the Catholic Church, hoping to bring back the true Gospel from within. Soon, you came to believe that was not possible. You saw your opponents as stodgy, old, hopelessly conservative, and only wanting to hang on to the power they wielded. Your cause—you thought—was a holy one of openness, freshness, and vitality. You wanted to clean up and "purify" your Church. You wanted to be on the side of progress. You understood that chaos might result, but you felt it was a necessary step to altering old, incorrect patterns. You believed the Christian Church would be stronger in the end for these struggles to break out of traditional constraints.

Terrified Teacher

Raised by Quaker parents, you were horrified by the institution of slavery. You became involved with a secret movement to teach slaves to read and write. Although it was illegal, you worked as a teacher under dangerous conditions. Often terrified, you felt compelled to continue knowing the stakes were even more deadly for the men and women who risked being tutored by you. At one point you were jailed for your activities. Another time a plantation owner caught you and had his minions beat you very badly. Your health never fully recovered from that, but you continued to risk your life. Your final passing was at the hands of an awful storm which caught you because your teaching was done under the cover of darkness.

♃ Jupiter in Libra ♎

Not for Sale

You were a judge during the imperial Spanish era in South America. Many of your opinions were attacked. You were also threatened physically by powerful people who were dissatisfied with some of your rulings. Your passion for justice, and willingness to struggle for the truth earned you the reputation of someone who could not be bought. Although your skills were good, you were blocked from moving into a more influential position. The authorities did not want you to gain any more power.

Need for Notice

You felt like the "invisible" child at home. Each of your siblings had a "special" place—the oldest, the youngest, the only girl—but you were the middle boy with no unique features. When you got to school, your hunger for attention was immense. You found recognition through the role of class clown. People liked you because you could make them laugh—even the teacher sometimes. Although you would have preferred applause for your mind or other skills, you felt you had to get the limelight in some fashion. So began a lifetime pattern of cracking jokes and covering over your serious feelings, of lacking love and attention from those close to you and seeking it through more distant relationships.

People Person

An amiable child, you were well-liked by your peers. Having affection around you was quite important to you. So, you gravitated to a position in retail sales. You were quite popular with the customers and your colleagues were fond of you personally. Your social needs, however, interfered with some of your duties. You tended to avoid paperwork and handling the official details of your job, because you preferred to be with people. You detested being alone, so put off chores which would be just between you and your desk. As result, you never did as well professionally as you could have. People appreciated you as a person, but felt your competence was less than it should have been.

More Meaning?

Your family was well-off and you lived in a community of upper middle class people. You all went to the same church — largely as a social function. People would plan recreation before and after services. You would meet your friends on Sundays. As you grew older, you felt a sense of yearning. You wanted more meaning in your life. You had an inkling that something more existed, but you weren't sure what it was and had no idea where to look. Everyone else around you seemed satisfied with their "good life" and you didn't understand why it wasn't enough for you.

Boss or Buddy?

You were a sweet child and continued to be kind-hearted as an adult. Very desirous of approval from others, you were quite susceptible to their opinions. You wanted everyone to like you. You hated to hurt anyone's feelings. In due course, you inherited the reins of the family business and it proceeded to go downhill. You couldn't fire anyone. You didn't really want to wield any authority because you wanted everyone to feel a part of the team—like you were just a friend rather than the boss. Some employees learned how to manipulate your desire for affection to get more than they earned. You just couldn't bring yourself to be a firm authority figure.

Customarily Compliant

A pretty, good-natured baby, you grew into a lovely girl and a beautiful young woman. Your parents encouraged you to develop social graces and you became very skilled at putting people at their ease. You also came to believe that your role in life was to get people to like you and find you attractive. You had great difficulty in dealing with people who were aloof or hostile. (In such cases, you usually retreated and avoided the miscreants as much as possible.) Quite compliant, you wouldn't dream of breaking the rules. You followed acceptable patterns of behavior and stifled much your individuality.

♃ Jupiter in Scorpio ♏

Mastering Moderation

Your life seemed like one long feast versus famine regime. You struggled for many years with an addiction to alcohol and finally became a teetotaler. You also swung back and forth, all that lifetime, between overeating and trying to cut back on your intake of food. Because your husband traveled for business, you had to deal with long periods of celibacy alternating with times of much sexual activity. Although your family had a reasonable income, you had to fight against your tendencies to go on spending "binges"—shopping excessively and purchasing things you didn't really need (or want). See-saw inclinations were strong; you spent most of your time striving for moderation.

Devoted to Detection

As a child, you were fascinated by what was hidden. Your parents were quite repressive and tried hard to squash your detective instincts, but never succeeded. If you sensed a secret was being kept, you did your best to uncover it. Once you started school, you studied all the topics your teachers preferred to avoid. You delved deeply into sexual matters, absorbing much misinformation along the way as few people knew (or would tell you) the truth. You explored cultural taboos. You asked questions about death, decay, excrement and other matters which were not considered appropriate areas of conversation or inquiry.

Sexual Suppression

A very sensual child, you loved the physical sensations of eating and soft, cuddly toys and clothes. As you grew older, you expanded your pleasure horizons. You discovered sexuality—by yourself and with other young adults. The process was exciting. You felt vital and alive. When your parents discovered what was going on, however, they hit the roof! Rather than trying to understand youthful experimentation, they called you names. Your self-esteem took a severe beating. Although you eventually married, you lost of the naive joy and easy release of your youth. Sexual activity was no longer exciting and fulfilling; it became something to be endured.

Minimal Marriage

You discovered your sensuous nature at a young age and became quite adept at the pursuit of pleasure. Rather good-looking, you engaged in a number of affairs. At length, family pressures to carry on the line persuaded you to marry. Your current lover had you enthralled. Against the better judgment of some of your friends, you married your lover and spent the next year in a wide variety of positions. You were quite amazed at her versatility and ended up quite sated sexually. You discovered, however, that your personalities outside of the bedroom were not particularly compatible, nor did you enjoy one anther's companionship. So you lived in a marriage which only had one redeeming feature in your eyes.

Protective Power

Growing up female in the Middle Ages, you were basically powerless. Through a friend, you were exposed to witchcraft. The idea of gaining some mastery over your life had great appeal. You began to study The Craft of the Wise. Your husband discovered your interest and beat you. That abuse did not stop you; it merely made you much more careful. You continued to delve into magic and spells of protection. When your husband failed to return from a fishing trip, you felt your rituals for your personal safety had worked. At that point, you became obsessive, begrudging moments spent on other activities.

Crossed Communications

Raised in a home full of mixed messages and double binds, you developed an early appreciation of nonverbal language and innuendoes. Forced to try to understand what was hidden, you relied heavily on your intuition. As you grew older, you found your inner wisdom an increasing source of strength and insight. After a time, you began to look beneath the surface of everything. You mistrusted appearances and assumed that people never said what they really meant. If something seemed to be simple, you became convinced it was truly complex. You made your life even more complicated at times, but also did tune into possible trouble spots before they developed into real problems.

♃ Jupiter in Sagittarius ♐

Wonderful Words

Your parents claimed that once you learned to talk, you never stopped! Once you discovered the glories of language, you were hooked. You studied and mastered a number of foreign languages. You gloried in discussing the nuances of various phrases. You could spend hours poring over dictionaries or other source books in selecting just the right wording. You talked with anyone and everyone about anything. Addicted to information, you sought it from every source. Often scattered and trying to study five or six subjects at once, you were a perpetual student and ceaseless conversationalist.

Fleeing Family

Home and hearth were central to your family, but you always felt a little claustrophobic as a child. When you discovered the wider world, you couldn't wait to explore it. Leaving home at an early age, you took to the open road, pursuing adventures in many different places. For you, going some place you had never been before was intensely exciting. The lure of a new land was immense. Although you periodically thought about "settling down" with a home and family, it just didn't feel right. You continued to travel into your old age, finding new and stimulating people to meet and places to see.

Grand Gambles

While still a youngster, you persuaded all the neighborhood children to pool their resources to dig a huge hole to turn into a swimming pool. Your parents stopped everything just before construction began. Unfazed, you were off on your career of wheeling and dealing. You learned the art of creative financing. You raised risk-taking to new heights. You had some wildly successful projects on a large-scale and some equally immense failures. Life was a roller-coaster when you were around. Speculation was in your blood and you were willing to take the down times along with the up ones.

Financial Fights

Born to a well-to-do family, you were raised to be a sweet young woman. With your training, you learned to spend lots of money on clothes, shoes, and being "fashionable." Extravagance came rather naturally to you, and your family background did not teach you any thrift. When you married, you continued to order expensive items as a matter of course. Your husband, however, was quite upset. Although he enjoyed your beauty and fashionable appearance, he had no intention of spending lots of "his" money on your "fripperies." Your marriage turned into a battleground over the issue of money.

Fighting Time

As a child, you were full of enthusiasms. Your energy was prodigious. If you were interested in something, you could be enthralled for several days, and tended to get all your friends involved. You had so many interests, however, that you were constantly pulled from one project to another. As an adult, you were chronically overextended. You always believed you could accomplish more in an hour than was truly possible. Time was your major barrier. You got in trouble with making promises to people only to find you'd been overly optimistic in anticipating completion of your contributions. Reality kept on hitting you in the face, but your optimism sprang back again and again.

Pushing Progress

Born into a staid, conventional family, you were sure someone had switched the babies at birth. Traditions had absolutely no appeal for you. From an early age, you wanted whatever was newest or most unusual. As a young man, you became a major proponent of westward expansion. You lobbied on behalf of new discoveries, support for science, and advancing technology as much as possible. Most people dismissed your ideas about how science could change the world as fanciful, but you were sure a new dawn was around the corner.

Occasionally, you got involved with movements which turned out to be crack-pot, but you figured that was the price of being truly on the cutting edge in life.

♃ Jupiter in Capricorn ♑

Earn and Own

Even as a youngster, you were ambitious. You began working at a very young age and dedicated yourself to success. Money became your measure. The more you made, the more powerful and significant you felt. What you did mattered less to you than how much money it brought in. Extremely patient, but forceful, you could prevail in almost anything you attempted. Soon, you gained a formidable reputation as a financier and mover and shaker in the world. You amassed more and more monetarily and continued to judge your worth in that regard.

Best of the Best

An energetic individual, you entered the working world at a young age, deter-mined to make your mark. Eager to achieve recognition, you worked very hard. With a good balance of confidence and caution, you were able to take necessary risks while doing the essential planning beforehand. As a result, your business endeavors flourished and you became more and more successful. Although you achieved quite a bit of admiration from the community, it was never enough. There was always someone else who was more famous, or more applauded, or more wealthy. Your need to shine and be special was so strong, that you chafed horribly at the thought of being in second place to anyone. Consequently, you were always going for more—of everything.

Perpetual Procrastination

Skilled with words and language, your parents thought you would grow up to be a professor. You, however, wanted to do something impressive in your career. Unsure what to dedicate yourself to, you passed the time by working in the family business. At length, you decided to write a masterpiece. You labored endlessly with your creation. You wanted it to be perfect, so kept on tweaking and adjusting, and re-writing, and editing. Friends eventually stopped asking when it would be finished because they recognized (although you did not) that you would never accept it as complete—because it would never be "perfect."

Business Blunder

A bright young woman, you learned quickly and easily. Although your father did not set out to teach, you managed to pick up an incredible amount of knowledge about how his business ran. After a time, he noticed your talents and began to train you in earnest. You quickly took the family empire to greater heights. Due to social conditions (and a desire to carry on a line), you knew you must marry. You chose a man you admired and he wished to become involved in the business. You gave him a section to run (after instruction) and left him in full charge of it. He drove it into the ground. He did not understand the business as you did and risked in the wrong areas while holding back at the wrong times. You maintained the remainder of the business very well, but your marriage was never quite as healthy after that.

Pressure Pot

In your family, personal worth was measured by material accomplishments. You learned early on to value someone on the basis of money and power. So, you naturally sought out successes in the realms of business and politics. A hard worker who was also willing to take the necessary chances to get ahead, you did flourish. You built an excellent business and began working your way up the ladder of local politics toward state (and, you hoped, national) positions. Emotionally, you coped by drinking a lot. The alcohol kept you numb enough so that you did feel the tremendous pressure and insecurity of your lifestyle. You did not consider yourself an alcoholic because you were functioning. Indeed, society viewed you as a great success. But you couldn't make it through any day without a few drinks.

Church Collections

Raised in a very religious household, you came to believe that your role in life was to serve God. You particularly wanted to create tangible testaments to the importance of the Lord. You became a fund raiser for building churches. You would travel from community to community, exhorting people to contribute funds to "raise a temple to the Lord." You use humor, guilt, peer pressure, shame, promises, bribes of Heaven and whatever it took to open people's purse strings. It didn't matter if people were rich or poor. You felt it only appropriate that everyone should give to your holy work.

♃ Jupiter in Aquarius ♒

You Did It Your Way

You were an adventurer and explorer who loved to roam to the ends of the Earth. You would work briefly at odd jobs until you had enough money to take off again. You avoided family or close ties in order to wander the world. You sidestepped responsibility as much as possible. You recognized very few rules and were willing to break the conventions of others if it suited you. You lived on your own terms, enjoyed being a loner and cherished your independence.

Prophetic Patterns

Your mind worked in very strange ways. You were able to see patterns which other people did not. You sometimes had flashes of genius. Even as a child, you were tuned into the future and had visions which turned out to be prophetic. In the beginning, however, your impressions were chaotic and difficult to interpret. As a consequence, your teachers treated you like an idiot and many of your peers viewed you as "crazy" or at the least, very strange. You had a hard time accepting your own thinking because it so often disagreed with what other people were saying. You had to struggle very hard just to follow through on such of your inspirations.

Varied Vocations

Your parents insisted that your first word was not "mama" or "dada" but "No." Rebellion flowed out of your pores. When people proclaimed truth or laws, you felt compelled to test, question, and break those "truths" and laws. Interested in everything, you could not settle into just one job. You tried writing, journalism, sales, advertising, the law, the ministry, and a number of other fields, but nothing held your interest long-term. You'd pursue a position for a bit, become bored, and move on to something else. Although you sometimes yearned to be more productive, in your heart of hearts you enjoyed the tremendous freedom of movement.

Rejecting Relationships

You grew up with a dictatorial father who abused your mother. Although he did not physically abuse you, he made it very clear that you had little worth in his eyes as you were female. When you were in your early teens, you left home and struggled to make enough to get training as a teacher. It was one of the few careers open to women and you were determined to be independent. Although you met a few men over the years, you would not allow yourself to get seriously involved. You were sure that marriage meant abuse and loss of yourself and were unwilling to risk it.

Forward to the Future

You were a young firebrand in what is now Kashmir. You preached for radical changes, for moving toward the future, for joining hands with other lands and leaving the past behind. The old guard was extremely resistant. Most people sided with the idea of preservation and conservation. The new seemed threatening to them. You continued to battle for the future, but realized the blockages were too strong. You could not overcome the ingrained inertia of the people of that time.

Rage to Rescue

You wanted to change the world. From a young age, you identified with the problems of humanity. You saw the inequities of your country and wanted to assist the cause of justice. You trained as a lawyer to gain tools in the struggle against oppression, but the battle was overwhelming. You saw the need for change everywhere and had trouble focusing on specific areas. You lived with much frustration because the problem was too huge for you to do much. Although you had a small impact, in general you had to watch a very large system continue to grind down upon people. Your idealism and urge to save the world made your failures much more painful.

♃ **Jupiter in Pisces** ♓

Self-Directed

You were an itinerant preacher in the 1800's. Although you dedicated your life to God, you also married and had a family. Survival was tough because you had very little money. Your charitable impulses led you to give away much of what little you had. Your family was very upset and often criticized you because they would go hungry when you gave money to a needy stranger. You felt guilty about not being able to provide fully for your family, but believed you answered to a Higher Power.

Absorbing Education

Your mind did not function in a linear fashion. You absorbed information in vast gulps and then needed a lot of time to process it. Much of your understanding came through nonverbal channels and you often had to work with imagery or symbols before you were clear about what you were taking in. The school system did not understand this and your teachers labeled you as stupid. You struggled life-long with a feeling of intellectual inferiority because you didn't follow the 1-2-3 steps of most people and because you knew some things but couldn't explain how or why you knew them.

Classic Caretaker

As a small child, you were enthralled by stories about the lives of saints. You loved hearing how various saints had sacrificed themselves for the good of the world. When anyone was ill in your family, you became the nurse. You adopted the role of family caretaker. Because you extended family was quite large, there was almost always someone who needed special assistance. You never got a chance to meet a young man or start a family of your own because you were always coming to the rescue of one or another of your cousins, siblings, aunts, etc.

Too Trusting

You believed in the goodness of life and human beings. Although you recognized that the world had its flaws, you trusted individual humans to be kind and caring. As a result, you were often let down, but it did not alter your basic trust and faith. Difficult times were sweeping the land. Religious intolerance was growing wildly. Your world view was a very personal and private one so you did not belong to the established religion. Nonetheless, you believed that your neighbors would let you live in peace. Alas no. You were killed—in the name of God — identified and murdered as a "heretic."

Arduous Art

Sensitive to beauty from an early age, you pursued a wide variety of artistic paths. Although life was extremely difficult and you made almost no money, you would not forsake your muse. Others counseled you to be practical and realistic and give up on your art, but you were determined. You continued to create though sales were few and small. You continued to count your blessing and noticed the glories of a sunset even when your stomach was empty. Although your physical suffering was great, you felt your soul had a rich, fulfilling life.

Heretical Herbalist

It seemed you were born compassionate. As a tiny toddler, you would try to soothe a hurt animal or a person in pain. As you grew older, you yearned to study medicine. This was not an acceptable path for a female, so you became a midwife an herbalist. Much of society rejected and ostracized you, but people would seek out your cures surreptitiously — sometimes in the dead of night. You learned that the people who avoided you in the day would come calling under the cover of darkness for your assistance. You never turned anyone away.

CHAPTER EIGHT

PAST LIFE SCENARIOS: URANUS

Find the sign Uranus was occupying at your birth and read the appropriate scenarios.

1934	Jun	6	3:42 pm	Taurus	1968	Sep	28	4:09 pm	Libra
	Oct	10	0:37 am	Aries	1969	May	20	8:58 pm	Virgo
1935	Mar	28	2:58 am	Taurus		Jun	24	10:30 am	Libra
1941	Aug	7	3:33 pm	Gemini	1974	Nov	21	9:30 am	Scorpio
	Oct	5	2:08 am	Taurus	1975	May	1	5:50 pm	Libra
1942	May	15	4:05 am	Gemini		Sep	8	5:14 am	Scorpio
1948	Aug	30	3:41 pm	Cancer	1981	Feb	17	8:53 am	Sagittarius
	Nov	12	1:27 pm	Gemini		Mar	20	11:27 am	Scorpio
1949	Jun	10	4:08 am	Cancer		Nov	16	12:04 pm	Sagittarius
1955	Aug	24	6:04 pm	Leo	1988	Feb	15	0:08 am	Capricorn
1956	Jan	28	1:58 am	Cancer		May	27	1:22 am	Sagittarius
	Jun	10	1:48 am	Leo		Dec	2	3:34 pm	Capricorn
1961	Nov	1	3:59 pm	Virgo	1995	Apr	1	12:08 pm	Aquarius
1962	Jan	10	5:56 am	Leo		Jun	9	1:47 am	Capricorn
	Aug	10	1:18 am	Virgo	1996	Jan	12	7:13 am	Aquarius

Example: Someone born in 1962 before Jan. 10 has Uranus in Virgo. If an individual was born in 1962 after 5:56 am EST on Jan. 10, but before August 10, his/her Uranus would be in Leo.

♅ Uranus in Aries ♈

Radical Revolutionary

You were a revolutionary in Latin America's early push toward independence. You preached equality, brotherhood, sharing, and freedom for all. The authorities were quite brutal in their attempts at suppression. Many of your comrades perished. Although somewhat reckless and hot-at-hand, your inventive streak helped you to stay alive.

Rush, Rush, Rush

Impatient as a child, you resisted efforts to teach you to take life more slowly. As an adult, you rushed from one project to the next. Drawn toward challenges, you seemed happiest when battle "impossible" odds. You never really settled in one place, so collected few possessions. It was rare for you to completely finish anything. Before the final touches, you had usually been lured away by a new enthusiasm. Stopping to smell the flowers, to relax and enjoy life, didn't occur to you.

Insistent Independence

A natural loner, you left home young to see the world. Although you met a number of attractive, interesting women, you couldn't imagine marrying anyone. You gloried in being free to come and go as you pleased with no responsibility to anyone else. Although you fell in love a few times, you were unwilling to give up your independence. So you remained basically solitary for all of your days.

Lousy Liar

Born into an aristocratic Mogul family, you had to deal with the pressures of court life. A naturally open and honest person, you had great difficulties with the power plays, scheming, and manipulation which were a part of daily life. You would have gladly left, but family obligations required your presence. So, you continued to struggle in an arena which was very uncomfortable — missing many of the innuendoes and receiving the peripheral damage that often came to innocent bystanders when several groups were vying for control.

Disbelieving Dogma

Compliance was not an easy path for you. From a young age, you questioned your parents and other people in charge. You had a particularly difficult time with religious authorities who believed your questions came perilously close to blasphemy. You suffered a degree of ostracism in the community because you didn't believe as others did. Many times, you were not sure what you did believe, but you knew the principles being promulgated by others just did not make sense to you.

Advising Adjustment

You were born in a time of change. New ideas were sweeping the land. When you were in your mid-teens, your tribe began to have contact with strange men from faraway places. The elders wanted to cling to the past, with no adjustment. You and many of your peers insisted that the tribe must alter its ways to survive this chaotic period. But the elders held the power. You and your friends could only watch and protest as everyone slipped closer to oblivion.

♅ Uranus in Taurus ♉

Preventing Poverty

You were a humanitarian in the 19th century. You worked with the poor and the dispossessed, striving to improve their lot. The inequalities of wealth and power in your society disturbed you. Although the people at the top would make occasional charitable contributions, they largely ignored or criticized your efforts. They preferred to blame the people involved—as if being poor was their own fault. Frustration dogged your footsteps, but you continued to work against the odds.

Decreasing Disruptive Damage

You became quite active and scholarly during the Age of Industrialization in England. You were concerned with the dislocations of many workers and the disruptions of the economy as society shifted away from an agrarian focus. You spent a lot of time analyzing trends and seeking innovative solutions to financial challenges and the question of resource allocation.

Mourning Mother

Very close to your family, you looked forward to when you would marry and have children of your own. In your late teens, you wed a local young man. You were blessed with a son two years later and twin daughters three years after your son's birth. In the year your son would have been eight, a plague swept the land. Despite your best nursing efforts, all three of your children perished. You were very ill and thereafter never conceived. You mourned your loss forever after.

Controlled Closeness

Born to a controlling mother, you felt stifled. She invaded your privacy constantly and expected to be told where you were, who you were with, and what you were doing. She warned repeatedly that men only wanted one thing and you must never provide it until married. She probed constantly into your feelings, seemingly convinced that you were enthralled by some man and trying to hide it. At length, you married almost the first man to ask just to escape your mother.

Agricultural Experiments

You grew up with two loves: science and the land. As an adult you blended them by experimenting with agricultural techniques and implements. You tested a variety of designs for hoes and plows, seeking the best. You bred various strains of plants, aiming to develop hardier varieties with greater resistance to disease. Feeling the soil and visualizing new tools and methods for getting the most from the earth was immensely gratifying.

Heavy Heart

You were the leader of a small band dependent upon the local river to survive. Over the years, the river had become dryer and dryer and it was reaching a crisis point. You felt the pressures of your position terribly. No one knew if the water would return. Scouts had not found good sites within any close distance. The best chance would be a difficult 20-day journey and it was not clear whether all your people could make the trek. You were terrified of making the wrong decision, but knew indecision could be as deadly. You elected to move your band and a few elderly and children died. You lived with the guilt thereafter.

♅ Uranus in Gemini ♊

Mutable Material

Extremely innovative, you were very hard on your possessions. You delighted in trying to get objects to fit purposes for which they had not been designed. You would take apart your toys and try to create a totally new toy—which was often not as satisfactory as the originals, but you enjoyed the challenge of the creative process. Your parents were annoyed and tried to teach you to be more careful but not giving you things, but you just turned your inventive mind toward the great outdoors and tried to make over the environment in various ways. You developed a life-long pattern of not having much materially because you were always altering it.

Ingenious Imagination

A brilliant young child, your thought processes were hard for other people to follow. Consequently, you were often dismissed or ignored as everyone was sure adults knew more than children. You were tempted at times to invent your own language because you felt your birth language was too inadequate to convey many of the concepts with which you were working. You studied other languages, but found none fully satisfactory. Your greatest frustration was that no one really understood you. Being unable to communicate your deepest perceptions was intensely frustrating.

Resourceful Reasoning

Your parents were well-meaning folks, but like most authorities, they believed that their ideas were the best. As a child, you had some unusual ideas — which your parents considered unacceptable. Although most individuals learned to be quiet and give in, you could not do so. You felt compelled to pursue your unconventional thinking, even when it got you into trouble. As a result, you left home at an early age. You continued to avoid close ties because your experience and observation led you to believe that people who were related to you or lived with you felt they had a right to tell you how to think.

Amusing Anecdotes

Blessed with a quick, perceptive, alert mind, you developed considerable verbal skills as well. You became noted for your wit and built quite a name for yourself within your community. People looked to you to tell funny stories, crack jokes, and keep people entertained. They knew your conversation would be peppered with sly digs, insightful comments, and amusing anecdotes. You were a star in your world—noteworthy for your light-heartedness and quick intellectual processing. You came to see your primary value as your ability to make people laugh and to respond speedily. You felt stupid if you couldn't come up with a quick quip or rapid repartee.

Varied Vistas

You found life fascinating. Learning was an adventure and you never tired of absorbing a new bit of information. Teaching came naturally to you and sharing your excitement with your students was gratifying. Although few of them had your facility for spotting alternatives and other ways of perceiving, you tried to instill in them a respect for the tremendous amount of knowledge which life has to offer. You lived an example of a mental adventurer who found the unknown vistas of the mind as gripping and life-and-death as any physical exploration.

Gadget Glut

A natural innovator, you were a great asset to your community. When people were stuck, they would come to you and you would bring in a unique perspective that broke the log-jam. When someone didn't know what to do, you saw an alternative. Always coming up with small but interesting gadgets, a few of your inventions were extremely helpful. You had trouble defining your place within your circle of people, but you knew you served a vital role.

♅ Uranus in Cancer ♋

Fluctuating Finances

Your family had considerable fluctuations. When you were born, your parents were extremely well off. When you were seven, political changes forced your family to flee, leaving almost all their material possessions behind. Your mother and father built back a business from scratch, only to lose everything again to a devastating earthquake (when you were twelve). Fortunately, all family members survived. But you learned a style of feast and famine in regard to finances and continued the up-and-down see-saw for the rest of that lifetime.

Lacking Learning

Your family had little stability. You traveled and lot, with a hand-to-mouth existence. Your parents would do day labor, help with harvests, make minor repairs—or anything for which they could get pay. Because you had no settled place to live, your schooling was practically nonexistent. Although you were very curious and eager to learn, your parents had no appreciation of "book learning." They believed what you learned by working at their sides was most valuable. But you felt a life-long yearning for the education you never got.

Cryptic Creativity

Highly creative, you were a great asset to your family. Blessed with considerable ingenuity, you could find a solution to almost anything. Minor repairs were a snap for you. When you were missing a tool, you improvised something from whatever was at hand. When people did not know what to do, you came up with an alternative. When someone felt constrained, you saw a path toward eventual freedom. You, however, did not recognize your own tremendous inventiveness. You saw yourself as a helpful person, but did not realize what incredible talent you had.

Rattled Routines

Born into poverty, you struggled to learn enough to be able to get a job. You ended up going into service. Then your mother got sick and there was no one else to nurse her. You neglected your duties and were fired with no references for a new position. After your mother passed away, you worked in an inn, but ended up caring for a sick sister. Then a niece ran away to you for protection from an abusive situation. It seemed whenever you were beginning to build up a decent work record, family matters disrupted your life again.

Scarce Security

Security did not exist in your childhood. If you weren't going hungry, the family was on the streets, looking for shelter. When you had a physical base, your father would disappear for a time. When your father was around, your mother would drink and become incoherent. As soon as possible, you left home. But rather than try to create a safe haven for yourself, you lived on the road. You traveled all over, never settling, believing in your heart of hearts that a stable family just was not possible for you.

Kinky Kindred

You worried sometimes that mental illness ran in your family, and decided not to have children, lest you pass on some defective gene. Both your parents were susceptible to sudden, erratic rages. They also drank to excess periodically (but one did not always cause the other). Some of the behaviors they insisted upon — such as wearing two pairs of socks — struck you as utterly senseless. Feeling totally estranged from them, you sought refuge with your friends. You fantasized that you'd been adopted and imagined that if you visited enough of your friend's houses you would eventually find your "true" parents. That never happened, but what nurturing you did get came through your friends.

♅ Uranus in Leo ♌

Frightening Finances

You had been among the "ruling class" of your country and done reasonably well financially. Most of your money, however, was tied up in land. When rumblings of revolution became outright danger for people like you, retreat became essential to survive. Your escape route required funds. Thinking they would arrive "any day," you delayed your departure, becoming more and more anxious. In the end, you died because the money did not arrive on time.

Speaking Out

You lived in very uneasy times. With several conflicting political groups vying for power, emotions were high. In your heart, you believed moderation was the best course, to seek a way to bring together that warring factions. Unable to contain your feelings, you began to speak out in public, calling for compromise and forbearance. Although you were perfectly willing to be reasonable, the more rapid proponent of various sides were not. You were assassinated at one public meaning as you called for mutual tolerance.

Limiting Laughter

You were a playful, fun-loving child. Charismatic, you were quite popular with the neighborhood children and a natural leader. You helped everyone look for adventures and kept them all entertained with your jokes and pranks. Although you grew up, you maintained your humor and light-hearted attitude. Your family arranged a marriage to a woman of good family. She was quite serious and they hoped she would "steady" you. Alas, she was also quite religious—and followed a sect that disapproved of any frivolity. Dancing was a lure to the Devil. Cards were a road to Hell, and even laughter was suspect. You life with her became very difficult and you stayed away as much as possible.

Alarming Activities

A bit of an excitement addict, you were drawn to adventures. When political unrest developed in your land, you became affiliated with one of the factions. You designed creative methods of passing on information. You enjoyed playing different roles to collect information and mislead the opposition. You found the challenges very stimulating and the danger of death added spice to the mix. Although you were not foolhardy, you were definitely a risk-taker. Your quick wits got you out of many tight spots, but in the end you were captured. Refusing to change your views, you were executed.

Hindering Hate

You spent the first half of your life as a soldier. You believed in your king and country and felt that the death-dealing which you did was appropriate. In your mid-forties, you had a religious conversion experience. You felt appalled at the blood on your hands and forswore aggression and war from that point forward. You retreated to a monastery, learned to read and write, and began to pen tracts about the evils of violence. You believed that God had spared your life in order for you to pass the work of the importance of choosing love over hate.

Endless Expectations

You learned early on that you had a persuasive streak. When you were excited about something, you could often talk other kids into it. As an adult, you became very involved with the plight of children. You became a reformer and advocate on their behalf. Although you raised quite a bit of money, you were chronically frustrated. You saw so much pain and suffering, so many hungry and abused children, and you could only affect a small percentage. Your best efforts were minuscule compared to the problem. You suffered terribly from your inability to rescue everyone.

♅ Uranus in Virgo ♍

Oppressive Obstacles

You were a farm worker who followed the harvests in Europe. Wages were minimal and living conditions were very poor. When your hand was damaged in a farming accident, life became even tougher. Mere survival was a challenge. You had no scope to pursue any of your personal desires; all your energy went into getting by each day. Your employers oppressed you, but you felt stuck. You saw no way out—with no future other than continual struggle.

Can't Keep

Raised in a family which strongly valued the material, you grew up assuming that getting, having, and holding was extremely important. Working hard at your business, you managed to amass a bit of property and some moderate wealth. Two of your family members, however, through a legal fluke were able to take your house away from you. Several of your servants stole money from you. Eventually you adopted that attitude of: "There is no point in having nice things because I won't be able to keep them anyway."

Finding Facts

You were an historian and archivist in Renaissance Europe. You spent long hours poring over hard-to-read records. You were utterly dedicated to precision and exactitude. Most of your life revolved around your work. You had few friends. Even those you worked with related to you mainly as the individual who could dig out information for them. Sometimes you imagined that you didn't exist, except to serve.

Science Studies

A natural scientist, you were driven to learn, to question, to examine from the earliest of ages. Although your parents did not particularly value education, you worked very hard to get the opportunity to master reading and then eventually to attend university. When you discovered the scientific method with its objective inquiry, you felt you had come home. You dedicated your life to studies, research, and inventions. You succeeded in coming up with a few useful devices, including a new form of nut cracker. More than any thing, however, you gloried in your ability to seek the truth.

Determined Dilettante

Your parents despaired of you, because you had not interest in following your father's footsteps as a cobbler. When asked what you wanted to do, you were unsure. Eventually, you realized that you did not want to do any ONE thing for all your life. You became a wanderer, learning the skills of several different trades. A few years was all you could manage, however, before you became bored and felt you had to move on. The idea of permanently committing to a career terrified you. The sense of responsibility and burden was something you continued to avoid.

Ready to Rescue

The daughter of a Danish clergyman, you knew about the "workhouses" for the poor. You understood that most people who entered them never exited alive. Disease was rampant. Hunger was extreme and conditions were awful. Although you had no real political power or monetary clout, you devoted your live to rescuing those whom you could. You taught a few people to read and write so they could look for positions as clerks. You hired many young women as servants at the vicarage until they polished their skills enough to get a good position. Although you often wished you could do more, your father (and later your husband, another clergyman) assured you that you were doing all you could.

♅ Uranus in Libra ♎

Monetary Madness

You were a business owner in Java. Although you would rather have become an artist, you felt constrained to please your parents. In addition, a number of relatives looked to you for support. You labored long and hard to provide materially for everyone. Despite your dedication, you felt unappreciated by your family. They had no real understanding of what you had given up for them, and were constantly demanding more of you. You became very resentful of their desire for more things and more money.

Death's Debt

As a child, you enjoyed roaming the woods near your village. You and your brother would race each other about. You would also play hide-and-seek and startle one another by leaping out suddenly from a behind a tree. One day your brother was teasing you and raced across the road. He was hit by a carriage and died. You felt extremely guilty. Your parents blamed you for the death of their only son. You never recovered from your sense of obligation—as if you owed your parents something (even though it was an accident) and as if you were indebted to your brother for still being alive.

Disregarded Designs
You built many castles in the sand growing up. As an adult, you turned to architecture. Design and construction fascinated you. Creative, you experimented with unusual materials and textures. You put balconies where no one expected them. You designed rooms with nonstandard shapes and dimensions. Most of your work was ignored. People were afraid to build something unconventional. What little work you did was very "ordinary" in your eyes. You felt frustrated that your creative genius was not acceptable within your society.

Loss and Longing
You had a childhood "best friend" with whom you shared everything. Feeling extremely close, you often slept together, whispering secrets far into the night. When you were twelve, your friend was killed in a freak thunderstorm. You were traumatized for some time, but eventually recovered. In your late teens, you married a man whom you loved very much. Your relationship was unusual for the times in that he gave you a great deal of respect and consulted you often when making decisions. You enjoyed each other's companionship. Then, he was killed by a runaway carriage. You went into mourning and decided to never again allow yourself to love. It hurt too much.

Awful Awakening
You led a sheltered life, raised as the only child of doting parents. When you were eighteen, you fell madly in love with a man 15 years your senior. Your parents forbade the match. Wildly attracted, you made plans to run away, when your maid betrayed you to your parents. Sorrowfully, they revealed that the man was your half-brother due to an affair your father had had some 16 years before. Nauseous at the thought of your near incest, you withdrew from relationships, vowing you would remain celibate for life.

Principled and Punctilious
You were a matchmaker in China. Families who came to you expected a perfect combination. Everyone wanted their children matched to a family of great wealth, power, and significance. People complained if they felt what you offered was less than ideal. You took your responsibilities very seriously and strove always to do the best job possible for everyone involved. When matters did not work out, or a couple proved infertile together, you felt very guilty. Unable to truly relax, you remained overly conscientious and carrying other people's burdens.

♅ Uranus in Scorpio ♏

Threatening Times
You were a tinker, wandering from place to place selling and repairing pots, pans, utensils and other tools. Times were poor and people just barely making it. People could not afford much, so your income was restricted as well. You were a convenient scapegoat for people's anger, so often got blamed if anything went wrong. People would accuse you of behaviors ranging from theft to spying. You ended up feeling incredibly defensive—as if you had to apologize for being alive.

Savoring Simplicity
You lived in a time of transition. Invaders battered at the borders of your country and no one was sure how long the barbarians could be repulsed. People were fleeing southward. Your parents were torn because they had a great deal of their wealth tied to items which were not portable. It was almost too late when you finally did escape; you got out with your lives and little else. There followed a period of years where you wandered about, looking for a safe place to settle to try to build back a modicum of security. Your parents never stopped mourning for what they had lost, but you learned to appreciate life's simple pleasures and get by with very few material things.

Undercover Understanding
While still quite young, you made the acquaintance of a local crone. She seemed immeasurably wise and you spent time each day with her, trying to understand how she learned what she knew. She taught you the art of full observation, the subtle clues which people put out without knowing. She instructed you in the art of focus, concentration, and directed will. You became adept at reading people's moods, faces, and actions. Among your peers, you were somewhat feared. They believed you used witchcraft to uncover secrets and scoffed at your explanations of pure observation. You became somewhat of an outcast.

Base Betrayal
You grew up with a neighbor boy and fell in love with one another in your teens. His parents, however, had very different plans for him—as did yours for you. He was sent on a journey to the New World to "broaden his horizons and check family investments" and you were bundled off to social activities where you could be paraded before other eligible bachelors. After two years, you were told your love had perished from a fever. Listless, you agreed to the marriage your parents wanted. A year later, your childhood sweetheart stormed into your presence. He, too, had been told you had died, and had just recently learned the truth. But neither of you would consider breaking your marriage vows. Instead, you made an internal vow not to love again as it just hurt too much.

Railroaded

You were born in China, but brought to the U.S. to work on the railroads. Along with back-breaking physical labor, you faced tremendous prejudice and abuse. People treated you as inhuman and made fun of your queue, your eyes, and your appearance in general. You felt rejected by everyone around you. Although promises of plenty and visions of "the Golden Mountain" had been used to lure you to the States, the reality you faced was terribly harsh. You barely survived the rigors of your stint on the railroad.

Severely Stressed

You were the chieftain of a Scottish clan—the Laird. Winters were long and harsh. Food was difficult to grow. Survival depended partly on raiding other clans. Many infants and children died from disease or hardship. Woman commonly perished in childbirth. Men were killed in fights with other clans. You felt the responsibility of leadership as a tremendously heavy burden. Struggle, frustration and set-backs were daily occurrences.

♅ Uranus in Sagittarius ♐

Insistent Invaders

You lived in the mountains of the Andes and were an adventurous young man. You traveled far and wide, enjoying new vistas. Unsure what you were seeking, your restlessness kept you on the move. One day you noticed strangers with hair on their faces who were dressed very oddly. Moving closer for a good look, you were captured. They kept you prisoner for several months, attempting to learn your language and to teach you theirs. At length, you learned they were obsessed with a search for a metal they called "oro." They demanded that you lead them to where they could find it. When you insisted you could not do that, they did not believe you and eventually killed you.

Exploring Everywhere

Born in a tiny Hunan village far from everywhere, you knew at an early age that you belonged in the wider world. As soon as you were old enough, you mapped out a course to the nearest town. After more hard work, discussion and planning, you were able to travel on to a city. The more you saw of the world, the less you cared about your birth place. You felt everyone "back home" was narrow-minded and very stuck in their ways. You gloried in the freedom to go anywhere, learn anything, and explore all ideas. You promised yourself that you would never tie yourself down to a place or a home. You belonged to the world.

Knowledge Over Needs

You were a German scientist and scholar during the 1700's. Keeping your connection to your university meant many long hours of effort with very little pay. You strained your eyes poring over ancient texts. You often worked in cold rooms and suffered from Chilblains and other ailments as a result. You assumed that physical discomfort was your lot in life. Unable to demand more supportive surroundings, you continued to suffer. You dedicated yourself to your quest for knowledge and refused to concern yourself with the impact upon your health and well-being. Pneumonia was your eventual fate.

Marrying Money

Driven by an insatiable thirst for knowledge, you studied everything that you could. Although your family was not well-off, they sacrificed much to pay for as much education as possible. When walking to university, you met by chance a young woman separated from her chaperone and struck up a conversation. She became fascinated with you and sought you out later. You learned she was the only daughter of a wealthy merchant. It was clear she would be happy to wed you if you asked. Although you did not love her, you resolved to propose in order to gain the funds to go further with your education.

Imprisoning Ideals

As a child, you loved the church—the stained glass windows, the burning candles, the pomp and ceremony of the rituals. Unlike most children, you loved attending. When you were a little older, you felt the calling and dedicated your life to God. Since your family was of the aristocracy, you were granted an excellent living and eventually became confessor to the king. The times were becoming difficult. Unrest stalked the land and rash statements by malcontents stimulated your ruler to very harsh responses. You spoke out on behalf of certain beliefs and ideals and were imprisoned. It mattered not that you had had the king's ear. He would brook no opposition. You languished in prison for many years.

Debating Doctrines

Questions consumed you as a child. The schooling you received was inadequate. Your teachers could not explain matters to your satisfaction. Nor could the Church. The older you grew, the less you believed the answers given to you by authorities. You began to study other religions. Your family and peers were shocked that you would risk "eternal damnation" to explore other explanations of the universe. You also studied science. It seemed everything you learned brought up more uncertainties. You embarked on a life-long quest for understanding and never did find Final Truth.

♅ Uranus in Capricorn ♑

Closed Shop

You were an independent businessman who continually sought out new ideas and products for trade. You would speak with anyone and everyone in regard to commercial possibilities. The authorities in control of your area saw your openness as a threat. They destroyed your business and banished you. You fought for years to regain your position, but it was simply impossible. You couldn't get the power needed to fight all the influential people involved.

Final Chapter

You "owed your soul to the Company store." Born in a Company town, you labored hard in the mines like your father before you. But you had to buy food (and drink) in the Company store and the bare necessities always cost more than your wages that week. So, each week you slipped more and more into debt. People grumbled about the life, but felt they didn't have any choice. You decided that the cycle would end with you and determined not to have any children who would suffer your fate.

Relative Revenge

The oldest son of a large and boisterous family, you had a relatively happy childhood. Your father trained you well in weaponry as the times were full of unrest. Bandits would attack travelers. Occasionally, former soldiers would band together to take over a small estate as their only way to gain land. Despite the need to be cautious, you all had good times as well. One day, after having been away for a week hunting, you returned to your family's manor to see many strange horses. Fearing the worst, you carefully snuck close enough to find out what was happening. Your mother, father, and all your brothers and sisters had been murdered. A landless "free sword" had brought together enough men to muster a killing wave so they could take over the lands. You swore yourself to vengeance, determined to live long enough to kill the leader and not caring what happened thereafter.

Modified Manners

An individualist, you presented a number of challenges to your parents in your youth. As an adult, your interests turned toward questions of health. Although the fashion was to keep ill, upper class women passive and in bed much of the time, you were convinced that a radical regime would be more effective. You established a country place as a "rest place" to which society women could retreat. You provided lots of fresh air and sunshine and encouraged everyone to walk and be as active as possible. A number of your patients improved markedly, but traditional physicians insisted they were just lucky flukes.

Skimming the Surface

Although you were very bright and a kind-hearted girl, you had the pox as a child so that your face was severely marked. In addition, your figure was dumpy—not in the current mode at all. You watched sadly as beautiful young women received many proposals and had their pick of husbands. It seemed no one noticed the beauty of your character. Everyone was too busy surveying outer appearances to look within. You began to search carefully for a man of good character—one who seemed kind and considerate—regardless of how he looked. After four years, you found such a man and had the opportunity to converse with him a few times. To your great joy, you discovered that he too had been disillusioned about people's superficialities and you two came to share a very special bond as well as a marriage.

Aristocratic Availability

Your mother came from a "good family," but your father made his money through trade so was considered at a lower rung of society. It was your parents' dream that you would marry into the aristocracy. You were groomed from a young age for the position of a fashionable nobleman's wife. Your individuality was carefully suppressed. You learned to speak only of commonplace, noncontroversial matters. You were trained not to be TOO smart, or TOO witty, or TOO different in any way. (Fortunately you were not TOO tall or TOO short.) Every effort was made to enhance and increase your beauty. Sometimes you felt hardly real—just a doll people were dressing and telling how to behave.

♅ Uranus in Aquarius ♒

Breaking Up

An idealist, you left your home and hearth behind to seek out like-minded people. You became involved with an intentional community (commune). No personal possessions were allowed. Everything was owned by the group. For several years, you enjoyed living there. As the founder aged, however, you noticed that certain people were moving into power positions. They ended up carving out personal "working areas" which were excused as for the good of the group. More and more things from the community made their way to those personal working areas. After a time, there was a clear split between the people controlling most of the resources and the people (like you) doing most of the work. Totally disillusioned, you left.

Curious Quirks

Curious and perceptive, you started taking things apart (and trying to reassemble them) at quite a young age. Your parents had enough money to allow you the luxury of tinkering and you invented a number of tools to save labor in the kitchen and in the fields. Totally uninterested in money, you let anyone copy your inventions. As soon as you had come up with a new idea and been able to put it into form, you were no longer interested. You wanted to pursue the NEXT new idea. Throughout your life you studied a multitude of subjects.

Roots of Rebellion

Born into a staunch American Tory family, you were initially a full supporter of England. As you were exposed to certain injustices, your feelings began to shift. Some of your friends had more radical tendencies. Eventually, you became a convert to the cause of revolution. This meant estrangement from your family. They were horrified and tried desperately to talk you out of your convictions, but it was not possible. You told them a conflict was coming soon and traveled away so as to minimize the chances that you might meet one of your brothers in the battles you were sure were to come.

Only Organizing

Economic opportunities were extremely limited where you grew up. You were bright, nimble and quick, so got hired for work in a diamond mine. Conditions were deplorable. You and everyone else were stretched to their limits physically. The bosses kept on demanding more and more labor — for wages which were a pittance. You thought that perhaps the workers could band together (strength in unity) for better conditions and pay. Most of your fellows were afraid to consider a union because many, many hungry people would be happy to replace them. Also, the bosses got wind of your intention and quickly sacked you—as well as arranging for you to be beaten. You had to go far away to get another job and survive.

Pure Potential

Reared on the philosophy of Jean-Jacques Rousseau, you decided to put his work into practice. Having inherited wealth, you established a school to teach children to reclaim their native goodness and purity. Spontaneity was encouraged. Teachers were supposed to aid children in returning to their natural state. When that natural state appeared to involve strife, competition, and meanness, you and your staff were convinced that parental and cultural contaminants were at work. So, you tried even harder to get to the inner souls of your pupils.

Early Advocate

You saw the need for change much earlier than anyone else. You began to talk of revolution ten years before it became a common topic. Your fervor made your friends and family uneasy. They worried about you. They also worried about themselves—that they would be assumed to be as radical as you and might be imprisoned or worse. You had scant sympathy for anyone as you were convinced of the necessity of a new path. You continued to agitate, to push for reform, and eventually saw the tide turn and many people join their voices with yours.

♅ Uranus in Pisces ♓

Slum Sufferers

You were a socialist reformer, eager to save the world. You labored long and hard in some of the worst slums of South America. Repeatedly frustrated, disillusioned, and disappointed, you nonetheless continued to try, to attempt to overcome blocks to people's opportunities. The power structure was completely opposed to your work. Your own existence was perilous at times. You often questioned as to whether your efforts really did make any difference.

Hidden Hints

When you were young, you saw bright colors around people. Thinking everyone could perceive them, you commented about the changing displays one day. Your aunt was horrified and told you that you were crazy. Thereafter, you didn't share your perceptions with others. However, you continued to tune into people's feelings and to see colors around them. Your ability to understand people was quite an asset in your business, but you never spoke about your talent to anyone again.

Maternal Majesty

Prince of a small kingdom in central Asia, you knew that your parents had married for reasons of state. Your mother's family of origin had strong political connections and she was constantly jockeying for more power within the court. Upon the death of your father when you were twelve, you knew that you would have to choose another regent quickly and forcefully, or your mother would take over. You were reluctant to move against your mother. She declared her regency, had you imprisoned within your quarters (for your "protection") and became de facto monarch.

Worn Out Working

Eager to be of service, you dedicated your life to the healing arts. You would work long hours in charity wards, trying to save the most wretched of the poor. Straining your eyes in poor lighting, you struggled to figure out how to cure the often incurable. An experimenter at heart, you would try unconventional—even desperate—measures on occasion. Once in a while, they worked! Your own health suffered because you drove yourself so much, striving to accomplish more and more. You almost became a martyr to the cause until some friends forcibly intervened and sent you to the country to recover.

Mind Over Mystery

Although quite intuitive, you also had an excellent logical, rational mind. This set up a conflict within you. One side wanted to rely solely on your intellect and didn't trust gut reactions or visions. The other side was content to accept nonrational information without analyzing it. Since your family steered you toward scientific training, you ended up repressing your imaginative side. Although you occasionally had unconscious breakthroughs, you largely ignored your hunches and psychic impressions. Your belief system emphasized trusting your mind over anything else.

Spiritual Saint

Born with the spirit of a warrior, you had also the heart of a saint. You would fight for a cause in which you believed. You suffered many wounds on behalf of spiritual principles or trying to protect and rescue people you felt needed assistance. You stood up for the downtrodden and spoke up for the dispossessed. You labored on behalf of the less fortunate in society. In the end, you perished in an attempt to guard people fleeing from persecution.

CHAPTER NINE
PAST LIFE SCENARIOS: NEPTUNE

Refer to the table to find your Neptune sign. I have not worked with any charts having Neptune in Aries, Taurus, or Pisces, so those placements are omitted for this chapter. Neptune in Aquarius is coming soon, so I've included a theoretical set of scenarios for that sign.

1942	Oct	3	4:59 pm	Libra	1970	Jan	4	7:53 pm	Sagittarius
1943	Apr	17	10:59 am	Virgo		May	3	1:35 am	Scorpio
	Aug	2	7:08 pm	Libra		Nov	6	4:30 pm	Sagittarius
1955	Dec	24	3:19 pm	Scorpio	1984	Jan	19	2:52 am	Capricorn
1956	Mar	12	1:57 am	Libra		Jun	23	1:16 am	Sagittarius
	Oct	19	9:26 am	Scorpio		Nov	21	1:18 pm	Capricorn
1957	Jun	15	8:13 pm	Libra	1998	Jan	29	2:46 am	Aquarius
	Aug	6	8:20 am	Scorpio		Aug	23	0:27 am	Capricorn
						Nov	28	1:09 am	Aquarius

Example: Someone born in 1957 before June 15 has Neptune in Scorpio. Someone born after June 15, 1957 (at 8:13 am EST) but before August 6, would have Neptune in Libra.

♆ Neptune in Gemini ♊

Identity Issues
As a child, you loved listening to fairy tales. Stories of magic and menace appealed to you. As you grew, you became more and more curious about the hidden side of the mind. You studied texts of magic. You investigated rumors of phantastical beasts and miraculous happenings. As you delved deeper into otherworldly images, your connections to physical reality became more tenu-

ous. Sometimes you lost track of who you were. You would identify with people of other times and places, or feel that a demon or person from the other side had taken over your body. You began to wonder if "you" even existed—or everything was a dream.

Made for Music

Beauty was your life. As a young child, you were drawn to music, nature, dance. You learned to play every musical instrument you could, enjoying all of them. As soon as you could afford to, you began purchasing instruments and filling your time with songs. Money was tight and you did not receive much recompense for your talents. But you gloried in the use of your muse. Life was harsh. You had almost no possessions (other than your instruments) and went to bed quite hungry at times, but you were inspired by your art and couldn't imagine any other life path.

Family Falsehoods

Growing up, something felt odd, although you could not quite pin it down. An only child of older parents, your material circumstances were reasonably comfortable, but emotionally you felt off balance. When you were ten, you were introduced to your Aunt Sally and immediately felt drawn to her, but you could tell your mother was uncomfortable with you spending time with your aunt. When the visit was over, life returned to normal. Then, your mother fell prey to a fever and died. In the midst of his grief and rage, your father told you that your aunt Sally was really your mother and he didn't know who your father was, but it wasn't he. Terribly distraught, you ran off, determined to make your way to Aunt Sally (who lived hundreds of miles distant). You perished on that journey, with your last thoughts that one could never trust family.

Boyish Botany

Growing up in the country, you were very close to nature. Particularly fond of butterflies, you could watch a meadow for hours, fascinated by the different forms of birds, insects, and wildlife. As you grew older, your parents expected you to learn the traditional skills of housewifery. Although you coped well with domestic demands, your heart remained in the out-of-doors. You met a young man who loved to tramp through the woods, and you fell in love. Once you were married, you discovered that your husband was a wonderful wilderness companion, but basically a small boy at heart. If you didn't work, manage the household accounts, and generally look after everything, nothing happened. Your husband was completely content to let everyone else—including you—take care of him.

Clandestine Christianity

Born in Japan, you were very close to your parents. They became involved with a Jesuit missionary from Portugal. After many discussions, your family decided to convert to Christianity. The Portuguese missionaries were having quite a bit of success in their endeavors. The shoguns of Japan became threatened. The Jesuits were expelled and Japanese society was closed from the "polluting" influences of the outside world. Some Christians were executed. Others, like your family, went underground, and kept their faith secretly.

Buried Blackness

Your mother was half white and half black, the product of a union of a slave owner and a slave. Your father was also white, so you were only one quarter black, but that was all that mattered in New Orleans where you lived. Quadroons were popular mistresses for the white planters, but that was not what you wanted. After much soul-searching, you decided to move north—to Illinois or Pennsylvania and "pass" (as white). Although you felt guilty at the deception, you were determined to have a chance at a better life. Throughout your time in the north, you feared being unmasked and felt different, but your secret was never discovered.

♆ Neptune in Cancer ♋

Wealthy Witness

Born with an artistic flair, you found your métier in sewing. Everyone was impressed with your creations, and you carved out a career as a designer to the wealthy. One day, one of your wealthy clients left your shop after a fitting, only to return crying "theft." She had lost her ruby brooch and was sure that you (or one of your shop assistants) had stolen it while she was trying on clothes. Although you allowed her to search and insisted you were innocent, she had you arrested. The judge did not imprison you, but your business was ruined. (Much later, your accuser found the brooch in a crack in the floor of her coach.) You retreated to the country, swearing to have nothing to do with riches or wealthy people.

Eroding Esteem

Sensitive and inward, you were a quiet, shy child. People often overlooked you and you grew up feeling a bit like you were invisible. As a young woman, you fell madly in love with an exciting young man. He was charismatic and very magnetic. A lot of women adored him. But he seemed drawn to your quiet serenity. He told you he felt peaceful around you. After you were married, he became more and more outgoing, and you withdrew. The more he shined, the more you shrank from the limelight. Your self-esteem shrank. You felt insignificant. He became the important one and your entire life revolved around him.

Fit For Farming

Born into a farming community, you learned to help out at an early age. When just a toddler, you were taught to distinguish weeds from vegetables so you could help look after family foodstuffs. You learned to shell peas and snap beans. When you were old enough, you learned to sow seeds, and plow fields.

Labor was from dawn to dusk. The weather could destroy most of a year's harvest if it turned wrong. Inadequate tools handicapped you further. Yet, when everything went right, or when you inhaled the rich scent of the fertile earth, all the effort was worthwhile.

Deadly Dogmas

Born into a merchant family in New Rochelle, France, your early life was quite comfortable. Then, your parents (and you) became involved with the Protestant movement. Many other merchants, artisans and even some nobles converted. The monarchy, which controlled the Catholic Church, was not pleased. Eventually, a civil war broke out. Your father was killed in the St. Bartholemew's Massacre (along with 3000 other people). You and your mother joined with other Huguenots to go to the New World, hoping you could worship in peace there.

Shifting Sands

You lived in North Africa—before the time of Rome, before the time of Carthage. A farmer, you wrested your livelihood from the earth. Each year, you watched the desert get closer and closer. Each year, you saw the winds bring more and more sand. You and your family had been on the land for generations, but you knew you would soon have to give up farming. Eventually, you faced reality, selling everything you could, and buying a small herd of goats. From then on, you drifted from place to place with your goats, no longer having land or structures of your own.

Priestly Persecution

With a strong mystical connection, you studied for the priesthood. During the realm of King Henry VIII and again under Elizabeth I, persecution of Catholics became quite severe. Several of your friends were martyred. You made use of the priest's holes in noble houses more than once to escape capture and execution. Although you were strongly motivated to pursue your vocation, living in hiding took its toll. You became seriously ill. Eventually, a combination of physical weakness and betrayal did you in. You were caught and lost your life.

♆ Neptune in Leo ♌

Temporary Things

Raised in the Caribbean by loving parents, you had a rather uneventful childhood. However, your island was directly in the path of hurricanes, so you learned that anything could be destroyed. Physical possessions were few because everything—including your house—might be torn away with the next severe storm. Your life was marked and recorded by these destructive winds: "the year the hurricane took Tante's house; the year the storm killed Gregor's goats," etc. You treated everything you owned as a temporary loan which you expected to have to return.

Birthing Barriers

Born into a farming community in the Ukraine, you grew up very attached to the land. The scent and feeling of the rich soil was wonderful. Seeing tiny green plants increasing in size thrilled you. When you were 17, you fell very deeply in love and were married. Your husband also adored you and the two of you planned on a large family. Your first birth was very difficult, but you and the babe survived. The second birth was even worse. The midwife warned you and your husband to cease marital relations lest you perish in childbirth. Your husband was willing to do so because he cared deeply about you, but you wanted at least one more child and seduced your beloved. Neither you nor the babe survived that birth.

Fool's Gold

You heard about the big strike in California and headed on out. A lot of people were searching for gold. Although you panned endlessly and dug many different places, you found nothing. Like many of your peers, you went broke buying food and supplies. A very small, occasional strike kept you going for years, struggling, working hard. But you never hit the big time. You spent your youth laboring away with no real results.

Bare Basics

You were born and raised in Babylon. Poor and politically powerless, you were persuaded to become a laborer working on the great hanging gardens. The palace was filled with greenery. An incredible number of plants were involved, and vast workers were needed to create the effect desired. You, however, were very puzzled that the powers that be were including all these inedible plants. As you and your fellow workers were often hungry, you could barely see the point of decorative projects. Pure survival was the focus.

Prejudice and Pogroms

You grew up in a small village in Poland. You knew you were Jewish, but had no concept of what it meant to the outside world until age 7. Somehow, the village got world that a pogrom was underway. Your grandmother smashed the windows of your house. She killed a chicken, smearing the blood around the walls, over the beds, ripping out the feather bed. She created bloodstains on the outside walls as well. When the house was completely demolished within, you and your entire family hid in a cavern in the earth with a midden above you. Outside, shrieks of mayhem could be distinguished periodically. You learned later that your grandmother had saved the house from burning. And you learned the price to be paid for being "different."

Paradise Lost

Born by the sea, you fell asleep to the rhythms of the waves. When you were young, you learned to recognize the voice of Mother Earth within the winds. Although you were not trained as a kahuna, you understood and respected the nature spirits. Then, men of pale skin came to your land. They insisted you must wear more cloth on your bodies—cloth which was itchy, binding, and flapped in the sea breeze. They demanded that you join their religion—threatening you with eternal fire if you refused. You retreated far inland to get away from their constant pressure, but their presence increased. Soon, you could not escape. Unwilling to forsake the old ways, you lived with much pain from the way these newcomers treated the land and your people.

♆ Neptune in Virgo ♍

Individual Impotence
You were a weaver in ancient Macedonia. All creations had to be funneled through your guild. The regulations were quite limiting and discouraged individuality. You often felt frustrated because you felt obedience was valued over efficiency. You appreciated competence and struggled with the system to make it more open to improvement. But the entrenched people in power were immovable. You ended up feeling that nothing you did made any difference.

Paucity of Possessions
Born into comfortable circumstances, you were a very empathic child. When you saw beggars on the street, you wanted to help. Your parents constantly chastised you for giving away your allowance or possessions to someone less fortunate. They implored you to be practical. When you were in your late teens, you felt the call of God and entered a monastery. You chose an order which had absolutely no personal possessions. Even the robes you wore belonged to the monastery—not to you. Food was sparse (and boring). The environment was limited—no pictures or rugs or anything to distract you from focusing on God.

Closed Communication Channels
Your parents believed that children should be seen and definitely not heard. Even as a baby, you cried less than most because you learned that crying didn't bring any response. By the time you were an adult, you rarely said anything. Out in the world, other people encouraged you to talk, but old habits were difficult to break. Even when you married and your wife desperately tried to initiate conversations with you, it was just too painful. Talking felt like a life-threatening act for you, so you continued to be reticent, leaving others to speak for you or to guess what was going on inside your head.

Ballet Over Boys
A vibrant, active child, you were a handful to raise. While still young, you discovered the world of ballet, and that became your life. You practiced as much as possible, addicted to the beauty of dance. You did odd jobs to earn money for shoes and extra classes. Your skill was sufficient that you found employment in the Corps de Ballet. Although pay was minimal and you lived in crowded apartments with other dancers, you were in heaven. Regularly, young men

would see you on stage and fall in love with your grace and beauty. You had no time for relationships, however. Everything was dedicated to your art.

Illicit Intimacy

A dutiful child, you were quiet and obedient. Your parents raised you within strict parameters including regular church attendance. You towed the line and rarely considered anything outside their expectations. In due course, they selected your husband—of good background and reasonably well off financially. Marriage was not easy. Your husband was very jealous and controlling. At the least hint of opposition, he would beat you. His work took him away from home, and he would question you closely when he returned. After one departure, you met a young man visiting the neighbors. You both were tremendously attracted to one another and managed to rendezvous in a cabin in the woods away from everyone. Looking for love, you ended up having an affair, and feeling terribly guilty about what you were doing, but needing something (someone) positive in your life.

Evading Ideology?

Born into a Puritan family, you learned young of the rigors of religious persecution. Certain jobs were closed to your family. Living quarters were restricted. Only some people would associate with you. A refusal to even get to know you was common. Although the discrimination hurt, you kept on striving for acceptance. After your sister was abused at the hands of ruffians who fancied themselves teaching a Puritan a "lesson," you and your family decided to leave. You departed for the New World, determined to find a place where you could pursue your own beliefs.

Peril in Protecting

An imaginative child, you spoke with invisible playmates and created whole worlds within your mind. When you became older, you became enthralled by the tales of saints and martyrs. You would study their lives intensely, and then seek out opportunities for you to rescue the downtrodden. Needless to say, this was rather dangerous at times. You perished, at age 22, when attempting to stop a mob from stoning a woman (identified as an adultress) to death.

♆ Neptune in Libra ♎

Surface Sweetness

You were a concubine in the Far East. Rules were very definite for the women of the harem. What you could and could not do was strictly controlled. You chafed under the limits of your situation. Any resistance on your part was swiftly punished. Attempts to assert your independence only brought troubles down upon you. You learned to be superficially obedient even when seething beneath the surface.

Begging Bowl

Born in India to a merchant family, you had a reasonably comfortable childhood. In your middle teens, you had a vision of Krishna. As a result, you gave away all your worldly possessions and began to wander. You traveled all over India with only a begging bowl. You mostly slept outdoors, sometimes in conditions of considerable hardship. You ate well when people were generous and not at all or poorly when they did not give. Although your physical life was very limited, you felt you were pursuing a vital spiritual path.

Romance Or Realism?

Your father died when you were very young, and your mother was quite a romantic. She told you wonderful tales, throughout your growing years, about how perfect your father was. To listen to her, one would believe he had been an ideal man—always loving, thoughtful, helpful, dedicated, and so on. As a result, your ideas about men and romance were rather impractical. When you started meeting men who were considering marriage, you suffered quite a shock. Nothing was as you'd dream it would be. No man measured up to the stories you'd heard about your father. Eventually, you decided that if you could not find your perfect, ideal soulmate love, you simply would avoid love completely.

Departed Darling

Sweet and loving, you were the only child of older parents. As a result, you spent much of your childhood with a neighboring family who had quite a few children. In your early teens, you fell in love with one of the sons. You tagged along with all his activities, admiring him and eager to spent all your hours with him. Although you adored him for years, he viewed you as just another sister and eventually married someone else. Heartbroken, you entered a nunnery and became a bride of Christ.

Naive Notions

A sweet and charming child, you grew into a lovely young woman. Aided by your great beauty and your father's clout within the aristocracy, you were assigned to be a lady-in-waiting to the queen. Life at court proved very challenging for you. Naive and idealistic, you did not understand all the undercurrents which went on around you. Believing everyone meant well, you missed all the plots and counter plots which took place. You believed that right would prevail over wrong. A group conspiring to assassinate the king involved you as a smokescreen for one of their women. Knowing nothing of these matters, you proclaimed your innocence, but they had laid the hints pointing toward you well. You were executed for treason.

Contrasting Communities

Born into an Amish community, you loved the artistic emphasis. Almost everyone was a craftsman of some sort. Many worked with wood. Others sewed. Beautiful (and practical) things were constantly under production.

Although you were very close to your community, you did sometimes visit in surrounding towns. You found the attitudes of outsiders difficult to deal with. They acted as though you were some strange being. You wanted them to like you, but most strangers eyed you as if you were a threat somehow. Children made fun of your clothes and speech. People treated you as if you were dull and stupid. Outside your community, you felt like a strange beast constantly on display—and ripe for teasing.

♆ Neptune in Scorpio ♏

Solitary Struggles

You were a government worker in New York City coping with waves of immigrants struggling against poverty and discrimination. Although you did not know her personally, you greatly admired the work of Jane Addams. Because you felt politics had a strong influence on the fate of your clients, you worked to change "the system." Most of your efforts brought only failure and frustration. Corruption, greed, and unfair practices continued. You felt discouraged, that the solitary individual had no power against the state.

Dispossessed

You were born on the sunny slopes of Spain. Although your ancestors had lived in Spain for 700 years, they followed the path of Islam. Called by the whites around you, Moors, you contributed much to the architecture, culture, and commercial life of the land in which you lived. Just as you were coming of age, a wave of intense, jingoistic Catholicism swept Spain. An edict went forth: you and all your kin were banished! After more than 700 years, you were told to depart Spain. And you were allowed to take almost nothing with you. Completely dispossessed, you and your family traveled to North Africa, starting over with almost no possessions.

Unwelcome Understanding

As a small child, you "saw" the village down the road devastated by a tornado and mentioned it to your mother. Three days later the tornado came. You saw the drowning of a neighborhood man, and the death of your father. By the time you were in your late teens, you hated your visions. Like Cassandra, you seemed to only perceive disasters. You begged God to turn off your "talent," as you hated living with it. This extra understanding felt like a curse to you and you prayed for it to go away. By your late twenties, your visions had ceased.

Brutal Betrayal

An insightful child, you often saw more than your parents realized. With a penchant for uncovering hidden information, you were better informed than most girls your age. Drawn toward the forbidden, you learned a bit of magic and yearned to study the occult more deeply. As was expected you married. It was impossible to keep your unusual interests entirely hidden from your husband, but you did not worry about it. Then, the fervor of the Inquisition swept the land. Your own husband turned you into the examiners. You were imprisoned, and eventually sentenced to die for your "heretical" beliefs.

Difficult Denial

Born into a very religious family, it was quite natural that you would be drawn toward the Church. With some funds and influential friends backing your career, you eventually rose to the position of bishop. Extremely conscientious, you fulfilled your duties well, but you did find yourself troubled in one regard. Even after years of celibacy, you found that the sight of women would incite your lust. You had to deal with many temptations and found it increasingly difficult to forswear the pleasures of the flesh. You knew that some of your colleagues had surreptitious affairs, but you wanted to keep your commitment to God. Although it was very difficult, you managed to restrain yourself throughout your long life and died a virgin, true to your vows.

Secret Circles

Born in Norway, you enjoyed the land of ice and snow as well as the grandeur of greenery in the spring. Your parents taught you an ancient way: the worship of the Mother and the turning of the wheel for the seasons. You celebrated the rites of spring (Beltane) and Midsummer, as well as Harvest. Then, the King converted to Christianity. He decreed that all his subjects must also convert. Death was to be the fate of those who resisted. Those who followed any other ways were called pagan and subject to persecution and execution. You and your family mouthed the words of conversion, but kept to your old ways in great secrecy, knowing you were risking your lives each time you paid your respect to The Lady at each full moon.

♆ Neptune in Sagittarius ♐

Frustrated Forcefulness

You were a rather unusual nun during the Middle Ages. You came to the convent later in life than most. Despite lacking a powerful family, you moved up the convent hierarchy rather rapidly. You gained positions wielding considerable authority and then hit a barrier. Your efforts to modernize (and make more efficient) the convent's production of herbs and tapestries (which were traded for other goods) were completely denied by the Mother Superior. You were heavily criticized for your "rebellious" mind and told to ask God for assistance in becoming more modest, cooperative, and sweet.

Real Renunciation

Born into considerable wealth, you were the only child. Although your parents were extremely sensual and materialistic, you had a strong mystical streak. You would spend hours with nature, feeling closer to God. When you inherited all your parents' worldly goods, you contributed them to the Church, keeping nothing for yourself. You could have purchased a place for yourself within a nunnery, but that did not feel right to you. Instead, you lived in great poverty to the end of your days.

Religiously Romantic

An extremely idealistic child, you had a hard time seeing the negative side of life. You wanted to believe everyone was good and kind, and were often disillusioned by people. Your parents tried to teach you to be more practical, but your first instinct remained trust and thinking that everyone meant well. You also developed romantic ideals about chivalry and relationships and were, your mother and father were convinced, ripe for tremendous hurt. Each person you admired inevitably fell off of his pedestal. Finally, disillusioned, but still seeking perfection, you decided to enter a nunnery and dedicate yourself to the Lord. Your parents breathed a sigh of relief and supported your decision.

Churchly Couple

A quiet and studious woman of good family, you were fortunate to have parents who believed in some schooling for women as well as men. Some of your studies were supervised by the family's priest. He had recently taken orders, so was only a few years older than you. Through shared ideas and interesting discussions, the two of you fell in love. You begged him to leave the Church and marry you, but he was adamant in remaining true to his vows. At length, you entered a nunnery resolved to have no man if you could not have the one you loved. You and he corresponded for the rest of your days, but never met face-to-face again.

Outrageous Opinions

Born into the Society of Friends, your parents and community taught you the ways of nonviolence and turning the other cheek. But the people surrounding you had no such ethical persuasion. Discrimination was fierce. Non-Quakers would deny you employment opportunities and some of the young men delighted in trying to pick fights or bullying Friends. Eventually, you decided England was not for you and emigrated to the New World. There, too, your faith was held against you until you journeyed to the area known as Pennsylvania. There, among like-minded individuals, you did your best to follow your loving creed.

Destination: Deseret

Your family followed the Church of the Latter Day Saints. You learned about discrimination at a young age. Other children would mock you. Adults whispered about your family, treated you as though you were all shameful people. Employment opportunities were very limited. Eventually, you decided to join Brigham Young's wagon train to find New Zion. Although the trip was very difficult, with the Indians, the harsh desert, and the privations of travel taking a toll, some of your made it to the Promised Land. In your hearts, despite the unprepossessing appearance of your destination, you knew you could build a utopia.

♆ Neptune in Capricorn ♑

Agoraphobia

Raised in a very religious home, you chose to take orders when you were old enough. The monastery which you entered was very self-sufficient. You raised your own food and wine and bartered with the outside world for other items. The quiet, contemplative life suited you very well. In fact, after several years, you began resisting leaving the premises. You felt very attached—as if it was your home, and got uncomfortable when away. Your abbot was understanding at first and didn't force you, but became concerned that you were becoming too dependent. By the time he got around to saying you needed to visit outside periodically, you were in no condition emotionally to do so. You spent the rest of your life in retreat behind the walls.

Supreme Service

A gentle child, you drifted through your early years. After a strong religious experience, you entered the Order of the Franciscans. Hard work and service became your focus. Serving the neediest among humanity meant often going without yourself. Although what you did could be quite draining, you knew that all your efforts were on behalf of the Lord. When you physical body was drooping with weariness and you had pushed yourself unmercifully, you tried to do just one more helpful act before resting.

Holy Vows

A boisterous child, you were the last person people expected to turn to religion. Yet, at age 13, you had a vision and felt that God had called you. When your mother questioned your certainty, you declared that marrying God would be far superior to any of the young men in your neighborhood! The Mother Superior at the local nunnery worried a bit that you were joining the church more to avoid marriage than due to a true vocation, but you were able to convince her of your dedication (and that you would do well in a community consisting solely of women).

Mystical Missionary

Nature drew you. Even as a toddler, you would go outdoors whenever possible. As you aged, you experienced a mystical connection. You found God in the waterfalls, in the mists on the mountain, in the wildflowers of the meadows, and more. You entered the church, but became a missionary. You would travel to faraway places, often with great deprivation, to carry the word of the Lord. Frequently rejected and reviled, you were buoyed by your faith. You felt the presence of the Infinite in everything and yearned to share that experience with all you met.

Authority and Arbiter

Born into poverty, you realized early on that money meant power. Understanding society's structure, you knew you had no real chance for great wealth, so you took the best path available and became a priest. Although appointments for bishops were largely political (and kept in the hands of second sons of the well-to-do), an active priest still wielded considerable clout. You enjoyed being the moral arbiter for your village and its environs. You found safety in becoming part of the power structure which told others what to do.

Psychic Suppression

Your parents prided themselves on their scientific minds and practical outlook. You were raised to believe in what you could see, hear, and touch. Yet, even from a young age, you had odd experiences. You talked to people who were supposed to be dead. You knew things before they happened. Your parents insisted it was all your imagination or "coincidence." Your learned that speaking about your "impressions" and "feelings" brought disapproval on your head. Soon, you suppressed yourself enough that you stopped having the psychic insights as well—becoming the little materialist your parents wanted.

♆ Neptune in Aquarius ♒

Covert Communication

Your family was not an easy one. Both your parents were unpredictably violent. As a self-protective measure, you spent much time with your brother who was just one year older than you. The two of you developed your own private language for communication. It provided part of your safety in a very dangerous environment. Often, you had no real interest in communicating with others. Outsiders didn't understand what your parents were like and your parents didn't want to listen to you anyway. So, almost all of your interaction was with your brother. The two of you shut everyone else out.

Nice and Easy

Born in Polynesia, you learned a laid-back style of life. Many fruits were available to pick and eat. A fishing line dropped in the ocean brought protein fairly rapidly. Erecting huts was a communal project and never took very long. The women worked longer hours weaving cloth and processing breadfruit. The men sat around telling stories, wandering along the beach, or sometimes working on canoes. When the white men came to your island, the were shocked and accused you all of being lazy. But you saw no reason to work on useless projects as the whites did. You were perfectly happy to live easily and harmoniously—with little labor.

Worried Wife

You grew up in a home where your father abused your mother. Although you were not beaten, you worried that the husband you would marry might treat you similarly. When you were old enough to wed, you examined your prospects very carefully. You chose a much older man who was enamored with you and appeared to be extremely doting. Shortly after the wedding, he became extremely ill and you ended up spending the next 20 years nursing him. With no real partnership, you had the privileges of a wife, but the responsibilities of a continual caretaker.

Withdrawing Within

Unusual and intuitive, you didn't quite fit in as a child. You preferred spending time with nature and animals to time with people. With a very rich inner life, you withdrew from the world to explore your own psyche. Becoming a hermit, you limited your contacts with the outside world. Mystical realms and magical concepts were part of your focus of attention. Although you felt sometimes that you were neglecting your personal growth in terms of intimacy, a solitary life suited you and was easier to manage.

Dangerous Differences

You were an Indian of the Plains and raised to appreciate the buffalo. From the buffalo came skins for your clothing and tipis, meat to eat, implements, rugs, and much more. You learned that many of the white men (who were becoming too numerous on the face of the Earth) saw killing buffalo as a path to eliminating Indians. In only about ten years, a few hundred hunters—encouraged by the U.S. military—killed over 40 million buffalo. A little of the meat was fed to railroad crews. Most of it rotted. You watched and knew that this was happening because you and your people were different and did not follow the ways of the white man.

Attacking Alterations

Born in what is now Czechoslovakia, your parents encouraged you to think for yourself. When you came of age, you heard a priest named Johann Huss. He spoke against the indulgences of the Catholic Church, the excesses, the lack of piety. Many other people listened as well. A movement began. Calling yourselves Hussites, you spoke up for the cleansing of the Church. Rebellion was in the air. The powers that be killed Huss. With his death, internal divisions arose and the movement floundered. You perished with many others and the quest for reformation died with you (to be resurrected later by another priest—Martin Luther).

CHAPTER TEN
PAST LIFE SCENARIOS: PLUTO

Find your Pluto sign and read the appropriate scenarios. Since I do not have a single case for those signs, there are no scenarios for Pluto in Aries, Taurus, Capricorn, Aquarius, or Pisces. Pluto in Sagittarius is pure theory.

1937	Oct	7	12:18 pm	Leo		1971	Oct	5	6:18 am	Libra
	Nov	25	9:03 am	Cancer		1972	Apr	17	7:46 am	Virgo
1938	Aug	3	5:59 pm	Leo			Jul	30	11:43 am	Libra
1939	Feb	7	12:56 pm	Cancer		1983	Nov	5	9:18 pm	Scorpio
	Jun	14	4:50 am	Leo		1984	May	18	2:19 pm	Libra
1956	Oct	20	6:18 am	Virgo			Aug	28	4:59 am	Scorpio
1957	Jan	15	2:39 am	Leo		1995	Jan	17	9:59 am	Sagittarius
	Aug	19	4:27 am	Virgo			Apr	21	2:08 am	Scorpio
1958	Apr	11	2:52 pm	Leo			Nov	10	7:40 pm	Sagittarius
	Jun	10	6:56 pm	Virgo						

Example: Someone born in 1972 before April 17 has Pluto in Libra. Someone born after April 17 (at 7:46 am EST) but before July 30 (11:43 am EST), would have Pluto in Virgo.

♇ Pluto in Gemini ♊

Will to Live

Born on the Carpathian plains in what is now Hungary, you had a rather ordinary childhood. Although your parents expected you to do chores and help out, you had some free time to get together with friends and play. You became quite adept at talking your peers into things. You could persuade them. The people you hung out with almost always ended up doing what you were interested in because you made it sound like fun. While you were still a teenager, a plague came to your village. It took your parents among the early victims. Eventually, you also succumbed to the illness. You fought long and hard. Finally, you passed on, with an overriding desire to LIVE stamped in your psyche.

Royal Raiding

Born a Jew in Europe in the Middle Ages, you knew from childhood on that you were alive only on sufferance. Although your family was hard-working, prejudice closed doors to you. Money-lending was one of the few permitted trades as Christians were forbidden from the practice. Some of your uncles were in that business, but your family focused more on crafts. Despite being taxed twice as heavily as the Christians, your family managed, through much effort on everyone's part, to make enough to buy a few nice things. The king, however, owed a fair amount of money to various Jewish money-lenders and elected to expel all Jews from the land. All your property was, of course, forfeit to the Crown. You had to leave and start completely over elsewhere.

Poetic Potential

From an early age, you were strongly moved by the glories of language. As a child, you loved to listen to people talk. You would gravitate to groups where discussions were taking place, and sit, fascinated, absorbed in the exchanges. When you discovered poetry, you became obsessed. Here was a tool for exploring the depths of life and the beauty of words. You created vast numbers of poems, but refused to show them to anyone. You were convinced they were meaningful only to you, and no one else would appreciate them. Further, you had strong doubts as to whether they were good enough to share. At length, you abandoned your verses, sonnets, and rhymes. Seeing no future there, you looked for something "sensible" to do.

Disinterest

Born at a time when marriage was the accepted path of a woman, you imagined nothing else when young. A rather inquisitive individual, you had a talent for drawing information out of people. They instinctively shared confidences with you and you were circumspect about what was revealed to you. At sixteen you were wed to a man of your parents' choosing. He was not a bad man, but he had little interest in women. All he wanted from you was an heir. If you tried to talk to him, he treated you like a foolish child. Eventually, for your own (somewhat bitter) amusement, you made a point of not initiating any interaction with him. By the time he died, fifteen years and passed and not once had he requested your opinion upon any subject.

Incomplete Information

Born with a burning curiosity, you questioned everyone around you. Sometimes people explained things to you; sometimes they did not. As a female, you were often told that your questions were inappropriate or that you didn't need to know about what you were asking. You felt a great deal of frustration at all the blocks that were put in the way of your learning. One of your brothers (who preferred sports to books) would loan you his textbooks in exchange for you hitting the highlights of what he was supposed to pick up in the reading. Eventually, your parents caught on to what was happening and you both were punished. It was "well-known" that too much book learning would spoil a woman for marriage. Your parents kept tight control after that and you were continually frustrated in your efforts to learn more.

Personally Persecuted

Raised in the traditions of Islam, you were exposed to the faith of the Bahai in your twenties. The loving tolerance preached by that faith had a great deal of appeal to you. The people around you, however, were not pleased. Most of your colleagues and neighbors were quite prejudiced against the Bahai faith. You bore the brunt of a great deal of minor unpleasantness by people who resented your religious positions. Then, during a period when scapegoating was at a particular high, you had to flee from threats to your very life. You learned the pain of being different!

♇ Pluto in Cancer ♋

Struggle to Survive

Your tribe spent winters on the banks of the Red River. At the end of your seventh year, there was a tremendous flood. Many people were swept away. Teepees were destroyed. Horses were lost. Individual acts of heroism abounded as family members and friends sought to rescue their loved ones. Most of the struggle was to no avail. You were caught in one of the rushes of water and swept into a raging current. Although you fought against it, struggling to keep your head above water and avoid the dangers of uprooted trees and corpses surrounding you, there was no way out. Despite all your efforts, you perished, feeling no matter how hard you tried, you would not succeed.

Yearning for Learning

Your father was a footman and your mother an upstairs maid in one of the houses of the aristocracy. Although they had a mere pittance on which to survive, they did marry and, in due course, you were conceived. With no other model, you were expected to enter service as well. You yearned to learn, but education was too expensive for a servant. Besides, no one could see the point of teaching a mere female such as yourself to read and write. You followed your mother's footsteps and became a maid, but listened at every opportunity to others, to broaden your knowledge base, and continued to hope that someday you would be able to read and write.

Childless

As a child, you adored your brothers and sisters and looked forward to a large family of your own. The man you wed also wanted a number of children. After a few years of marriage, and no pregnancy, you began to worry. Finally, after 10 years, you had a son! You and your husband rejoiced, but no other child appeared to grace your life. When your son was 10 years old, a serious plague swept through the children of the village. Despite your round-the-clock care, he perished after a few days. Broken-hearted, you decided that you were not meant to ever have any children.

Eating to Anesthetize

When you were young, your mother developed a wasting disease and slowly got sicker and sicker. The neighborhood women made up by feeding you as often as possible. The less your mother could keep down, the more everyone urged you to eat. Getting really full seemed to help anesthetize you against the pain of your mother's slow death. By the time she passed away, you were addicted to overeating. Food was your panacea for any difficulties. You developed a number of health problems as a result, but stuffing yourself worked very well as a reassurance and substitute pleasure.

Mother or Mate?

Your father died when you were very young, so you were raised solely by your mother. She was very loving, but oddly dependent upon you. She discouraged you from visiting friends and being with other people, seeming to prefer that you remained close to her. She encouraged you to discuss all your feelings with her, and to come to her whenever you needed to work anything out. She did not forbid you to get to know young men, but seemed to find flaws in any of the men you discussed with her. Despite this, you fell in love and got married. Your mother insisted she had to live with you; she couldn't bear to be all alone. You took her in, but tensions increased between your mother and your husband. You were constantly in the middle. It seemed each of them demanded that you choose him (or her) over the other. Your marriage got rockier and rockier and your relationship with your mother became quite uncomfortable. Soon, you found yourself avoiding everyone, wishing you could be left alone!

Resented Revelations

A quiet child, you rarely disturbed the people around you. Occasionally, you would voice a remark which shocked your family. "How did you know that?" was their usual response. You could never explain to their satisfaction that you just understood the inner workings of people, with great insight into their motivations. When you predicted certain behaviors (which came to pass), people spoke of "witchcraft" and "trafficking with the Devil." You became more and more silent, but could not contain all your observations. Finally, an influential neighbor had you imprisoned for sorcery. (His wife left two days after you had told your brother in the marketplace that she had the look of a slave fleeing her master.)

♇ Pluto in Leo ♌

Non-Attachment

You were born near the "smoking mountains" of central Mexico. Your father was headman of the village, so you were relatively well off. You and your family ate well and had some lovely and valuable objects in your home. When you were twelve, the smoking mountain began to flow. Most villagers had barely enough time to escape with their lives. Your mother shepherded you and your younger siblings, but your father stayed, desperately trying to same of his cherished possessions. He perished in the lava flow and you vowed never to become attached to things!

Controlling Children

Born into an aristocratic Cornish family, you were raised to know what you owed to your lineage. In due time, you married and became a father. As the patriarch of the clan, you were very forceful. Your heir received the most pressure in regard to how he was expected to behave, but the other children came in for their share as well. You expected the girls to grow up to make excellent marriages with the "right" sort of man. Several of the children opposed your will. Your heir battled over his allowance, his friends, his military interests. Your oldest daughter made a runaway marriage with a man you viewed as a neer'do'well. The more you tried to control, the more they resisted. You became increasingly frustrated and often quoted King Lear: "Sharper than a serpent's tooth is a thankless child."

Social Spouse

Born female, you learned that your only worth lay in the marriage you would eventually make. Your family had important political connections and wished to maintain and strengthen them. Eventually, you were wed to an older man whose connections at court matched your family's ambitions. Although you were expected to be the gracious hostess, any significant discussions were held by the men. Your major role was ornamental and occasional light entertainment. Frustrated by the lack of any substance, you would have preferred to retreat to your painting, but even that was denied as you had to be visible and charming as a political wife. You learned how to present in a room and acting like a proper wife when your spirit and imagination were far away.

Protective Policeman

You were a police officer who really cared about his community. You attended weddings, Christenings, and funerals in your neighborhood. When kids got in trouble, you talked to them, and did all you could to steer them toward the law. If theft was committed, you hardly rested until you could apprehend someone. You took your duties extremely seriously and felt the weight of your position on your shoulders. If you could not solve a crime, you were horribly embarrassed and felt you had failed your "people."

Always Apart

Your white parents perished in an Indian raid, but you were young enough to be adopted by the tribe. You were raised within the culture of the Comanche Indians. Although you became quite bronzed by the sun, with your blue eyes and fair hair, you always looked different. You were given the same opportunities as other youths—to prove yourself. Your adoptive parents did not distinguish between you and the children of their body, yet you felt out of place. Although you wanted desperately to belong, you believed you would never fit in completely. A part of you would always be the outsider.

Community Concept

While you were still a teen-ager, you became caught up in the idea of an intentional community. Convinced you and your fellows would establish a utopia on Earth, you followed your leader and set up a commune in Iowa. Everyone labored long hours to establish your spiritual community. Spirits were high. You were convinced that you were part of a new wave which would change the world. With the death of your founder, however, the dream faltered. In-fighting began. People could not agree. Disappointed and tremendously disillusioned, you eventually left—at age 50—hoping to find a new vision.

♇ Pluto in Virgo ♍

Punitive Pressure

You were an early medical student who studied illegally obtained cadavers to polish your understanding of anatomy and bodily functions. Although you felt gaining the knowledge was essential, a part of you regretted breaking the law and felt guilty. You pushed yourself unmercifully go grow in training and expertise. You demanded total comprehension and recall of facts. If you could not meet your demanding standards, you were extremely self-critical. Because you dealt with life and death issues, you felt a tremendous responsibility and burden.

Fatal Famine

Your Irish parents were very poor and worked as tenant farmers on the estate of an absentee (English) landlord. The soil was hard and rocky, and the growing season was limited, but they scraped by most of the time, never managing to get out of debt to their landlord. Then a blight struck the potato crop. Devastation was widespread. Whole counties had their food supply wiped out. There was no place to go. Although many who could scrape together funds emigrated (to America and elsewhere), most stayed—your family among them. You and your parents tried and struggled desperately, but in the end, you starved to death.

Healing or Husband

Drawn toward healing, you were able to pursue your inclinations and got training as a nurse. It gave you tremendous satisfaction to be able to help repair wounded or ill bodies. Although the work was very physically demanding, you felt satisfaction in being able to make a difference. Then you met a man who was very attractive and interested in you. When he proposed, however, he made it very clear that you would have to choose between nursing and him. He was unwilling for his wife to work in a hospital—or anywhere else. After great soul-searching, you turned him down, knowing you could not give up your opportunity to help people.

Sexual Strain

Like most girls, you knew that marriage was to be your lot in life. You dreamed of a pleasant husband with whom to spend your days. The man whom your family approved was financially comfortable and seemed a nice enough fellow. Once you were married, however, you discovered he was a sex addict. He wanted intercourse five and six times a day. He would come home and expect you to be ready to immediately have sex—no matter what you were doing. If you refused him, he became furious and hit you. When you spoke to your pastor, haltingly, about your husband's demands, he reminded you of a wife's "duty" to her husband. Whenever your husband was not around, you dreamed of a time when you would never have to have sex again.

Broken Promises

Born into the Cherokee Nation, your parents raised you to follow a high ethical standard. Those were dark times for your people. Several times treaties were made with the white man, and several times they were broken by the white man. Then, the great White Father in Washington made his decree and the white man's army came to your land. You were forced to leave everything you owned and all that you knew to embark upon what became known as the Trail of Tears. During that difficult journey, you watched your mother and then your brother die. In the end, you and your father tried to begin a new life, sick—barely surviving, in a land far from the land of your ancestors.

Dedicated Doctor

When you were two, you got bitten trying to stop a fight between older children. Then you went on to try to heal all the wounded animals in your neighborhood. Eventually you went into medicine. Extremely dedicated, you put in long hours. Although your stamina was excellent, you wore yourself down trying to care for everyone. Many of your patients were poor and could not pay you for your services. Often, you'd get some vegetables or eggs, or a promise of later payment. Your health suffered from irregular meals, high stress, and not enough sleep. But you would not give up your mission!

♇ Pluto in Libra ♎

Beauty Over Brains

As a small child, you were very attractive. People oohed and ahed over your beauty. Even as you became a teen-ager, you skipped the awkward stages experienced by most young girls. You went from being a lovely baby, to a pretty child, to a beautiful young woman. Because everyone was always exclaiming over your looks, you didn't try very hard in school. You found, in fact, that most people expected you not to try. They seemed to assume that you must be rather stupid since you were so beautiful. Your teachers let you coast. As a consequence, you started to doubt your own mind. Not having really exercised it, you wondered whether you really were intelligent or not. Although you appreciated the positive attention you got through your physical appearance, you felt very unsure of yourself intellectually.

Terrible Twosome

Your parents made the great love match of the ages. All their friends talked about how obsessed with one another they were, how they had eyes only for one another—after all these years. That was certainly true, but it was also true that they had no real interest in their children. You and your siblings were largely ignored. It seemed your parents begrudged every instant caring for you took away from their time together. You spent many hours in the nursery with only each other and no parental response even when one of you cried. Eventually, you all learned to cope, but you also learned not to trust or depend upon anyone.

Dismal Drudgery

As soon as you were old enough to push a needle, your mother taught you the rudiments of lace-making. The work was very demanding. Every stitch had to be painstakingly accurate. Small, tiny seams were essential. The delicate fabrics were easily damaged (and the seamstress had to pay terrible fees). You often worked with poor light, into the night, because your family needed the money. Despite the arduous effort involved, the pay was minimal. You spent many hours laboring to earn enough for a simple meal. Life became a grinding drudgery, with no escape in sight.

Misleading Marriage

As a child, you were different. Other little girls played with dolls; you climbed trees. Other young women simpered and giggled and batted their eyelashes at beaus. You spoke seriously, asked questions about "male" subjects, and looked them straight in the eye. Of course you were left unmarried! At age 30, you were at the beck and call of your relatives as the "spinster" of the family. A gentleman you knew slightly proposed a marriage of convenience. You would get more freedom and he would have a wife which he explained would solve certain problems in his life. A marriage in name only was preferable to being an unpaid servant to your relatives. You accepted. After seeing some of the male visitors of your husband, and his good-looking male friends, you understood why he needed a marriage of convenience. But the appearance of normality was enough for you as well. You had no desire for a true marriage.

Faithless Father

Your mother died at your birth. Although he never admitted it, you realized much later that your father blamed you for her death. All your memories, from the earliest age, are of trying—and failing—to please your father. He set you many difficult tasks. With great effort, you managed to accomplish some of the difficult challenges he set before you, but he always found fault with the result. As you grew older, you asked yourself sometimes why you kept on trying, when you knew the result would be disappointment. You couldn't figure out the answer, but continued to strive—fruitlessly—for your father's positive regard.

Living as Lepers

While still a child, you traveled west with your family. Your father and mother dreamt of establishing a ranch of their own. In the beginning, however, all they could afford was a very minor spread with a small herd of sheep. You settled, however, in the midst of cattle country. Your neighbors all despised sheep. Your family was treated as outcasts. People avoided you—even in church. Although your ranch was not big enough to present a threat, no one wanted to take the chance that you could enlarge (or others might join you). You grew up feeling totally rejected by everyone other than your own flesh and blood.

♇ Pluto in Scorpio ♏

Countless Questions

As a small child, you were fascinated by the hidden and taboo. You asked awkward questions about bodily processes. You wanted to understand death—and sex. Your parents were horrified. They felt your childish queries were a sure sign that the devil had you in his hands. They tried to beat the curiosity out of you. They failed in that, but did manage to convince you that talking (especially asking questions) was not a safe activity. You became a silent child—extremely observant, but very reticent. Even as an adult, you never used two words when one would do. People became accustomed to your quiet presence.

Alarming Attraction

Shy as a child, you had just a few friends, but they were very close. Extremely loyal, once you committed to someone, you were their friend for life. As you grew older, you turned into an exceptionally lovely young woman. All the young man started hanging around. Not terribly comfortable with the attention, you avoided giving any preference to anyone. One young man became obsessed with you. He would haunt your neighborhood, hanging around for hours. He would attempt to monopolize you at dances. One day, he tried to abduct you when you walking over to visit a friend! (Fortunately, people heard you crying for help and came to your rescue.) The next time you saw him, he forced his way into your house, brandishing a gun, declaring that if he couldn't have you, no one could. Although you did your best to remain calm and talk to him soothingly, he was wild and out of control. He shot you—and then himself. You died thinking, "Love is much too dangerous."

Mutilated Marriage

When you were in your late teens, your parents decided to take advantage of opportunities out west. On the frontier, you met a dashing army officer and married him. One day, you and a friend were out riding and were captured by Indians. Rather than killing you, one of the braves raped you and decided to keep you as a second wife. You were responsible for doing much of the drudgery of keeping the household: scrubbing, gathering firewood, pounding rawhide, etc. Although you were alert for opportunities to escape, you had no real chance as the other wives kept close watch on you. One day, your encampment was overrun by cavalry. They were busily killing—even women and children—but fortunately your skin was still white enough to be recognized. When you were reunited with your husband, he rejected you, declaring he wouldn't take the "leavings" of a savage. With marriage an impossible dream, you had to find some other purpose for your life.

Banished Beliefs

Drawn to mysteries, you became a student of the occult while still quite young. Hidden matters fascinated you. You sought to discover old ways, and questioned people who might have knowledge of magic, herbs, nature spirits, and the web of life. Words of your interests spread and the Church did not approve. Your priests lectured you about the dangers of your "ungodly" pursuits. Ignorant people in the village muttered "witch" behind your back and quoted the Bible as not suffering a witch to live! Although you recognized your danger, you would not forsake your studies. Eventually, matters came to a head. Had the priest not intervened, you might have died at the hands of a mob, but the end result was your banishment—never to return to the place of your birth.

Religiously Responsible

Born the eldest son to a respectable estate, your father spent all his later years gambling and wenching. Once you were old enough to understand what was going on, you watched helplessly as he frittered away what would have been your patrimony. By the time you inherited, the estate was considerably encumbered by debt. You labored mightily to make the land profitable again. Although you made some progress, a year of bad weather would set you back alarmingly. Upkeep and maintenance on the tenant cottages was difficult with negligible funds. Your own household was extremely spartan. Life consisted of one test after another. Sometimes you dreamt of running off to the Indies to seek your fortune, but you felt an obligation to the people dependent upon the estate, to try to make a got of it all.

Harmless Hermit

A very simple child, you had difficulty with life as you grew older. A natural truth-teller, you had great trouble understanding that people would lie to you. Your pattern was to believe whatever you were told, and you often ended up in complicated contretemps because you had believed everyone, and each person was twisting things just a bit (for their own ego or advantage). Eventually you decided the interacting with others was too painful. You retreated to the country, determined to become a hermit and avoid all the challenges of trying to comprehend human beings.

♇ Pluto in Sagittarius ♐

Severe Scarcity

Born in Japan, you were raised in comfortable circumstances. Your family had a tea set going back 500 years and filled their house with lovely lacquer items. Well educated for the times, you nonetheless absorbed many of the old beliefs. When you were eleven, a devastating earthquake swept the land. Your house and everything in it was destroyed. Everyone except your father (and you) perished. He insisted that this was the gods' punishment for becoming too comfortable. Thereafter, you two had almost nothing. You learned to survive with virtually no material goods, and to consider yourself more worthy the longer you could last without food and drink as well.
and nimble fingers had been used that way.

Constant Caretaker

The oldest of nine children, you often helped your mother with the younger ones. Then, when your parents became ill, you were the "natural" caretaker in the family. While you were looking after everything, a few of your siblings married. After they had children, you were the doting aunt expected to fill in with child care whenever needed. Eventually, at age 50, you realized that you had lived your entire life for your family. Everything you had done had been for someone else. You could hardly imagine what you would do if you thought only of yourself.

Rigorous Researcher

As a child you would study bugs and dissect leaves. You looked at all the little pieces of life, trying to make sense of it all. Discovering the written word was a great joy. You threw yourself into reading and became a voracious student. Eventually, your interest and focus came to the attention of a local university. You were able to gain a research position. The pay was terrible—just enough to live on. But it allowed you to spend all day in libraries. You could hunt down obscure bits of information. You could dig up answers to queries. You could spend years on a particular historical project. Though you had no social life, no luxuries, and essentially no money, you were totally absorbed in your work.

Manipulative Maneuvers

Born into the minor nobility in India, you had a pampered childhood. As you developed into a great beauty, plans were made for a significant marriage. At length, your parents arranged for you to wed a nobleman living far away in Persia. After an arduous journey, you arrived at the land of your husband to be. Once married, you found that court life was very peculiar. You learned that pursuing goals directly was not effective. You had to develop skills of misdirection, manipulation, and maneuvering. Similarly with your husband, you had no overt power. The only impact you could achieve was through indirect means of persuasion.

Faraway Fancy

Born in the lowlands of Scotland during tough times, you and your family tried to scrape a living from a limited growing season and an unforgiving climate. Your land was subject to English rule. While you were in your teens, the Enclosure Act was passed. As a result, many people were unable to survive. You and your family left for the New World, having no choice. The journey was long and difficult. You ended up in the Appalachian hills of western Virginia with other Scottish families and started a new community. Although you were in a foreign land, you carried forth with Gaelic and your traditional ways, unwilling to lose the hopes and dreams of your youth.

Pushing and Persevering

Even as a child, you had a very strong will. You fought long and hard for what you believed in. When you became older, you got very involved with the idea of free, compulsory education for everyone. You were convinced that educating the masses—instead of just the elite—would provide for humankind's salvation. You even wanted to educated women, which was a radical notion at the time. You fought with the powers-the-be. You tried to change the established structures. You identified with the mythological Sisyphus—constantly rolling a rock uphill only to have it slide back down again. You kept failing, and you kept trying again and again.

CHAPTER ELEVEN

SATURN: MAJOR KARMIC KEY

The planet Saturn is a major key to "karma" (consequences) in the horoscope. The placement of our Saturn speaks particularly to our past patterns in regard to authority, power, rules, structure, and definitions of reality. Also called the "Great Teacher," Saturn represents an area where we must learn to be realistic and practical. In past existences, we may have ignored the regularities which Saturn symbolizes, or we may have taken them too much too heart and placed too many limits on ourselves.

There are two major uncomfortable paths people experience with Saturn. The more common road is taken by people who experience the position of Saturn in their horoscope as one of insecurity, lack of power, blockage, frustration, inadequacy, and failure. An inner sense of not measuring up — lifetime after lifetime — may be quite strong. The less common road is traveled by people who experience the position of Saturn in their horoscope as representing external limits, rules, strictures, or physical (and cosmic) laws which the individuals on this path are resisting. Such people resonate to descriptions of many lives spent fighting authority and authority figures as well as time and the realistic constraints of a physical body and health needs.

A more comfortable path involves a strong, internal sense of competence, healthy responsibility (neither too much nor too little), and a willingness to work **within** the rules (inside the system) to achieve one's ambitions. Many of us try one (or both) of the paths above before we reach this middle position.

Even in this lifetime, most of us initially experience the power of the world where Saturn is placed. This often results in feelings of personal insecurity, inadequacy and self-doubt. These emotional reactions are not limited to this lifetime, but are carried in from the past as well. Saturn is often a symbolic key to feelings of failure or blockage — and experiences in the past when we couldn't, wouldn't, or didn't achieve or get what we wanted.

People on the first path (feeling inadequate) then tend to work on their insecurities, in order to try to master them. Once people have internalized the power symbolized by Saturn, they recognize that it is their own ability to take control, take charge and be responsible in the world. They are no longer at the mercy of authority figures and the power of the universe. They are power centers themselves. At this point, people begin to teach others and to give to the world where their Saturn is placed. (Then they usually find another Saturn lesson, on another level, to learn—repeating the cycle.)

People on the less-traveled path, who internalize the power early (in previous lives, presumably), need to learn the limits of what is possible. Their Saturn lesson is to live within the limits of human and cosmic laws, not to overreach, trying to make their own will into law, trying to do more than is reasonable and possible in this physical universe.

Thus, Saturn's lessons may be a case of too much, too little, or in the wrong place, but the issues are reflected by the house, sign placements and aspects of Saturn. For example, Saturn conjunct Mercury or in the third house or (less strongly) in Gemini can indicate a challenge around learning, thinking, communication, and early peer relationships.

For some people, the issue is around the intellect. With the first path, people doubt their mental ability (especially when young) or experience communication problems (stuttering, phone phobias, etc.). They may have to work to believe in their own good mind. (Occasionally, this placement indicates a real mental limitation and restriction. More often, it indicates an individual who experiences a sense of inadequacy, but actually has a fine mind.) The other path (much more rare, but it does occur) is people who have spent too many lifetimes giving power to the mind. They have relied excessively on rational skills. They overintellectualized. They sought power through detachment and have to work on balancing a mental life with the physical, emotional, and spiritual.

For some people, the issue is around communication. One group of people is learning to communicate easily and freely. Others need to learn to communicate less. Or, our major learning may take place with early relatives (e.g., if we feel mentally deficient, we are confronted with a very bright sibling who forces us to deal with our intellectual capacities. Or, we learn to be responsible through a sibling or other relative for whom we care.)

Once the lesson of Saturn is learned, we can give to others through our professional role with Saturn. Thus, many people with Saturn conjunct Mercury or in the third house end up professional communicators: in teaching, television, radio, sales.

There are twelve major lesson areas depicted by Saturn. These are revealed by the "astrological alphabet" (discussed thoroughly in *Astrology: The Next Step* [formerly *Complete Horoscope Interpretation*]). For the reader working with an actual horoscope, I will cite the "cosmic state" (house and sign placement as well as aspects) of Saturn which relate to each of these 12 major lesson areas. If your Saturn has any of the listed placements or aspects, read the paragraphs which follow. For the reader interested purely in the lessons involved (without astrological details), there are three choices:

(1) Read all twelve Saturn sections and see which ones resonate most for you. (In general, people will be working on an average of about three to five Saturn lessons.)

(2) Order your free chart from the back of this book which lists, in English, the Saturn sign, house and aspects for this chapter and also for your personal karmic gifts, debts, etc. (chapters 14 and 15).

(3) Use the table to indentify your Saturn sign which will point to one of your lessons. The first Saturn lesson ("To Thine Own Self Be True") applies to the first sign (Aries) and so on.

1932	Feb	24	2:47 am	Aquarius	1971	Jun	18	4:10 pm	Gemini
	Aug	13	11:15 am	Capricorn	1972	Jan	10	3:43 am	Taurus
	Nov	20	2:10 am	Aquarius		Feb	21	2:53 pm	Gemini
1935	Feb	14	2:09 pm	Pisces	1973	Aug	1	10:21 pm	Cancer
1937	Apr	25	6:30 am	Aries	1974	Jan	7	8:28 pm	Gemini
	Oct	18	3:41 am	Pisces		Apr	18	10:34 pm	Cancer
1938	Jan	14	10:31 am	Aries	1975	Sep	17	4:57 am	Leo
1939	Jul	6	5:46 am	Pisces	1976	Jan	14	1:17 pm	Cancer
	Sep	22	5:18 am	Aries		Jun	5	5:09 am	Leo
1940	Mar	20	9:41 am	Taurus	1977	Nov	17	2:42 am	Virgo
1942	May	8	7:40 pm	Gemini	1978	Jan	5	0:48 am	Leo
1944	Jun	20	7:48 am	Cancer		Jul	26	12:02 pm	Virgo
1946	Aug	2	2:42 pm	Leo	1980	Sep	21	10:48 am	Libra
1948	Sep	19	4:36 am	Virgo	1982	Nov	29	10:29 am	Scorpio
1949	Apr	3	3:40 am	Leo	1983	May	6	7:32 pm	Libra
	May	29	12:58 pm	Virgo		Aug	24	11:53 am	Scorpio
1950	Nov	20	3:50 pm	Libra	1985	Nov	17	2:10 am	Sagittarius
1951	Mar	7	12:14 pm	Virgo	1988	Feb	13	11:51 pm	Capricorn
	Aug	13	4:44 pm	Libra		Jun	10	5:24 am	Sagittarius
1953	Oct	22	3:36 pm	Scorpio		Nov	12	9:26 am	Capricorn
1956	Jan	12	6:45 pm	Sagittarius	1991	Feb	6	6:52 pm	Aquarius
	May	14	3:47 am	Scorpio	1993	May	21	4:58 am	Pisces
	Oct	10	3:11 pm	Sagittarius		Jun	30	8:31 am	Aquarius
1959	Jan	5	1:33 pm	Capricorn	1994	Jan	28	11:44 pm	Pisces
1962	Jan	3	7:02 pm	Aquarius	1996	Apr	7	8:50 am	Aries
1964	Mar	24	4:18 am	Pisces	1998	Jun	9	6:08 am	Taurus
	Sep	16	9:05 pm	Aquarius		Oct	25	6:42 pm	Aries
	Dec	16	5:39 am	Pisces	1999	Mar	1	1:26 am	Taurus
1967	Mar	3	9:32 pm	Aries	2000	Aug	10	2:26 am	Gemini
1969	Apr	29	10:24 pm	Taurus		Oct	16	0:47 am	Taurus

Example: Someone born in 1964 before March 24 has Saturn in Aquarius. Someone born after March 24 (at 4:18 am EST) but before September 16, has Saturn in Pisces. If born after September 16 (at 9:05 pm EST) but before December 16 (at 5:39 am EST), Saturn would be in Aquarius.

Saturn Lessons

To Thine Own Self Be True Υ

Letter One of Astrological Alphabet: Saturn conjunct Mars or Ascendant or any ruler of 1st house; Saturn in 1st house or horoscope; Saturn square, opposite or quincunx Mars, Ascendant, or any 1st-house ruler; Saturn in Aries; Capricorn on 1st house cusp. (Give more weight to factors which appear earlier in this list. Closer aspects are more significant.)

Karmic challenges center around themes of assertion, self-expression, personal identity and will, independence, and one's right to exist physically in this world. Anger and action may be a focus of learning. You probably are too hard on yourself; self-criticism is apt to be overdone. You may be imbalanced in regard to responsibility—taking on way too much in some regards, and avoiding it like the plague in other instances. You could be full of rage at times, but have trouble expressing it. You may limit yourself in regard to what you pursue in the world, feeling that authority figures or the structure of society will block you from what you want. You could fight with the powers-that-be, struggling to get your own way. You could feel you only "exist" when working, or define yourself too much in terms of what you do (your achievements). You are apt to be very familiar with sensations of blockage, frustration, limitation, and restriction.

Past lives contributed to feelings of personal inadequacy or lack of worth. In some cases, you were given constant critical messages, so that you did not feel good about who you were. In some instances, you were told that your only importance was what you could do—the responsibilities and burdens you took on for others. In some situations, your physical integrity was attacked in circumstances (e.g., slavery) where defending yourself was well-nigh impossible. You've had to deal with direct physical threats and with attacks on your identity and sense of self. Some circumstances required almost constant battle with your environment and encouraged you to believe you always had to fight to survive in life. In some settings, you were not allowed to express anger or independence; the familial and cultural setting attempted to quash your personal will.

Your challenge is to clearly define yourself and your personal rights within the structure of a society of other people. Your growth goal is to be able to clearly, courageously, and directly pursue your own personal desires while still considering the rules and regulations which protect the rights of others. With integration, you can express appropriate and healthy anger (and not sit on it or let it build unreasonably). You can find a profession (or series of vocations) which allow you personal satisfaction, freedom, excitement and accomplishment. You feel vital and alive in your work, but know that you are much more than what you do! You are able to be yourself, express yourself, and take courageous actions in responsible, practical, and effective ways.

Gratifying & Satisfying ♉

Letter Two of the Astrological Alphabet: Saturn conjunct Venus (or any ruler of 2nd house); Saturn in 2nd house; Saturn square, opposite, or quincunx Venus (or any 2nd-house ruler); Saturn in Taurus; Capricorn on 2nd house cusp. (Give more weight to factors which appear earlier in the list. Closer aspects are more significant.)

Karmic challenges center around themes of sensuality, pleasures, possessions, finances, indulgence, beauty, comfort, and material security. Handling the appetites (for food, sex, spending, etc.) may be a focus of learning. You could restrict yourself from perfectly reasonable indulgences through a desire for self-control, or a self-denying "I have to work hard and then I'll relax and enjoy myself" attitude. You may inhibit pleasures unnecessarily. The opposite is also possible: you may become enmeshed in materialism. You could be too concerned with amassing money, possessions, or indulgences. A poverty consciousness might exist—whereby you are overworked and underpaid and never seem to get ahead financially and in terms of enjoying the physical world. Your capacity to stop and smell the flowers—to appreciate and indulge in the myriad forms of beauty and pleasure in the world—may be limited by feelings of self-criticism, undeservingness, excessive responsibility, or an overdone desire for control.

Past lives contributed to your ambivalence about material resources. You took vows of poverty in some. You were involved with very ascetic, self-denying religious groups. You experienced severe deprivation where there was never enough food and felt hunger every day for years. You starved to death one time or were a deliberate family sacrifice to a famine. You dedicated yourself to art and never made much money one lifetime. Perhaps you were the pampered child of rich parents who gave you everything materially, but you saw the hunger and want around you and always felt guilty. You died too young to give all your worldly goods to charity. You might have been an aristocrat who felt the tremendous burden of a large estate, with many families dependent on you for survival and grew to hate the onus of ownership. You were a member of a persecuted groups whose worldly goods were confiscated and you were sent into exile.

Your challenge is to be able to enjoy the sensual, material, financial and artistic world without being consumed by it. Your growth goal is to be comfortable with your own sensuality and feeling for beauty and to be measured and practical in your approach to the world of money and possessions. With integration, you earn a reasonable salary and are at ease with what you have. You neither feel deprived (constantly striving for more) nor overburdened by material responsibilities. You are able to express your sensuality and still feel the master of your appetites. You can make money, spend money, give money, receive money, and share money comfortably. You can relax into the world of nature, appreciate beauty, enjoy a good back rub and know that your basic security is taken care of.

Witty & Wise   ♊

Letter Three of the Astrological Alphabet: Saturn conjunct Mercury (or any ruler of 3rd house); Saturn in 3rd house; Saturn square, opposite, or quincunx Mercury (or any 3rd-house ruler), Saturn in Gemini; Capricorn on 3rd house cusp. (Give more weight to factors earlier in the list. Closer aspects are more significant.)

Karmic challenges center around themes of thinking, communicating, learning, dexterity, curiosity, and light-heartedness. Your relationships with siblings, aunts, uncles, cousins, other relatives, or with people right around you may be a focus of learning. You probably had self-doubts (at least when younger) about your mental capacities or communication skills. Or, perhaps you put too much weight on the mind, relying too heavily upon logic. Your curiosity may have been unnecessarily restricted. You could have been too objective and cool at times, and lacked perspective and detachment at other moments. You may have felt people did not "listen" to you, or could not understand you. You may be uncomfortable talking in front of groups, on the telephone, or just talking! Listening could be difficult, because your inner "self-talk" is so strong and self-critical.

Past lives contributed to your sense of blockage in the mental realm. You had several lifetimes as a younger sibling, always striving to "catch up" mentally to your older brothers and sisters. You could have spent one lifetime as a curious child during the time of the Inquisition and your eager thirst for knowledge was squelched first by your family and then by the Church's representatives. You may have spent one life as a trader traveling from place to place and learning many different languages, but never really settling. You may have been killed for what you thought or what you said. You could have had lifetimes where you were given intolerable mental choices to make and felt mentally and emotionally paralyzed (e.g., the parent asked to choose which child to sacrifice). You could have spent one lifetime as a slave who was expected to constantly talk about her experiences in the "strange and curious" (in the eyes of your captors) land from whence you came. A few times you scattered your forces, never really settling on a career or life purpose. Now and again you had a dry lifetime, focused purely on the mind without the richness of emotional connections. You had some lives when schooling was denied on the basis of your sex, race, class or caste.

Your challenge is to put your knowledge into tangible form. Writing or working in a field of learning and communication allows you to prove to yourself how much you do know. Grounding your verbal and mental skills allows you to overcome past limits. With integration, you know when it is safe to be curious, and when caution is called for. You know when to speak and when to listen. You can identify the appropriate times to be logical, objective and a bit detached. You can value—but not overvalue—your mental prowess. Your flippancy and dry wit can be used wisely.

Interdependence $\mathcal{S}$

Letter Four of the Astrological Alphabet: Saturn conjunct the Moon, I.C., or any ruler of 4th house; Saturn in 4th house; Saturn square, opposite, or quincunx Moon, I.C., or any ruler of 4th house, Saturn in Cancer; Capricorn on 4th house cusp. (Factors earlier in the list are more significant. Closer aspects are more significant.)

Karmic challenges center around themes of dependency, nurturing, home, family, nesting urges, children, emotions, and the quest for safety. Family matters are likely to be a focus of learning. You may be a natural caretaker who easily adopts more than your share of family responsibilities. You could have parented (one or both of) your own parents. You may be the strong, capable one in the home—and dependency frightens you. Your freedom needs may be so pronounced that you view nurturing or emotional attachments as a trap. Alternately, you might be quite dependent, needy, emotionally possessive. You may seek total security in your familial relations, striving to keep everything safe, predictable, and supportive. Questions of who does what for whom within the family are significant. You are likely to feel you did not get the kind of unconditional love, nurturing, protection, and support that every child wants and needs. In some way, you had to face reality young.

Past lives could have contributed to feelings of emotional insecurity. In some cases, you were abandoned at birth. Sometimes you survived; other times you did not. At times, your mother could not nurse you, which you took as a rejection. In several harsh lifetimes, you suffered numerous miscarriages and all your babies died at a young age, causing you to reject mothering as too painful. At times, you left the cherished homeland in search of greater opportunities, while other lives involved you being "cast out" into exile. In several lifetimes, your parents died or were killed and you took over responsibility for the entire family, often at great personal cost. In some circumstances, you were trained to be a totally dependent on your master (such as a Chinese concubine with bound feet).

Your challenge is to keep a balance between learning on others and being leaned on—able to do both comfortably. Integration means you are able to care for others, to support and look after them—but not too much. (You avoid the role of constant caretaker.) You are also able to be vulnerable, to ask others for assistance, to allow others to help you. You create a nest which is solid, practical, and reliable. You choose to share your home with people who encourage you to care, and to take turns supporting and being supported emotionally.

Loving Your Inner Child $\mathcal{N}$

Letter Five of the Astrological Alphabet: Saturn conjunct the Sun (or any ruler of 5th house); Saturn in 5th house; Saturn square, opposite, or quincunx the Sun (or any 5th-house ruler); Saturn in Leo; Capricorn on 5th house cusp.

(Placement earlier in the list are more significant. Closer aspects should be weighted more.)

Karmic challenges center around themes of self-esteem, creativity, risk-taking, being center stage, children, speculation, and any form of pouring out from your own center to gain love, attention, admiration, or applause from the world. Your quest for the adrenaline rush may be a focus of learning. You are working on the balance between being King/Queen of the Hill and hiding your light under a bushel. You may block your own creativity, downgrading your achievements, critiquing your productions. Issues of responsibility, authority, control, and caution may arise with children and loved ones. Questions of how, when, who, and how much to love could abound.

Past lives contributed to your self-esteem issues. In several cases, you were a struggling artist, barely maintaining yourself on what your art earned. In a couple circumstances, even though you had artistic talent, you elected to enter a family business because you didn't feel you were "good enough" to be a professional artist. You could have been caught in a financial crash in one lifetime and developed an abhorrence of speculation and investment. You were, perhaps, a skilled actor, but financially you barely survived, feeling art was hardy worth it. You may have had several lifetimes as a mother of a child with special problems, so you came to associate children with heavy responsibility. Love relationships brought varying degrees of unhappiness due to obsessions, low self-esteem, over idealization, or other handicaps.

Your challenge is to develop good self-esteem, to be comfortable with your special talents. Your growth goal is to be able to create—whether on-stage, through art and aesthetics, teaching, selling, coaching, having children, etc.—and feel joy and reward in your self-expansive efforts. With integration, you can take risks, speculate appropriately, and enjoy being the center of attention at times. You are sensible and responsible (but not overly so) in respect to children and loved ones. You can give and receive love easily, with a healthy balance. Your career (or contribution to society) involves an element of creativity, love, magnetism, charisma, applause, persuasion or cheer leading. You appreciate yourself and can help others appreciate themselves. Your inner child is alive and full of zest.

Service—Not Servant ♍

Letter Six of the Astrological Alphabet: Saturn conjunct Vesta or Ceres (or Mercury if you decide Mercury is more Virgo than Gemini in a chart) or Saturn conjunct ruler of 6th; Saturn in 6th house; Saturn square, opposite or quincunx Ceres or Vesta (or Mercury or any 6th-house ruler); Saturn in Virgo; Capricorn on 6th house cusp. [Give more weight to close aspects and items nearer the beginning of this list.]

Karmic challenges center around themes of efficiency, productivity, health, work, and common sense. Themes of service, humility, concern with details and competence are in focus. Your lesson revolves around working enough—

but not too much and taking good, practical care of your physical body. You may be imbalanced around work—falling into workaholic extremes on occasion and avoiding work at other times. You might be facing a health challenge with a need to be clear about what you can and cannot do physically (to realistically know your limits). Work may feel like a burden, a duty, an onerous necessity. Colleagues may be involved in the situation with issues of responsibility, power, criticism, and control emerging between you.

Past lives contributed to issues of efficient functioning in the body and on the job. In several lives, you were totally driven in your career. You pushed yourself too hard physically and eventually had health breakdowns. In several circumstances, employers took advantage of you. You had excessive duties, were constantly laboring, and carried the bulk of the work at your job, with none of the credit. A few lifetimes as a servant added to your feeling that perhaps you didn't deserve anything better—that it was your role to be of humble service in life. There were probably other lifetimes in which you refused to work. You may have wanted to run the show, to avoid the "petty details," so simply did not work. A series of lives spent in poverty and unremitting labor could have contributed to a pattern of ill health. Accidents damaging certain bodily parts (or death through those areas) could carry a residue into this life.

Your challenge is to adopt good health habits and to be clear and reasonable in the demands you put upon your body. Your growth goals is to know what you can, cannot, and should do to remain healthy and functioning well. Another challenge is to find satisfying work in which you can be an expert—without giving up convinced you'll fail and without falling into an overwork mode. You need to eschew the extremes of workaholism (or a servant mentality) or total avoidance of work. You need a vocation which exercises your pragmatism, dedication, strength, and drive to make a tangible contribution to the world.

Fair is Fair   ⌒

Letter Seven of the Astrological Alphabet: Saturn conjunct Pallas or Descendant (or Venus in cases where Venus is more Libran than Taurean) or Saturn conjunct any ruler of 7th house; Saturn in 7th house; Saturn square, opposite, or quincunx Pallas, Descendant (or Venus or any 7th-house ruler); Saturn in Libra; Capricorn on 7th house cusp. (Give more weight to closer aspects and items near the beginning of this list.)

Karmic challenges center around themes of equality, balance, beauty, aesthetics, teamwork, sharing, and partnership. Marriage and other committed relationships may be a focus of learning. You may demand much of yourself, your partner, or the people who share your life. You may avoid relationships for fear of being hurt, limited, restricted, dominated, controlled, or criticized. Responsibilities may be unevenly distributed between you and a spouse or partner. The career of either partner might interfere with feelings of love and attachment. Authoritarian tendencies could derail intimacy. You may attract older (or younger) people who push the same emotional buttons as your authority parent did. You could fall into a parent/child association rather than an equalitarian arrangement. The stress involved may incline you to just avoid relationships! Relationships can be made on the basis of status, or what one can get from a partner. Beauty, grace, and harmony may seem incompatible with the demands of the "real world." Issues of prejudice, fair play, justice, and equality may be significant.

Past lives contributed to your insecurity around partnership. You spent a few lifetimes as a female sold into marriage for material or political reasons. You spent several lives as a woman in a very patriarchal society where your husband had total power and control over you. You probably had at least one lifetime as a highly ambitious woman who had to choose between a partner and a career and selected the career. At least once, you were married to the soul who became your father in this lifetime. You were sometimes the dominant partner. You and a mate may have gone back and forth between roles of master/slave; beloved/mistress; master/concubine. Differences in caste, class, power, or education could have been prominent in your past relationships. In some instances, you had to deny your artistic or aesthetic leanings in order to survive in life. At other times, you chose to be true to your need for beauty and balance, even when poverty accompanied it. You faced prejudices from both sides (the oppressed and oppressor).

Your challenge is to clearly own your own power and choose a partner who is also strong. Your growth goal is to be able to share responsibilities, tasks, and authority with someone. With integration, you can take turns being strong, in-charge, and taking care of business. You may enhance each other's careers and could even work together. You each put your critical, judgmental, controlling side into affecting the physical world and accomplishing tasks—not into dissecting one another. You can enjoy competence as well as relaxation and ease. You can have both beauty and practicality in your life. You can treat people as peers and equals, being fair to everyone involved.

Psychological Power ♏

Letter Eight of the Astrological Alphabet: Saturn conjunct Pluto (or Juno or any ruler of the 8th house); Saturn in 8th house; Saturn square, opposite or quincunx Pluto (or Juno or any 8th-house ruler); Saturn in Scorpio; Capricorn on 8th house cusp. (Give more weight to closer aspects and to items nearer the beginning of this list.)

Karmic challenges center around themes of self-mastery, self-control, addictions, compulsions, depth insights, intimacy, sexuality, shared resources, transformation, and occult interests. Joint finances, pleasures, and possessions may be a focus of learning. Being able to forgive, let go, and move on could be difficult. Issues of anger or resentment may arise. Intense emotions and all-or-nothing tendencies are possible. You may be drawn into life-or-death situations. Power issues—its use, abuse, and misuse—could abound. Manipulation, emotional blackmail, intimidation, and power plays might exist. Your urge to dig out secrets, to probe beneath the surface and uncover hidden knowledge might be overdone—or ignored and suppressed.

Past lives contributed to fears and anxieties in regard to intimacy. Several lifetimes spent as a religious celibate require effort from you now in order to relax and enjoy intimacy. Hermit tendencies won over the need for a mate on some occasions. Several lifetimes in various violent settings accustomed you to constant warfare and struggles for dominance through raiding of each other's resources. You may have experienced (or meted out) abuse, violence, torture. Your circumstances in the past could have included battles to overcome addictions to opium, alcohol, and tobacco. Perhaps female lives as a victim of rape tie your experience of sex to fear. A lifetime at a European court might have given you a tremendous disgust of scheming, manipulation, and underhanded techniques but also gave you a talent for récognizing them in practice. You dabbled in magic, witchcraft and occult studies across many lifetimes. In some, you suffered for your fascination. In some lives, you gave all your power away to other people, subject to their control, intimidation, or manipulation. In others, you fought to gain or maintain power within your own sphere.

Your challenge is to clearly define the degree of self-mastery you wish to achieve. You need to distinguish between excessive control (an ascetic self-denial) and too much appetite indulgence in order to find the middle ground. Clarify your position in regard to shared resources and possessions. What can you live with; what is practical? You may have to do some work separating out power issues from sexuality. You need a constructive outlet for a power drive—through your work, in sports, in games, in fighting for causes. You need to be able to exert force, seek control, have an impact on the world in socially acceptable veins. You're working on the balance between personal privacy and the need for a deep, intimate connection with a partner. You are capable of tremendous depth, great perseverance, focus, and concentration. Loyalty is emphasized. Once you commit, you will do everything possible to maintain and enhance your commitment.

Faith, Hope & Charity ♐

Letter Nine of the Astrological Alphabet: Saturn conjunct Jupiter (or Chiron or any ruler of 9th house); Saturn in 9th house; Saturn square, opposite, or quincunx Jupiter (or Chiron or any 9th-house ruler), Saturn in Sagittarius; capricorn on 9th house cusp. (Give more weight to closer aspects and to items near the beginning of this list.)

Karmic challenges center around themes of faith, exploration, adventure, education, idealism, values, and the search for ultimate meaning. Religion, philosophy, spiritual quests, or world views may be a focus of learning. You may experience too much faith (gullible, easily persuaded to go along with dreams and schemes); too little faith (agnostic, wondering if life has any purpose) or faith in the wrong place in life (turning money into an ultimate value; putting total faith in a partner; making a child your reason for being, etc.).

You are likely to face feelings of frustration, limitation, responsibility, and demands in regard to meaning, travel, visions, and the quest for bigger and better.

Past lives contributed to potential anxiety regarding seeking and searching behavior. In several lives, you were an explorer who went far off the beaten track and died during your adventuring. In a number of lifetimes, you were involved in the controversy between religious and scientific beliefs; sometimes you were on the scientific side; sometimes on the religious. You probably spent one lifetime in worship and pursuit of power, authority, and control. You experienced religious persecution in various forms. In several instances, you were a female filled with a hunger for knowledge, but blocked by the culture from pursuing education. In some circumstances, your perennial optimism or naive belief in the goodness of others led to your death. Difficult lifetimes could have affected your feelings about travel, foreign lands (and foreign people) and the pursuit of one's dreams.

Your challenge is to clearly define your beliefs, values, and long-range goals. You need a solid faith in yourself (neither rash and foolhardy nor anxious and depressed) as well as a faith in a Higher Power. With integration, you have idealism by which you live, but you trust in the universe to take over after you've done your part. Your growth goal is to reach for more knowledge, inspiration, purpose and enlightenment in practical, grounded ways which can be applied to real-world results.

Reasonable Responsibilities   ♑

Letter Ten of the Astrological Alphabet: Saturn conjunct Midheaven or any ruler of 10th house; Saturn in 10th house; Saturn square, quincunx, or opposite Midheaven or planets in or ruling 10th; Saturn in Capricorn; Capricorn on 10th house cusp. (Give more weight to closer aspects and to items nearer the beginning of this list.)

Karmic challenges center around themes of authority, control, responsibility, ambition, status, reputation, parental archetypes, competence, performance, dominance, and realism. Your career and/or relationships with authority figures could be focuses for learning. You may have to deal with dictatorial, controlling, overbearing individuals. You may be too hard on yourself. One extreme is the workaholic—the person who is driven, who takes on excessive responsibility, who carries the whole world on his/her back, who pushes unmercifully. (The usual outcome is exhaustion and perhaps even physical breakdown because one cannot do everything.) The other extreme is the person who feels inadequate, insecure, blocked, frustrated and afraid to try. That individual is convinced the world, the establishment, parents, authority figures will stop him/her—or that s/he will fail or fall short in any effort. So why even try? Often people exhibit both sides at different times and places in their lives.

Past lives contributed to your confrontation with demands, duties, and drudgery. Some lives involved back-breaking labor that never ended. A few involved positions of great power, but the responsibility was equally great and the consequent pressure (to always make the "right" decision) was almost more than you could bear. In several cases, you had to undergo arduous testing in order to prove your competence. Things rarely came easily; it seemed your path always involved hardship, or tremendous effort. The power structure may seem set against you. In several cases you were father to your father (of this lifetime). Outside circumstances (due to your class, race, gender, class, etc.) often blocked you from rising in life. In a number of situations, your mere survival was a great accomplishment.

Your challenge is to gain a firm sense of expertise. You may need to prove your competence to yourself—by doing things. The more you do, the more you recognize your strength and abilities. You need to act to accomplish—even when you doubt yourself. Integration involves a balanced approach to responsibility—taking on your fair share without carrying too much. Rising above your karma entails clear separation from your authority parent—acknowledging useful contributions and being appropriately different. It means owning your power, competence and capability and not seeing all the power as in the outer world. Your growth will include making a contribution to society.

Future Shock

Letter Eleven of the Astrological Alphabet: Saturn conjunct Uranus or any ruler of the 11th house; Saturn in 11th house; Saturn square, opposite, or quincunx Uranus (or any 11th-house ruler); Saturn in Aquarius; Capricorn on 11th house cusp. (Give more weight to closer aspects and items near the beginning of this list.)

Karmic challenges center around themes of individuality, uniqueness, freedom, rebellion, detachment, objectivity, restlessness, change, and variety. Friends, groups, or associations may be a focus of learning. You may deal with anxiety, fear, insecurity in regard to the future, technology, or being different. You could be imbalanced in regard to your uniqueness—too rebellious or eccentric in some areas and allowing your special flavor and individual insights to be squashed by society or peer pressure in other instances. You could feel torn between conventionality and unconventionality; between the old and the new; between the traditional and the avant garde or progressive.

Past lives contributed to any current limitations, frustrations, and inhibitions in regard to being a unique individual. Most previous cultures were very intolerant of those who stood out from the crowd and you suffered rejection, ejection, and even death in different lifetimes. Too often, the color of your skin, your religion, or your sex was the basis for people attacking you. You were an inventor in several lifetimes, but probably died in an explosion or other accident in one of those. You spent several lifetimes on different sides of the eternal struggle between the conservative elders of the tribe and the rebellious youth. In some lives, you took too many risks, while other lives were spent in stifling conformity.

Your challenge is to firmly establish your own individuality, to be able to stand against a crowd if you believe it is right. Part of your gift to the world is your ability to change perspectives, be original, and shake up people's assumptions and preconceptions. You can help groups, friends, and associations be practical, grounded and realistic in their pursuit of unusual goals. You can help bring the future into being.

Universal Understanding ♓

Letter Twelve of the Astrological Alphabet: Saturn conjunct Neptune (or any ruler of the 12th house); Saturn in 12th house; Saturn square, opposite, or quincunx Neptune (or any ruler of 12th); Saturn in Pisces; Capricorn on 12th house cusp. (Give more weight to closer aspects and items near the beginning of this list.)

Karmic challenges center around themes of idealism, fantasy, magic, illusions, deception, escapism, compassion, healing, union, mysticism, spirituality, and beauty. Meditation, solitude, being with nature, merging with the Infinite could be focuses for learning. You may have to cope with institutions, lies, or confusion. You may feel anxious, phobic, insecure—unsure what to trust and what to believe in. Or, you could have a firm and grounded faith. You may inhibit or block your intuitive side. You could fear your unconscious understanding. Feelings could sometimes be overwhelming, leading you to limit your compassion and urge to succor.

Past lives contributed to your frustration regarding the pursuit of infinite love and beauty. Some lifetimes were spent as a starving artist. In several instances, you were a hopeless idealist, striving to improve the world and chronically frustrated by its intransigence. Martyrdom was your lot in several lives; you gave so much of yourself that you ended up dying young or being attacked by people who did not agree with your desire to rescue the downtrodden. Imprisonment (in various circumstances) occurred. One lifetime was spent watching the world and dreaming about better ways without doing anything. Your imagination was strong enough that you could lose yourself within it on occasion. Several lives saw you in a healing role—repairing wounded bodies, minds, and souls. A religious vocation was your focus many times as well.

Your challenge is to clearly define your dream—how you want to make the world a better, more beautiful, more loving, more fulfilling place. Then you need to clarify the steps necessary to achieve your dream — and take them, one at a time. Your growth goal is to become a realistic mystic, a practical helper, a grounded artist or a pragmatic savior. Rather than running away from an imperfect world, or living with chronic dissatisfaction, you enjoy the process toward perfection. You take the first step toward improving, uplifting, inspiring, and beautifying our universe.

CHAPTER TWELVE

PAST LIFE SCENARIOS: SATURN

Since Saturn is a karmic indicator no matter where it appears in the horoscope, the scenarios in this chapter are based on the house and sign placement of Saturn. Because astrology so often focuses on the "dark side" of Saturn, I deliberately included Saturn past-life scenarios which are mostly constructive. Once we master the challenges represented by Saturn, it symbolizes our inner power, expertise, and authority.

Saturn in 1st House

in Aries – Self-Sufficient
You were a very active, courageous child and quickly came to excel at a number of sports. Challenges invigorated you and you tried a number of activities once—just to prove to yourself that you could do them. Your father wanted you to carry on the family business. As much as you loved your parents, you knew you couldn't stay. The dangers of the Siberian frontier drew you. Quickly mastering the basics of living off the land, you did quite well in hunting and trapping ermine for their fur. You also served as an occasional guide, scout, guard and hunter for travelers. You visited your family once every few years, but travel was arduous and you much preferred the wilderness to civilization. You were very happy being on your own and remained active, healthy, and independent to the end of your days.

in Taurus – Cultural Continuation

As much as you loved your family, you knew you could not stay. From an early age, you felt a need to be independent. As a young man, you took, off for the "Wild West." You became fascinated with different Indian cultures and studied the tribes which were at peace with the whites. You were particularly drawn to their arts and handicrafts. Among the Hopi, you met and fell in love with a young woman. Despite her family's reluctance, you were married. Your wife was a skilled potter, creating bowls, jugs, and cups of great beauty. You were determined to help preserve at least a portion of Indian culture, so built up a business selling rugs, pottery, and beadwork to rich Easterners. You and your wife established a comfortable living and your two daughters and a son also were drawn to the arts. Your whole family found joy and fulfillment in financial and cultural independence through beauty.

in Gemini – Rapid Repartee

Known for a quick tongue, tact was not your strong suit. Your parents appreciated your excellent mind, encouraging you to exercise it. They also set good examples in being caring, considerate people. Although patience was not always easy, you learned kindness and understanding—even when people could not keep up with your mental processing. You decided to train for the law and did quite well in the field. Using your intellectual gifts to support justice had great appeal. You could be extremely forceful on a client's behalf. You wife was the daughter of a man you represented in a property dispute. The two of you fell in love and she became quite an asset to you. Her empathic understanding of people helped you to see more facets to each case and provided valuable insights. Over time, you had four children and enjoyed playful debates around the dinner table. These honed everyone's verbal skills and reasoning power, but love underlaid it all.

in Cancer – Building Boom

Born into one of the "first families" of Boston, you never liked being identified with them. Although you loved and respected your parents, you knew that your path was elsewhere. Independence beckoned. After an excellent education, you made your way to the frontier. A few shrewd investments convinced you that real estate in boom towns was your forte. You had a knack for sensing the area that was likely to go up in value. Several times, you brought property relatively low and sold it high a few years later. When you met your wife, she was running a boarding house (where you stayed). She happily adapted to your lifestyle. The two of your enjoyed going to a new town, surveying it and choosing what to buy. You'd live there for one to four years, make your sale (profitably) and move on. It was varied, challenging, and satisfying. You both thrived on it!

in Leo – A Purely Personal Path

Your father was a highly successful businessman and began to dabble in politics when you were young. Your mother was very active socially and with charity work. Although you loved them, you recognized that being "the son of" was not your path in life. You struck out on your own. Skilled at sales, you went into the insurance business. Providing protection and peace of mind to people had great appeal. You met your wife when selling her parents an insurance policy. Very much in love, the two of you did well in your early years of struggling. When you became more established, your first child (a daughter) was born—with much rejoicing. Your wife and you had only one more child, a son, almost ten years later. Laughter was common in your home and love pervaded the family circle.

in Virgo – Earned Expertise

Orphaned at a young age, poverty and an early death were very real possibilities. You were determined, however, to become master of your own fate. You made yourself as useful as possible around the orphanage. You became known as someone willing to help out. When an opportunity arose for apprenticeship to a cobbler, you immediately took it. Conscientious and thorough, your skills were well suited to making shoes. Your measurements were precise and your stitching was very even and regular. Customers were very pleased with the quality of your work. As you grew older, you learned more and more until your master had passed on all that he could. He was tiring, so you offered to buy out his business over the next few years, allowing him to rest more. Once you had a stake in the firm, you felt free to marry and raise a family. Knowing that your hard work, patience, competence and dedication to doing a good job had led to your success gave you great satisfaction!

in Libra – The Dance of Love

Movement was important to you. According to your mother, you danced almost as soon as you could walk. Although your Lombard family had limited resources, they scraped together enough money to pay for the ballet lessons you desperately wanted. Your teacher was amazed at your natural talent. You seemed almost a creature of air and spirit. When dancing, you felt wholly alive. After an amazingly short period of time, you were employed by the premiere theater in Milano. Your husband saw you dancing and fell in love. You resisted his courting for almost a year, as many men fell in (and out of) love with you. Giorgio, however, convinced you of his sincerity and your long years together were very emotionally rich and rewarding. Despite the demands of your profession, you managed to have and raise two wonderful daughters. Although you danced into your 80's, you stopped professional work in your 30's and turned to teaching and choreography.

in Scorpio – Breaking Bonds

Raised in an atmosphere of shame and secrecy, as a small child you had no idea what the problem was. Eventually you learned that you were illegitimate and that the person you thought was your mother was actually your aunt. Your mother had been addicted to alcohol and died from neglecting her safety and nutritional needs. Your aunt was emotionally abusive and believed that telling you how sinful you were might keep you from following your mother's path to ruin. (But deep inside, your aunt was convinced that "blood would tell" and you would "sin" as well.) Fortunately, your best friend lived next door and her mother was very nonjudgmental. She just loved you, so you spent as much time as possible in her house. When you were old enough, you got a position serving in a bar. You wanted to prove to yourself that you were **not** your mother—with regard to both alcohol and men. You succeeded very well. Shortly thereafter you met the man who became your husband. After a short, but intense, courtship where you asked him some very probing questions, you were married. You settled in a town far enough away from your aunt that visits would be rare and happily raised a family of your own. Your husband understood and supported your determination to be extremely honest with your own children. His loyalty and commitment meant as much to you as his love.

in Sagittarius – Wonderful Wilderness

Yours was a normal family. Your siblings were content to stay where all of you had been born, but you knew that your future lay elsewhere. Everything you heard abut the outer world fed your desire to see it. While still in your teens, you took off. Working your way across the world, you did whatever you could to make money for the next destination. You took ships (and rowboats), rode horses (and asses and camels), and walked a lot. The wonders of nature inspired you: incredible snow-swept vistas, majestic canyons, rushing rivers, waterfalls reflecting rainbows, and desert sunsets. You wrote home about your experiences, but continued to wander the world. You felt that travel was your destiny. Never lonely—you met lots of people—you knew you were happiest on your own, in the wilderness. You managed to achieve that ecstasy often.

in Capricorn – Regaining Respect

Born with a club foot, you were threatened at birth. Your father wanted to destroy you, believing you could never be a successful warrior of Macedonia, but your mother begged for your life. From an early age, you learned that you had to try harder physically to master many challenges other boys took as a matter of course. Your mother also encouraged you to develop your mind. You became very adept at strategy. As others began to notice your talents, you were put in charge of planning more and more raids, forays and battles. With you as the general, victory was usually assured. You gained more and more respect—and a portion of the spoils. Young women began to pay more attention to you, but you chose a shy young woman—who had been your friend from childhood—as your bride. You had many happy, healthy children and your wisdom was even more revered when you became a grandfather.

in Aquarius – Innumerable Implications

Raised in a restrictive environment, spontaneity was forbidden. Children were expected to be seen and not heard. Anything less than instant obedience was ground for a beating. Although you didn't really know any other way, inside your heart, you felt a need to be different. In your late teens, you made your way—with difficulty—to the city. You saw people with much freedom. Quite skilled with animals, you managed to find a position at a dairy just outside the city. Then followed a period of exploration—finding out about your new territory and discovering who you really were. Once you were on your own, your quick wit surfaced. People laughed with you. You also had an ability to look ahead and helped people to plan for the future. You discovered a large fund of tolerance within yourself, and an eagerness to learn about everyone (and everything) in the world. Each day brought for self-discoveries and the pleasure of developing your potentials—and meeting interesting people—was immense.

in Pisces – Happy Household
Your father was a bluff English squire who loved to hunt. Often ill as a child, you became very drawn to books and literature. In your early teens, you began writing poetry. Appalled at the thought of such "unmanly scribblings," your father forbade you to write. Your muse was too strong. so you continued to write in secret for a time. Just after you came of age, you received a small inheritance from a childless uncle. You set up your own modest household and asked your childhood sweetheart to marry you. She taught piano to neighborhood children and some of your poetry was published, brining in a bit more income. Although your father was horrified, you and your wife were idyllically happy in your tiny house filled with music, poetry, and love.

Saturn in 2nd House

in Aries – Innovative Investments
Born into a comfortably middle class family, you had a rather calm, ordinary childhood. The only son, you were expected to carry on the family dry goods business. You advised your parents to bequeath it to your older sister instead, as she had much more of a knack for it than you. Besides, you wanted to find your own fortune. Along with a number of friends, you pooled your resources to invest in a ship traveling to the Spice Islands. When she returned safely with a full cargo, profits were large. You chose other opportunities to make money with money, and parlayed your stake into considerably more. After marrying the daughter of the captain of your first successful venture's ship, you started a family. You enjoyed lively discussions at dinner of where else money might be made. Your whole family played with investment idea and was serious about loving one another.

in Taurus – Principally Pleasing
As the queen of a minor North Indian principality, you had much position with little real power. You dedicated yourself to making your life and your husband's as comfortable as possible. You made sure that the gardens were kept up with lots of sweet-smelling blossoms in the spring. You brought in beautiful carpets

and tapestries to please the eye and the touch. They also helped to moderate extremes of heat and cold in your rooms. You encouraged artists, architects and artisans of all sorts to bring more beauty into court life. You instructed the chef to insure meals were as sensually satisfying as possible. Good food and drink became the norm and you had the comfort of a very gratifying life that brought beauty and pleasure to others as well.

in Gemini – Wry Writing

From your earliest baby babbling, you enjoyed language. You played with words, seeking the most attractive phrase or the most beautiful intonation and description. Although your parents and siblings belonged to the "Might Makes Rights School, you knew that your most important battles would be mental. Leaving home early, you turned to writing. You experimented with journalism, novels and short stories. You tried drama, farce, comedy, tragedy, biography, and just about everything. In the end, your wry comments and observations about life (especially as it went on around you) became very popular. You developed into a valued columnist. Once you were financially established, other avenues (such as fiction) became viable as well. You married a fellow writer and had twins. Soon you had the house of your dreams with a bright and interesting partner and lots of opportunities to learn and discuss anything.

in Cancer – Happy Housewife

A pleasant child, you were very close to your mother. You enjoyed learning the skills of housewifery: how to shop for the best cuts of meat, how to tend your kitchen garden, how to sew and cook and clean properly. At a relatively young age, you had mastered the myriad talents necessary to run a household well and economically. Shortly thereafter you fell in love with a rising young banker. Although only 16, you were pronounced by your mother as quite capable of handling your own home, so your father gave permission for the wedding. You spent even more time on domestic tasks, enjoying the challenge of making your home as comfortable and attractive as possible—without spending much money. Your husband admired and appreciated your special talents and the births of three children enlarged your circle of love.

in Leo – Making Money with Money

Although it was not considered "ladylike," you had quite a talent for numbers. Eager for learning, you were able to persuade your parents to extend your education beyond the minimum given to most girls. In your teens you learned about the Stock Exchange and began to study it. Convinced you understood certain patterns, you wished to invest, but women were not allowed at that time. You persuaded your best friend to invest a little nest egg you had from a great aunt and it multiplied. Soon, you were managing funds for a number of friends. Shortly thereafter you met a young man at a party and the attraction was instant. Although afraid to reveal your special talent, you did tell your beloved. He took it quite in stride and you were able to continue your money-making hobby throughout your long and happy marriage.

in Virgo – Honest Healing

Drawn to healing, you made all necessary sacrifices to attend medical school. Your family helped somewhat, but their resources were limited. You made it through the demanding internships and began to work at a hospital while building up your private practice. You knew that wealthy patients would bring in the best income, but you were determined to treat only the truly ill. Many society matrons, you believed, suffered from boredom rather than physical ailments. So you served all your patients with great integrity no matter what their walk of life. A wealthy mill owner was impressed with your skills and dedicated and founded a hospital (to be named after him). You were appointed director and finally had the salary you deserved, work to fit your ideals, and the wherewithal to support a wife and family. The latter you found quickly in an idealistic Quaker woman who helped you serve with love.

in Libra – Comfortable Couple

Raised to be an obedient child, you became a sweet, agreeable young woman. Very drawn to music, you could spend hours practicing the piano and feeling the beauty of the sound. As was the case with your peers, your first duty was to make a good marriage. Your parents carefully examined the prospects of each available young man and let you know who was worth cultivating. Blessed with an easygoing nature, you got along with almost everyone. When a polite, pleasant young man asked (with parental permission) for your hand, you accepted. You had made up your mind to be a good wife and set yourself to discovering his preferences and pleasures. He was financially well-off which contributed to the comfort of the household. You found that keeping him happy also contributed to your contentment. He was more considerate and kind to you when you went out of your way to make him comfortable. You developed a strong affection for one another and a companionable bond that lasted many years. Your music became a shared pleasure. Life was easy, relaxed, and enjoyable.

in Scorpio – Prospective Planning

When you were young, you didn't have much other than a roof over your head. Your parents had a small farm, but with ten siblings, resources were stretched a bit thin. When you turned sixteen, your father let you know that if you were not going to get married, you would have to find employment, so you left for the city. With mostly farming skills, you weren't suited for much, but you did have natural grace and beauty. You got a bit part in a play and decided to take the only available career path: mistress to a wealthy "protector." You didn't shift "protectors" very often, carefully choosing men who were generous. You saved money every year against your eventual retirement and carefully scouted out a banker who was good at investments. By the time you were too old to easily find a desirable parti, you had enough saved to live comfortably. At that point, you indulged yourself with good food, wine, and chocolate. You lived, modestly but with great gusto—to a ripe old age.

in Sagittarius – Gratifying Garden

Nature called to you. As a young girl, you loved spending time out of doors. You felt a connection to the creatures of he wild and imagined you could sometimes hear God's voice on the wind. You felt called to the Lord and became a postulant at a Benedictine nunnery. In due course, you made your vows to Christ. Mother Superior assigned you to the garden. You loved being outside and able to work with green, growing things. The sensual experience of the rich earth was very gratifying to you. Eager to enrich the lives of your fellow nuns, you planted many herbs and spices and varied seeds whenever you could get them. You and the cook worked out a very rich, diverse menu which was quite sensually satisfying. Your life was good, with agreeable companions, physical indulgences, spiritual dedication, and an appreciation of simple pleasures.

in Capricorn – Comfortable Compliance

Born into a family which traced its roots to the Norman Conquest, you were very conscious of tradition. Your father expected you to attend his university and you did. After your graduation, it was assumed that you would enter the family banking business, and you complied. A dedicated worker, you labored for a year in each department until you thoroughly understood how everything functioned. You fell in love with a highly suitable young woman of good family and were married in an impressive ceremony with all the "right" people attending. In due course, two children arrived, which pleased you and your wife and thrilled both sets of grandparents. You followed the road laid out, taking over when your father retired. You had a very successful, comfortable, pleasant life.

in Aquarius – Innovative Inventor

A rather odd child, you were fortunate in having relaxed parents who let you go your own way in many respects. You developed a hobby of tinkering quite young and kept it throughout your life. You were sufficiently innovative to come up with some inventions which brought in income. Your other love was art. You painted wild pictures which almost never sold, but gave you great satisfaction to create. You were lucky enough to find a woman who found your eccentricities endearing. (She even liked your paintings.) The two of your married and set up a very non-structured household where you lived contentedly for many more years.

in Pisces – Making Melodious Music

When you first heard music, you knew your lie path. As soon as you were old enough to train, you found a voice teacher. Your parents scraped together enough money for lessons. Your talent was prodigious and you were one of the youngest singers to perform at Milan's great La Scala. You had a number of successful years as a diva. Although you had never wanted children—having poured all of your creativity into another channel—you did eventually marry one of your ardent admirers. You two enjoyed the best of food, wine, and music, Pampering one another brought great pleasure. Life was generally on a high note.

Saturn in 3rd House

in Aries – Extensive Erudition
The world around you was intensely fascinating. As a child you loved observing your environment. Once you learned to talk, you unleashed your curiosity on everyone. A new acquaintance would be treated to a barrage of questions about his or her age, family situation, profession, feelings about the world, etc. You loved learning and found every part of life fascinating. In school, you were voracious in absorbing every speck of information and reading many, many books. Although choosing a profession was challenging, due to your interest in everything, you became a curator at the Museum of Natural History. That allowed you to continue to study almost anything. One of the frequent visitors to the museum was a scholarly young woman and you struck up a friendship which led to a long, happy marriage where each of you shared all kinds of information with the other.

in Taurus – Serene Scholarship
Born into a highly competitive family, your siblings didn't understand you. They were constantly striving to outdo one another, jockeying for superior positions, and you weren't even keeping score! Although a bright and alert child, you were relaxed about learning and mental pursuits. You preferred comfort to contests. With considerable dexterity, you could juggle and play several musical instruments, but you had no desire to outshine your more audience-hungry brother and sisters. So you continued to quietly enjoy life and learning. You were content to often be the audience and selected a spouse who was likewise of an easygoing disposition, but got great pleasure from mental activities. You created an affectionate, low-key home.

in Gemini – Love Letters
Born with a speech impediment, you had to work very hard to make yourself understood. But you labored to become a good communicator. You found a real gift in writing. With a knack for a telling phrase, a playful twist of wording and a gift for rich descriptions, your novels proved quite popular. As was the style for many women of that time, you used a nom de plume. You felt you had two lives: the admired writer and the woman who had to speak slowly and carefully to be understood. You fell in love with your husband when he looked you straight in the eye and did NOT try to finish your sentences for you. Your marriage was full of joy and generated many, many love notes and love letters.

in Cancer – Expanding Education

Your earliest memories were of wanting to know! Burning curiosity was a common state for you. Once you started school, you realized that you had found your life's purpose. Being able to nurture the lives of others (while continuing to learn yourself) felt like the highest calling of all. Although teachers were not paid a lot and had to do other tasks of drudgery, you were thrilled to be training to teach. Finding an loving a man who shared your interest in education was an unexpected bonus. You spent many glorious years instructing your own children as well as other people's kids. You delighted in seeing the spark of awareness light up someone eye. You lived and taught the excitement of learning (and love).

in Leo – Lively Learning

Fun-loving and carefree, you laughed a lot in your youth. Although you enjoyed learning, you didn't take anything too seriously. You were fortunate to gain an education far beyond the norm for women at that time. Then, both your parents were killed in a boating accident and you had to support yourself. You found a position in a select school for young, aristocratic women. Your charged loved you because you were so entertaining and playful. Their parents were grateful because your unusual approach resulted in more actual retention of knowledge by the young women you tutored. You exercised your creativity by constantly getting your young ladies excited about learning.

in Virgo – Quality Crafts

Born into a family of Cremona craftsmen, you followed your father's footsteps and became a maker of violins. He taught you great care and conscientiousness. The process began with selecting just the RIGHT wood. The sanding had to be perfect. Measurements had to be precise to the smallest fraction. Your Dad taught you reverence for your creations. You loved and respected the instruments you built. Your family's name was synonymous with quality. You married a very musical woman who supported your dedication and helped you to carry on the traditions of your ancestors. You took good care of each other and loved with a strong, deep bond.

in Libra – Hand in Hand

Born into an ordinary family, you had a rather quiet childhood with parents older than average. Realizing that you must train for a trade, you became an assistant to a glove maker. At first he used you only to help customers try on gloves and to make deliveries. After a bit, you noticed how fine your sewing was and began to teach you the stitching of various gloves. Through shared labors, you became closer. He proposed marriage and you accepted. you continued to assist in the shop, albeit discreetly, through your four pregnancies. You had four fat, sassy babies who survived to be contented adults. you and your husband had a long association of love, joint efforts, and dedication to family.

in Scorpio – Magnificent Memory

A quiet child, you noticed everything. A keen observer, few facts slipped by you. Whenever anyone lost anything, the called went out to "Ask Alex; he'll know." Although your family teased you about "supernatural powers," it was only your meticulous observation and excellent memory which were at work. As an adult, you were drawn to law enforcement. Your special skills were valuable assets in detection. You also developed an inner 'truth meter" so that you could almost always tell if a witness or suspect was lying to you. Soon you were an extremely valued member of the police force. Although your wife worried about your life of work, the two of you had a long, happy married, blessed with two children who learned to be utterly honest!

in Sagittarius – Lasting Legacy

Rudderless as a young adult, you had no real sense of direction. With a vague impulse to travel, and no real path to follow, you joined the Army. You were posted to a remote desert fort with nothing around for many miles. Bored, you began to read. You became fascinated by history, then philosophy. Finding used books (which cost less) became a major preoccupation. Your mind was expanding and you found information utterly exciting. After the army, you became involved in the development of the frontier—and made quite a bit of money. Although your marriage was long and rewarding, you and your wife had no children, so you set up a foundation to build and maintain a library of history in your name.

in Capricorn – Stressful Stutter

When you learned to speak, you developed a bad stutter. It made communication challenging, and your parents really didn't know how to cope. Fortunately, your fourth grade teacher was a very sensitive and loving individual. She spent extra time with you, hours after school on occasion, and helped you to relax and feel better about yourself. The two of your practiced different techniques and you were able to largely eliminate your stutter. Under conditions of great stress, it would recur. Your teacher was such a wonderful exemplar for you that you decided to train to be a teacher as well. You ten found a position working with children who had various problems learning. Naturally you did not succeed in every case. But through much love and hard work, you brightened the lives of a number of children. You were particularly touched when your old teacher visited and admired your accomplishments.

in Aquarius – Limitless Learning

Your parents considered you a very strange child and called you their cuckoo—left in the wrong nest. Born into a family that spent most of the time drinking beer and watching fits (cock fights, dog fights, people battling), you had no interest. As soon as you discovered the written word, you begged and borrowed as many books as you could. Several teachers took pity upon you and fed your voracious hunger for knowledge. You worked at any jobs you could to save a few pennies toward you education. One of your teachers help you to get a scholarship to the university and you became a minor star there. Invited to stay on as a lecturer, you eventually worked your way to fill professorship, thrilled to be an environment where learning was the priority.

in Pisces – Abundant Assimilation

You spent most of your childhood feeling overwhelmed. Extremely sensitive, you were alike a psychic sponge in a chaotic, confusing environment. It took quite a while for you to figure out that some of your feelings were not really yours, but you had absorbed them from a sibling or school mate or some such. Other times, you learned to developed your own shielding techniques. Meanwhile, your family defined you as first disturbed, then silent, then overly imaginative. Fortunately, you found a friend who has a similar problem so that two of your provided reality checks or each other. You swore to be "blood brothers" to one another and went into business together as adults. Using your intuitive skills, you did very well in tuning into fashion and trends. You two became highly successful and found sensitive, lovely wives after careful searching. Life was very rewarding.

Saturn in 4th House

in Aries – Home and Hearth

Restless as a child, you always had an inner sense of wanting to be someplace else. In your late teens, you fell in love with a man eager to move west. Hearing about the Homestead Act, you were ready to leave. To have land of your very own had great appeal. You and your husband found a spread quite far from your nearest neighbor. The isolation meant going without a lot of things, but you loved the independence. Whatever you and your spouse could not grow, make or improvise, you had to give up having—or waiting for the twice-a-year trek into town. You had six children and felt blessed that all survived to thrive as adults. Although the life you led was very physically demanding, it was soul-satisfying. You had found your true home.

in Taurus – Gifted with a Green Thumb

As your father before you, gardening was your profession. You learned to distinguish all the different flowers which your father cultivated on his master's estate. You grew to love the smell and feel and taste of the rich earth. Your father taught you the secrets of growing certain fruits in the succession houses. You learned how to hasten ripening when the mistress wanted strawberries on the breakfast table. You mastered the arts of weed-killing, pruning, and training. Even topiary design became one of your talents. You seemed to have a particular propensity for your work and were known in the local area for your "green thumb." You married a cheerful young maid and raised one son of your own amidst the glories of man-made and natural vegetation.

in Gemini – Foster Families

Growing up in a large, active and lively household, you thrived on the movement and variety. When you married, you hoped for a large family. In the meantime, you followed local custom and fostered children from other homes. Your numerous siblings were happy to send one of their various broods to be raised by you and your husband. You cared for all as tenderly as if they were from your own body. As the years went by, you failed to conceive. The times blames you, but looking at all your sisters' large families, you wondered. Your beloved husband was the only son, born late in life, to his parents. But you both found great joy in fostering the children of others. Eventually your spouse designated as his heir a nephew you had raised. You and your husband continued to love and care for children to the end of your days.

in Cancer – Plentiful Progeny

When you were old enough to toddle, you wanted to hold and rock your younger sister. Feeding, tending, entertaining younger children was a joy for you. Uninterested in dolls, you were fascinated by real babies. As you came of age, you evaluated the young men courting you on the basis of family background and whether you thought they would be loving toward children and could support a large family. The man you accepted in marriage was very gentle and caring. To your great delight, you got pregnant almost immediately, giving birth to a daughter, whom you named Joy, 10 months after your wedding. Thereafter, you had a child almost every other year for 20 years. You felt your life was full of love and warmth and looked forward to many grandchildren with great anticipation.

in Leo – Best Background

The only daughter of an aristocratic Bavarian family, you were taught great pride in your heritage. Tales of the glory of your ancestors were common. You learned to dress as attractively as possible. You mastered the pianoforte and the harp and basked in your parents' compliments on your performances. Your mother tutored you thoroughly in the duties of a chatelaine and praised your attention to and comprehension of the myriad duties involved. You ran your parents household smoothly for a year before your marriage—to their great delight. Your husband had been raised in a chaotic holding and he was extremely pleased with your organizational skills and knack for bringing out the best from the servants. He felt you transformed his manor into a heavenly palace with good music, sparkling surroundings and wonderful meals. Everyone assured you that you were a credit to your lineage and you enjoyed rising to the highest level that you possibly could.

in Virgo – Solicitous Service

You were a tenant farmer on a duke's estate. Unlike some of his peers, he charged a fair rent. Although you hard to work hard and bad weather threatened your livelihood, you made just enough to support yourself and your family. Your wife was extremely good-natured and taught all your children to be courteous and helpful. She earned a little extra through the special, healing herbs she raised and sold. Although you had few luxuries, your family life was satisfying. Contentment came easily to all of you. Satisfaction is a job well done was important to each of you, and staying close to the land fed your psyche.

in Libra – Marvelous Mother

Very close to your mother, you were in no hurry to leave home. You married later than your peers—to a widower well established in the village. This ensured you could remain near to your family. Although you did have children of your own and a strong affectionate bond with your husband, you still visited your parents regularly. When your father's health began to fail, you took your parents into your home and helped your mother to care for him. He passed after about a year, but you coaxed your mother to stay, enjoying her company. You did all you could for her, valuing the opportunity to give back a little bit of the tender, loving care she bestowed upon you. Even when she became very ill at the end of her long life, you did not begrudge the hours of care required. You were happy to look after her. Your family filled your life on every level.

in Scorpio – Totally Truthful

Shadows stalked your family home. Your parents sometimes exchanged hate-filled glances or retreated into sullen silences. You knew something was wrong, but had no idea what. When you were older, you learned that your older sister was actually your half-sister because your father was not her father. As a result of your experiences, you were determined to choose a mate who would be honest and loyal. You examined all your marital prospects carefully and engineered a few subtle tests by maneuvering circumstances and conversations. Your future husband called you upon your manipulations, asking what you were doing. You explained and he asked, "How can you look for honesty in a partner through dishonest means?" Impressed, you got to know him better and ended up marrying. Each of you was faithful to the other throughout your long and fruitful marriage. You discussed everything honestly and openly and he was your best friend.

in Sagittarius – Dream Days

Born on the wide prairie of western Canada, you grew up hearing your mother yearn for England. She regretted leaving the land of her birth and missed her parents terribly. She painted an idyllic picture of England as a civilized, refined place while Canada was rough and tough. You loved nature. The great outdoors felt free to you. One of your favorite activities was to go for long walks with your father while he pointed out wildlife and named the flowers and the trees which you passed. He even taught you how to hunt—horrifying your ladylike mother. When you married, you chose a man who also loved the land. You settled out in the country to raise a family. Although there was much hard work in living on the frontier, everyone in your house pitch in to help. You all loved one another and encouraged each other to do everything possible. You lived your dream and helped your children to develop the faith and confidence to pursue their own visions.

in Capricorn – Orderly and Organized

The oldest of 10 children, you were fourteen when your mother was partially paralyzed in a fall. You took over the household. You organized everyone and assigned chores so that each person would be contributing. You did the lion's share of the cooking, much of the cleaning, some of your mother's daily care, and all of the planning. Without you at the helm, chaos reigned. Other matrons gave you pitying looks and 'tsk-tsked" about the burdens placed on such young shoulders, but you adored your sense of accomplishment and gladly gave back to your mother a measure of the love and care she had provided you. Even after you were happily married with a well-run home of your own, your siblings would periodically request you visit to reorganize their households and bring order out of anarchy. If a neighbor had troubles, you were first with a helping hand. Caretaking satisfied you and everyone in your life appreciated your knack for solving problems.

in Aquarius – Unconventional Upbringing

You knew there was something odd about your Prussian family, but didn't grasp it until you saw some of the families of your schoolmates. Your father discussed everything openly with your mother. He respected her opinion and decisions were made jointly. In public, she deferred to him, but in private, equality reigned. This became your model for relationships and you had to search for quite some time before you found someone of the caliber of your father. Once you married, you were thankful you had been so careful. You and your husband were friends. You found each other interesting and your marriage was exciting and stimulating. Children were a new challenge, but you both enjoyed the additional of fresh, young minds to the mix. Your home was a place of growth, of much conversation, many discoveries and an environment which encouraged individuality and openness to unconventional ideas. You all loved stretching your minds.

in Pisces – Special Sanctuary

As a child, you felt invaded. One of eight siblings, your house was too small for its many inhabitants. Privacy didn't exist and you were never alone. You loved going off into the woods for some time by yourself—and for quietude (except for the birds). Your mother, however, was a worrier. If you were gone more than a few minutes, she would dispatch one of your siblings to check upon you. Most of your childhood was spent dreaming of escape. A very attractive young woman, you had quite a few beaus. You talked seriously with each man who asked your hand in marriage and wed the one who understood your needs. Within your new house was a room all your own. You filled it with plants and pretty things. That was your sanctuary. When you went in and closed the door, your husband agreed not to disturb you unless the house was burning. Each of your children learned that rule as well. Consequently, you were serene, relaxed, refreshed, and a loving partner and mother. Life flowed beautifully.

Saturn in 5th House

in Aries – Ample Anxieties

Your mother died in childbirth with your younger brother. He did not survive either. Your father blamed himself, talking endlessly of the dangers of child-birth and how he should never have subjected his beloved wife to such agonies. Thus, you grew up with a distorted image of what having children entailed. Your father, irrational about the idea of you (his last link to his beloved wife) leaving, encouraged your anxieties. In your mid-twenties you fell madly in love with a young man. He was able to persuade you to marry him, but promised you could avoid children if desired. He took you to his aunt who explained a technique for trying to avoid conception, but warned it was fallible. She also spoke long and frankly about the realities of childbirth. That could not allay the fears of a lifetime, but did get you to rethinking about what you had been taught. Your husband remained very loving and reassuring, and his aunt provided much nurturing and mothering to you. Eventually, you decided you must overcome your fears and got pregnant. It was harder than you expected, especially as you wanted to be very courageous and not lean always on your husband for emo-tional support. When the actual birth came, it was much easier than you had expected. Your daughter was a great joy and deepened the love between you and your husband. You had three more wonderful children and lived to a happy, healthy, old age.

in Taurus – Chrysalis

Very drawn to music, you felt fortunate that your Viennese parents could afford piano lessons for you. Too much exhibition of talent, however, was unladylike. You were not expected to be TOO good. That might shock people. When you felt compelled to write down the music in your mind, you were informed that women could not be composers—period. You had to practice in secret at times because your parents felt you neglected your needlework, deportment, and other essential skills for your music. Although most of the young men you met had interests in little other than sports, riding, or hunting, you did manage to meet a skilled flutist. Of course you fell in love and were married. You spent many happy hours playing together. You could freely compose. You felt like a butterfly escaping a cocoon prison.

in Gemini – Comfortable Conversations

You grew up in a household where a respectful child was a silent child. You loved babies and hating seeing the transformation of each of your younger siblings from a cooing, friendly, happy infant to a silent, anxious, "invisible" child. When boys came courting, you gravitated toward the ones who enjoyed conversation. You eliminated the ones who expected to dominate with only an occasional sound of agreement required from you. The man you married was bright, curious, and eager to experience life. You had three children and adored reading to them. You and your husband held interesting discussions at meals and the children learned to join in as soon as they could. Your home was happy. People could talk about anything and you spoke of your love for one another often.

in Cancer – Cherishing Children

From your earliest moments, you knew you wanted to be a mother. When people asked you about your plans as a child, you said, "I'm going to be a mommy." Naturally the man you married was also eager for a family—and comfortably well-off with a large home. You were thrilled and excited with your first pregnancy—and with your last—the fourteenth. You felt awe whenever a new life emerged from within you. Each of your children was a special gift. You adored and admired them all, taking a moment each day to notice each one's specialness. Life was sometimes chaotic, and often noisy, but you loved it.

in Leo – Kind Kinfolk

As a child, you learned not to upstage your father. He was an entertaining, larger-than-life personality who needed an audience. If you accidentally impinged upon a "performance," you would be embarrassed and humiliated or discover later he had "slipped and fallen" on your favorite possession or toy and destroyed it. Although you had considerable dramatic talents, you learned to suppress them. Then you fell in love with a young man from a volatile Italian family. They loved to make grand gestures, to exaggerate, to strike a stance. You found it was acceptable to be expressive and emotional. Better yet, they admired your abilities and applauded (sincerely) some of your performances. You had found your heart's desire. You and your young man were taken into the bosom of his family and loved vociferously. When you provided the first grandson quickly—but not TOO quickly—you were even more the darling of everyone. You flourished, giving and receiving love with gusto.

in Virgo – Creative Crafts

An enterprising child, you felt a drive to create from an early age. You loved working with your hands and had quite an eye for detail. Over the years, you made many beautiful things, hats, dresses, lace, embroidery, decorated eggs, Christmas ornaments and much more. Handicrafts were a joy to you. The man you grew to love and marry was an excellent salesman. He persuaded a local store to carry some of your crafts. People bought them. Soon you had an extra income which provided household luxuries. Through your four pregnancies, you continued to create attractive knickknacks for the public. One of your children joined your efforts in her early teens. Everyone in your household helped everyone else. Love meant service and assisting as needed. You felt very fortunate to have a good husband, healthy, helpful children and creative work which was fun to do.

in Libra – Painting Pleasure

When you learned to paint, a whole new world opened up. The creative act sparked by a blank canvas was amazing. You felt incredibly vital and alive when engrossed in your art. As a female, you knew recognition was unlikely and your parents expected you to marry. You found an easygoing young man who had no objections to an artistic wife and married him. Determined to build a happy relationship, you were a good wife. You and your husband developed a strong bond of affection and when you had children, the circle of love widened. Throughout your life, you fed your soul with your painting and felt grateful that you had a loving family which supported your need to express.

in Scorpio – Sexual Satisfaction

Seduced and abandoned by your father, your mother taught you to fear and repress your sexuality. Nonetheless, you had a strong passion for life and tended to do everything whole-heartedly. Naturally when you did fall in love, it was quite intense. You own anxieties and your mother's paranoia led to many secret meetings after she was abed. You did not make love (although you came close), but had many intimate discussions, talking over fears and feelings, and what you each wanted in life. After baring your souls you decided to marry. Your mother had little use for any man but grudgingly conceded marriage was an honorable bond. When the two of you began exploring your sexuality, your bond strengthened and deepened more. You built a passionate connection that lasted a lifetime. Each of you could revitalize the other with a loving look, a caress, a wink, or an acknowledgment.

in Sagittarius – Late Bloomer

You were an only child, born late in life to your parents after they had almost given up hope. You loved babies and eagerly tended children of other squaws when you were a young maiden. You worried that your mother's barrenness would be carried by you. Very honest, you reminded each brave who courted you of your family history and asked him how he would feel if you could give him no sons. The third brave said he wanted to marry you, not the mother of possible sons. You wed him happily. After five years, each one adding to your inner insecurity, you conceived. Your first born was a daughter who you named the Iroquois equivalent of God's Gift. Just one year later, you delivered a son and your happiness was complete. Your family ended up including your beloved husband, two cherished sons, and two beloved and valued daughters.

in Capricorn – Valiant Victories

Eager to marry and start a family, you wed your childhood sweetheart. Your first born was a gentle, loving infant. Over time, it became clear that his mental faculties were limited, so you and your husband resolved to keep him with you always so you could provide loving care, direction, and structure to his life. The doctor told you that your son was likely to die young. You and your husband gave him every opportunity for a range of experiences within his limits and greatly admired his sweetness and lovability. Your next child, a daughter, became a fearless tomboy. She dared anything. An accident rock climbing left her bed-ridden for a year. The doctor said she might never walk again, but you and she refused to give up. You helped her to devise exercises for her muscles while she recuperated in bed. You supported her through endless crutches and attempts at walking until she succeeded. In the end, she recovered 95% of her former level of functioning. A neighbor asked you how you coped with the "extra burdens" of your children. You told her truthfully that your children were joys, not burdens. You loved both of them fiercely and felt your life had been immeasurably enriched through knowing them. The whole family took great satisfaction in each tiny victory, each step toward more. You felt wealthy in love and blessed with your family and its closeness.

in Aquarius – Nonpossessive Nurturing

Your parents were very dear to you and you looked forward to a loving bond with children of your own. You married a man who was also very focused on family. You had three children: two sons and one daughter, each very different. You loved them all, yet had to release them all as well. Your eldest son fell in love with the sea and sailed all over the world. Understanding his need for freedom, you set no barriers and received letters written in faraway lands with much loved expressed. Your daughter fell in love with a young man who wanted to emigrate to New Zealand. You said farewell with sadness, but loving support of her decision. Thereafter, you and she expressed your love and caring through letters. Your final son was an idealist and spent years in various countries helping the less fortunate improve their lot. Although a part of you wanted to tie your children close, you knew that their growth required independence. You lovingly made farewells, affirming their need to find their own ways. In return, you received written verification of their enduring love—and occasional, much-cherished visits. Your husband and you deepened your own love bond and took great joy and pride in the excellent job of parenting you had done and the wonderful children you had raised.

in Pisces – Infinite Images

As a child, you saw fairies and communed with nature spirits. Growing older, you were frustrated by the gap between your perfect, ideal, inner world and the limited world of physical reality. You couldn't sing or compose the celestial music you heard in your altered states. You could not create in charcoal or paint or pencil the inspired beauty you saw in your imagination. No sculpture felt or looked exactly like you wanted it to. For a time, you let your utter frustration stop you from creating. "If I can't do it perfectly, I won't do it at all." was your inner lament. But with increased maturity, you recognized the limits of the material plane. You chose writing as your medium. You learned to let your creativity flow and stopped trying to perfect it. You understood that inspiration was always greater than reality. You let your public see works that were less than ideal. You gained great satisfaction from mastering the "good enough" stage which allowed your work to be appreciated and you to keep alive the excitement of new projects.

Saturn in 6th House

in Aries – Considerable Cooperation
Your father was killed in a gin-bar fight when you were two and your mother struggled to put bread on the table. You helped from an early age. Running errands and delivering messages were your first tasks to bring in a few pennies. Big for your age, you got a job loading and unloading at the docks. Conditions were often unsafe with poorly balanced cargo that could shift and bury a man, and slippery decks and wharves to traverse. You spoke out strongly suggesting teamwork. You felt a combined voice would be most effective and were a pioneer in the long struggle that led to an eventual union to protect the workers from the more dangerous aspects of your job. You led the way and could take pride in helping to improve the lives of people who came after you.

in Taurus – Consolidating Cooperation
You and your family worked the grape harvest. You would move in to pick the vintner's grapes and then move on to the next harvest. Although wine makers could command impressive prices for their premier wines, you and your family were paid almost nothing. You talked with other families to seek solidarity. You looked for ways to organize your fellows. Although nothing so official as a union was formed, a few vintners made concessions. Better accommodations were created for migrant workers. Salaries were raised a bit. You had the satisfaction of knowing that you had improved the lot of many workers and stimulated the thinking of others.

in Gemini – Collective Cooperation
Driven to know, you turned to intellectual pursuits early on. You worked hard to gain an excellent education and then adopted teaching as a profession. Teachers were very poorly paid and often had to provide unpaid janitorial services as well. Women teachers were not allowed to marry in many areas. You felt conditions were unreasonable and began to feel out, very cautiously, some of your fellow educators. You explored the idea of a union to protect a few basic rights and perhaps to improve pay scales. Although no actual organization was

formed, you could see your suggestions were getting people thinking and moving them toward a stance of collective power.

in Cancer – Championing Children

You were a progressive member of the House of Commons who became a strong advocate of Reform (laws regarding child labor). Appalled at the abuse of young children by chimney sweeps, mill owners, and other employers, you lobbied hard for two bills. One would set a minimum age before a child could be hired. The other would limit the number of hours a child could be required to work. You made those reforms your major focus. When they finally passed, you, your family, and your fellow humanitarians celebrated the beginning of a more humane era!

in Leo – Attentive to Animals

As a child, you were fascinated by the magic of the circus. As an adult, you became concerned with the treatment of the animals. You began a personal crusade, making random visits and nosing around circuses. You reported abuses to local animal welfare societies: the starved lions, the beaten elephants, the abused horses pulling heavy wagons, and more. When you could get attention in the newspapers, you took your case to the public, trying to drum up outrage. Although progress was slow, you took great satisfaction in your cause. Your family also aided your efforts and you all learned to take pride and joy in each small step forward.

in Virgo – Protecting Pets

You loved animals, adopting many pets in your youth. Horrified by the conditions under which many animals (barely) survived, you became on advocate on their behalf. You were one of the founders of the Royal Society for the Prevention of Cruelty to Animals. Total elimination of barbaric practices such as dog fights and bear baiting were among your goals. You began establishing shelters to deal with the problem of overpopulation of pets. You and your colleagues strove to educate people and rouse their sympathies on behalf of animals. You felt great satisfaction and purpose in being a voice for animals who could not speak for themselves.

in Libra – Collective Contributions

You were a "mill girl" working long hours for low wages in a cotton mill. The machines were large and a tired worker risked injury that might damage an arm or worse. The owners didn't care what happened to their girls and simply fired anyone who was hurt. Riled by the injustice, you began talking with other young women about banding together in some fashion. Feeling that a group would have more power than an individual, you sought ways to develop a collective voice. Although an official union took years to form, you were influential in helping everyone to clarify goals such as some kind of injury insurance and shorter hours of work. You knew that your life had made a real difference to people, that your actions had counted for something.

in Scorpio – Union Unity

Born into a coal mining community, you worked as soon as you could—as did everyone. As you grew to adulthood, you noted the unfairness of the company town that made virtual slaves out of most miners. You began talking with others about combining your forces. The idea of a union was mentioned in whispers. You knew that if word got back to the bosses, you risked a beating or worse. Nonetheless, subtle efforts at organizing continued. When the first union was formed, you took great pride in being one of the major architects of the movement. You and your family knew that it was a great moment in history and an opportunity to improve the health and fortunes of all miners.

in Sagittarius – Advantageous Association

Injustice made you angry and uncomfortable, even as a child. As an adult, you turned to the law as your path to truth and righteousness. You observed that the standards in your profession were extremely varied and that some of your fellows used unethical methods and procedures. So you became one of the movers behind the establishment of the American Bar Association. Your goal was a group that could scrutinize its members and take action against those who did not follow good moral and ethical principles. You also envisioned a group that could rate the quality of its members and make recommendations to administrators or others in need of a high-level lawyer. You were very pleased to be a catalyst in this new chapter for American law.

in Capricorn – Massing Mailmen

As a child, you loved to speak, write, and get letters. As an adult, you became a postal worker. Mail delivery was physical arduous and sometimes dangerous (due to weather, people, or animals on one's route). It occurred to you that a union would be helpful. Collective bargaining might bring some protection to you and your fellows—especially those for whom on-the-job injury had led to loss of a job. You spoke to everyone you could and your wife spoke to as many wives as she could. You both believed strongly in your labor on behalf of everyone's health, well-being, and livelihood.

in Aquarius – Urgent Organizing

You grew up in the area around Manchester, England. When you were in your teens, unrest was growing. Abusive labor practices were widespread. Injured workers could starve to death. Hours of labor were horrendous and pay was minimal. You joined with many others in calling for a strike. Believing the winds of change were blowing, you felt a show of power to the authorities was essential. The powers that be overreacted with their usual hysteria and killed unarmed people who were simply listening to speeches. Sickened and saddened, you kept on working on behalf of organized labor and had the satisfaction of knowing that your long life of hard work had helped to improve the working life of the "common" man and woman.

in Pisces – Asylum Assistance

Raised in a gentle and loving family, you were drawn toward the healing arts. Medicine was unheard of for a woman of that time, but you had the funds and social position to pursue charity work. After someone described Bedlam Hospital to you, the plight of the mentally ill became your cause. People in asylums were chained, beaten, abused and often teased by visitors who mocked them or even threw rotten fruit and worse. You wrote letters, talked to people, sponsored educational seminars and lobbied members of Parliament on behalf of the insane. Although progress was inch by inch, you had the satisfaction of helping to alleviate the suffering of people who had few protectors.

Saturn in 7th House

in Aries – Accommodating Association

Although your parents had a reasonably pleasant marriage, you noticed that a number of spouses did not. As you grew into young adulthood, unlike most of your contemporaries who dreamed of marriage, you dreamed of independence. Knowing your parents did not want to support a spinster daughter, you took stock of the available young men. You eliminated all you knew who had a temper or drank to excess. You crossed off anyone whose father beat his wife or children. You delayed committing as long as you could. Finally, you accepted a slightly older man who was good-natured and easy to please. You accommodated him as much as possible because you believed your fate could have been much worse. The two of your built a good, affectionate relationship. You gave to rely on and treasure one another.

in Taurus – Challenging Choices

Your family's fortunes dwindled as you matured. Since your turned into a very beautiful young woman, you were under tremendous pressure to "marry rich" and provide for your parents. Concerned about the price your might have to pay for money, you considered your prospects. One of the men courting you was much older than the rest and shared your love of music. He also seemed kind and gentle. Your parents were happy to encourage his suit as he was quite wealthy, so you were wed. To your great relief, your husband proved to be a truly good man. He loved to pamper you and continued to assist your parents periodically. You and your spouse became known for your musical evening, and he treated you always with affection, tenderness, and respect. Soon you came to love and value him deeply, cherishing your 20 years together. You were proud, as a widow, to follow his loving example.

in Gemini – Mental Meandering

You fell in love with your husband's mind. Impressed by his powerful intellect, attraction on other levels followed. Since both sets of parents had no objections, a match was made. Your spouse was a rare man for he did not find intelligence in a woman threatening or abnormal. He encouraged you to continue learning. You two shared many happy hours in your library and in discussions. In the beginning, he was more often your tutor, but as time went on, you were able to convey new insights and information to him. Although you and your husband had only one son, your union was very happy. The whole family explored mental vistas and treated one another with loving respect and interested attention.

in Cancer – Loving Lineage

You and John were born on neighboring manors. Both of you were trained to respect and value family traditions. Betrothed in your cradles, you were to be the link between two estates. As nearest neighbors, you and John grew up together, although both of you spent some years away at school as well. When you returned from finishing school with your hair up and figure developed, he was struck dumb at the change in his former playmate. You were equally impressed with his manly proportions. Both of you became quite eager for the wedding. Your similar backgrounds proved to be excellent preparation for the marriage. Your tastes were alike and your thinking parallel. You happily continued family traditions with your brood of children.

in Leo – Loving Laughter

You spotted your husband-to-be at a party. He was the center of attention with people laughing at his repartee and admiring his quick wit. Having grown up in a family full of fun and no small measure of play-acting, you wanted a marriage full of laughter and excitement. After ascertaining that the man you wanted was not cruel in his humor, the chase began. Catching his attention was not difficult. Then a subtle flirtation cum competition ensued. You two would trade quips and admiring glances at parties. Although he was older and a "hardened bachelor," he proposed after ten months, and you accepted. Your judgment was proved excellent for he was a loving husband ever eager to play with you. Your long years together were filled with good times.

in Virgo – Loving Labor

Raised on the edge of poverty, you went to work very early to help your family make ends meet. As a young woman, you first admired your husband-to-be for his industriousness. Getting to know him better confirmed your opinion that he was a conscientious, hardworking individual. He also appreciated your willingness to assist. Shortly, you were married. You saved enough and borrowed a bit from relatives to take over a dilapidated inn. Your husband and brothers refurbished it. You cleaned thoroughly and began making delicious meals for wayfarers. Your food became quite a draw and the inn's facilities were soon noted for comfort, convenience, and cleanliness. Your custom increased. Soon you and your husband had a bustling business which employed a number of relatives and even your own children when they were old enough. The bond of shared efforts and success through teamwork strengthened the love between you all.

in Libra – Flight to Freedom

A bright young woman, you felt great trepidation about your future. Marriage appeared to be nothing but legalized slavery in your eyes, but being a spinster in your society was not an appealing prospect either. You devised a plan. Getting to know the young men in uniform, you arranged to be betrothed to a reckless young lieutenant just before he left to serve in the forces sent to quell the American rebellion. As you had suspected, he perished in the fighting, and you (naturally) had to go into mourning for a year. (You had a fall-back plan in case he had returned.) Your next choice was a man who could have been your grandfather. He was fond of you, but a bit senile, so another engagement was not difficult. Fond of him, you looked after him very well in your marriage. He was quite content for the next ten years and passed away peacefully. As a widow, you were granted considerable independence and able to live the life you wanted—studying at the library, talking with friends, gardening, and playing your harp. Life was very pleasant.

in Scorpio – Deja Vu

When you touched Michael's hand for the dance he requested, you felt something akin to a shock. By the end of the dance, you both knew that you must marry. Older, "wiser" heads counseled caution, but you explained to your mother that your body "recognized" Michael in a way you could not explain. Passion flared brightly in your union, but being together was also like a homecoming. You could discuss everything with Michael—and did. At some point, you two became fascinated by comparative religion. When you began reading about Hinduism, you each turned to the other and said: "We've been together before."

in Sagittarius – Wanting to Wander

Restless in your youth, you had quite reasonable parents and a comfortable childhood, but always an inner yearning for something more. When you read about Lady Hester Stanhope's adventures in Arabia, you had an inkling of what you wanted. But what was permissible for a rich old eccentric was not acceptable for a young debutante. Shortly thereafter you attended a party graced by the Wandering Earl—noted for his travels and archeological studies. Upon arranging an introduction, you told him he could saw your life by marrying you. Amused, he sought you out for further conversation. Upon realizing your hunger for exploration and faraway lands, he did his best to dissuade you with detailed descriptions of real perils and great discomfort. You assured him that you could handle it all and the experience would be quite worthwhile. He persuaded your parents to join a "house party" aboard his yacht and you spent two weeks in close (but chaperoned) quarters. At the end of the two weeks, he spoke with you seriously about the age difference between you (15 years), and proposed. You accepted. Your life together was full, exciting, and happy. You saw many of the sites you'd dreamed about—and more. Your fresh perspective also deepened your husband's pleasure.

in Capricorn – Caretaking Couple

As a girl, you sighed over romances with your peers and dreamed of tall, dark, and handsome heroes. In real life, you knew that your parents would arrange your marriage. You obediently wed the man they selected and did your best to be a good wife. Your husband was a bit of a daredevil and spent much time riding wildly. One year after you were married, he broke his neck on the hunting field. After the obligatory year of mourning, your parents informed you that they had selected another candidate for your hand. Although you could have settled into widowhood, you still hoped for companionship, so agreed to meet the man involved. You were relieved to discover that your intended second husband had no real vices and was a responsible, considerate person. Feeling that a good marriage would be possible with him, you were wed. He duly informed you of his plans every day, and consulted you about your wishes. He did what he could to please you and was appreciative of your efforts to learn his preferences and to make his life and household comfortable. You two found yourselves gradually growing into love. Children strengthened your connection. Your concern and care for one another built a very strong bond and you enjoyed a long, fulfilling union.

in Aquarius – Friends Forever

Your best friend growing up was the boy next door. Although he was a few years older, he allowed you to tag along for many of his activities. You made an admiring pupil, so he taught you to fish, wade, climb trees, understand bird calls, and much more. In his late teens, he became infatuated with several unsuitable women and was briefly bewitched by a sophisticated widow. In each case, he eventually came to his senses, but he told you a bit more than your parents would have approved of sullying a young maiden's ears. Your faithful admiration helped to reinforce his confidence after having his heart broken. When you started gaining admirers of your own, he teased you initially, then began insisting that none of the young men were suitable. (Your parents disagreed.) Finally he realized that it was you he wanted for a wife and proposed. Naturally you had recognized your love bond much earlier, so you accepted his proposal. Having husband who was both lover and best friend was wonderfully rewarding and your many years together were quite happy.

in Pisces – Charitable Couple

You chose your husband when you saw him stop his carriage to rescue a dog wounded by the driver of a curricle. Your heart was touched. Once you learned his name, you were able to be introduced,. To your delight, he was also a member of one of your favorite charitable organizations, so you had much in common to discuss. Your feelings were very compatible and your love deepened over time. He came to appreciate your sensitivity, empathy, and caring nature. He proposed with great tenderness. Your marriage was long and you had the satisfaction of contributing together to a better world. The love you felt for one another poured out in assistance to society's less fortunate. You counted your many blessings often.

SATURN IN 8TH HOUSE

in Aries – Time for Temperance

You observed the ravages of alcohol firsthand in your own family. Your father would drink away much of his salary and become belligerent when he got home. You learned to avoid him as much as possible. Your mother could not always do so. When you came of age to marry, you very deliberately chose a teetotaler of whom you were also fond. Eager to help others escape what you had endured, you became active in the Women's Temperance Union. You spoke and wrote and lobbied to limit access to alcohol. You encouraged people to pledge temperance in their lives. Your husband whole-heartedly supported your efforts. Able to build a marriage of love, affection, and shared ideals, you felt extremely fortunate.

in Taurus – Rich Reserves

Your father dissipated your patrimony on wine, women, and song, but you were raised by your mother on the country estate. You got to know all your tenants and their suffering as your father tried to squeeze more income for his indulgent lifestyle. Inheriting at 18, you knew marrying money was the only chance—not only for you, but for all the people whose livelihood depended on running the estate. You surveyed the daughters of rich merchants who might be interested in "buying" a title. You felt fortunate to find a quiet young woman well trained in household management and very fond of gardening. A bargain was stuck and you began the long, slow process of building back the land from your father's depredations. Your wife proved skilled and very helpful, increasing your affection for her. You were very circumspect about using "her" money (that came with the marriage) because you wanted to put it to the most effective use, and maintain a reserve for emergencies. You also feared that a part of you could become as abusive of others and indulgent as your father had been. Instead, you found each year strengthening the love between you and your wife and improving the estate. You built your family and rebuilt your heritage together.

in Gemini – Secret Spy

Quite a mimic as a child, you easily picked up accents and dialects. Language fascinated you and you mastered several tongues in your teens. When war with the French broke out, your government solicited your services as a spy. Ferreting out information could save English lives and you gladly risked yours for that purpose. Some of your compatriots were daredevil types and they perished. You survived by being cautious, scouting your territory and arranging a bolthole whenever possible. When the war was over, you were honored for your service. Shortly thereafter you married a bright young miss. You and your wife entertained yourselves by playing with codes and ciphers. You designed an elaborate system which you offered to the government. Although they officially declined, you wondered if perhaps they were using it without the knowledge of you and your wife. A happy home, a history of service to your country, and a complex, intellectual hobby kept you quite contented.

in Cancer – Dearest Defender

A complex young man, you had considerable sporting prowess which gained you the respect of your peers, but an inner core of gentleness. You championed the underdog and rescued and healed many a wounded animal. From age 11 on, you and a young girl you grew up with knew that you loved each other devotedly. That love deepened over the years, and you were betrothed at age 18, even though she was virtually penniless. Just then, your father's condition became severe. He had been subject to rages and black-out periods, but they were becoming so common that you and your mother realized he would have to be confined. It was then that you were told the family secret: your father's father had suffered from the same condition. Horrified, you had to think, then sat down for a long talk with your fiancee. She was willing to chance marriage and children (as your mother had been), but you could not risk that for someone you loved so much. You made an agreement. You would extend the betrothal for five years. Your father's first symptoms had emerged by age 21. If you showed no signs by 23, you would marry your beloved and risk children. In the meantime, you and your fiancee would share your passion discreetly in the privacy of the countryside in a manner which would not risk pregnancy and would leave her a virgin if the worst occurred. The symptoms did begin when you were 21. At first, your despair was great, but you set your course. Every safe moment was spent sharing love with your fiancee. You discussed much and urged her to find happiness after you were confined. You willed all your possessions to your beloved, ensuring her financial security no matter what happened to you. An unexpected black-out overtook you when you were out riding one day (a pleasure you had not wanted to give up). As your soul passed from your body, you felt it was for the best. You had not wanted the experience of a lingering descent into madness, and you knew that you had shared all possible with your betrothed and left her well provided. Despite its brevity, your life had been rich and full and you had been able to look after the interests of your beloved.

in Leo – Promoting Progress

Your parents were dramatic individuals who made "entrances" rather than walking into a room. They taught you confidence and the belief that you could do anything you set your mind to. As a young man, you were excited by progress and believed that growth and development would be accelerated by technology. When you learned about steamships, you used your persuasive skills to gather a group of investors to utilize this new tool. Your venture was quite successful and you became a catalyst. You would research a number of possibilities and present the best opportunities to people with money. They would pool resources to back a particular project. You almost always made money for yourself and your investors. You also had the satisfaction of aiding humanity's progress.

in Virgo – Revitalizing Research

Drawn to the healing arts, you trained as a doctor in your youth. A small inheritance allowed you to keep your practice minimal and devote yourself to research. You pored over case studies and talked much with other physicians. You observed the courses of certain diseases. Your wife shared your fascination with the functioning of the human body and assisted your research. You published papers and sought to clearly identify factors that led to a strong constitution and resistance to disease. Although recognizing a hereditary factor, you were determined to isolate other causes so doctors could save more lives. As you and your wife pursued trails leading to diet, to air, to exercise, you felt the excitement of discovery, the satisfaction of sharing a worthy task with the woman you loved, and the hope of making the world better.

in Libra – Treasure Hunts

As a child, you were fascinated by tales of pirates and buried treasure. The only child of well-off parents, you were able to pursue your interest as a hobby. You began to research tales of old or lost treasures and relics. You even managed to collect a map or two. You met your wife-to-be in the library—backing into her as you perused the shelves. It was love at first bump. After your marriage, she became involved in your quests as well. Her perspective was different, so proved invaluable in considering alternatives when trying to decipher deliberately vague or coded clues and directions. You actually mounted a few expeditions to areas which were not dangerous. Your wife came along and you had the great excitement and fulfillment of discovering buried treasure in one case!

in Scorpio – Dealing with Death

Your family never really understood you. Inclined to question areas they preferred to leave undisturbed, you made them a bit uncomfortable. You had a knack for uncovering secrets. Even when young, you could and would face topics others were afraid to address. One of your fascinations was with the processes of birth and death. You believed that how one entered and exited from life was very important. As an unmarried woman, there was more disapproval about you investigating childbirth, so you began doing volunteer work in hospitals. You found a real gift in working with the dying. Many seemed eased just by being in your presence. Some would talk with you even if sullen and silent with everyone else. Many told you that you had helped them to prepare for death with dignity. They appreciated your care. Even after you married and were happily involved with your own children, you would visit the hospitals occasionally and help people (with noncontagious diseases for the sake of your children) to prepare for the transition.

in Sagittarius – Ensuring Education

A child of privilege, you were born into a wealthy Brahmin family. Your parents took the responsibility of their position seriously and you were taught to consider the impact of your actions on those dependent upon you. After some thought, you decided education was a goal you wished to promote. You persuaded your parents to donate some funds and began to set up schools to help train tenants in rudimentary reading and writing skills. You married a man who also had idealistic leanings and worked together to increase education among the "common" people. You quest was much more gratifying than the heedless parties pursued by many of your peers. You and your husband increased your love and respect for one another through your shared efforts and successes.

in Capricorn – Soul-Seeking

You lived in a time when careless hedonism ruled the day. People rushed from party to party with gay abandon. They sough excesses regularly. Self-indulgence was carried to extremes. Moderation appeared unknown. Despite the seductive pull of a life devoted to pleasure, you resisted. You felt the need for something of more substance in your life. You spent hours probing your feelings, trying to ascertain what was fundamentally significant in your life. At times, a sense of meaninglessness and despair overwhelmed you. During your "dark night of the soul," you met the woman who became your wife. She was dedicated to doing her small part to battle the evils of opium addiction in your society. An understanding clicked into place for you, and you recognized your life's path: to encourage people to awaken, to eliminate addictions and distractions from their lives in order to peel down to their true inner selves and thus uncover their vital contribution. You and your wife pursued your efforts on behalf of self-control and self-mastery, simultaneously enriching your own love relationship.

in Aquarius – Assisting Advances

Living after the American Revolution was exciting. Experimentation was in the air. People knew they were pioneers and were eager to blaze a new political path. Although women were not directly involved in decision-making, they did have input through their families. Political discussions were common at your dinner table growing up and your married a Virginia planter who served for a time in the legislature. Although busy raising a family and helping to oversee everything related to your husband's lands, you kept current with political developments. Through osmosis, some of your ideas traveled from you to your husband to other law-makers. You also hosted two parties a year to bring together many of the movers and shakers of society and did your best to promote progressive concepts. Although you wanted more change than your husband, you respected one another and had a loving marriage. You were able to see that your viewed influenced him even more than he acknowledged, and knew that you had helped to birth the future, providing more opportunity for your children and your children's children.

in Pisces – On Behalf of Orphans

Raised in the Quaker traditions of nonviolence, you were very sensitive to the misfortunes of people. As a young child, you donated the few pennies you earned from sewing to a charity for abandoned women. You married your childhood sweetheart and worked very hard raising children and maintaining a household. Yet you knew you had to serve as well. Orphans particularly tugged your heartstrings, so you devoted a few hours every week to trying to raise money for a local foundling hospital. You could not host big bashes for society people. But you could and did persuade newspapers to occasionally run a touching story and pleas for assistance. You spoke with friends, neighbors, and even strangers. You made presentations to any organizations which would allow you to speak on behalf of the orphans. Your obvious sincerity opened some wallets and purse strings. You continued your campaigns throughout your long life.

Saturn in 9th House

in Aries – Expanding Erudition

Excited by the prospects of a new land, you emigrated to America. Many things were beginning, and anticipation was strong everywhere. You became involved with the cause of education. Knowing that colleges and universities were essential for an educated—and successful—populace, you helped to work toward the founding of Princeton University. The day that dream became reality was tremendously moving. The university was the second love of your life— after your wife, who shared the high value you placed on education. You both built toward the future.

in Taurus – Goddess Goodness

You grew up in the age of Earth religions. Your priestesses marked the passing of the seasons. Rituals celebrated the equinoxes and solstices, particularly through the symbolism of first seed/ sprout/ growth/ harvest/ decay/ seed. As bodies came from Mother Earth, they were cherished. Food was prepared with love and care to be beautiful and delicious. Skins and grasses were used to build soft beds. Hot springs provided sites for long baths with mild sex play. life was good. You understood the order and patterns of the universe, and you felt your connection to the Whole. You knew that the Goddess was with you and loved you always.

in Gemini – Prized Professor

Raised in an intellectual family, you found great pleasure in the pursuit of knowledge. Like your father, you fell in love with a bright woman—already an author when you proposed. Your marriage was very mentally stimulating as well as passionate. Since learning was your life, you accepted a position at Harvard with the understanding that you could become a full professor over time. Your father, ensconced at Yale, teased you a bit about the rivalry between your schools. Your research and teaching went well, and you gained that full professorship. Life to you was precious, and you spent every possible moment learning, loving, writing, or teaching.

in Cancer – Blessed Be

The religion of the Great Mother prevailed in your time. Women were clearly the source of life and connected to the mysteries of death for you bled monthly but did not die. As a young woman, you were trained in nurturing and child care as well as gardening and plan care. The land was your mother and would provided everything you needed if you tended her with love and respect. You married a man of your tribe whom you had eyed for several summers. He proved to be a strong and gentle mate and a good father to your six children. Your harvests were usually good and you dwelt in love and the light of the Goddess, thanking Her for Her Blessings.

in Leo – Restful Rituals

You felt God's calling quite early and went to seminary as soon as you were old enough. The rituals of the Orthodox Church were soothing to you—the liturgy, the music, candles, incense. When the time came to choose from among the two careers paths, you knew that you were destined to marry and be a priest of the people. Some in your class chose the black robes of the celibates, to live removed from the world. God was served through both means. You found a loving, devout woman to marry and spent many years pleasing each other and working for the glory of God.

in Virgo – Married Missionaries

When you were 14, you realized that you had to devote your life to God's service. Your parents did not fully understand, you but trained to become a missionary. While in training, you met a young woman who shared your vision, and you were married. The church posted you to Africa. Although conditions were spartan, you and your wife learned to do much with little. You became a carpenter, like your Lord. Your wife sewed all your clothes and hers as well and cooked all the meals, often improvising in regard to ingredients. You both took satisfaction in your accomplishments and the strengths you developed. Although you could not save all souls, you had enough success among the natives to feel you were doing God's work. You and your wife had a loving bond, meaningful tasks, and a higher purpose You needed nothing more.

in Libra – Rigorous Rulings

Interested in everything as a child, you absorbed a great deal of information about many different subjects. A keen observer, you also developed good insight into human nature. After settling on the law as a profession, you married into one of the local, powerful families. Due to your wife's family's influence, you were soon appointed a judge. Extremely conscientious, you weighed your decisions carefully. Supporting justice and integrity was essential to you, and you fought corruption on all levels. Your wife was an equal partner in your marriage and in full support of your toughest rulings. You had an excellent marriage and the knowledge that your life had supported fairness.

in Scorpio – Hidden History

As a child, you were fascinated by tales of Julius Caesar. History became a natural focus for you in school. You spent many happy hours in the library pouring over ancient tomes and comparing different sources regarding past events. Analyzing the patterns and cycles in human affairs utterly enthralled you. Although you knew history was written by the winners, you did your best to track multiple versions, and get as many and varied perspectives as possible. Your work earned you a position at William and Mary College and you gratefully expanded your research and writing. You also met the daughter of a much older colleague, and fell in love. She was a considerable scholar in her own right, so your union was fruitful in producing both books and children. Your life was long and happy; you enjoyed observing the small slice of history in which you had a part.

in Sagittarius – Far, Far Away

Born into a Viking family, you knew you were to be a traveler. You made your first voyage at five years, and many more thereafter. Eager to find new vistas, you inspired a few of your fellows to take a small, sleet ship father than anyone had gone in recent memories. To the south and west, you discovered seemingly endless schools of fish often massed together for easy capture. Your discovery was very welcome at home, for a steady supply of salted fish meant survival through the harsh winters. Basking in a bit of hero worship, you married a young maiden you'd been admiring. She accepted your frequent absences, caring for the children and the household while you were away. You continued to wander, to seek far vistas, to view what had not been seen by others. You thanked Odin and Thor for your fortunate life.

in Capricorn – Holy Word

When the printing press became widely available, you saw a vast opportunity and borrowed enough money to print The Bible. Anyone with just a little bit of cash and a little bit of learning wanted God's Word to improve his reading skills and to help insure his place in heaven. You felt very responsible for conveying God's precise Words to the masses. Religious traditions were very vital to you, and you felt having written, permanent records would prevent distortions. You married a woman who shared your respect for the old ways and did your best to support The Father in every respect. You knew your work, your marriage, and your life were dedicated to the Lord.

in Aquarius – Trying and Tinkering

Science fascinated you from the day your first read about Ben Franklin's experiments with electricity. You became a tinkerer, trying different approaches and building different gadgets you dreamed up. Fascinated by the idea of putting water to work, you rigged contraptions by a rushing stream to churn butter, wash clothes, and (not a success) peel potatoes. Your family was amused, but did not interfere. The man who became your husband was impressed with several of your inventions and encouraged you to keep innovating while married. A few of the items you patented and brought in income. What pleased you most, however, was the creative process. That and the love of your husband made your life complete.

in Pisces – Spiritual Sight

When you were ten, you felt God's calling. You were in an apple orchard and the impression was absolutely clear. Your parents were well-off so you could choose from among several nunneries. You chose a place where the sisters could be close to nature. All your training just reaffirmed the rightness of your decision and you took permanent vows at 18. You felt the glory of God's love daily. The atmosphere at your convent was serene and beautiful and you loved almost all of the other sisters. When you took your daily walk in the woods, you occasionally saw the face of the beloved Virgin Mother. You often heard her gentle tones conveying her love to you and once or twice, her hand briefly touched your hair in a gesture of blessing. The Abbess believed your experience, but cautioned you that everyone felt the grace of Our Lord and Savior differently, so you should not expect your sisters to see or hear what you did. Your life was full of beauty and serenity.

Saturn in 10th House

in Aries – Frontier Foodstuffs

As the number of westward-bound settlers increased, you recognized an opportunity and sold supplies. Your store was the last for many, many miles, so people would get a few more foodstuffs or items they realized they had forgotten to stock. You built up quite a good business and moved west in a few years as the patterns of emigration shifted. Where people were on the move in large numbers, you made sure you were a significant supplier. After you married, your wife helped you to choose items which would sell most quickly and bring in greater profits. She also helped you to recognize when it was time to move to a new location. you enjoyed the challenges and changes of your work and particularly liked being your own boss.

in Taurus – Sweet and Submissive

Born female in a Japanese family, you absorbed subservience with your daily rice. A sweet, good-natured child, you were well suited to become a compliant young woman. You liked making people comfortable, so easily settled into a lifetime of pleasing men. Your family selected your husband, and you obeyed. Once you were married, you worked hard at determining your husband's preferences. You served his favorite foods often. You massaged him when he came home tired. In return, you received his affection and protection. When you produced a son, you received praise as well. His mother was even kind to you, so you considered yourself most fortunate.

in Gemini – Profitable Partnership

Married to an ambitious young man, you were both working hard and saving pennies so he could start his own business. Noticing how public education was burgeoning, you suggested perhaps selling school supplies (slates for writing and blackboards, and chalk) would be a lucrative field. Your first tentative investments paid off very well. Soon you had a distribution network to many schools as well as colleges and universities. You and your husband worked well together, often sparking ideas off one another. "Two heads are better than one' became your inside joke and you designed business cards with merged profiles. Both your commercial ventures and your marriage flourished.

in Cancer – Minimizing Mourning

Born into a family of undertakers, you expected to continue the business as a matter of course. Although outsiders shuddered and wondered, "How could you?" you valued the family traditions. Your job was to take care of matters other people could not face emotionally. You also served to orient people in the grieving process. You took pride in making a funereal as easy as possible for the loved ones left behind. You married a man whose background was similar and raised many happy children continuing your familiar ways.

in Leo – Moral Magistrate

Born into a "good family," you knew there were few paths to power for a female. Marrying well was your first step. Conveniently, it happened that you were very much in love with your husband. Through judicious planning, friend-ships, and cultivation of blood and other ties, you became an arbiter of fashion-able society. Your glare could intimidate a young debutante. Your cold shoulder was a death knell to the hopes of a fortune hunter. Naturally dramatic, you wielded your power with flash and dash. Joining together with a few other matrons, you became a moral force. You used your influence to persuade people toward a path of integrity and decorum. You eschewed drunkenness and lewd behavior, and sent clear messages of disapproval to those who caroused. You felt this was your contribution to the betterment of society and did your best to be a positive, ethical force.

in Virgo – Registry Referral

You and your wife ran a registry business in London. You interviewed potential housekeepers, butlers, maids, and other servants. Wealthy individuals checked with your registry (or their secretaries checked for them) when they needed servants to run their houses. Particularly for people who lived in the country and only opened their London houses for a few months, your services were very valuable. You and your wife prided yourselves on your conscientiousness. All the servants you listed were well trained and good workers. Employers guaranteed a minimum wage for the workers and, of course, you received fees for your services. The business provided the means for you, your wife, and your three children to be materially comfortable. Love and caring provided the other necessities for a happy life.

in Libra – Designing for Debutantes

Beginning with doll dresses, you were a designer. Girlfriends coveted your clothes because any dress you made was striking and capitalized on the wearer's good points. You knew instinctively how to flatter any figure. Unsure if you wanted to marry (and not liking any of your prospects in the country), you persuaded an indulgent uncle to invest in your talents. Opening a shop in Bath, you catered to wealthy visitors to the city. After a new start, you became wildly popular as mothers realized your dresses could transform the plainest of daughters into a moderately appealing feminine vision. You viewed yourself as a fairy godmother who turned ugly ducklings into swans. When you met, fell in love with, and married a successful young man, you happiness was complete.

in Scorpio – Meticulous Manager

You were an estate manager for the local lord. Like his father, he spent much time at the Saxon court while you managed his country estate and invested any extra funds. You were a conscientious steward, husbanding his resources, but generating income for his living and entertaining expenses. You also strove to be very fair to all tenants and people living on the estate. You believed you did the best for everyone concerned. Your wages were not stupendous, but enough to marry a local girl you admired, and to support the four children you had. Life was busy, but very fulfilling.

in Sagittarius – Sailing Store

Beginning your career as a sailor, you picked up some interesting items in your travels. Selling them for quite a profit back home persuaded you to enter the import/export business. Your instincts as a buyer were excellent and you built up a network of wealthy clients in Amsterdam who relied upon you to provide one-of-a-kind conversation pieces for their homes. When you married, you thought about delegating the buying so you could spend more time with your beloved wife. Instead, she persuaded you to take her along. Flouting superstitions about females on ships, her companionship resulted in purchases highly appealing to the wives of your clients, and your business boomed even more.

in Capricorn – Judicious Jeweler

Your father was a jeweler and you apprenticed in his shop. After a long training period, he turned everything over to you. Building on his reputation for quality, you slowly expanded. Although you kept his classic designs, you also tried a few new approaches. Interested in rocks and minerals, you created some lovely paperweights utilizing crystals and geodes. They proved very popular, and brought in a younger crowd, further enlarging your client base. Feeling secure and established, you married your patient fiancee who had waited five years for the wedding). Your family began shortly thereafter and you looked forward to being a prosperous, pampered patriarch.

in Aquarius – Satirical Sketches

The only daughter of a noted scholar, you received an education far beyond the average male (much less female) of your time. Your mother was also very bright and keenly interested in current events. From her, you learned to follow political developments. Along with your father's private tutoring, you received extensive training in household management from your mother and mastered the requisite embroidery and musical skills of a young lady of your time. You also took lessons in dancing, sketching and deportment. You discovered quite a talent for satire and indulged in scathing sketched which skewered the pomposities of public figures and politicians. Secretly submitting a few, under a pseudonym, to a political journal (among those to which your mother subscribed), you were quietly delighted to see them published. You tried a few articles and most of them were accepted as well. A fellow writers whose work you admired begged (by letter) the favor of an introduction (thinking you male, of course). Nervous, but eager to meet him, you revealed your "secret life" to your parents. Initially taken aback at your acerbic wit, they ended up quite proud of you and arranged a meeting with your identity initially concealed. Love at first sight struck both you and the young man who admired your articles, so you joined in matrimony and happily wrote political commentary and cartoons for many years.

in Pisces – Maestro of Music

Born into a musical Neapolitan family, you showed early talent. Willingly undergoing the rigorous raining and discipline required, you became a concert pianist. You toured Europe, moving people everywhere with your power performances. In your twenties, you began to compose as well. Falling into (unrequited) love slowed your creative output. Falling into fully reciprocated love increased your rate of composition. In your thirties, you retired from public performing to spend more time with your beloved wife and children. You continued to compose and was happy with your balanced and harmonious life.

Saturn in 11th House

in Aries – Breaking Barriers
You were not an ordinary little girl. Very active and fearless, you tried almost everything. An instinctive tomboy, you found no acceptance from little girls making tea parties in frilly dresses. As you got older, the boys rejected your presence in their games, determined to be completely separate from girls. Having former comrades turn you away hurt, but you learned self-reliance. You began to measure decisions and actions against your inner integrity meter. You could stand firm against public opinion if you knew your course was right. As a result you became a ground breaker for other women. You proved women could do things they were considered too weak or too fragile to do. Your example gave other women the courage to go outside "normal" boundaries. You made new, important friendships, and found love as well.

in Taurus – Sweet Success
Other children made fun of you because your clothes were ragged and you often had no shoes. Your mama taught you that what was on the outside of a person was surface gloss that rubbed off quickly while the inner light of a good soul shone through forever. You took advantage of every opportunity to earn a few pennies to help out your mother. After working in a sweets shop, you saved enough to make an experimental batch of candy. It sold very well. You made two more batches from your profits—and built an empire from there. It was your custom to hire workers who were "misfits"—who were "different" in some way. you believed you could help them to get their inner lights shining, and you often did!

in Gemini – Deaf, Not Dumb!
Born deaf to hearing parents, you were an outcast in many ways. You learned to lip read on your own as your parents didn't really know how to deal with you. Regular schooling was impossible, but you devoured books, reading as much as your parents would allow. Eventually, you taught yourself to speak somewhat, although your diction was never as good as would have been desirable. Your parents assumed you would be dependent all your life, but you were determined to make your own way. You found a job as a proofreader at a newspaper— where your quick, eagle eyes were an asset. You also met your wife there; she came into the offices to place an ad. She was a warm, loving person and fully supported your "other [unpaid] job:" lobbying, writing, and agitating for better educational opportunities for the deaf. Your life was satisfying and complete. You wanted everyone to enjoy such opportunities.

in Cancer – Caring Community

Your parents were rigid people, unable to demonstrate affection and note quite sure to do with their unexpected, change-of-life baby. As soon as you were old enough to play outside, you started making friends. Many of your friends lacked support at home as well. A band of you swore fealty as "blood brothers and sisters." As you grew older, you heard of various groups establishing "intentional communities" (communes) in the areas of present-day Illinois, Wisconsin, Nebraska, etc. Your group decided this was for you and everyone worked at whatever they could and saved their pennies for seven years. The most eloquent among you also sought a wealthy sponsor to help fund your dream. An eccentric millionaire contributed three thousand dollars. You invited others who shared your philosophy (nurturing and love of children was paramount) to joint forces. Everyone had to bring a skill and basic tools and minimal household goods. Establishing your community was touch, but the camaraderie was incredible. Man of the "blood brothers and sisters" married each other. You chose a husband from among your early chums and doted delightedly on him and on your four beloved children.

in Leo – Magical Moments

As a child, you didn't fit in. Often lost in your inner world, you made mistakes in class. Worse in the eyes of your peers, you were not up to date on appropriate cliques, favorites, and gossips. Being an outcast bothered you somewhat, but your vivid imaginations often took you away anyway. In your teens, you got an opportunity to try acting and quickly found your niche. You moved the audience to tears and laughter equally well. In an amazingly short period of time, you were among the most admired actresses in French theater. Young men and women who had snubbed you just a few years before were now eager to claim life-long friendship. You didn't hold grudges, having no time for such nonsense, as you were consumed by your craft. Becoming a new character, inside-out, was enthralling but demanding work. You took great satisfaction in your ability to lift people out of their ordinary lives and allow them to visit a magical world for a couple hours. When you found a fellow actor to share love, your cup of happiness overflowed even more.

in Virgo – Optimizing Oddities

A slight and sickly child, you were over protected by anxious parents who feared you would die. As a result, other children saw you as alien and to be avoided. Your buried yourself in books and your imagination. As you matured, your body strengthened. You wanted to become a writer and tried novels, essays, and poetry with no success. At length, you decided to capitalize on your "oddities" rather than trying to minimize them (still seeking acceptance). You wrote some imaginative children's books about a magical land with colorful whimsical characters (all of whom were odd in one way or another). Your books became best-sellers. People clamored for more. You created a series and had the ultimate satisfaction of reading them, with your beloved wife, to your own son.

in Libra – A Model Year

You were an awkward child—gawky and tall, often tripping over your own big feet. Freckled, you somewhat resembled a spaniel. Slow to develop, you were still flat and scrawny while other girls had definite curves. Although you had one very dear friend, most of the other girls made fun of your looks and the boys called you scarecrow behind your back. Discovering you in tears one day, your mother sent you away for one year, assuring your that you would blossom. She sent you to visit your uncle in Paris who had just had a big break as a designer. He was delighted to have you visit, telling you that you had "great bones" and were tall enough to model. Some of his friends taught you make-up and how to walk. You did model in his fall show. His whole fall line, and you, were a great success. You could have returned to your home town in dazzling triumph, but elected to continue a modeling career for a time, and to learn enough about design to try your hand at that when you were "too old" to model. You had indeed left behind the ugly duckling and become the swan, just as your mother had promised.

in Scorpio – Generating Goodness

Scandals swirled in your village of birth. Destructive gossip would result in people being ostracized for a time, until the next victims took their places. You felt such pain and cruelty was pointless and spoke out against the process—only to suffer long-term "invisibility" for daring to attack a favored form of recreation. Disillusioned, you left your village for the city. Beginning with church work, you eventually found employment writing tracts designed to show sinners the errors of their ways and to inspire waverers to stay on the straight and narrow path. Rather than creating more moralistic diatribes against evil, you told stories. You wrote tales clearly illustrating the damage done by gossip, by lies, by laziness. Your parables were a rousing success and compared to Aesop's Fables. You delighted in helping to promote good in the world.

in Sagittarius – Pleasant and Peaceful

Raised in Puritan traditions, you followed a rather narrow creed as it was what you were taught. When some Quakers wanted to settle nearby, the elders among you were up in arms. Such a heathen sect should not be allowed to "pollute" the area near you. "They should be driven out!" was one of the cries. When you saw Quakers on the street, you fully expected them to have horns like the devil. A chance rainstorm found you sheltering with a Quaker girl (Jane) about your age. Bored, you fell into conversation. To your surprise, she seemed perfectly normal, even very nice. You became friends. After a time, your friendship came to the attention of the powers that be, and they demanded you stop associating with Jane. In fear and trembling, you refused to give up your friend. You were not struck by lightning, but you were ostracized by many in the Puritan community. Fortunately, the Quakers were not so exclusionary. They gladly opened their homes and hearts to you. In the end, you married a Quaker man and found much happiness in a creed of openness and tolerance.

in Capricorn – Narrow Notions

Your parents believed there were two choices in life: their way and the wrong way. Naturally you were expected to follow their way at all times. They structured your life and left little room for variance. Believing the discipline would be good for you, they sent you away to school, choosing one they were convinced would continue their work of molding you into a respectable young lady. In school, however, you discovered a wider world. Although most of the teachers were colorless individuals, they were individuals. And each student was unique. You got to observe many unusual people in the village were the school was located. These experiences put you in touch with your own inner self. You discovered that you actually had opinions which differed from your parents. Careful consideration led you to be circumspect in regard to your new discoveries. You learned how to pursue you interests and curiosities (including reading forbidden books) while appearing obedient on the surface. You mastered the art of preserving your independence within the structure your parents demanded. Deception was not pleasant, but the alternatives were worse. You got to know a very dear friend at school and you each determined that, if you could not find husbands who would allow a modicum of freedom, you would hold firm to spinsterhood. As "hopeless" spinsters, you expected to be able to set up a household together by your late twenties and be free to pursue your true interests and studies. You were fortunate to find an open-minded gentleman interested in marriage, so had love and kept your dearest female friend as well.

in Aquarius – Toward Tolerance

When you were young, you were impatient. Injustices enraged you and you would fight fiercely to right the slightest of wrongs. Although your parents had a strong desire to reform society, you thought they were much too conservative. They were willing for change to come at a snail's pace, and you couldn't wait! As a youth, you fell in with various lost causes and fought in a few wars of independence. With maturity, you realized that life has many shades of gray. You came back and made peace with your aging parents. You began work together to open up the political process. Whenever possible, you spoke with groups of people, attempting to sway them. You felt that group action was the most effective, and wanted everyone to understand the need for tolerance and equal access. You took great joy in each progressive measure which passed.

in Pisces – Philosophical Forays

As a child, you were taught to defer to adults. As a young woman, you were taught to defer to men. The more you suppressed yourself and did what everyone else wanted, the sicker you got. One day, a friend asked you what you wanted in your life. Your mind went completely blank. That shocked you, so you decided to do some inner work. Since you had lots of time while recuperating in bed, you began reading philosophy. You started asking yourself questions and examining your feelings on a wide variety of topics. As you began getting some answers, you were less willing to be as accommodating to others. You remained tactful, but sometimes did what YOU wanted rather than what other people wanted. You began to build back your health. You stopped succumbing to every cold or infection around. Eager to maintain your health, you learned to stand up for your individuality, to protect your rights (as well as other people's). Life became an exciting adventure and the possibilities open to you multiplied.

Saturn in 12th House

in Aries – Secret Solitude

Although your people were very kind and gregarious, you never felt quite comfortable. Inhabitants of the islands were quite sociable. Since food gathering and preparation was relatively easy, much time was available for discussions and play. You were drawn toward silence. From an early age, you took long walks to the center of the island. You sought out secret pools where you would swim and meditate. The more time you spent alone, the closer you felt to God. Finally, you decided to withdraw completely. You chose a site far away from everyone. Fishing was good all around the island, and you had breadfruit and coconuts available. Mystical experiences became commonplace for you. The solitary lifestyle was exactly what you needed to deepen your spiritual life.

in Taurus – Budding Botanist

Shy as a child, you spent much time outdoors, away from people. With ready access to the woods and meadows, you educated yourself about different trees, flowers, shrubs, and herbs. Pursuing an interest in botany, you also developed talent for sketching, and rendered quite lovely charcoal drawings of much of the plant life which you observed. It was not difficult to convince your parents that your nerves precluded any city life. You were able to stay in the country, leading a life full of contemplation and quietude. An introduction by mail led you to correspond with one of the botanical writers of the day. He was ecstatic over your precise but beautiful drawings and persuaded you to create the illustrations for his next book. Thus was born a long-standing collaboration. Between your work, your reading, your time with nature, and your meditative moments, you had exactly the life you wanted.

in Gemini – God's Gift

After a fairly ordinary childhood, you felt a spiritual pull and knew that your life path lay with God. You investigated a number of different monasteries before choosing an isolated sanctuary where vows of silence were taken. The experience of quiet was particularly moving for you. Your senses deepened when chatter was eliminated from your life. You found other channels of communication opened up when the verbal was eliminated. You were amazed to discover "other" senses seemingly developing out of nowhere. You could sense people's emotions. You could sense presences around you—visible and invisible. Your precognitive abilities increased. Most important of all, your still inner voice was much easier to hear without the distraction of conversation. You rejoiced in your closeness to God.

in Cancer – Capital Cook

Born in the West, you learned to love the land. Your coordination just couldn't manage getting a lasso around a steer, or riding herd on a bunch of cattle. So, you learned to cook. As an excellent chef, your services were in demand. Cowboys and ranch hands ate a lot, and being well fed was expected. You could also manage well with a chuck wagon on long cattle drives. Your famous, flaky biscuits could be created even on the trail. Ranch people felt like family to you. There was a sense of acceptance among them that touched you deeply. You also realized you had to be in the country. You needed to be able to see the stars at night, feel the breezes, and walk among the sage brush. Prayer came easily to you when you were out in the desert, and your almost mystical connection to the land soothed you. With good comrades, a skill which brought appreciation and recognition, and a spiritual life which filled your soul, your life was rich.

in Leo – Holy Healing

Your persuasive skills were considerable, even when you were quite young. If you believed in something, you had a knack for convincing others it was a wonderful idea. As you grew older, your thoughts turned toward religion. You became swept into a charismatic sect. Ritual and drama were prominent within the practices. As you became involved, you discovered you had healing talent. You became a traveling preacher, holding revivals and faith healings in large tents. Although your talent was not infallible, you did change people's lives. You gloried in doing God's work and felt incredibly fortunate that your life was full of excitement, travel, and the ability to assist others. When you met and married a woman who was also very religiously oriented, your life moved to a new high.

in Virgo – Religious Rewards

From an early age, you knew that your life would follow a different path. You had no interest in the games of most children. You were fascinated by books and eager to absorb knowledge. Almost unsociable, you drew instinctively into yourself, with a rich imagination, and avoided relationships with others. Your scholastic ambitions helped to earn you a position within an order dedicated to contemplation and research. You found the monastic life extremely rewarding. Celibacy was very easy for you as long as you were away from the world of women. You happily spent hours poring over original sources in the library and tracing histories. Your rare conversations with other brothers usually centered around some fine point of religious dogma. Very attuned to music, you were deeply moved by the choir and chanting which were a significant part of your life. Being removed from the world was a wonderful thing in your eyes. You could dedicate all your time to God's glory, your music and scholarly investigations, and letting your imagination roam free.

in Libra – Private Poetry

You were quite shy as a child, but your parents did not force you to interact with the outer world. Spending many happy hours in your imagination, you traveled to magical places and experimented with imagery. Your dreams were rich with imagery and metaphors. As you grew, you became fascinated by language. English fascinated you with its multiple words for similar concepts and its alliterative qualities. Soon, you were writing poetry. Preferring your reclusive lifestyle, you avoided the public, even when your poems earned a degree of recognition. Your home was your sanctuary and shutting most of the world out allowed you to be immensely creative. Your poems were full of spiritual concepts as well as imagery from nature. Poetry was your major channel to God.

in Scorpio – Reverence and Respect

Your mother was quite knowledgeable about herbs and taught you all she knew. You maintained an extensive supply of medicaments, growing many items to insure a reserve. The still room (where potions were mixed and poisons were kept) was your private domain. No one else had a key. You also inherited a large notebook from your mother. The women of your household had kept notes, for many years, regarding the uses of various items in different circumstances. They hoped, through the notebook, to be able to identify patterns, and to increase the efficacy of their cures. You carried on that tradition and accumulated other resources as well. You began to track down occult tomes, uncovering old traditions which had been forgotten. You delved deeply into ancient mysteries—any source which might help you to save a life! Your were highly respected and revered for the healing assistance you provided to many.

in Sagittarius – Solitary Seeking

Questions haunted you from a young age. You wanted to know the meaning of life. You wanted to understand how everything began and how it all functioned. Your parents did their best to answer your queries, but many of the issues you brought up were far beyond the capabilities of your mother and father. You turned to books, reading a myriad of authors in a vast array of topics. You became most drawn toward philosophy and metaphysics. Determining that you learned best when away from worldly distractions, you built a small home near a pond. It was simple and rustic, but enabled you to focus entirely on your seeking. Occasionally like-minded friends would visit for significant philosophical exchanges. Mostly, you wrote and studied; thought and imagined, putting your focus on seeking ultimate meaning. You felt connected to God through Nature, but yearned for a deeper, broader understanding than you had achieved as yet. The quest for vastly satisfying; you knew this was the only path for you.

in Capricorn – Profitable Parables

Very close to your grandfather, you loved sitting on his knee and listening to him tell stories. Most of his stories were based on the New Testament. He would tell you tales of Jesus and the Apostles and of Mary, but he made them richer and more interesting. He told you what food was probably eaten at The Last Supper. He described the clothes that Mary might have worn. He brought religious history alive for you. When you were older, you decided that putting religious stories into form was the career you wanted to pursue. You consulted with experts and arranged funding, then launched a company which produced books about The Bible. In those books, people could see sketches of The Holy Land. They could read about clothing, houses, foods, and other daily details about Biblical figures. The series proved very successful and you were pleased have a remembrance of your beloved grandfather and to be earning a good living from doing the work of the Lord.

in Aquarius – Teaching Tolerance

Brought up in a gentle and loving home, you were quite an idealist. Married to your best friend, you spent some time organizing your household and bringing grace and beauty into your home. Through one of your maids, you discovered the terrible treatment under which many immigrants suffered. Discrimination was widespread. Unemployment was a real problem and physical abuse also occurred. You resolved to work for tolerance. You became active in several civic organizations. You arranged for women's groups to hear people speak on the topic of immigration and the equality of mankind. You spoke out at parties when people made ethnic slurs. Although you could not change the world, you had a definite impact in your community. Friends admitted to you that they had not really thought about their behavior until you brought it to their attention. They became more open-minded and willing to extend a helping hand. Your volunteer work, along with your happy marriage and children, gave your life meaning and purpose.

in Pisces – Christian Charity

A very sensitive child, you were deeply moved by the story of Jesus. You resolved to live your life upon Christ's principles. You did your best to return good for evil. Naturally there were times when irritation or frustration or fear overcame your good intentions, but you were largely successful. Living rather retired from most of the world, your life included much time with nature and much meditation. You also embroidered beautifully, bringing more loveliness into the world. Marrying late in life, you accepted a husband who was also quite idealistic. Although you were too old to have children, you provided nurturing to children in a nearby village who lacked it in their homes. Your circle of influence was relatively small, but your impact was great. Your example was noted by others and was an inspiration to all to practice love in their lives.

CHAPTER THIRTEEN
EMOTIONAL RESIDUES FROM PAST LIVES

Several parts of the horoscope point to emotional residues from past lives which are still significant in our current functioning. The first major keys are the Nodes of the Moon—two sensitive points in the horoscope[1].

The two Nodes are always directly opposite one another (180 degrees apart)—across the zodiac. As such, they define important polarities in our lives: present lives **and** past lives. Relating back to the Moon, the Nodes symbolize strong emotions. They are keys particularly to emotional residues which we have carried forward from past lifetimes. They point to ingrained patterns which we tend to repeat over and over again. Old insecurities are depicted here—ways in which we seek safety and try to protect ourselves and others. Relationship issues are often prominent. People who "push our emotional buttons" often have Nodal connections between our horoscope and theirs.

There are three major paths people take in coping with the emotional residues of the Nodes. Most of use try the first two paths before discovering the third.

Path One: some people experience the Nodes as a **seesaw**: they swing from one extreme to the other. For example, with the Nodes across Aries/Libra, some people vacillate between being alone and being together. They get lonely, want a relationship and get involved. Once they're involved, they start to feel trapped, hemmed in, and eventually leave. Then they start to get lonely again, and repeat

---

1The Nodes are defined by the intersections of the Moon's orbit and the Earth's orbit. The North Node's position is based on the Moon moving into north declination (above the celestial equator) while the South Node's position is based on the Moon moving into south declination (below the celestial equator).

the cycle. Typically, people with each Nodal polarity have had some past lifetimes living out one extreme and other lifetimes living out the opposite extreme.

Path Two: some people identify with one Node and "project" the other Node. That is, they are unconsciously attracted to people who will live out the qualities symbolized by that opposite Node. The problem is, if we express only one side of a polarity, the people we attract are likely to express the opposite in excess. They will overdo it! With the Aries/Libra example, if an individual identifies with the Libra end ("I want a relationship"), s/he may repeatedly attract "free souls" who won't commit, married people who aren't available, or self-centered individuals unwilling to make the comprises necessary in a healthy relationship. One person is overdoing the Libra need for an "other;" the other person is overdoing the Aries need for self-assertion and personal freedom. Conversely, the individual who identifies only with the Aries Node wants to live life on his/her own terms, be independent, and keeps on attracting people who want to marry, settle down, be together, share everything (overdoing the Libra).

Path Three: people find the happy medium between the Nodal polarities. They realize that life is an "and" not an "or" and fit the drives of both Nodes into their lives. They turn potential enemies into allies by not going to either extreme. They face their inner insecurities (including those from experiences in past lifetimes) and muster the emotional courage to reach a constructive balance point. By bringing together the best of both sides, they are more effective and more emotionally poised. A positive equilibrium is reached.

The Nodes are considered important keys to where we've been and where we are going. They indicate issues we are learning to balance—polarities we've faced in the past and have the opportunity to integrate in this lifetime. The polarities defined by the Nodes relate to the houses and signs they occupy. For most people, two polarities are involved: one relating to the two signs occupied by the North and South Nodes; the other relating to the two houses occupied by the North and South Nodes. In some cases, the house and sign polarities relate to the same letters of the astrological alphabet. That is a repeated theme, indicated those emotional residues are particularly strong and deeply rooted for the individual involved.

The house positions of the Nodes depend on the place and time of birth, so we can only provide house positions if you order the free horoscope in the back of the book. Sign positions can be figured from the table on page 237.

Here's a look at what the horoscope positions of the Nodes reveal about past lifetimes.

Assertion Vs. Accommodation
(NODES ACROSS 1ST/7TH HOUSES AND/OR ACROSS ARIES/LIBRA)

You have been working on the balance between self and other over many lifetimes. In some lives, you were too intent upon getting your way and resisted compromises. You were quite fierce in your independence. In other lives, you were too needy and other-directed. You gave your power over to the hands of a partner who used and abused it. You could have been the victim of physical violence. Your needs were disregarded; your partner demanded everything. In some lives, you went in and out of relationships. You avoided commitment and emphasized independence until you got lonely and rushed into a relationship. Then you felt trapped, stifled and confined and had to get out. So, you ran away—or fought with your partner til one or the other of you gave up and left. Then you stayed alone for a time, until the need to share again became overwhelming and the cycle repeated. Questions of assertion versus accommodation; how much to please yourself and how much to please and appease others, permeated your associations. You couldn't make up your mind whether it was better to be alone or be together with someone.

Your karmic challenge is to reach a balance between separation and togetherness. You are learning to meet your own needs **within** the framework of a relationship. You are mastering the art of compromise—neither demanding nor giving up too much. Your growth goal is to maintain a long-term committed relationship which feeds the independence, courage, and self-direction of both you and your partner.

North Node Positions 1930 - 2000
(South Node opposite)

1930	Jul	7	16:01 pm	Aries		1970	Nov	2	8:12 am	Aquarius
1931	Dec	28	5:15 am	Pisces		1972	Apr	27	8:04 am	Capricorn
1933	Jun	24	4:36 pm	Aquarius		1973	Oct	27	1:60 am	Sagittarius
1935	Mar	8	5:40 pm	Capricorn		1975	Jul	10	1:22 am	Scorpio
1936	Sep	14	6:29 am	Sagittarius		1977	Jan	7	6:07 pm	Libra
1938	Mar	3	11:17 pm	Scorpio		1978	Jul	5	10:42 am	Virgo
1939	Sep	11	10:47 pm	Libra		1980	Jan	5	3:52 pm	Leo
1941	May	24	7:47 am	Virgo				7	2:25 am	Virgo
1942	Nov	21	5:55 am	Leo				12	6:30 pm	Leo
1944	May	11	2:36 pm	Cancer		1981	Sep	20	6:47 am	Cancer
1945	Dec	2	6:33 pm	Gemini				21	10:24 am	Leo
1947	Aug	2	10:23 am	Taurus				24	5:59 am	Cancer
1949	Jan	25	11:37 pm	Aries		1983	Mar	16	2:06 am	Gemini
1950	Jul	26	8:56 pm	Pisces		1984	Sep	11	5:03 pm	Taurus
1952	Mar	28	10:45 am	Aquarius		1986	Apr	6	5:29 am	Aries
1953	Oct	9	4:29 am	Capricorn			May	5	11:04 pm	Taurus
1955	Apr	2	11:12 pm	Sagittarius				8	5:34 pm	Aries
1956	Oct	4	9:37 am	Scorpio		1987	Dec	2	5:07 am	Pisces
1958	Jun	16	11:44 am	Libra		1989	May	22	11:56 am	Aquarius
1959	Dec	15	5:37 pm	Virgo		1990	Nov	18	7:23 pm	Capricorn
1961	Jun	10	8:08 pm	Leo		1992	Aug	1	10:10 pm	Sagittarius
1962	Dec	23	3:32 am	Cancer		1994	Feb	1	9:09 am	Scorpio
1964	Aug	25	10:23 am	Gemini		1995	Jul	31	12:37 pm	Libra
1966	Feb	19	4:41 pm	Taurus		1997	Jan	25	0:50 am	Virgo
1967	Aug	19	5:23 pm	Aries		1998	Oct	20	5:52 am	Leo
1969	Apr	19	6:54 am	Pisces		2000	Apr	9	0:09 am	Cancer

Mine Vs. Ours

(NODES ACROSS 2ND/8TH HOUSES AND/OR TAURUS/SCORPIO)

You have been working on the balance between self-indulgence and self-control over many lifetimes. In some lives, you pursued a policy of "eat, drink and be merry" to excess. In others, you were quite self-denying—perhaps to the point of asceticism. Feast versus famine over food, alcohol, sex, etc., was possible. You swung between lives as a philanthropist and a miser; a playboy and a celibate; a hedonist and a Calvinist. In some lifetimes, you provided total financial and material support for a partner; in others, you were totally dependent. In some lifetimes, you lost all your possessions to flood, hurricane, tornado, volcano, or other natural disaster. You went from rags to riches to rags more than once.

Power became an issue with sexual expression in some lifetimes—in your favor at times and to use and abuse you in other instances. Questions of who earns the resources; who owns the possessions; and who enjoys what in bed abounded in your relationships. In some circumstances, you sought comfort, ease, and an unchanging familiarity. In other lives, you constantly probed, looked deeper, sought out complications, dug up secrets, disclosed unpleasantness, and confronted the dark side of yourself and those around you.

Your karmic challenge is to reach a balance between comfort and confrontation—to know when to relax and enjoy and when to face the not-so-nice side of life. You are learning to give, receive, and share pleasures, possessions, money, and sexuality with another human being. You are learning to alternate supporting and being supported in a comfortable exchange. Your growth goal is to be able to enjoy the physical, sensual world — without being consumed by it or worrying endlessly about losing it—and to maintain an intimate connection which brings great satisfaction and mutual pleasure to you both.

Information Vs. Wisdom

(NODES ACROSS 3RD/9TH HOUSES AND/OR ACROSS GEMINI/SAGITTARIUS)

You have been working on the balance between knowledge and wisdom over many lifetimes. In some lifetimes, you were intent on picking up tons of trivia, every bit of information you could absorb. In other lives, you were totally focused on pursuing Ultimate Truth—often through a religious vocation. You swung back and forth over several lives between believing that constant activity and learning in the near environment would satisfy your curiosity versus a drive to explore, adventure, wander the world, convinced that real meaning lies over the next hill. You alternated between lives devoted to a great, overwhelming vision and lives enmeshed in tiny bits of information. You spent numerous lifetimes as a teacher, a student, a bard, a teller of tales, a traveler, and a seeker. You were often torn between science and religion, between an intellectual and emotional pursuit of the truth. Questions of faith and belief (or lack of) in a Higher Power were quite significant.

Your karmic challenge is to reach a balance between the big, inspiring vision and the everyday details which make it possible. You are learning to identify your faith (while keeping it open to further revision), to be able to communicate it clearly to the people around you, and to live it in everyday, mundane life. You are likely to continue the roles (officially or unofficially) of student and teacher; gathering information and insight is a way of life for you. Your goal is to constantly expand your mental and physical horizons in ways which further your life's Highest Purpose.

Dominance Vs. Dependency
(NODES ACROSS 4TH/10TH HOUSES AND/OR CANCER/CAPRICORN)

You have been working on the balance between the mother and father archetypes over many lifetimes. In some lives, you were too supportive, endlessly protective, nurturing, and nourishing. The end result was that you felt drained and consumed, because no one took care of you. In other lives, you were focused on performance, on doing the right thing. Then you ended up exhausted and overworked because you took on too much responsibility. At times, you were the cherished, overprotected child who had to struggle to develop strength and independence. At other times, you were the restricted, dominated, criticized child—overburdened with rules and regulations who felt unloved (and sometimes unlovable) due to the harsh upbringing. Your parents, across many, many lives, had a hard time getting a good balance between conditional and unconditional love. In several lifetimes, you faced choices between devoting yourself to your family versus committing yourself to vocational ambitions. Sometimes you chose family over career; other times you choose outer-world success over family. Issues of abandonment, responsibility, and protection came up often.

Your karmic challenge is to reach a balance between dominance and dependency. You are learning how to have a close, emotional connection and significant home life along with making a sincere contribution to the world. You are reaching a compromise between your internal mother and father. Your growth goal is to be able to be vulnerable and dependent when appropriate, able to connect to others and receive their support; to be the strong, in-control expert when called for; and to be the nurturing protector when needed.

Being Special Vs. Being Equal
(NODES ACROSS 5TH/11TH HOUSES AND/OR LEO/AQUARIUS)

You have been working on the balance between head and heart over many lifetimes. In some lives, you chose to pursue an intellectual life—focused on logic, reason, and an interest in developing technology. In other lives, you chose to focus on love affairs, children, or matters of romance and excitement. In some lives, you wanted desperately to have children, but were unable—or you lost your life in childbirth or lost many children to death and disease. Some karmic residues of fear around children and childbirth may yet remain. During some lifetimes, you felt constant tension between the time and energy you devoted to loved ones versus the time and energy you devoted to friends, humanitarian causes, and an interest in the future. Often, you delayed long-term commitments to marriage and children because you did not want to give up your freedom and independence to pursue unusual interests..

Your karmic challenge is to achieve a balance between passion and detachment; between freedom and closeness; between loved ones and transpersonal concerns. You are learning to love with an open hand, to turn family into friends (open, tolerant) and friends into family. You are mastering the art of passionate detachment, intellectual passion, and loving logic. Your growth goal is to maintain a committed relationship and creative outlet(s) along with individualistic pursuits and interests which expose you to the wider world.

Inspiration Vs. Perspiration
(Nodes Across 6th/12th Houses and/or Virgo/Pisces)

You have been working on the balance between idealism and realism over many lifetimes. In some lives, you focused entirely on the role of idealist—pursuing dreams; living a religious vocation; creating art, etc. In other lives, you focused entirely on the role of realist—concerned with what you could see, hear, touch, and measure. You spent some lifetimes in meditation, in a convent, ashram, or monastery. You spent other lifetimes absorbed in the world of business, medicine, craftsmanship, or construction. At times, you swung between global, intuitive, metaphorical thinking and linear, step-by-step, detail-oriented thinking. Some lifetimes were full of "cosmic discontent" because no matter how much your pursued your dream of infinite love and beauty, your physical approximations fell short of your vision. (The sculpture, painting or other art form was not identical to what you saw in your imagination. Your healing efforts could not save the whole world.) Other lifetimes, you gave up and didn't try: "If I can't do it perfectly, I won't do it at all." You also vacillated between a naive faith and trust and great cynicism and criticism. You were unsure whether God's grace came through trust and faith or through concerted effort and good works.

Your karmic challenge is to reach a balance between dreams and reality, to make your visions tangible. You are learning to have artistic or idealistic goals and to identify the steps necessary to attain each goal. You are mastering the art of enjoying life as a process. You can move toward perfection without expecting to ever arrive. Your growth goal is to bring more beauty, healing, caring, compassion, or inspiration into the world in ways that affect people's lives for the better.

Stellia

Another major focus in the horoscope is indicated by a stellium: three or more planets occupying one sign or three or more planets in one house. Significant issues, ingrained from "practice" in prior lives are revealed by stellia (plural of stellium) in your horoscope. Stellia point to concerns, feelings, reactions, and drives with which we have dealt before. A stellium also points to potential talents as it pinpoints areas where we've had practice and opportunity to hone our skills.

A stellium is one way a horoscope repeats a theme. With a stellium, a horoscope is saying —three or more times— "This sign (or this house) is important." Using the astrological alphabet, it is possible to spot other repeated themes in a horoscope. Themes which are reiterated by astrology also indicate areas of focus and concern in past lives (as well as potential abilities for this one). The next section looks at what stellia and themes reveal in regard to past lifetimes.

Self-Definitions
(THREE OR MORE PLANETS IN 1ST HOUSE OR IN ARIES)

Gaining clarity about assertion and who you are is essential. In some past lives, you experienced people trying to obliterate you. Your physical existence, personal integrity, or sense of identity may have been at risk. In some, you pushed too hard at the world. You are working on a clear, strong sense of self and understanding your personal rights, needs and desires in balance with the rights of others. Constructive handling of anger will help. The further you progress, the more energy you will feel.

Pleasure Principle
(THREE OR MORE PLANETS IN 2ND HOUSE OR IN TAURUS)

Attaining moderate pleasures is part of your karmic quest. In some past lives, you felt deprived and denied in regard to sensual pleasures—and could have suffered greatly. In some, you overindulged. You are learning to enjoy the senses: eating, drinking, making love, creating beauty, etc.—without being ruled by them. A balanced approach to material security, comfort, and pleasure is indicated. The further you progress, the more you will enjoy life.

Masterful Mind
(THREE OF MORE PLANETS IN 3RD HOUSE OR IN GEMINI)

Enjoying the world of the mind is a central karmic issue. In some past lives, you were totally scattered in your seeking of knowledge. In others, you made major contributions through your thinking, communication, or handling of information. Flexibility, dexterity, and multiple talents are highlighted. Your challenge is to be open to information from all sources, while sufficiently focused to achieve in a few areas. The further your progress, the more you will laugh and learn.

Home & Hearth
(THREE OR MORE PLANETS IN 4TH HOUSE OR IN CANCER)

Issues of dependency and nurturing are karmic for you. In some past lives, you were too needy, too vulnerable, too dependent upon others. In other lives, you were a super parent: protective, nourishing, supportive, and sometimes doing too much. Warmth and caring have been keynote themes for you. Your challenge is to create a balance between caring for others and allowing them to care for you, between leaning and being leaned upon. The further you progress, the more emotionally secure you will feel.

Vibrant & Vital
(THREE OR MORE PLANETS IN 5TH HOUSE OR IN LEO)

Issues of ego, self-esteem, recognition and applause are your karmic focus. In some past lives, you had a royal, special attitude, believing yourself a superior being. In other lives, you were miserably self-conscious, insecure, and vulnerable to the opinions of others. You desperately wanted people to love and admire you. In some lives, you had a healthy sense of self-esteem, expressed your creativity, and gained positive regard and attention for your talents. That is your goal for this life. The further you progress, the more charismatic, magnetic, and vibrant you will become.

Competent Capability
(THREE OR MORE PLANETS IN 6TH HOUSE OR IN VIRGO)

Practicality, health, and common sense are highlighted as karmic issues. In the past, you have been too hard on yourself or on others—seeking flaws, looking for what needed to be fixed. In a few lives, you did not take care of yourself physically and faced health challenges. In some lifetimes, you were overworked, underpaid, and labored long and hard—over invested in being of service. You are learning in this lifetime to direct your efficiency instincts toward your health habits and your job: to analyze and nit-pick work routines, but not people. The further you progress, the more capable, efficient, and healthy you will become.

Balanced Bonds
(THREE OR MORE PLANETS IN 7TH HOUSE OR IN LIBRA)

Balance, equality, fair play and sharing are among your karmic issues. In a few lives, you gave too much importance to appearances. In other lives, you fought hard for justice and equality. In some past lives, maintaining a committed relationship was quite a challenge; you felt torn between personal and interpersonal needs (your wants and needs versus your partner's). Beauty, grace, and aesthetics were often an important part of your lives. This time around, you are learning to maintain a significant partnership, keep beauty an important part of your daily life, and model for other people the ability to share and take turns.

The further you progress, the more balanced, attractive, and bonded with another you will become.

Inner Insight
(THREE OR MORE PLANETS IN 8TH HOUSE OR IN SCORPIO)

Issues of obsession, compulsion, emotional intensity, challenges, confrontation, and deep, transformational growth abound among your karmic past. In some lives, you dealt with addictions—sometimes mastering them and sometimes not. Most of your past lives have included an element of intensity; you thrive on emotional experiences and learn most fully when dealing with issues of power. Life-and-death issues have been a focus more than once. Sharing sex, resources, finances, and pleasures has often been challenging. Your current growth goal is to explore your inner depths and be able to give, receive, and share the sensual and material world with another person. The further you progress, the stronger you will become, and the deeper levels of intimacy and self-insight you will reach.

Wider World
(THREE OR MORE PLANETS IN 9TH HOUSE OR IN SAGITTARIUS)

Questions of faith, truth, meaning, and morality abound in your past. Many of your lives have involved a quest—a seeking of answers. You have had times of total doubt in a Higher Power and times of total trust. You have idealized many different areas. Restlessness has been a challenge. Occasionally, you succumbed to intellectual arrogance or unwillingness to commit. Often, you were concerned with justice, ethical principles, and philosophy, religion, metaphysics or any system which offered a sense of meaning. In this lifetime, you learning to identify clear goals, firm yet flexible principles, and a world view which offers hope, inspiration and enough openness to be able to change at any time. The further you progress, the more optimistic, fun-loving, and trusting you will feel.

Defining Duties
(THREE OR MORE PLANETS IN 10TH HOUSE OR IN CAPRICORN)

You have dealt strongly in your karmic past with issues of structure, control, authority, limits, and rules. At times, you have been restricted, inhibited, and beaten down by life and authority figures. In other lives, you have been the power figure, the expert, the responsible individual. Realism was often highlighted. Learning what you can do, cannot do, and must do has been a challenge. In this lifetime, your focus is to own your own strength and power and to do what is necessary and essential on a practical level. You also need to identify unnecessary duties and "obligations" and say "No" to them. The further you progress, the stronger, safer, more capable and achieving you will become.

True Tolerance
(THREE OR MORE PLANETS IN 11TH HOUSE OR IN AQUARIUS)

Your karmic issues revolve around individuality, freedom, tolerance, and the new. In some past lives, you have carried the role of rebel too far. At times, you pushed too hard for the new, the different, the unusual, the unconventional. You may have taken excessive risks. In a few lives, freedom became an absolute and other essential human qualities were lost. Occasionally, you suppressed your different qualities and tried to fit in to no avail. In this lifetime, you are learning to own your inventive, innovative side, to use your feeling for the future wisely. The further you progress, the freer, more open, more excited you will feel.

Ecstatic Escapes
(THREE OR MORE PLANETS IN 12TH HOUSE OR IN PISCES)

Issues of compassion, sensitivity, Union, beauty, and escapism lurk in your karmic past. In some lives, you were a consummate artist, bringing beauty to the world. In many lives, you helped or healed others. In a few lives, you ran away from reality—through drugs, alcohol, fantasy or other imaginative by-ways. You sought a sense of God, of inspiration, of cosmic consciousness in most of your lives. You tried to open yourself psychically, intuitively. In this lifetime, you are learning when and where it is safe to be a channel to the Universe—and when and where to protect yourself and your sensitivities. The further you progress, the more inspired, uplifted, and connected to the Source you will feel.

Repeated Themes in the Horoscope

Freedom
(STRONG ASPECTS TO MARS, JUPITER, URANUS, CHIRON; SEVERAL PLANETS IN 1ST, 9TH, 11TH HOUSES; SEVERAL PLANETS IN ARIES, SAGITTARIUS, AQUARIUS)

Maintaining your freedom without disrupting your life has been a challenge. Sometimes you've just run away (literally). Sometimes you've ended up feeling stifled and claustrophobic. Sometimes you've pushed people away, unable to maintain your individuality and relationships as well. Intimacy seemed too threatening. Occasionally, you've forced yourself to follow the structures of others.

Your challenge in this lifetime is to be yourself, to be true to your inner uniqueness and still keep room for significant attachments. Be free **and** caring.

Closeness/Interpersonal
(STRONG ASPECTS TO THE MOON, THE SUN, VENUS, PLUTO, PALLAS, JUNO; SEVERAL PLANETS IN 4TH, 5TH, 7TH, 8TH HOUSES; SEVERAL PLANETS IN CANCER, LEO, LIBRA, SCORPIO)

Handling your emotional attachments has been a challenge. Sometimes you've been "swept away" in relationships and lost yourself. You've been carried away by dependency or a "need to be needed." In the past, you've been too attached, too interconnected. You've sometimes moved past the point of loving care into martyrdom and loss of individuality. Occasionally, you've just retreated from the whole question because it felt like too much!

Your challenge in this lifetime is to create truly caring, mutually supportive interactions with others. You are learning to balance vulnerability and caretaking, to meet people in the middle, forming an equalitarian exchange.

Relationships (One-on-One)

(STRONG ASPECTS TO VENUS, PLUTO, JUNO, PALLAS; SEVERAL PLANETS IN 7TH AND 8TH HOUSES; SEVERAL PLANETS IN LIBRA, SCORPIO)

Committed partnerships have been a challenge. In the past, you've had multiple relationships. You've also had lives when you avoided the whole question, feeling unable to cope. You've retreated into being a hermit or religious celibate on occasion. Sometimes you demanded your relationships be totally on your terms. Other times you gave all your power to the other and became co-dependent. You've evaded commitment, and felt lost without it. Your expectations have been much too high at times. Accepting the human limits and foibles of yourself and your partner is essential.

Your challenge in this lifetime is to establish a significant, caring partnership. You are learning to form a true team: taking turns, sharing with one another, each giving in different areas of strength. You can gain great pleasure from the dance of give-and-take with another human.

Intellectual Stimulation

(STRONG ASPECTS TO MERCURY, JUPITER, URANUS, CHIRON; SEVERAL PLANETS IN 3RD, 6TH, 9TH, 11TH HOUSES; SEVERAL PLANETS IN GEMINI, VIRGO, SAGITTARIUS, AQUARIUS)

The world of the mind has been a strong lure for you in the past. Many times, part of your gift to the world involved your knowledge, insight, and understanding. Yet, you have also led some lives where you scattered your forces, trying to master everything and consequently not accomplishing much of anything. You have sometimes rationalized and intellectualized feelings away. Your curiosity and need to know have often been a driving force.

Your challenge in this lifetime is to feed your mind, without letting it rule your life. You have much to learn, including clear priorities in what is central to your pursuit of truth, and what is just for fun to pick up and drop. You are practicing balance between your head and heart, recognizing that life involves the physical, emotional, and spiritual as well as the mental.

Artistic

(STRONG ASPECTS TO VENUS, NEPTUNE, PALLAS, JUNO; SEVERAL PLANETS IN 2ND, 7TH, 12TH HOUSES; SEVERAL PLANETS IN TAURUS, LIBRA, PISCES)

The world of beauty has been within your grasp many times in the past. In some lives, you did not believe enough in your own skills. In others, you chose a path of family, or earning a living rather than trying to follow your muse. On occasion, you have gloried in the aesthetic and shared your talent with the world.

Your challenge this time around is to incorporate beauty into your daily life. Whether you experience the artistic as a vocation, avocation, or for personal enjoyment is not significant. Appreciating the grandeur of nature, of all the myriad forms of beauty, is essential. Expressing your own abilities is also part of your karmic quest. Believe in your capacity to bring grace into the Earth. Make your world lovelier.

Idealistic

(STRONG ASPECTS TO JUPITER, NEPTUNE, CHIRON; SEVERAL PLANETS IN 9TH AND/OR 12TH; SEVERAL PLANETS IN SAGITTARIUS AND/OR PISCES)

You've been an idealist for a number of lifetimes. Your instinct is to seek the best, to pursue the highest in life. This has led you to many lives which helped to make the world a bit better. It has also led to times of martyrdom, depression, and disillusionment when your dreams were higher than could be achieved. At times, your idealism was well directed: toward art, nature, God, healing activities, and principles for living. At other times, you sought perfection in yourself, your partners, your work, your children, or other areas where human imperfection (and consequent disappointment) was inevitable.

Your challenge in this lifetime is to identify a worthy dream and pursue it. You need goals and visions. You need a sense of inspiration—and to do something to help change the world and leave it a bit better than when you arrived.

Security

(STRONG ASPECTS TO VENUS, MOON, VESTA, CERES, PLUTO, SATURN; LOTS OF PLANETS IN 2ND, 4TH, 6TH, 8TH, 10TH HOUSES; LOTS OF PLANETS IN TAURUS, CANCER, VIRGO, SCORPIO, CAPRICORN)

In the past, you have sometimes held on too long, reluctant to change. Security has felt very important to you. Supporting structures and stability appealed.

Your challenge this time around is to build inner security. This includes a firm faith in the goodness of the universe and a solid trust in your own abilities. Then you can choose to dissipate outer security if necessary. You are not being asked to give up all security, merely to choose wisely. Your growth goal is to know what is vital and deserves to be preserved—and when, as well as knowing what can be released without regrets as you move toward the new.

Risk/Creativity/Change

(STRONG ASPECTS TO MARS, SUN, JUPITER, CHIRON, URANUS; SEVERAL PLANETS IN 1ST, 5TH, 9TH, 11TH HOUSES; SEVERAL PLANETS IN ARIES, LEO, SAGITTARIUS, AQUARIUS)

In the past, you have often been a pioneer. You have broken new ground, taken risks others were unwilling to do. At times, this has resulted in rash behavior, and sometimes the results have been quite uncomfortable. Occasionally, you have been too restless, upsetting structures or moving on before it was really time. Usually, you have been a figure of courage.

Your challenge this time is to continue to model healthy creativity and openness to change. You can teach others to risk, to know when to leave security behind and grasp the future with both hands. You can exemplify choosing wisely, knowing when to build and when to alter and move forward into something new.

Power

(STRONG ASPECTS TO SUN, PLUTO, SATURN; SEVERAL PLANETS IN 5TH, 8TH, 10TH HOUSES; SEVERAL PLANETS IN LEO, SCORPIO, CAPRICORN)

Many of your past lives have highlighted the issue of power, authority and control. Sometimes you have been the authority figure. In those lives, you have often wielded power wisely and well. Occasionally, you have slipped into uncaring or destructive use of power. Sometimes, you have been a victim of power-trippers, unable to claim your own strength.

Your challenge this time around is to first own your own power. Next, you need to find a constructive channel of expression for using it. Sports, games, business, politics, fighting for causes, and other outlets are all appropriate. You need to win, to have an impact, to make a difference in the world.

Transpersonal

(STRONG ASPECTS TO JUPITER, SATURN, URANUS, NEPTUNE, CHIRON; SEVERAL PLANETS IN 9TH, 10TH, 11TH, 12TH HOUSES; SEVERAL PLANETS IN SAGITTARIUS, CAPRICORN, AQUARIUS, PISCES)

In the past, you have been very drawn toward larger issues. You have affected the wider world often. Activity which involves the big scene was central. A few times, you felt overwhelmed by the immensity of your ambitions and did nothing. On occasion, you chose inaction rather than doing something less than "the best" or the "most impressive." Once in a while, you used your concern with the wider world as an escape from personal relationships. Generally, seeing the overview and understanding your place in history and the larger scheme has been vital.

Your challenge this time around is to identify a cause, to choose a path by which you can make a difference in the world. It need not be earth-shaking, but it must resonate with you personally. You must avoid the trap of procrastination because you don't think you can affect anything. Small ripples can have large impact. You are learning to acknowledge and pay homage with your concern for the bigger picture, without neglecting important, loving connections in your life!

Self Versus Other

(1/7 POLARITY: SEVERAL PLANETS IN 1ST AND 7TH HOUSES; SEVERAL PLANETS IN ARIES AND LIBRA; MARS [OR ASCENDANT, OR ANY RULER OF 1ST] SQUARE, OPPOSITE OR QUINCUNX VENUS [OR DESCENDANT OR ANY RULER OF 7TH])

In the past, you've been torn between focusing on personal needs and independence versus focusing on relationships and pleasing others. You may have swung between being lonely and feeling trapped; between separation and too much attachment, between assertion and accommodation. You are learning to compromise, to allow some space in your loving. Karmically, you are working on the balance between self and other: not to give too much to others; not to demand too much for yourself. Be true to yourself and open and willing to cooperate with others. As your balance improves, you feel better about yourself and about your relationships.

Giving & Receiving

(2/8 POLARITY: SEVERAL PLANETS IN THE 2ND AND 8TH HOUSES; SEVERAL PLANETS IN TAURUS AND SCORPIO; VENUS [OR ANY RULER OF THE 2ND] SQUARE, OPPOSITE, OR QUINCUNX PLUTO [OR ANY RULER OF THE 8TH])

In the past, you've had swings involving self-indulgence and self-control. Some lives involved extreme deprivation—starving, sensual denial, celibacy, etc. Other lives were hedonistic. At times, you went from one extreme to the other in handling physical appetites (food, sex, alcohol, etc.). Financial balance may have been challenging as well: spending versus saving or earning your own way versus relying on or providing for someone else. You are learning to enjoy the world of the senses without being consumed by it. The more you can give, receive, and share power, possessions, and pleasures comfortably, the better balance you have achieved.

Near & Far

(3/9 POLARITY: SEVERAL PLANETS IN 3RD AND 9TH HOUSES; SEVERAL PLANETS IN GEMINI AND SAGITTARIUS; MERCURY OR ANY RULER OF 3RD SQUARE, OPPOSITE OR QUINCUNX JUPITER OR ANY RULER OF 9TH)

In the past, you've had lifetimes of wandering, seeking, searching, studying. You've been a perpetual student, teacher, and traveler. With itchy feet and a curious mind, settling down was not easy. You've often felt torn between a desire to gather any and all information and a need to focus on ultimate meanings and Higher Knowledge. In some lives, you were torn between spending time with the people right around you versus wandering to faraway lands and other cultures. Your multiple interests made it easy to scatter. Your challenge at this time is to keep your curiosity about life alive, while having clear priorities about what is most important for you to learn and understand. The more you balance between knowledge and wisdom, the clearer you goals, visions, and beliefs become.

Caring & Career

(4/10 POLARITY: SEVERAL PLANETS IN 4TH AND 10TH HOUSES; SEVERAL PLANETS IN CANCER AND CAPRICORN; MOON, IC, OR ANY RULER OF 4TH SQUARE, OPPOSITE, OR QUINCUNX SATURN, MC, OR ANY RULER OF 10TH)

In the past, you've often been torn between the demands of the outer world (in terms of business, earning a living, coping with reality) and the needs of your family. In some lives, you sacrificed worldly success for those you loved. In other lives, you gave up the possibility of a home and family in order to rise to the top of your position in society. In many, you felt tension between the two realms. Your challenge in this life is to make room for both: a moderately successful contribution to society along with caring connections and a domestic base which helps you feel secure.

Heart & Head

(5/11 POLARITY: SEVERAL PLANETS IN 5TH AND 11TH HOUSES; SEVERAL PLANETS IN LEO AND AQUARIUS; SUN OR ANY RULER OF 5TH SQUARE, OPPOSITE, OR QUINCUNX URANUS OR ANY RULER OF 11TH)

In the past, you sometimes had to choose between your heart and your intellect. Some paths of learning required you give up passionate attachments. Some loving relationships left you insufficient time to inquire, to question, to go further with your mind. You've also swung between feeling exciting, enthralled, and captivated by love, to wanting to break loose, break free, and be on your own. On occasion, you've been forced to choose between having children and being involved in causes to affect the wider world. Your current challenge is to find a middle ground: to be able to love with openness; to guard your own individuality and the uniqueness of children and loved ones; to be able to blend your heart with your head for optimum results.

Parts Vs. Whole

(6/12 POLARITY: SEVERAL PLANETS IN 6TH AND 12TH HOUSES; SEVERAL PLANETS IN VIRGO AND PISCES; MERCURY, CERES, VESTA, OR ANY RULER OF 6TH SQUARE, OPPOSITE, OR QUINCUNX NEPTUNE OR ANY RULER OF 12TH)

In the past, you've reached for the stars. In some lives, you were an inspired artist, a celebrated healer, a compassionate, helpful individual. In some, you were a frustrated idealist—endlessly unhappy because the world did not measure up to your hopes and dreams. In a few, your only visions came through escapist paths—drugs, alcohol, chronic daydreaming, etc. You've worked on the integration of a wholistic viewpoint with nitty, gritty details. You've faced the challenge of blending linear and global approaches. This time around, you are learning to bring your dreams to earth, to do something tangible to make the world a bit better or more beautiful. You can be a practical mystic and a capable idealist.

CHAPTER FOURTEEN
KARMIC DEBTS

This chapter examines your karmic debts according to astrological tradition. Karmic debts refer to obligations you may feel as a result of past actions. Sometimes you find yourself "going that extra mile" for people to whom you are karmically indebted — without knowing why. At times, part of your karmic debt is to know when to **stop** giving. And sometimes people seem compelled to be extra generous to you — presumably paying off old debts of their own. Most debts refer to old, repeated patterns. The idea of "clearing up debts" is to break the cycle—to halt the repetition. By recognizing the past, we can learn to do differently in the future.

Astrologically, placements and aspects to Saturn and the South Node are examined to give insight into area where we have an underlying sense of emotional pressure to give, to overcome, or to carry out a "duty" or "obligation." The South Node appears a bit more "karmic" than the North, in that people often feel extra insecurity, anxiety, or pressure where their South Node is placed. The house positions of Saturn and the South Node are most significant, with aspects also playing a part.

House Placement of Saturn and/or South Node

You Owe Yourself (and Your Body)
(SATURN IN 1ST OR SOUTH NODE IN 1ST)

You have a karmic debt to yourself—to stay alive, to cope, to be clear about what you want in life. You spent too many lifetimes just struggling to survive or sacrificing your desires to other people. Occasionally, you went to the opposite extreme and stepped on the rights of other people. Your challenge is to master "enlightened selfishness:" to put yourself number one without diminishing anyone else; to give yourself healthy priority; to defend your rights and pursue your needs in the world. Your debt requires you learn to be assertive in a balanced fashion.

You Owe Your Capacity to Relax and Be Comfortable
(SATURN IN 2ND OR SOUTH NODE IN 2ND)

You have a karmic debt to your sensuality—to enjoy, to be moderate, to appreciate the material world. You spent too many lifetimes in self-denial, starving the senses, depriving yourself materially, or struggling with poverty. Occasionally, you went to the opposite extreme and overindulged in hedonism or materialism. Your challenge is to master simple pleasures: to enjoy nature, the physical senses, possessions, and money without being owned by them. Believe in your worth—that you deserve to feel good.

You Owe Your Mind (& Perhaps People Near at Hand)
(SATURN IN 3RD: OR SOUTH NODE IN 3RD)

You share a karmic debt with siblings, neighbors, relatives and a debt to your own mental capacities. You spent many lifetimes intertwined with these people and their intellectual abilities affected yours. You may go out of your way for the people around you; be sure it is truly justified. Your challenge is to indulge your curiosity, interest in the world, and need to communicate without being **too** scattered or superficial. You are learning to trust your intellectual and verbal capabilities. It is time to reclaim your own wit and wisdom.

Debts Exist in Parental Associations
(SATURN IN 4TH OR SOUTH NODE IN 4TH)

You share a karmic debt with your parents (nurturing figures). You spent too many lifetimes taking care of them or being overwhelmed by them. It is time to nurture yourself; provide internal security and emotional support. Your challenge is understand when you are to be the nurturer and when you are to lean on others and allow yourself to be vulnerable. An exchange of caretaking is essential. You are learning to become comfortable with emotional closeness and not concerned about control. Allow yourself to feel, to make warm connections with others.

Debts Exist with Loved Ones
(SATURN IN 5TH OR SOUTH NODE IN 5TH)

You share a karmic debt with children, lovers. You spent too many lifetimes working for them, being responsible—or avoiding them. It is time to revitalize your inner child, to rekindle your excitement, zest, enthusiasm, and love of life. Your challenge is to feed your inner creativity while affirming the zest and joy within your loved ones. Building everyone's self-esteem is important. Focus on positives; practice appreciation and be lavish with giving and receiving praise and admiration. Let yourself radiate!

You Owe Your Health (& Perhaps Colleagues)
(SATURN IN 6TH OR SOUTH NODE IN 6TH)

You share a karmic debt with colleagues, coworkers, and a debt to your own personal health. You spent too many lifetimes being of service to others (or avoiding it). You abused or neglected your physical body in some lives. It is time to focus on your well-being, to strengthen your competence, efficiency, practicality, and health. Your challenge is to be practical without excessive nit-picking; to be helpful without carrying the whole load. Paying attention to issues of nutrition, exercise, and relaxation (which affect health) is vital. Notice what you do well and affirm your skill and capability.

Debts Exist in Partnerships
(SATURN IN 7TH OR SOUTH NODE IN 7TH)

You share a karmic debt with your partner(s). You spent too many lifetimes dominating or being dominated by them. You may do too much and easily slip into feeling obligated in your relationship(s). It is time to reach equality, sharing, balance, and the ability to take turns and share responsibilities. Your challenge is to relate to someone who is strong without controlling or being controlled. Making sure you both have tasks and ambitions on which to focus is helpful. Trusting your own capacities is vital. Clarify your true responsibilities and release old emotional baggage. Share efforts and you can establish an enduring relationship in which you both make significant contributions.

Debts Exist in Intimacy
(SATURN IN 8TH OR SOUTH NODE IN 8TH)

You share a karmic debt with your mate and have a therapeutic bent. You spent too many lifetimes involved in power struggles with a significant other—or emotionally intimidated. It is time to share deeply, respect each other's boundaries, release obsessions, and establish a healthy sexual and financial exchange. A focus on self-understanding and transformation is highly appropriate. Your challenge is to take enough—but not too much—responsibility in regard to shared resources, intimacy, obsessions, and work on your own psyche.

Debts Exist in Regard to Seeking Truth
(SATURN IN 9TH OR SOUTH NODE IN 9TH)

You have a karmic debt to your (inner and outer) teachers, spiritual leaders, and personal faith. You spent too many lifetimes in anxious pursuit of faith or self-righteous proclamation of your beliefs. It is time to establish a firm, workable connection to a Higher Power. Your challenge is to avoid the extremes of too much or too little faith and to establish firm values which are testable in the "real world." Education, philosophy, religion, travel, or spiritual quests can help you to create a world view which serve you well this lifetime.

Debts Exist in Parental Associations
(SATURN IN 10TH OR SOUTH NODE IN 10TH)

You share a karmic debt with your parents (authority figures) and owe your inner expert. You spent too many lifetimes being under their thumb, or having to be responsible for them. It is time to do **only** appropriate responsibilities, to be reasonable about what you take on. Your tasks is to avoid the extremes of feeling blocked about everything or falling into a workaholic mode. Being practical and planning ahead for achievement is advisable. Exercising your expertise and making a contribution to society are essential.

Debts Exist with Friends or Groups
(SATURN IN 11TH OR SOUTH NODE IN 11TH)

You share a karmic debt with friends, organizations, and owe your own individuality. You spent too many lifetimes following other people's rules, struggling to be yourself, or rebelling in chaotic, disruptive ways. It is time to be who you are (while still respecting the rights of others and of society). Your challenge is to find individuality within a group; to encourage your own uniqueness while tolerating the foibles and eccentricities of your friends. Objectivity and detachment can be two-edged swords: use enough, but not too much. March to your inner drummer!

You Owe Your Higher Self
(SATURN IN 12TH OR SOUTH NODE IN 12TH)

You have a karmic debt to humanity, nature, the world. You spent too many lifetimes feeling the need to magically make the world better—or running away from a less-than-ideal world. It is time to be moderate in your quest to bring more love, beauty, and inspiration into our universe. You cannot rescue the universe, nor are you supposed to retreat (fantasy, escapism) when life is less than perfect. Your challenge is to bring a dream down to earth: to make an artistic vision manifest or to help and heal the planet. Responsible compassion is your focus.

Aspects to Saturn and the South Node

The aspects used were conjunction (8 degrees), square (6 degrees), opposition (6 degrees), quincunx (3 degrees), and 1 degree for the octile (semi-square) and tri-octile (sesqui-square).

Shine On!
SUN ASPECTS

You are discharging a karmic debt to your child (of this life or an earlier one) by dealing constructively with ego issues, personal pride, self-esteem, prominence, positive attention, recognition, creativity, and leadership potentials.

Sense and Sensibility
MOON ASPECTS

You are working on a karmic obligation to your mother by integrating emotional security needs; keeping a balance between nurturing and dependency; establishing a healthy home base; acknowledging your roots; and accepting your feelings.

Lots of Lore
MERCURY ASPECTS

You're paying off your debt to a sibling (of this life or a previous one) by developing your mind; encouraging communication, flexibility, a light touch; eagerly seeking out new experiences; collecting and disseminating information; and increasing your store of knowledge.

Rapprochement
VENUS ASPECTS

You're meeting your obligation to women or to a particular woman in your life by taking turns in life; supporting equality and fair play; promoting balance, grace and harmony; developing artistic skills; practicing the art of compromise; and enjoying life.

Assertive Acts
MARS ASPECTS

You are discharging a karmic debt to yourself by practicing reasonable self-assertion; identifying your rights and defending them; encouraging your spontaneity, willingness to act, ground-breaking instincts, directness, independence and courage.

Seeking Meaning
JUPITER ASPECTS

You are working on a karmic obligation to an (inner or outer) teacher by seeking constant growth; traveling, studying, asking questions, looking for answers about life; developing values; living moral and ethical principles; and encouraging broad-mindedness.

Accountable Authority
SATURN ASPECTS

You're paying off your debt to your father by being responsible (but not overly so), dedicated, organized, pragmatic, achievement-oriented, willing to wield power constructively, develop expertise; face reality and take care of business.

Impartial
URANUS ASPECTS

You're meeting your obligation to a friend by staying aware of the big picture; being true to your unique nature; practicing tolerance, openness, and objectivity; looking to the future; enjoying the new and different; and developing networks.

Meditative Mysticism
NEPTUNE ASPECTS

You are discharging a karmic debt to a dreamer you know by bringing more beauty, grace, love, and healing to the planet; practicing compassion and a spiritual path; connecting with the Source; encouraging high ideals; and living an inspired life.

Metamorphosis
PLUTO ASPECTS

You are working on a karmic obligation to your mate OR an intense competitor by developing emotional courage; transforming negatives into positives; probing deeply into your own motives; bringing secrets into the light; releasing what is dead; sharing power, possessions, and pleasure with another person.

CHAPTER FIFTEEN
KARMIC GIFTS (TALENTS BROUGHT IN FROM THE PAST)

This chapter examines talents you may have developed in the past. Your horoscope reveals abilities which are part of your gift to the world, attributes which you need to share with others. (Your gifts, by their nature, create an internal pressure to put them out into the world.) In other lifetimes, you probably have struggled to integrate the qualities discussed here. Through your challenges, you have gained the strength and the true vision to become an example and a beacon to others in these areas.

The interpretations here are based on astrological traditions, some of which have been confirmed by clients who have had past life memories, flashbacks, or regressions. The astrological traditions examine planets which are retrograde or intercepted (both seen as looking backward or inward) and planets in or ruling the 4th, 8th or 12 houses (the houses associated with the past, including past lives).

Outer planets positions (at least when retrograde, intercepted, or involved with water houses) seem to correlate with "karmic groups"—individuals who have chosen to share a time period to reincarnate together. Similar issues are shared by the people within those groups. Clients have strongly identified with the themes from some of these Jupiter, Saturn, Uranus, Neptune, and Pluto placements.

Use the following interpretations ("planet" in sign) if your "planet" (including Sun, and Moon) occupies an intercepted house, the 4th, 8th, or 12th, is a ruler of the 4th, 8th, or 12th or is retrograde. If the same planet fits several categories, these themes and issues are likely to relate to several past existences.

Intercepted, Retrograde, Occupying
or Ruling 4th, 8th, or 12 Houses

SUN

Sun in Aries: The Pioneer

Your past labors helped to develop your valor, assertion, urge to be first and willingness to lead the way. You have strengthened your personal will, initiative, spontaneity, eagerness and integrity. This lifetime, you are to be an important role model to others for bravery, directness, confidence, immediacy, vitality and action.

Sun in Taurus: The Sensualist

Your past efforts helped to develop your dependability, a relaxed, easygoing manner, sensuality, and skill with resources. You have strengthened your reliability, ability to enjoy the material world, endurance and comfort level. This lifetime, you are to be an important role model to others for stamina, gratification, and ability to handle money, possessions, comfort, and beauty.

Sun in Gemini: Versatile

Your past lives have helped to develop your fluency, versatility, rationality, and flexibility. You have strengthened your curiosity, logic, communication skills and interest in the world around you. This lifetime, you are to be an important role model to others for the intellect, verbal skills, adaptability, light-heartedness and multiple talents.

Sun in Cancer: The Caretaker

Your past struggles have helped to develop your nurturing warmth, caretaking skills, sympathy, and home focus. You have strengthened your roots, emotional attachments, and security-seeking. This lifetime, you are to be an important role model to others for appropriate dependency, protection, nesting, family focus, and safety issues.

Sun in Leo: The Star

Your past experiences have helped to develop your creativity, dramatic instincts, generosity, and charisma. You have strengthened your self-esteem, confidence, willingness to risk and urge to motivate others. This lifetime, you are to be an important role model to others for excitement, healthy pride, persuasion, praise and stage presence.

Sun in Virgo: The Analyst

Your past labors have helped to develop you competence, interest in health, focus, skill with details, and an analytical eye. You have strengthened your practicality, common sense, modesty, and discretion. This lifetime, you are to be an important role model to others for helpfulness, service, pragmatism, dedication, organization and doing a good job.

Sun in Libra: The Negotiator

Your past lives have helped to develop your cooperative attitude, relationship focus, diplomacy, and aesthetic eye. You have strengthened your feeling for balance and harmony, grace, and one-on-one interactions. This lifetime, you are to be an important role model to others for compromise, taking turns, charm, visual forms of beauty, and seeing both sides.

Sun in Scorpio: The Catalyst

Your past efforts have helped to develop your passion, power drive, penetrating focus, and persistence. You have strengthened your psychological awareness, depth understanding and self-mastery. This lifetime, you are to be an important role model to others for self-control, intensity, perseverance, potency, and powerful impacts.

Sun in Sagittarius: The Seeker

Your past experiences have helped to develop your optimism, enthusiasm, idealism, and whole-hearted leap into life. You have strengthened your benevolence, urge to broaden horizons, and need to seek the Truth. This lifetime, you are to be an important role model to others for humor, philosophy, Higher Truths, independence, and growth.

Sun in Capricorn: The Executor

Your past struggles have helped to develop your sense of responsibility, authority instincts, need for tradition and formality. You have strengthened your ambition, drive for status, control, and achievement. This lifetime, you are to be an important role model to others for hard work, expertise, strength, careful planning and dogged determination.

Sun in Aquarius: The Inventor

Your past efforts have helped to develop your uniqueness, inventiveness, independence and futuristic insight. You have strengthened your tolerance, humanitarian instincts, and interest in the new. This lifetime, you are to be an important role model to others for innovation, progress, justice, change, and objectivity.

Sun in Pisces: The Mystic

Your past labors have helped to develop your compassion, spiritual or mystical leanings, and visionary potentials. You have strengthened your sensitivity, intuition, aesthetic skills, and sense of Unity with Life. This lifetime, you are to be an important role model to others for creating beauty, love, harmony, healing, transcendence, and Oneness.

MOON

Moon in Aries: Fast Feelings

In previous lifetimes, you emotionally dedicated yourself to courage, action, assertion, and self-reliance. You fed your moods, quick emotional reactions, and urge for freedom within family. This time around, you can nurture high spirits, pioneering, warmth with independence, and eagerness within other people.

Moon in Taurus: Mellow Moods

In previous lifetimes, you emotionally dedicated yourself to enjoying the physical world of beauty, the senses, and possessions. You fed your fidelity, affectionate nature, dedication, and patience. This time around, you can nurture dependability, comfort, pleasure, material indulgence, and simplicity within other people.

Moon in Gemini: Mercurial Moods

In previous lifetimes, you emotionally dedicated yourself to exploring the world and people right around you. You fed your curiosity, communication skills, versatility and quick perceptions. This time around, you can nurture the intellect, alertness, learning, teaching, multiple interests, and flexibility within other people.

Moon in Cancer: Strongly Sensitive

In previous lifetimes, you emotionally dedicated yourself to home, family, protection, and cherishing. You fed your emotional attachments, roots, and need to be needed. This time around, you can nurture caring, warmth, family feelings, safety, security, feelings, and absorption within other people.

Moon in Leo: Extravagantly Expressive

In previous lifetimes, you emotionally dedicated yourself to drama, being on-stage, applauded and admired. You fed your magnetism, charisma, generosity, and enthusiasm to do more than you'd done before. This time around, you can nurture the sparkle, zest, excitement, self-esteem and personal pride within other people.

Moon in Virgo: Calm and Competent

In previous lifetimes, you emotionally dedicated yourself to service, taking care of business, practicality, and essential duties. You fed your self-discipline, analytical skills, and urge to fix things, people, or situations. This time around, you can nurture technical abilities, repairing instincts, flaw-finding, and competence within other people.

Moon in Libra: Even-Tempered Emotions

In previous lifetimes, you emotionally dedicated yourself to beauty, grace, balance, and harmony. You fed your aesthetic impulses, graciousness, empathy, and urge for fair play. This time around, you can nurture equality instincts, beauty needs, charm, affection, popularity, and attractiveness within other people.

Moon in Scorpio: Potent Passion

In previous lifetimes, you emotionally dedicated yourself to intensity, reading hidden messages, probing, and going to the limit. You fed your psychological insight, survival instincts, and tenacity. This time around, you can nurture emotional depth, self-mastery, perseverance and potency within other people.

Moon in Sagittarius: Jovial Jester

In previous lifetimes, you emotionally dedicated yourself to adventures, questing, seeking, and growing. You fed your urge for freedom, travel, learning, promotion, and expansion. This time around, you can nurture ideas, ideals, independence, faith, outreach, and spiritual searching within other people.

Moon in Capricorn: Serious and Stable

In previous lifetimes, you emotionally dedicated yourself to caution, planning, responsibility, and conscientiousness. You fed your ambitions, security needs, urge for structure and preference for the known. This time around, you can nurture achievement, business skills, power drives, and practicality within other people.

Moon in Aquarius: Uniquely Unconventional

In previous lifetimes, you emotionally dedicated yourself to humanitarian causes, friends, groups, and looking ahead. You fed your individuality, freedom instincts, unusual perspective, and flashes of insight. This time around, you can nurture openness, tolerance, progress, independence, and objectivity within other people.

Moon in Pisces: Idealized Impressions

In previous lifetimes, you emotionally dedicated yourself to helping, healing, creating beauty, or seeking God. You fed your compassion, mysticism, artistic abilities, and idealism. This time around, you can nurture philanthropy, sensitivity, intuition, imagination, serenity, aesthetics, and spirituality within other people.

MERCURY

Mercury in Aries: Courageous Communication

One of your skills, on which you have worked hard, is promoting directness and integrity. You can generate pioneering ideas. Your life presents an example to others of intellectual courage. You can be a constructive role model in terms of speaking one's mind.

Mercury in Taurus: Comfortable Communication

One of your skills, on which you have labored long, is grounding concepts. Your life presents an example to others of feeling comfortable with thinking and with communicating. You can be a constructive role model in terms of assisting simplicity in life.

Mercury in Gemini: Casual Communication

One of your skills, to which you dedicated lives, is stimulating ideas. Your life presents an example to others of encouraging learning and communication. You can be a constructive role model in regard to supporting variety and promoting a childlike freshness.

Mercury in Cancer: Caring Communication

One of your skills, developed with much dedication, is feeding people's minds. Your life presents an example to others of encouraging empathic interactions. You can be a constructive role model for using words with compassion and tuning into feelings.

Mercury in Leo: Charismatic Communication

One of your skills, on which you labored long, is presenting exciting ideas and dramatizing concepts. Your life presents an example to others of using words to motivate people. You can be a constructive role model who highlights humor and a fun-loving spirit.

Mercury in Virgo: Careful Communication

Using precise and judicious language has been a focus for you. Your life presents an example to others of encouraging common sense and practical ideas. You can be a constructive role model of efficiency in thought and communication with an organized mind.

Mercury in Libra: Counseling Communication

One of your skills, developed with much dedication, is diplomatic language and graceful phrasing. Your life presents an example to others of encouraging communication and the exchange of ideas. You can be a constructive role model for balancing listening with speaking.

Mercury in Scorpio: Cathartic Communication

One of your skills, to which you dedicated much effort, is deep thinking. Your life presents an example to others of encouraging therapeutic analysis and furthering investigative tendencies. You can be a constructive role model in regard to understanding obsessions.

Mercury in Sagittarius: Questing Communication

One of your skills, the focus of many lifetimes, is a philosophical outlook and an optimistic attitude. Your life presents an example to others of a wide-ranging intellect. You can be a constructive role model in regard to seeking life's meaning.

Mercury in Capricorn: Cautious Communication

One of your skills, on which you have worked hard, is putting ideas to work and creating mental structures. Your life presents an example to others of persevering with concepts and facing facts. You can be a constructive role model for realistic communication.

Mercury in Aquarius: Creative Communication

One of your skills, on which you labored long, is original thinking. Your life presents an example to others of intellectual objectivity. You can be a constructive role model in terms of encouraging brainstorming and networking and supporting tolerance.

Mercury in Pisces: Quixotic Communication

One of your skills, developed with much dedication, is affirming intuition and wholistic thinking. Your life presents an example to others of poetic language or skill with metaphors and imagery. You can be a constructive role model who encourages transcendent thinking.

VENUS

Venus in Aries: Ardent Admirer

In the past, you have put effort into loving openly. You can stimulate others to take risks in relationships. Your example of spontaneous personal pleasure can inspire others. You can live emotional courage and instinctive enjoyment. You encourage others to love themselves.

Venus in Taurus: Sensually Satisfying

In the past, you have put effort into loving faithfully. You can encourage others to solidify and strengthen relationships. Your example of natural sensuality can inspire others. You live emotional reliability and comfortable gratification. You help others to feel good.

Venus in Gemini: Love and Learning

In the past, you have put effort into loving intelligently. You can encourage others to communicate within relationships. Your example of love of learning can inspire others. You adore new input and seek out fascinating experiences. You stimulate others to recapture their youthful curiosity.

Venus in Cancer: Compassionate Caresses

In the past, you have put effort into loving support. You can encourage others to be nurturing within relationships. Your example of protection and sustenance can inspire others. You help people to take care of one another and to gain a sense of security and safety.

Venus in Leo: Larger than Life

In the past, you have put effort into loving magnificently. You can encourage others to be cheerleaders within relationships. Your example of charisma and generosity can inspire others. You help people to excite one another and enjoy feeling proud of each other.

Venus in Virgo: Endearing Efficiency

In the past, you have put effort into loving sensibly. You can encourage others to be practical within relationships. Your example of good sense and taking care of business can inspire others. You help others to take stock of what they enjoy and how they love.

Venus in Libra: Poised Partner

In the past, you have put effort into loving harmoniously. You can encourage others to be accommodating within relationships. Your example of grace and charm can inspire others. You help others to appreciate their partners, to seek beauty and to enjoy balance.

Venus in Scorpio: Intense Intimacy

In the past, you have put effort into loving passionately. You can encourage others to be intense and loyal within relationships. Your example of depth and psychological understanding can inspire others. You help others to reach new levels of intimacy and sharing.

Venus in Sagittarius: Extravagantly Exciting

In the past, you have put effort into loving expansively. You can encourage others to be open-hearted and fun-loving within relationships. Your example of gregariousness and an adventurous spirit can inspire others. You help others to reach for the stars.

Venus in Capricorn: Serious and Sensible

In the past, you have put effort into loving carefully. You can encourage others to choose wisely and plan well in relationships. Your example of realism and willingness to work can inspire others. You help others to put effort into building and maintaining connections.

Venus in Aquarius: Pals in Partnership

In the past, you have put effort into loving unconventionally. You can encourage others to allow space and individuality within relationships. Your example of tolerance and openness can inspire others. You help people to enjoy their differences with a partner.

Venus in Pisces: Inspired Intimacy

In the past, you have put effort into loving idealistically. You can encourage others to be sensitive and empathic in relationships. Your example of forgiveness and focusing on the Higher Self can inspire others. You help others to visualize and co-create the best.

MARS

Mars in Aries: First and Foremost
In earlier lives, you focused on being yourself. You worked on putting yourself first and defending your own rights. You now have the opportunity to teach others about assertion, directness, spontaneity, movement, bravery, and doing your own thing in the world.

Mars in Taurus: Enduring and Easygoing
In earlier lives, you focused on being slow, steady, and persistent. You worked on earning your own resources and enjoying personal pleasures. You now have the opportunity to teach others about gratification, handling the material world, appropriate indulgence and endurance.

Mars in Gemini: Agile and Adaptable
In earlier lives, you focused on being alert, perceptive and quick-witted. You worked on being bright, flexible, eager to learn and move. You now have the opportunity to teach others about agility, dexterity, rapid observation, and thinking on your feet.

Mars in Cancer: Concerned and Caring
In earlier lives, you focused on being protective, gaining security, and guarding the home. You worked on emotional expression, your relationship to the maternal archetype, and moods. You now have the opportunity to teach others about nurturing with freedom, expressing anger kindly, and smoothing and soothing emotional impulses.

Mars in Leo: Lavish and Lively
In earlier lives, you focused on being exciting, magnetic, dynamic, and on-stage. You worked on gaining the limelight, being admired, and motivating others. You now have the opportunity to teach others about thrills, developing self-esteem, appreciation and zest.

Mars in Virgo: Healthy and Hardworking
In earlier lives, you focused on being productive, pragmatic, and efficient. You labored hard, always striving for tangible results in work and health. You now have the opportunity to teach others about practicality, healthy habits, and getting the job done.

Mars in Libra: Natural Negotiator
In earlier lives, you focused on face-to-face interactions with other people. Some were cooperative; some were competitive. You worked on the balance

between self and other, and now have the opportunity to teach others about sharing power, taking turns, and acting with grace.

Mars in Scorpio: Deep Desires

In earlier lives, you focused on sexuality, relentless pursuit of your desires, and self-mastery. You worked hard to control yourself, direct your intensity, and make a passionate connection. You now have the opportunity to teach others about intimacy, taking life to the limit, and finding a constructive, competitive outlet.

Mars in Sagittarius: Active and Athletic

In earlier lives, you focused on fun, frolic, travel and teaching. You worked hard at seeking enlightenment, expanding your horizons, and laughter.. You now have the opportunity to teach others about faith, finding the silver lining, seeking, searching, and growing.

Mars in Capricorn: Controlled and Capable

In earlier lives, you focused on defining limits, creating structures, and confronting rules and authorities. You worked hard to get what you wanted within the established structure. You now have the opportunity to teach others about balancing self-will and societal constraints and combining initiative and planning for lasting results.

Mars in Aquarius: Unusual and Unique

In earlier lives, you focused on rebelling, finding your own individuality, and being outside the "norms" of society. You worked hard to be original, inventive, open, and progressive. You now have the opportunity to teach others about freedom, welcoming change, acting from one's own center, and being unique.

Mars in Pisces: Sweet and Sensitive

In earlier lives, you focused on meditating, contemplating, rescuing, and empathizing. You worked hard to be sensitive, compassionate, intuitive, and graceful. You now have the opportunity to teach others about philanthropy, beauty in motion, fighting for the underdog, and tuning into life.

JUPITER

Jupiter in Aries: Beyond the Lost Horizon

You and a group of people your age were active in the Age of Exploration—wandering the world. Part of your quest was a search for life's meaning. Some of you went too far and slipped over the edge to true believers: "My way is the **only** way." Because physical prowess was valuable, some of you fell into a "Might makes Right" attitude. You have a group goal for this lifetime to live optimism, faith, and trust in something higher without righteousness. Your task is to be courageous, active, confident and adventurous, without trampling on other people's rights. Your spiritual job is to be idealistic without trying to convert others; to encourage growth, confidence, and putting one's beliefs into action.

Jupiter in Taurus: "Go West, Young (Wo)Man"

You and a group of people your age were active in the development of the American West. A connection to nature was made for many of you. Some of you went too far and slipped over the edge to rampant materialism: turning money, goods and goodies into ultimate values. You have a group goal for this lifetime to live simplicity, comfort and in harmony with the Earth without over consuming. Your spiritual job is to enjoy the material world without giving it too much weight; to encourage pleasure within an ethical framework and to support the continuance of Nature's bounty and beauty.

Jupiter in Gemini: The Flowering of Knowledge

You and a group of people your age were active during the Renaissance. The seeking of knowledge and information flourished incredibly. Some of you went too far and slipped over the edge to turn rationality and logic into idols. The human mind was put above anything else. You have a group goal for this lifetime to learn voraciously, to pursue knowledge tirelessly while realizing that there is always more to know. Your spiritual job is to enjoy language, communication, and intellectual stimulation without expecting them to answer all of life's needs; to realize that a full life has a physical, emotional and spiritual (as well as mental) dimension.

Jupiter in Cancer: Clans and Caring

You and a group of people your age formed a kin-group in pre-Christian Asia. Tied by blood to one another, you had a close bond to the land on which you lived. When an invading culture appeared, you were unwilling to move or compromise. The clan decided to fight to the death against other ways. Eventually you all starved to death. You have a group goal for this lifetime to value warmth, family, land, country, feelings, food, and roots without making them all-important. Your spiritual job is to enjoy security, safety, the familiar and your nest, without putting all your emotional eggs in those baskets.

Jupiter in Leo: Aristocracy and Admiration

You and a group of people your age were fellow aristocrats in a French court. You enjoyed the drama and pageantry of your positions. Generous with one another, you viewed life as a fun-filled opportunity. Although some of you held to high standards of personal integrity, others of you were seduced by the power you wielded. You have a group goal for this lifetime to value charisma, admiration, and applause while able to share it with others. Healthy self-esteem is vital—neither an overblown ego nor a squashed self-appreciation. Your spiritual job is to understand the importance of positive feedback—for yourself and others—and to share generously your appreciation of other people.

Jupiter in Virgo: Health and Healing

You and a group of people your age were active in the early development of nursing and cleanliness standards in medicine. Eager to improve the situation, you dedicated yourselves to service. Some of you got carried away with a focus on petty details, insisting that procedures must be done **just so** in order to be right. Others continued to value competence without getting hung up in excessive fault-finding. You have a group goal for this lifetime to value hard work, effort, and dedication—without carrying it to an extreme and also without looking forever for that "perfect" career that does not exist. Your spiritual job is to understand the balance between nit-picking and having the faith to act (even though life is not yet ideal); to be able to see the big picture as well as the small details.

Jupiter in Libra: Spousal Support

You and a group of people your age were sent to be wives in the development of America. Out into the "wilderness" you went to find a spouse. Many of you came to value your marriages and appreciate the contributions made by both you and your husband. Others of you put your spouse on a pedestal and deferred excessively for "the sake of the relationship." Some of you kept an idealistic image of what marriage was "supposed" to be and could never really settle into the real thing. Those individuals remained restless and dissatisfied, always feeling there should have been "something more." Your spiritual job is to share a quest for something Higher in life with a spouse, close friend, or associate. Your quest is to bring together people and ideals in a constructive way—to seek truth together, to be generous to one another, and to build each other's trust in life's goodness.

Jupiter in Scorpio: Inquiry or Inquisition

You and a group of people your age were active during the Inquisition. For some of you, it was a time of deep, religious searching. You asked penetrating questions and sought to understand spiritual truths on the deepest levels. For some, it was a time of religious fanaticism. Intense emotions were involved, and the urge to control was sometimes expressed negatively against other people. Manipulation and abuse in the name of religion took place. You may have experienced torture because of your principles. Your spiritual job is to make a commitment to investigate the depths of your psyche; to know that the deeper you go within, the more you connect to the Light from above. Your quest is to understand that true spiritual growth includes accepting (not rejecting) the darkest corners of yourself (and others). Your path to enlightenment involves the emotional courage to face the dark within yourself, and to transform and transmute it into light. A part of your task is to not judge the darkness or light of others, but to allow them to choose their own path, preventing only actual harm to others.

Jupiter in Sagittarius: Where is Truth?

You and a group of people your age were active among the missionaries to the New World. Some of you were motivated by a desire to spread the word of God and to bring more opportunities to the people you met. Others of you were convinced that your "truth" was the only acceptable one. The more someone resisted your religion, the harder those group members pushed it! Some of you were generous to the native dwellers and eager to share ideas. Others were intent on promoting one particular brand of "education" and morality. Your spiritual job is to support education, broadened horizons, and a quest for enlightenment in the world. Your task is to feed a hunger for Ultimate Knowledge wherever you find it. If you do your quest well, you understand that every answer brings new questions, and that we are all on a path toward the Light—but no one has arrived yet!

Jupiter in Capricorn: Physical Versus Spiritual

You and a group of people your age were active in the rise of materialism. You contributed to the development of science—and believed it would be the answer to all of humankind's problems. You furthered the cause of big business and looked to the material world for final answers. Some of you maintained a corner of questioning and wondering—particularly as you looked into the night sky and the endless vistas of the universe. Many of you were convinced that physical forces would be found to explain everything. Your spiritual job is to create a marriage between the physical and spiritual, to make peace between faith and fear (or doubt). Your task is to work sensibly in the material world while developing a trust in Higher Meaning. By clearly defining your goals, beliefs, and values, you can work sensibly toward making them manifest.

Jupiter in Aquarius: Breaking Loose

You and a group of people your age were active in the Age of Revolutions (American, French, Mexican...). You placed a high value on the individual person, on the right to freedom. You promoted justice and humanitarian principles. Some of you went to extremes and got involved with very bizarre, eccentric political movements. At times, you placed too much faith in the "common man or woman." Because detachment was important, some of you fell into a stance of encouraging revolution even if it meant everyone would die on the barricades. Your spiritual job is to develop a firm set of ethical, moral, and political principles. Part of your task is to encourage healthy freedom, growth, equality, and justice. Teach yourself and people when and where it is appropriate to break the rules. Value your inventive, progressive spirit.

Jupiter in Pisces: Romantic Reveries

You and a group of people your age were active in the Romantic period in England. Music, poetry, song, dance, and nature worship were important elements of your lives. A connection to the Source pervaded your works. A sense of meaning and purpose was instinctual; you just "knew" that there was something more to life. In some instances, values were cloudy, confused, diffused as people tried to absorb and assimilate too much. A few individuals took self-sacrifice to an extreme. Most of you were concerned with making your best contribution to inspiring the world. Your spiritual job is to continue to uplift others, to help them find meaning and purpose in the world. Your task is to spread faith, belief in a Higher Power, compassion, and a connection to nature and beauty.

SATURN

Saturn in Aries: Sensible Self-Direction
Previous life lessons have focused on issues of independence, action, assertion and being first. You've put much effort into physical challenges and learning how to be self-focused in a healthy manner. You can help others learn to be practical about how they direct personal drives and desires, the ways they get want they want in the world.

Saturn in Taurus: Calm and Comfortable
Previous life lessons have focused on issues of sensuality, finances, pleasures and possessions. You've put much work into learning to enjoy the material world without being consumed by it. You've dealt with excesses and deprivation and found a comfortable middle ground. You're here to teach others sensible sensuality, practical money management.

Saturn in Gemini: Career Communicator
Previous life lessons have focused on issues of thinking, talking, and learning. You've put a lot of work into dealing with the world of the mind. You've had challenges around intellectual inadequacy and blocks as well as excessive rationality or flippancy. You're here to teach others to enjoy curiosity, mental byways and communication.

Saturn in Cancer: Family Duties
Previous life lessons have focused on issues of nurturing, protection, reassurance, and emotional support. Trials and tribulations regarding excessive dependency as well as too much caretaking have occurred. You've put much effort into being responsible about emotional ties and came back this time to teach others.

Saturn in Leo: Satisfying Self-Esteem
Previous life lessons have focused on issues of pride, shame, attention, ego, performance, and creativity. You've worked hard on being able to pour out from your own center (in love, speculation, drama, etc.) and seek a positive response from the world. You can teach others the hard lessons of self-esteem and sensible risk-taking.

Saturn in Virgo: Efficiency Expert

Previous life lessons have focused on being grounded, efficient, and helpful. You've put effort into maintaining a healthy body and being conscientious and productive in your work. You've reaped tangible results from your labors. You've come in this time to help teach others about effectiveness, focus, and doing something **well**.

Saturn in Libra: Taking Turns

Previous life lessons have focused on being fair. Striving for justice, balance, and beauty have been major concerns. You've put much effort into marriages, business partnerships, other peer associations and aesthetic activities. Striving for a balance of power has been challenging. You can help teach others about the importance of equality.

Saturn in Scorpio: Intimate Interactions

Previous life lessons have focused on power, intensity, secrets, and intimacy. You've worked hard to learn to share power, possessions, and pleasures with a mate. Self-mastery has been an ongoing concern. Control issues have abounded. You've returned to help teach others to master appetites, share deeply, understand fully.

Saturn in Sagittarius: Powerful Philosophies

Previous life lessons have focused on idealism, truth-seeking, wanderlust, and your quest for the best. Religious, moral, ethical principles have been a concern often. You've worked hard on developing a usable world view, a set of beliefs and values which works. You can help others to reach philosophies which function in the real world.

Saturn in Capricorn: Rules and Regulations

Previous life lessons have focused on figuring out the rules of the game. You've learned to be dedicated, responsible, practical, and reliable. Concerned with society, you've put effort into affecting the material world and making a contribution. Part of your gift is to teach others how to face facts and work sensibly within the system.

Saturn in Aquarius: Rule-Breaking and Rule-Making

Previous life lessons have focused on freedom, rebellion, detachment, and the new. You've learned to move toward the future, to promote individuality, to support tolerance and openness. Chaos sometimes reigned over community. You've put effort into constructive nonconformity. You can teach others to see more alternatives and options.

Saturn in Pisces: Ideal Versus Real

Previous life lessons have focused on integrating the ideal and the real. As artist, craftspeople, and healers, you worked on the blend between visions and practicality. You learned to combine inspiration and perspiration, to make your dreams manifest. You can help others eschew escapism and become practical mystics, realistic visionaries.

URANUS

Uranus in Aries: "Give Me Liberty..."

You and some of your peers were active in various liberation movements. You pushed on behalf of personal freedom and individuality. Loner instincts were often prominent among your group. Most of you gloried in being first, in breaking new ground and presenting new ideas. A few of you carried rebellion to an extreme. You and your peers have incarnated now to show the world how to be truly yourself. Each of you is to be model for self-sufficiency, independence, and active originality. Your goal is to live self-actualization as an example to others.

Uranus in Taurus: Money and Material

You and some of your peers were active in periods when humankind's relationship to Mother Earth was changing. You helped people to reassess their handling of material resources. When mediums of exchange were altered, you were there. Your group of peers provided the innovative attitude needed to construct a different approach to the material world. You have incarnated now to help us recapture our connection to the earth. Your experience will prove valuable as we change our attitudes toward money. You can contribute to new and different definitions of beauty, comfort, and pleasure. You can redefine sensuality.

Uranus in Gemini: Changing Concepts

You and some of your peers were active in times of changing paradigms. When old ideas began to give way, and new ideas to flourish, you were there. Part of your soul purpose was to help people see new perspectives. Your capacity to brainstorm, to consider alternatives, to change and alter concepts makes a vital contribution to today's world. Your past experiences strengthened your inventiveness and ability to convey new information to others. You can make the most of modern forms of communication and innovative approaches to learning. You can help disseminate a new way of looking at the world.

Uranus in Cancer: New Nurturing

You and some of your peers were active in times when attitudes toward family were shifting. When one set of roles was melting away, you helped to provide something new to take its place. Your ability to take a broad view of family helped you and your peers to transform definitions of domestic units. Your expanded, transpersonal perspective will be particularly valuable in our swiftly changing world. Your past experiences increased your ability to see family within a humanitarian perspective. You incarnated to help people learn that the Earth is one family; that our interconnections are much more vital than our differences.

Uranus in Leo: Liberating Love

You and some of your peers were active in times when attitudes toward love and romance were shifting. When old ideas about love, sexuality, chivalry, and glamour were fading, you helped to provide a new viewpoint. Your ability to love with an open hand; to making an exciting connection without losing your individuality helped you and your peers to transform definitions of falling in love. Your larger perspective will be particularly valuable now. Your past experiences mean you are more able to love without possessiveness. You incarnated to help people to learn that caring for someone means supporting their ability to shine, their uniqueness, and encouraging that person to become all s/he is capable of becoming.

Uranus in Virgo: Working Way

You and some of your peers were active in times when attitudes toward work and productivity were shifting. The places where work was performed altered. The ways in which work was done changed. You helped people deal with the transitions. As they felt their everyday world was falling apart around them, you and your peers provided new models for efficiency, practicality, and doing a good job. The work ethic was redefined. The meaning of work within a full and fulfilling life also altered. Your past experience is particularly valuable now. As our ways of working and the job available change rapidly, you can help people adapt. You incarnated to be of assistance in the changing workplace.

Uranus in Libra: Fairness in Flux

You and some of your peers were active in times when attitudes toward partnership and beauty were shifting. New ways of looking at the world brought in new perspectives in art and altered classic definitions of what was attractive. The relationships between the sexes were in flux. You helped people to deal with the transitions. You and your peers provided models for equality, justice, fair play, and balance. You helped to present a different perspective for associating with others. Your past experience is particularly valuable now as people strive toward fuller equality with one another. You have incarnated into this period to help us deal with changing paradigms in terms of one-on-one interactions.

Uranus in Scorpio: Shifts in Sharing

You and some of your peers were active in times when attitudes about ownership and resources were shifting. How people dealt with money and property was in flux. How power was distributed between different groups was changing. Questions between "haves" and "have nots" arose. You helped people deal with that time of stress. You and your peers provided models for equality of access, for living the importance of each person mastering him/herself and recognizing the rights of others. You set an example of sharing finances, pleasures and possessions with respect for everyone involved. Your past experience is particularly valuable now as people strive to share the resources of our planet. You have incarnated into this period to help us deal with changing views in regard to power and property.

Uranus in Sagittarius: Religious Reversals

You and some of your peers were active in times when attitudes about religion were changing. The old beliefs were being challenged, and new ideas presented. Traditions were being swept away and revolutionary concepts advanced. Ideas about God, Truth, and Ultimate Meaning were shifting. You helped people to deal with their search for meaning. You and your peers provided role models for an objective look at different philosophies, religions, and world views. Your past experience is crucial now, as our world is in another period of spiritual flux. You have incarnated into this time to help us deal with new concepts of religion, new ways of seeking answers, new forms of worship, and new understanding.

Uranus in Capricorn: Altering Authorities

You and some of your peers were active in times when the established structures of society were changing. The old ways were being challenged. Revolutions— in thought and deed—were active. Some established forms crumbled under the weight of excessive authority and age. Others were pushed by people eager for the new. You and your peers provided models for building new structures. You helped to level excessive hierarchies. You cooperated to build more equality and opportunity into the new organizations. Your experience is essential for us now. As the old forms are giving way around us, chaos and anarchy threaten. You have incarnated now to help us find new, healthy, individualistic forms of structure that support progress and personal growth.

Uranus in Aquarius: Change and Chaos

You and some of your peers were active in times of chaos. When the world seemed unpredictable and erratic, you were there. When revolutions were breaking down and breaking up nations, religions, and economic systems—you were there. As others felt lost, demolished, confused, and distraught, you and your peer group presented a model for operating within ambiguity. You promoted healthy change without determining an absolute ending point. Your experience is valuable now. As our world stays in flux; as future shock builds, you can help us cope. You have incarnated to teach us to be open to change, to prize individual experience, to keep many choices and options available, and to support progress and more equality.

Uranus in Pisces: Spiritual Shifts

You and some of your peers were active in times of spiritual shifts. As old ideas about how to talk to God dissolved, you were there. As mystical experiences leapt into consciousness, you were there. As radical, revolutionary forms of communicating with the "other side" were tried, you were there. You promoted an attitude of open-mindedness. You encouraged people to find their own, personal, unique connection to a Higher Power. You and your peers provided a model for the individual human to relate to the Cosmos. Your experience is quite valuable now. As our ideas about spirituality are changing once again, you can encourage people to be open to new ideas, to explore new methods, to seek new answers.

NEPTUNE

Neptune in Aries: Higher Selves
You share with a group of age-mates ideals about courage, assertion, and independence. Your role is to inspire the world in terms of pioneering and being willing to act. The shadow side of your group is a glorification of force and personal will. The highest potential of your group is to feed the Divine Spark within each person.

Neptune in Taurus: Life's Simple Pleasures
You share with a group of age-mates ideals about comfort, pleasure, indulgence, and material resources. Your role is to inspire the world in terms of earthly matters and sensual connections. The shadow side of your group is a glorification of materialism and hedonism. The highest potential of your group is to demonstrate the beauty of the Earth and the simplicity of living in harmony with our land.

Neptune in Gemini: Wonderful Words
You share with a group of age-mates ideals about thinking, communication, logic, and flexibility. Your role is to inspire the world with language, concepts, and a multi-faceted approach. The shadow side of your group is superficiality and being scattered. The highest potential of your group is to create beautiful, flowing language, metaphors and symbols to convey Spiritual Truths.

Neptune in Cancer: Spaceship Earth
You share with a group of age-mates ideals about home, family, the nest, and roots. Your role is to inspire the world in terms of nurturing, protection, and emotional safety. The shadow side of your group is to overvalue kin and emotional security. The highest potential of your group is to live the experience of humanity as one family, within the embrace of an all-loving Higher Power.

Neptune in Leo: Affirming Each Other
You share with a group of age-mates ideals about power, love, applause, and positive regard. Your role is to inspire the world with drama, magic, allure, and persuasion. The shadow side of your group is to glorify aristocratic or elitist

trends and put love of a pedestal. The highest potential of your group is to live the healing power of love and demonstrate the power of positive self-esteem.

Neptune in Virgo: Healing Hands

You share with a group of age-mates ideals about work, health, competence, and efficiency. Your role is to inspire the world by repairing, enhancing, fixing, and making healthier. The shadow side of your group is to slip into workaholism, excessive details, or extremes around health. The highest potential of your group is to take practical steps to make the world more beautiful and more ideal, to promote aesthetics, to help and to heal.

Neptune in Libra: Inspirational Interactions

You share with a group of age-mates ideals about relationships, equality, fair play and balance. Your role is to inspire the world by sharing, taking turns, and spreading justice. The shadow side of your group is to idealize partners or partnership or fall into savior/victim relationships. The highest potential of your group is to use Divine forgiveness wisely to make the best of your one-on-one relationships, to create beautiful, flowing interactions.

Neptune in Scorpio: Emotional Encounter

You share with a group of age-mates ideals about sexuality, intensity, self-mastery, and hidden matters. Your role is to inspire the world by probing deeply, being intimate and emotionally courageous. The shadow side of your group is to turn sex, money, or power into God. The highest potential of your group is to touch the Higher Self within you and within your mate through intimate caring and sharing, and to respect the rights of all who share planetary resources.

Neptune in Sagittarius: Enlightenment

You share with a group of age-mates ideals about education, travel, knowledge, and religion. Your role is to inspire the world by seeking and searching for the Highest Truth. The shadow side of your group is to believe that you have found absolute answers and promote One Way. The highest potential of your group is to recognize the inspired elements within many paths to the Light and to affirm them all.

Neptune in Capricorn: Continuing Contributions

You share with a group of age-mates ideals about structure, responsibility, authority, and control. Your role is to inspire the world by achieving, becoming an expert, and coping with rules. The shadow side of your group is to glorify limitations, hierarchical structures, and tradition. The highest potential of your group is to live dedicated to serving society, making a contribution, and leaving a lasting legacy to the world.

Neptune in Aquarius: Teaching Tolerance

You share with a group of age-mates ideals about freedom, innovation, individuality, and humanitarian causes. Your role is to inspire the world by being inventive, independent, and unique. The shadow side of your group is to glorify chaos, anarchy, or change for the sake of change. The highest potential of your group is to live a life of spiritual openness, to facilitate healthy change, and anything which gives humanity more access to mystical understanding.

Neptune in Pisces: Yearning toward Unity

You share with a group of age-mates ideals about spirituality, Oneness, beauty, and perfection. Your role is to inspire the world by healing, creating beauty, assisting, and empathizing. The shadow side of your group is to flee into escapism, rose-colored glasses or disconnected dreams. The highest potential of your group is to live a transcendent life, to feel and share the connection of All Life and to convey the joy and grace of becoming one with The Source.

PLUTO

Pluto in Aries: Mastery of Self

You share with others of your generation past lives involving power wielded in pursuit of independence. You focused on breaking new ground, maintaining separate space, and being in charge of yourself and your world. You carried courage, integrity, and directness to profound depths. You came back now to provide an intense example of self-mastery, inner concentration and personal transformation.

Pluto in Taurus: Mastery of Materials

You share with others of your generation past lives involving power wielded in pursuit of comfort, pleasure, and material gain. You concentrated on dealing with the physical world and carried beauty, indulgence, and gratification to deeper levels. You came back now to master the senses, to gain increased self-control and to help transform the world around you.

Pluto in Gemini: Mastery of Mind

You share with others of your generation past lives involving power wielded in pursuit of knowledge and information. You focused on issue of research, depth insights, the strength of logic, and the power of facts. You came back now to participate in a powerful thrust toward increased communication and a shift to a higher level of thinking.

Pluto in Cancer: Mastery of Emotions

You share with others of your generation past lives involving power within the family circle. You focused on learning to wield power with and for kin. Connection to the homeland was often strong. Blood ties were central. You came back now to broaden the definitions of family, and to learn to use power on behalf of Mother Earth.

Pluto in Leo: Mastery of Power

You share with others of your generation past lives involving power as a source of excitement. Your group was energized by wielding power. The drama of struggles for supremacy was thrilling. Children and other loved ones were often pulled into political maneuvers. You were sometimes the user and sometimes the abused where power was involved. You came back now to learn the true power of love, to discover your vitality is built even more by **sharing** the power with others.

Pluto in Virgo: Mastery of Body

You share with others of your generation past lives involving power harnessed for material results. You were motivated to push and push until you finished your tasks. Being efficient, maintaining health, and getting results were vital. You came back now to reach profound depths in understanding the workaday world and the essentials of good health, nutrition, and personal (lifestyle) habits.

Pluto in Libra: Mastery of Balance

You share with others of your generation past lives involving power issues in relationships. You butted heads with partners. Negotiation and the art of compromise had to be learned. Intense confrontations occurred. You came back now to share your understanding of true depth in relating, to carry the dance between self and other to deeper levels of intimacy.

Pluto in Scorpio: Mastery of Inner Psyche

You share with others of your generation past lives involving power experienced through sexuality, money, or the sharing of possessions. Power struggles over resources—and intense emotions—are familiar to you. You came back now to reach a deeper level of your being, to probe your inner psyche, to master obsessions and compulsions, and to reach a profound level of intimate attachment.

Pluto in Sagittarius: Mastery of Philosophy

You share with others of your generation past lives involving power experienced through education, philosophy, or religion. You have dealt with issues of Divine Right and Absolute Morality. You have probed and asked deep questions about ultimate meaning. You came back now to help humanity reach into the recesses of our souls and gain a deeper insight into spirituality.

Pluto in Capricorn: Mastery of Structures

You share with others of your generation past lives involving power experienced as a part of the Establishment. You have dealt with issues of control, authority, and executive position. You have hung in and persevered to do whatever must be done to gain desired tangible results. You came back now to help transform current power structures, to know what is worth keeping and what is dead and should be buried (and emotionally released).

Pluto in Aquarius: Mastery of Chaos

You share with others of your generation past lives involving power experienced as part of the Out Group. You wielded authority as a rebel, revolutionary, or resister of the status quo. You have concentrated on revealing alternatives. You have focused on issues of equal access. You came back now to uncover hidden issues, to force confrontations regarding humanitarian principles, and to deepen people's understanding of "justice for all."

Pluto in Pisces: Mastery of Illusion

You share with others of your generation past lives involving power directed toward dreams, ideals, beauty, and philanthropy. You wielded power for a cause. You concentrated and persevered to generate compassion, grace, forgiveness, and intuition. Escapism and addiction were sometimes seductive. You came back now to reach deeper levels of mystical insight, reveal hidden spiritual truths, and strengthen people's willingness to face the dark and transform it into Light.

Additional Gifts

Astrologically, when karmic factors (Saturn and the Nodes) make harmonious aspects (sextile, trine) to other planets, they symbolize additional gifts and talents brought in from past lives. Here is a list of the associated gifts for each planet.

Sun: generosity, magnetism, creativity, dramatic skills
Moon: warmth, caring, domestic tendencies, supportiveness
Mercury: logic, curiosity, communication skills, humor, flexibility
Venus: artistic talent, grace, charm, sensuality, easygoing approach
Mars: courage, initiative, directness, integrity, willingness to act
Jupiter: intellectual focus, love of travel, gregariousness, spiritual or religious focus
Saturn: discipline, responsibility, executive instincts, practicality
Uranus: an open-mind, inventiveness, individuality, skill with technology
Neptune: compassion, intuition, artistic inclinations, imagination.
Pluto: depth psychological insight, tenacity, self-control, skill with hidden matters

Further gifts are indicated by grand trines in the chart (three planets each 120 degrees from the other two, making a triangle within the horoscope). These talents are defined by the element (fire, earth, air, water) of the planets involved as well as the signs and houses occupied by the three planets. (If a grand trine has mixed elements, combine the abilities listed here.)

Fire Grand Trine:	confidence, energy, recuperative ability, initiating skills
Earth Grand Trine:	competence, skill at handling material world, sensuality
Air Grand Trine:	skill with ideas and people, objectivity, curiosity, logic, detachment
Water Grand Trine:	empathy, sensitivity, psychic openness, ability to see process/patterns

The gifts you bring from your past are easy to access in your present (and future). Enjoy!

CHAPTER SIXTEEN

CONCLUSION

I hope that this book has opened a door for you to explore issues which may relate to past lives (or may simply be metaphors for your present life). A past-life connection might allow you to desensitize in regard to fears and phobias; to forgive old, karmic, repeating family patterns; to break a trend of poverty, dysfunction, and pain; to leave marital strife in the past and concentrate on the now; to understand the roots of sexual blockages and work to fulfillment; to make sense of depression, guilt and violence from earlier lives and move on. If you've been living out a script from habit and "repetition compulsion," you now have the opportunity to change! Understanding your roots often gives you the strength to outgrow what is holding you back.

If you wish to explore further, astrology is one tool you can use. Hypnotic regression or guided imagery is also an option. Body work helps to trigger flashbacks (memories) for some people. Others find that they can receive important unconscious material by asking their psyche for a dream.

Many paths are available to you at this point. I hope you will explore the alternatives which empower you, inspire you, strengthen your ability to rise above old patterns, and encourage you to seek the most positive outcomes.

May this life and your future ones be full of love, laughter, and enlightenment!

APPENDIX
PLANETARY POSITIONS

The following pages include tables for when the planets Mercury, Venus, and Mars enter each sign for the years 1930 through 2010. Use these tables to locate the postion of these planets at your birth and read the appropriate scenarios in the chapter for each planet.

Times given in all planetary tables are Eastern Standard Time (EST). If you were born on the West Coast, add three hours to your birth time to get the EST equivalent. If you were born in the Mountain time zone, add two hours. If you were born in the Central time zone, add one hour.

Example: People born after January 2,1930 (at 5:25 am EST) but before January 22,1930 have Mercury in Aquarius. People born after January 22,1930 (at 7:30 pm EST) but before February 15,1930 have Mercury in Capricorn, and so on.

Mercury Positions 1930 – 2000

1930

Jan 2	5:25 am	Aquarius
Jan 22	7:30 pm	Capricorn
Feb 15	10:08 am	Aquarius
Mar 9	5:39 pm	Pisces
Mar 26	6:36 pm	Aries
Apr 10	12:05 pm	Taurus
May 1	12:31 am	Gemini
May 17	6:06 am	Taurus
Jun 14	3:09 pm	Gemini
Jul 4	5:10 pm	Cancer
Jul 18	9:44 pm	Leo
Aug 3	9:38 pm	Virgo
Aug 26	1:04 pm	Libra
Sep 19	9:16 pm	Virgo
Oct 10	11:45 pm	Libra
Oct 29	9:35 am	Scorpio
Nov 17	12:31 am	Sagittarius
Dec 6	3:57 pm	Capricorn

1931

Feb 11	7:27 am	Aquarius
Mar 2	12:28 pm	Pisces
Mar 18	2:31 pm	Aries
Apr 3	8:38 am	Taurus
Jun 11	2:27 am	Gemini
Jun 26	8:49 am	Cancer
Jul 10	2:56 pm	Leo
Jul 28	6:24 pm	Virgo
Oct 4	1:27 pm	Libra
Oct 21	9:08 pm	Scorpio
Nov 9	11:27 pm	Sagittarius
Dec 1	7:00 pm	Capricorn
Dec 20	2:59 am	Sagittarius

1932

Jan 14	7:47 am	Capricorn
Feb 4	9:36 pm	Aquarius
Feb 22	7:50 pm	Pisces
Mar 9	3:21 pm	Aries
May 15	5:49 pm	Taurus
Jun 2	6:05 pm	Gemini
Jun 16	5:30 pm	Cancer
Jul 2	3:16 am	Leo
Jul 27	3:38 pm	Virgo
Aug 10	2:32 am	Leo
Sep 9	2:20 am	Virgo
Sep 25	8:15 pm	Libra
Oct 13	10:41 am	Scorpio
Nov 2	3:28 pm	Sagittarius

1933

Jan 8	5:25 am	Capricorn
Jan 27	5:39 am	Aquarius
Feb 14	12:06 am	Pisces
Mar 3	5:49 am	Aries
Mar 25	4:49 pm	Pisces
Apr 17	10:27 am	Aries

May 10	2:42 am	Taurus
May 25	9:27 am	Gemini
Jun 8	9:12 am	Cancer
Jun 26	8:12 pm	Leo
Sep 2	12:44 am	Virgo
Sep 17	10:48 pm	Libra
Oct 6	10:04 am	Scorpio
Oct 29	11:27 pm	Sagittarius
Nov 15	9:07 pm	Scorpio
Dec 11	10:43 pm	Sagittarius

1934

Jan 1	1:40 pm	Capricorn
Jan 20	6:44 am	Aquarius
Feb 6	12:24 pm	Pisces
Apr 14	11:14 pm	Aries
May 2	1:45 pm	Taurus
May 16	6:43 pm	Gemini
Jun 1	3:22 am	Cancer
Aug 9	8:49 am	Leo
Aug 24	9:18 pm	Virgo
Sep 10	6:29 am	Libra
Sep 30	9:46 am	Scorpio
Dec 6	1:42 am	Sagittarius
Dec 25	9:59 am	Capricorn

1935

Jan 12	8:20 am	Aquarius
Feb 1	6:16 am	Pisces
Feb 14	10:02 am	Aquarius
Mar 18	4:53 pm	Pisces
Apr 8	1:40 pm	Aries
Apr 24	7:29 am	Taurus
May 8	12:20 pm	Gemini
May 29	2:26 am	Cancer
Jun 20	12:58 pm	Gemini
Jul 13	5:22 pm	Cancer
Aug 1	8:48 pm	Leo
Aug 16	3:39 pm	Virgo
Sep 3	4:33 am	Libra
Sep 28	10:52 am	Scorpio
Oct 12	1:03 pm	Libra
Nov 9	8:24 pm	Scorpio
Nov 29	2:05 am	Sagittarius
Dec 18	3:28 am	Capricorn

1936

Jan 5	10:32 pm	Aquarius
Mar 13	1:40 am	Pisces
Mar 31	12:08 am	Aries
Apr 14	8:45 pm	Taurus
Apr 30	8:30 pm	Gemini
Jul 8	3:47 pm	Cancer
Jul 23	10:39 am	Leo
Aug 7	5:59 pm	Virgo
Aug 27	12:43 pm	Libra
Nov 2	6:00 am	Scorpio
Nov 20	7:39 pm	Sagittarius

Dec 10	1:40 am	Capricorn

1937

Jan 1	11:41 am	Aquarius
Jan 9	4:28 pm	Capricorn
Feb 13	7:26 pm	Aquarius
Mar 6	9:06 am	Pisces
Mar 22	10:41 pm	Aries
Apr 6	8:09 pm	Taurus
Jun 13	5:28 pm	Gemini
Jun 30	9:21 pm	Cancer
Jul 14	11:11 pm	Leo
Jul 31	4:07 pm	Virgo
Oct 8	5:12 am	Libra
Oct 25	8:14 pm	Scorpio
Nov 13	2:25 pm	Sagittarius
Dec 3	6:51 pm	Capricorn

1938

Jan 6	4:37 pm	Sagittarius
Jan 12	5:30 pm	Capricorn
Feb 8	8:17 am	Aquarius
Feb 26	10:01 pm	Pisces
Mar 14	7:02 pm	Aries
Apr 1	8:24 am	Taurus
Apr 23	8:56 am	Aries
May 16	12:46 pm	Taurus
Jun 7	7:32 pm	Gemini
Jun 22	8:09 am	Cancer
Jul 6	10:21 pm	Leo
Jul 26	5:55 pm	Virgo
Sep 2	9:58 pm	Leo
Sep 10	10:38 am	Virgo
Sep 30	11:19 pm	Libra
Oct 18	7:43 am	Scorpio
Nov 6	6:33 pm	Sagittarius

1939

Jan 12	2:57 am	Capricorn
Feb 1	12:57 pm	Aquarius
Feb 19	3:09 am	Pisces
Mar 7	4:14 am	Aries
May 14	8:43 am	Taurus
May 30	9:45 pm	Gemini
Jun 13	6:01 pm	Cancer
Jun 30	1:41 am	Leo
Sep 6	11:58 pm	Virgo
Sep 23	2:48 am	Libra
Oct 11	12:20 am	Scorpio
Nov 1	2:03 am	Sagittarius
Dec 3	2:22 am	Scorpio
Dec 13	2:16 am	Sagittarius

1940

Jan 6	2:56 am	Capricorn
Jan 25	5:14 am	Aquarius
Feb 11	9:01 am	Pisces
Mar 4	5:09 am	Aries

Mercury Positions 1930 – 2000

Mar 7	8:25 pm	Pisces
Apr 16	11:56 pm	Aries
May 6	4:14 pm	Taurus
May 21	8:59 am	Gemini
Jun 4	5:29 pm	Cancer
Jun 26	9:32 am	Leo
Jul 20	8:39 pm	Cancer
Aug 11	12:06 pm	Leo
Aug 29	6:11 am	Virgo
Sep 14	6:34 am	Libra
Oct 3	7:14 am	Scorpio
Dec 9	7:45 am	Sagittarius
Dec 29	4:35 am	Capricorn

1941

Jan 16	5:36 am	Aquarius
Feb 3	8:08 am	Pisces
Mar 6	9:22 pm	Aquarius
Mar 16	7:26 am	Pisces
Apr 12	2:19 am	Aries
Apr 28	6:09 pm	Taurus
May 12	7:50 pm	Gemini
May 29	12:32 pm	Cancer
Aug 6	12:57 am	Leo
Aug 21	12:18 am	Virgo
Sep 6	6:58 pm	Libra
Sep 28	4:21 am	Scorpio
Oct 29	3:34 pm	Libra
Nov 11	3:11 pm	Scorpio
Dec 2	7:11 pm	Sagittarius
Dec 21	10:54 pm	Capricorn

1942

Jan 9	10:24 am	Aquarius
Mar 16	7:10 pm	Pisces
Apr 5	2:06 am	Aries
Apr 20	8:42 am	Taurus
May 4	11:37 pm	Gemini
Jul 12	3:24 pm	Cancer
Jul 28	11:24 pm	Leo
Aug 12	8:48 pm	Virgo
Aug 31	3:27 am	Libra
Nov 6	8:44 pm	Scorpio
Nov 25	3:26 pm	Sagittarius
Dec 14	5:21 pm	Capricorn

1943

Jan 3	3:27 am	Aquarius
Jan 27	6:42 pm	Capricorn
Feb 15	2:00 pm	Aquarius
Mar 10	11:59 pm	Pisces
Mar 28	6:19 am	Aries
Apr 11	11:56 pm	Taurus
Apr 30	10:56 am	Gemini
May 26	5:04 am	Taurus
Jun 13	7:46 pm	Gemini
Jul 6	4:05 am	Cancer
Jul 20	11:08 am	Leo

Aug 5	5:33 am	Virgo
Aug 26	7:36 pm	Libra
Sep 25	4:56 am	Virgo
Oct 11	6:27 pm	Libra
Oct 30	6:37 pm	Scorpio
Nov 18	8:39 am	Sagittarius
Dec 7	8:47 pm	Capricorn

1944

Feb 12	9:17 am	Aquarius
Mar 2	9:45 pm	Pisces
Mar 19	2:43 am	Aries
Apr 3	12:29 pm	Taurus
Jun 11	6:46 am	Gemini
Jun 26	10:40 pm	Cancer
Jul 11	2:41 am	Leo
Jul 28	6:44 pm	Virgo
Oct 4	10:17 pm	Libra
Oct 22	6:33 am	Scorpio
Nov 10	6:09 am	Sagittarius
Dec 1	10:31 am	Capricorn
Dec 23	6:21 pm	Sagittarius

1945

Jan 13	10:04 pm	Capricorn
Feb 5	4:20 am	Aquarius
Feb 23	6:25 am	Pisces
Mar 11	1:45 am	Aries
May 16	10:21 am	Taurus
Jun 4	5:30 am	Gemini
Jun 18	7:27 am	Cancer
Jul 3	10:39 am	Leo
Jul 26	9:48 am	Virgo
Aug 17	3:50 am	Leo
Sep 10	2:21 am	Virgo
Sep 27	7:08 am	Libra
Oct 14	7:13 pm	Scorpio
Nov 3	6:06 pm	Sagittarius

1946

Jan 9	9:09 am	Capricorn
Jan 29	2:22 am	Aquarius
Feb 15	10:43 am	Pisces
Mar 4	4:26 am	Aries
Apr 1	1:16 pm	Pisces
Apr 16	9:54 am	Aries
May 11	9:29 am	Taurus
May 26	11:13 pm	Gemini
Jun 9	9:00 pm	Cancer
Jun 27	2:07 pm	Leo
Sep 3	11:29 am	Virgo
Sep 19	9:34 am	Libra
Oct 7	4:21 pm	Scorpio
Oct 30	6:23 am	Sagittarius
Nov 20	3:16 pm	Scorpio
Dec 12	7:03 pm	Sagittarius

1947

Jan 2	8:46 pm	Capricorn
Jan 21	4:06 pm	Aquarius
Feb 7	8:31 pm	Pisces
Apr 15	11:31 pm	Aries
May 4	1:03 am	Taurus
May 18	8:33 am	Gemini
Jun 2	8:40 am	Cancer
Aug 10	12:40 pm	Leo
Aug 26	9:50 am	Virgo
Sep 11	3:54 pm	Libra
Oct 1	10:26 am	Scorpio
Dec 7	7:32 pm	Sagittarius
Dec 26	6:17 pm	Capricorn

1948

Jan 14	5:06 am	Aquarius
Feb 1	7:46 pm	Pisces
Feb 20	6:08 am	Aquarius
Mar 18	3:14 am	Pisces
Apr 8	9:26 am	Aries
Apr 24	8:38 pm	Taurus
May 8	11:38 pm	Gemini
May 28	5:50 am	Cancer
Jun 28	12:57 pm	Gemini
Jul 11	3:56 pm	Cancer
Aug 2	8:54 am	Leo
Aug 17	3:44 am	Virgo
Sep 3	10:47 am	Libra
Sep 27	2:19 am	Scorpio
Oct 16	10:33 am	Libra
Nov 9	9:19 pm	Scorpio
Nov 29	10:09 am	Sagittarius
Dec 18	11:46 am	Capricorn

1949

Jan 6	3:53 am	Aquarius
Mar 14	4:52 am	Pisces
Apr 1	11:02 am	Aries
Apr 16	9:55 am	Taurus
May 1	9:19 pm	Gemini
Jul 9	10:19 pm	Cancer
Jul 25	12:20 am	Leo
Aug 9	4:04 am	Virgo
Aug 28	10:48 am	Libra
Nov 3	1:58 pm	Scorpio
Nov 22	4:06 am	Sagittarius
Dec 11	8:37 am	Capricorn

1950

Jan 1	7:39 am	Aquarius
Jan 15	2:35 am	Capricorn
Feb 14	2:12 am	Aquarius
Mar 7	5:04 pm	Pisces
Mar 24	10:52 am	Aries
Apr 8	6:13 am	Taurus
Jun 14	9:33 am	Gemini
Jul 2	9:57 am	Cancer

Mercury Positions 1930 – 2000

Jul 16	12:08 pm	Leo
Aug 1	9:44 pm	Virgo
Aug 27	9:17 am	Libra
Sep 10	2:16 pm	Virgo
Oct 9	9:40 am	Libra
Oct 27	5:36 am	Scorpio
Nov 14	10:10 pm	Sagittarius
Dec 4	8:57 pm	Capricorn

1951

Feb 9	12:50 pm	Aquarius
Feb 28	8:04 am	Pisces
Mar 16	6:53 am	Aries
Apr 1	10:27 am	Taurus
May 1	4:25 am	Aries
May 14	8:40 am	Taurus
Jun 9	3:43 am	Gemini
Jun 23	10:13 am	Cancer
Jul 8	8:39 am	Leo
Jul 27	10:24 am	Virgo
Oct 2	9:25 am	Libra
Oct 19	4:52 pm	Scorpio
Nov 7	11:59 pm	Sagittarius
Dec 1	3:41 pm	Capricorn
Dec 12	7:39 am	Sagittarius

1952

Jan 13	1:44 am	Capricorn
Feb 2	8:38 pm	Aquarius
Feb 20	1:55 pm	Pisces
Mar 7	12:10 pm	Aries
May 14	9:43 am	Taurus
May 31	10:26 am	Gemini
Jun 14	7:22 am	Cancer
Jun 30	5:27 am	Leo
Sep 7	7:02 am	Virgo
Sep 23	1:45 pm	Libra
Oct 11	8:05 am	Scorpio
Nov 1	12:34 am	Sagittarius

1953

Jan 6	8:24 am	Capricorn
Jan 25	2:10 pm	Aquarius
Feb 11	6:57 pm	Pisces
Mar 2	2:21 pm	Aries
Mar 15	4:16 pm	Pisces
Apr 17	11:48 am	Aries
May 8	1:24 am	Taurus
May 22	10:58 pm	Gemini
Jun 6	3:23 am	Cancer
Jun 26	6:01 am	Leo
Jul 28	8:40 am	Cancer
Aug 11	9:04 am	Leo
Aug 30	5:59 pm	Virgo
Sep 15	4:45 pm	Libra
Oct 4	11:40 am	Scorpio
Oct 31	10:49 am	Sagittarius
Nov 6	5:19 pm	Scorpio

Dec 10	9:48 am	Sagittarius
Dec 30	12:14 pm	Capricorn

1954

Jan 18	2:43 am	Aquarius
Feb 4	1:03 pm	Pisces
Apr 13	6:34 am	Aries
Apr 30	6:26 am	Taurus
May 14	8:57 am	Gemini
May 30	11:13 am	Cancer
Aug 7	9:44 am	Leo
Aug 22	12:42 pm	Virgo
Sep 8	3:05 am	Libra
Sep 28	11:06 pm	Scorpio
Nov 4	7:37 am	Libra
Nov 11	5:25 am	Scorpio
Dec 4	2:02 am	Sagittarius
Dec 23	7:10 am	Capricorn

1955

Jan 10	6:05 pm	Aquarius
Mar 17	3:49 pm	Pisces
Apr 6	11:15 am	Aries
Apr 21	9:57 pm	Taurus
May 6	8:05 am	Gemini
Jul 13	9:44 am	Cancer
Jul 30	12:22 pm	Leo
Aug 14	8:08 am	Virgo
Sep 1	7:06 am	Libra
Nov 8	1:57 am	Scorpio
Nov 26	11:34 pm	Sagittarius
Dec 16	1:06 am	Capricorn

1956

Jan 4	4:16 am	Aquarius
Feb 2	7:18 am	Capricorn
Feb 15	1:34 am	Aquarius
Mar 11	5:27 am	Pisces
Mar 28	5:41 pm	Aries
Apr 12	12:10 pm	Taurus
Apr 29	5:41 pm	Gemini
Jul 6	2:02 pm	Cancer
Jul 21	12:35 am	Leo
Aug 5	2:06 pm	Virgo
Aug 26	8:30 am	Libra
Sep 29	4:25 pm	Virgo
Oct 11	2:30 am	Libra
Oct 31	3:19 am	Scorpio
Nov 18	4:42 pm	Sagittarius
Dec 8	2:11 am	Capricorn

1957

Feb 12	9:30 am	Aquarius
Mar 4	6:34 am	Pisces
Mar 20	2:48 pm	Aries
Apr 4	6:37 pm	Taurus
Jun 12	8:40 am	Gemini
Jun 28	12:08 pm	Cancer

Jul 12	2:41 pm	Leo
Jul 29	8:44 pm	Virgo
Oct 6	6:09 am	Libra
Oct 23	3:50 pm	Scorpio
Nov 11	1:00 pm	Sagittarius
Dec 2	6:19 am	Capricorn
Dec 28	12:30 pm	Sagittarius

1958

Jan 14	5:03 am	Capricorn
Feb 6	10:21 am	Aquarius
Feb 24	4:44 pm	Pisces
Mar 12	12:31 pm	Aries
Apr 2	2:17 pm	Taurus
Apr 10	8:51 am	Aries
May 16	8:53 pm	Taurus
Jun 5	3:59 pm	Gemini
Jun 19	9:20 pm	Cancer
Jul 4	6:46 pm	Leo
Jul 26	5:08 am	Virgo
Aug 23	9:31 am	Leo
Sep 10	8:10 pm	Virgo
Sep 28	5:45 pm	Libra
Oct 16	3:52 am	Scorpio
Nov 4	9:36 pm	Sagittarius

1959

Jan 10	11:48 am	Capricorn
Jan 30	10:41 am	Aquarius
Feb 16	9:15 pm	Pisces
Mar 5	6:52 am	Aries
May 12	2:48 pm	Taurus
May 28	12:35 pm	Gemini
Jun 11	9:11 am	Cancer
Jun 28	11:31 am	Leo
Sep 4	9:28 pm	Virgo
Sep 20	8:20 pm	Libra
Oct 8	11:02 pm	Scorpio
Oct 30	8:16 pm	Sagittarius
Nov 25	6:53 am	Scorpio
Dec 13	10:42 am	Sagittarius

1960

Jan 4	3:24 am	Capricorn
Jan 23	1:16 am	Aquarius
Feb 9	5:13 am	Pisces
Apr 15	9:22 pm	Aries
May 4	11:45 am	Taurus
May 18	10:27 pm	Gemini
Jun 2	3:31 pm	Cancer
Jun 30	8:14 pm	Leo
Jul 5	8:22 pm	Cancer
Aug 10	12:49 pm	Leo
Aug 26	10:11 pm	Virgo
Sep 12	1:29 am	Libra
Oct 1	12:17 pm	Scorpio
Dec 7	12:30 pm	Sagittarius
Dec 27	2:21 am	Capricorn

Mercury Positions 1930 – 2000

1961
Jan 14	1:58 pm	Aquarius
Feb 1	4:39 pm	Pisces
Feb 24	3:22 pm	Aquarius
Mar 18	5:16 am	Pisces
Apr 10	4:22 am	Aries
Apr 26	9:34 am	Taurus
May 10	11:34 am	Gemini
May 28	12:23 pm	Cancer
Aug 3	8:15 pm	Leo
Aug 18	3:52 pm	Virgo
Sep 4	5:32 pm	Libra
Sep 27	7:16 am	Scorpio
Oct 21	9:29 am	Libra
Nov 10	6:53 pm	Scorpio
Nov 30	5:54 pm	Sagittarius
Dec 19	8:04 pm	Capricorn

1962
Jan 7	10:08 am	Aquarius
Mar 15	6:43 am	Pisces
Apr 2	9:32 pm	Aries
Apr 17	11:10 pm	Taurus
May 3	1:05 am	Gemini
Jul 11	2:36 am	Cancer
Jul 26	1:50 pm	Leo
Aug 10	2:29 pm	Virgo
Aug 29	10:48 am	Libra
Nov 4	9:20 pm	Scorpio
Nov 23	12:31 pm	Sagittarius
Dec 12	3:51 pm	Capricorn

1963
Jan 1	8:10 pm	Aquarius
Jan 19	11:59 pm	Capricorn
Feb 15	5:08 am	Aquarius
Mar 9	12:26 am	Pisces
Mar 25	10:52 pm	Aries
Apr 9	5:03 pm	Taurus
May 2	11:17 pm	Gemini
May 10	3:39 pm	Taurus
Jun 14	6:21 pm	Gemini
Jul 3	10:00 pm	Cancer
Jul 18	1:19 am	Leo
Aug 3	4:20 am	Virgo
Aug 26	3:33 pm	Libra
Sep 16	3:29 pm	Virgo
Oct 10	11:44 am	Libra
Oct 28	2:54 pm	Scorpio
Nov 16	6:07 am	Sagittarius
Dec 6	12:17 pm	Capricorn

1964
Feb 10	4:30 pm	Aquarius
Feb 29	5:50 pm	Pisces
Mar 16	6:54 am	Aries
Apr 1	7:57 pm	Taurus
Jun 9	10:45 am	Gemini

Jun 24	12:17 pm	Cancer
Jul 8	7:38 pm	Leo
Jul 27	6:35 am	Virgo
Oct 2	7:12 pm	Libra
Oct 20	2:11 am	Scorpio
Nov 8	6:02 am	Sagittarius
Nov 30	2:30 pm	Capricorn
Dec 16	9:31 am	Sagittarius

1965
Jan 12	10:12 pm	Capricorn
Feb 3	4:02 am	Aquarius
Feb 21	12:40 am	Pisces
Mar 8	9:19 pm	Aries
May 15	8:19 am	Taurus
Jun 1	10:47 pm	Gemini
Jun 15	9:04 pm	Cancer
Jul 1	10:55 am	Leo
Jul 31	6:24 am	Virgo
Aug 3	3:09 am	Leo
Sep 8	12:14 pm	Virgo
Sep 25	12:49 am	Libra
Oct 12	4:15 pm	Scorpio
Nov 2	1:04 am	Sagittarius

1966
Jan 7	1:26 pm	Capricorn
Jan 26	11:10 pm	Aquarius
Feb 13	5:17 am	Pisces
Mar 2	9:57 pm	Aries
Mar 21	9:34 pm	Pisces
Apr 17	4:31 pm	Aries
May 9	9:48 am	Taurus
May 24	12:59 pm	Gemini
Jun 7	2:11 pm	Cancer
Jun 26	2:05 pm	Leo
Sep 1	5:35 am	Virgo
Sep 17	3:19 am	Libra
Oct 5	5:03 pm	Scorpio
Oct 30	2:38 am	Sagittarius
Nov 12	10:26 pm	Scorpio
Dec 11	10:27 am	Sagittarius
Dec 31	7:52 pm	Capricorn

1967
Jan 19	12:05 pm	Aquarius
Feb 5	7:38 pm	Pisces
Apr 14	9:38 am	Aries
May 1	6:26 pm	Taurus
May 15	10:27 pm	Gemini
May 31	1:02 pm	Cancer
Aug 8	5:09 pm	Leo
Aug 24	1:17 am	Virgo
Sep 9	11:53 am	Libra
Sep 29	8:46 pm	Scorpio
Dec 5	8:41 am	Sagittarius
Dec 24	3:33 pm	Capricorn

1968
Jan 12	2:19 am	Aquarius
Feb 1	7:57 am	Pisces
Feb 11	1:54 pm	Aquarius
Mar 17	9:45 am	Pisces
Apr 6	8:01 pm	Aries
Apr 22	11:18 am	Taurus
May 6	5:56 pm	Gemini
May 29	5:44 pm	Cancer
Jun 13	5:32 pm	Gemini
Jul 12	8:30 pm	Cancer
Jul 31	1:11 am	Leo
Aug 14	7:53 pm	Virgo
Sep 1	11:59 am	Libra
Sep 28	9:40 am	Scorpio
Oct 7	5:46 pm	Libra
Nov 8	6:00 am	Scorpio
Nov 27	7:47 am	Sagittarius
Dec 16	9:11 am	Capricorn

1969
Jan 4	7:18 am	Aquarius
Mar 12	10:19 am	Pisces
Mar 30	4:59 am	Aries
Apr 14	12:55 pm	Taurus
Apr 30	10:18 am	Gemini
Jul 7	10:58 pm	Cancer
Jul 22	2:11 pm	Leo
Aug 6	11:21 pm	Virgo
Aug 27	1:50 am	Libra
Oct 6	9:57 pm	Virgo
Oct 9	11:56 am	Libra
Nov 1	11:53 pm	Scorpio
Nov 20	1:00 am	Sagittarius
Dec 9	8:21 am	Capricorn

1970
Feb 13	8:08 am	Aquarius
Mar 5	3:10 pm	Pisces
Mar 22	2:59 am	Aries
Apr 6	2:40 am	Taurus
Jun 13	7:46 am	Gemini
Jun 30	1:22 am	Cancer
Jul 14	3:06 am	Leo
Jul 31	12:21 am	Virgo
Oct 7	1:04 pm	Libra
Oct 25	1:16 am	Scorpio
Nov 12	8:16 pm	Sagittarius
Dec 3	5:14 am	Capricorn

1971
Jan 2	6:36 pm	Sagittarius
Jan 13	9:16 pm	Capricorn
Feb 7	3:51 pm	Aquarius
Feb 26	2:57 am	Pisces
Mar 13	11:46 pm	Aries
Apr 1	9:11 am	Taurus
Apr 18	4:52 pm	Aries

Mercury Positions 1930 – 2000

May 16	10:32 pm	Taurus
Jun 7	1:45 am	Gemini
Jun 21	11:25 am	Cancer
Jul 6	3:53 am	Leo
Jul 26	12:03 pm	Virgo
Aug 29	3:42 pm	Leo
Sep 11	1:45 am	Virgo
Sep 30	4:19 am	Libra
Oct 17	12:49 pm	Scorpio
Nov 6	1:59 am	Sagittarius

1972

Jan 11	1:18 pm	Capricorn
Jan 31	6:46 am	Aquarius
Feb 18	7:53 am	Pisces
Mar 5	11:59 am	Aries
May 12	6:45 pm	Taurus
May 29	1:46 am	Gemini
Jun 11	9:56 pm	Cancer
Jun 28	11:52 am	Leo
Sep 5	6:36 am	Virgo
Sep 21	7:11 am	Libra
Oct 9	6:11 am	Scorpio
Oct 30	2:27 pm	Sagittarius
Nov 29	2:08 am	Scorpio
Dec 12	6:20 pm	Sagittarius

1973

Jan 4	9:41 am	Capricorn
Jan 23	10:23 am	Aquarius
Feb 9	2:30 pm	Pisces
Apr 16	4:17 pm	Aries
May 5	9:55 pm	Taurus
May 20	12:24 pm	Gemini
Jun 3	11:42 pm	Cancer
Jun 27	1:42 am	Leo
Jul 16	3:03 am	Cancer
Aug 11	7:21 am	Leo
Aug 28	10:22 am	Virgo
Sep 13	11:16 am	Libra
Oct 2	3:12 pm	Scorpio
Dec 8	4:29 pm	Sagittarius
Dec 28	10:14 am	Capricorn

1974

Jan 15	10:56 pm	Aquarius
Feb 2	5:42 pm	Pisces
Mar 2	12:49 pm	Aquarius
Mar 17	3:11 pm	Pisces
Apr 11	10:20 am	Aries
Apr 27	10:10 am	Taurus
May 11	11:55 pm	Gemini
May 29	3:03 am	Cancer
Aug 5	6:42 am	Leo
Aug 20	4:04 am	Virgo
Sep 6	12:48 am	Libra
Sep 27	7:20 pm	Scorpio
Oct 26	6:21 pm	Libra

Nov 11	11:05 am	Scorpio
Dec 2	1:17 am	Sagittarius
Dec 21	4:16 am	Capricorn

1975

Jan 8	4:58 pm	Aquarius
Mar 16	6:50 am	Pisces
Apr 4	7:28 am	Aries
Apr 19	12:20 pm	Taurus
May 4	6:55 am	Gemini
Jul 12	3:56 am	Cancer
Jul 28	3:05 am	Leo
Aug 12	1:12 am	Virgo
Aug 30	12:20 pm	Libra
Nov 6	3:58 am	Scorpio
Nov 24	8:44 pm	Sagittarius
Dec 13	11:10 pm	Capricorn

1976

Jan 2	3:22 pm	Aquarius
Jan 24	8:30 pm	Capricorn
Feb 15	2:03 pm	Aquarius
Mar 9	7:02 am	Pisces
Mar 26	10:36 am	Aries
Apr 10	4:29 am	Taurus
Apr 29	6:11 pm	Gemini
May 19	2:21 pm	Taurus
Jun 13	2:20 pm	Gemini
Jul 4	9:18 am	Cancer
Jul 18	2:35 pm	Leo
Aug 3	11:41 am	Virgo
Aug 25	3:52 pm	Libra
Sep 21	2:15 am	Virgo
Oct 10	9:47 am	Libra
Oct 28	11:55 pm	Scorpio
Nov 16	2:02 pm	Sagittarius
Dec 6	4:25 am	Capricorn

1977

Feb 10	6:55 pm	Aquarius
Mar 2	3:09 am	Pisces
Mar 18	6:56 am	Aries
Apr 2	9:46 pm	Taurus
Jun 10	4:07 pm	Gemini
Jun 26	2:07 am	Cancer
Jul 10	7:00 am	Leo
Jul 28	5:15 pm	Virgo
Oct 4	4:16 pm	Libra
Oct 21	11:23 am	Scorpio
Nov 9	12:20 pm	Sagittarius
Dec 1	1:43 am	Capricorn
Dec 21	2:18 am	Sagittarius

1978

Jan 13	3:07 pm	Capricorn
Feb 4	10:54 am	Aquarius
Feb 22	11:11 am	Pisces
Mar 10	7:10 am	Aries

May 16	3:20 am	Taurus
Jun 3	10:26 am	Gemini
Jun 17	10:49 am	Cancer
Jul 2	5:28 pm	Leo
Jul 27	1:10 am	Virgo
Aug 13	2:05 am	Leo
Sep 9	2:23 pm	Virgo
Sep 26	11:40 am	Libra
Oct 14	12:30 am	Scorpio
Nov 3	2:48 am	Sagittarius

1979

Jan 8	5:33 pm	Capricorn
Jan 28	7:49 am	Aquarius
Feb 14	3:38 pm	Pisces
Mar 3	4:32 pm	Aries
Mar 28	5:39 pm	Pisces
Apr 17	7:48 am	Aries
May 10	5:03 pm	Taurus
May 26	2:44 am	Gemini
Jun 9	1:32 am	Cancer
Jun 27	4:51 am	Leo
Sep 2	4:39 pm	Virgo
Sep 18	1:59 pm	Libra
Oct 6	10:55 pm	Scorpio
Oct 30	2:06 am	Sagittarius
Nov 17	10:08 pm	Scorpio
Dec 12	8:34 am	Sagittarius

1980

Jan 2	3:02 am	Capricorn
Jan 20	9:18 pm	Aquarius
Feb 7	3:07 am	Pisces
Apr 14	10:58 am	Aries
May 2	5:56 am	Taurus
May 16	12:06 pm	Gemini
May 31	5:05 pm	Cancer
Aug 8	10:31 pm	Leo
Aug 24	1:47 pm	Virgo
Sep 9	9:00 pm	Libra
Sep 29	8:16 pm	Scorpio
Dec 5	2:45 pm	Sagittarius
Dec 24	11:46 pm	Capricorn

1981

Jan 12	10:48 am	Aquarius
Jan 31	12:35 pm	Pisces
Feb 16	3:02 am	Aquarius
Mar 17	11:33 pm	Pisces
Apr 8	4:11 am	Aries
Apr 24	12:31 am	Taurus
May 8	4:42 am	Gemini
May 28	12:04 pm	Cancer
Jun 22	5:51 pm	Gemini
Jul 12	4:08 pm	Cancer
Aug 1	1:30 am	Leo
Aug 16	7:47 am	Virgo
Sep 2	5:40 pm	Libra

Mercury Positions 1930 – 2000

Sep 27	6:02 am	Scorpio
Oct 13	9:09 am	Libra
Nov 9	8:14 am	Scorpio
Nov 28	3:52 am	Sagittarius
Dec 17	5:21 pm	Capricorn

1982

Jan 5	11:49 am	Aquarius
Mar 13	2:11 pm	Pisces
Mar 31	3:59 pm	Aries
Apr 15	1:54 pm	Taurus
May 1	8:29 am	Gemini
Jul 9	6:26 am	Cancer
Jul 24	3:48 am	Leo
Aug 8	9:06 am	Virgo
Aug 27	10:22 pm	Libra
Nov 2	8:10 pm	Scorpio
Nov 21	9:28 am	Sagittarius
Dec 10	3:04 pm	Capricorn

1983

Jan 1	8:32 am	Aquarius
Jan 12	1:55 am	Capricorn
Feb 14	4:36 am	Aquarius
Mar 6	11:23 pm	Pisces
Mar 23	3:09 am	Aries
Apr 7	12:04 pm	Taurus
Jun 14	3:06 am	Gemini
Jul 1	2:18 pm	Cancer
Jul 15	3:57 pm	Leo
Aug 1	5:22 am	Virgo
Aug 29	1:07 am	Libra
Sep 5	9:30 pm	Virgo
Oct 8	6:44 pm	Libra
Oct 26	10:47 am	Scorpio
Nov 14	3:56 am	Sagittarius
Dec 4	6:22 am	Capricorn

1984

Feb 8	8:50 pm	Aquarius
Feb 27	1:07 pm	Pisces
Mar 14	11:27 am	Aries
Mar 31	3:25 pm	Taurus
Apr 25	6:49 am	Aries
May 15	7:33 am	Taurus
Jun 7	10:45 am	Gemini
Jun 22	1:39 am	Cancer
Jul 6	1:56 pm	Leo
Jul 26	1:49 am	Virgo
Sep 30	2:44 pm	Libra
Oct 17	10:01 pm	Scorpio
Nov 6	7:09 am	Sagittarius
Dec 1	11:29 am	Capricorn
Dec 7	4:46 pm	Sagittarius

1985

Jan 11	1:25 pm	Capricorn
Feb 1	2:43 am	Aquarius

Feb 18	6:41 pm	Pisces
Mar 6	7:07 pm	Aries
May 13	9:10 pm	Taurus
May 30	2:44 pm	Gemini
Jun 13	11:11 am	Cancer
Jun 29	2:34 pm	Leo
Sep 6	2:39 pm	Virgo
Sep 22	6:13 pm	Libra
Oct 10	1:50 pm	Scorpio
Oct 31	11:44 am	Sagittarius
Dec 4	2:23 pm	Scorpio
Dec 12	6:05 am	Sagittarius

1986

Jan 5	3:42 pm	Capricorn
Jan 24	7:33 pm	Aquarius
Feb 11	12:21 am	Pisces
Mar 3	2:22 am	Aries
Mar 11	12:36 pm	Pisces
Apr 17	7:33 am	Aries
May 7	7:33 am	Taurus
May 22	2:26 am	Gemini
Jun 5	9:06 am	Cancer
Jun 26	9:15 am	Leo
Jul 23	4:51 pm	Cancer
Aug 11	4:09 pm	Leo
Aug 29	10:28 pm	Virgo
Sep 14	9:28 pm	Libra
Oct 3	7:19 pm	Scorpio
Dec 9	7:34 pm	Sagittarius
Dec 29	6:09 pm	Capricorn

1987

Jan 17	8:08 am	Aquarius
Feb 3	9:31 pm	Pisces
Mar 11	4:55 pm	Aquarius
Mar 13	4:09 pm	Pisces
Apr 12	3:23 pm	Aries
Apr 29	10:39 am	Taurus
May 13	12:50 pm	Gemini
May 29	11:21 pm	Cancer
Aug 6	4:20 pm	Leo
Aug 21	4:36 pm	Virgo
Sep 7	8:52 pm	Libra
Sep 28	12:21 pm	Scorpio
Oct 31	8:57 pm	Libra
Nov 11	4:57 pm	Scorpio
Dec 3	8:33 am	Sagittarius
Dec 22	12:40 pm	Capricorn

1988

Jan 10	12:28 am	Aquarius
Mar 16	5:09 am	Pisces
Apr 4	5:04 pm	Aries
Apr 20	1:42 am	Taurus
May 4	2:40 pm	Gemini
Jul 12	1:42 am	Cancer
Jul 28	4:19 pm	Leo

Aug 12	12:29 pm	Virgo
Aug 30	3:25 pm	Libra
Nov 6	9:57 am	Scorpio
Nov 25	5:04 pm	Sagittarius
Dec 14	6:53 am	Capricorn

1989

Jan 2	2:41 pm	Aquarius
Jan 28	11:06 pm	Capricorn
Feb 14	1:11 pm	Aquarius
Mar 10	1:07 pm	Pisces
Mar 27	10:16 pm	Aries
Apr 11	4:36 pm	Taurus
Apr 29	2:53 pm	Gemini
May 28	5:53 pm	Taurus
Jun 12	3:56 pm	Gemini
Jul 5	7:55 pm	Cancer
Jul 20	4:04 am	Leo
Aug 4	7:54 pm	Virgo
Aug 26	1:14 am	Libra
Sep 26	10:28 am	Virgo
Oct 11	1:11 am	Libra
Oct 30	8:53 am	Scorpio
Nov 17	10:10 pm	Sagittarius
Dec 7	9:30 am	Capricorn

1990

Feb 11	8:11 pm	Aquarius
Mar 3	12:14 pm	Pisces
Mar 19	7:04 pm	Aries
Apr 4	2:35 am	Taurus
Jun 11	7:29 pm	Gemini
Jun 27	3:46 pm	Cancer
Jul 11	6:48 pm	Leo
Jul 29	6:10 am	Virgo
Oct 5	12:44 pm	Libra
Oct 22	8:46 pm	Scorpio
Nov 10	7:06 pm	Sagittarius
Dec 1	7:13 pm	Capricorn
Dec 25	5:57 pm	Sagittarius

1991

Jan 14	3:02 am	Capricorn
Feb 5	5:20 pm	Aquarius
Feb 23	9:35 pm	Pisces
Mar 11	5:40 pm	Aries
May 16	5:45 pm	Taurus
Jun 4	9:24 pm	Gemini
Jun 19	12:40 am	Cancer
Jul 4	1:05 am	Leo
Jul 26	8:00 am	Virgo
Aug 19	4:40 pm	Leo
Sep 10	12:14 pm	Virgo
Sep 27	10:26 pm	Libra
Oct 15	9:01 am	Scorpio
Nov 4	5:41 am	Sagittarius

Mercury Positions 1930 – 2000

1992

Jan 9	8:46 pm	Capricorn
Jan 29	4:15 pm	Aquarius
Feb 16	2:04 am	Pisces
Mar 3	4:45 pm	Aries
Apr 3	6:52 pm	Pisces
Apr 14	12:35 pm	Aries
May 10	11:10 pm	Taurus
May 26	4:16 pm	Gemini
Jun 9	1:27 pm	Cancer
Jun 27	12:11 am	Leo
Sep 3	3:03 am	Virgo
Sep 19	12:41 am	Libra
Oct 7	5:13 am	Scorpio
Oct 29	12:02 pm	Sagittarius
Nov 21	2:44 pm	Scorpio
Dec 12	3:05 am	Sagittarius

1993

Jan 2	9:47 am	Capricorn
Jan 21	6:25 am	Aquarius
Feb 7	11:19 am	Pisces
Apr 15	10:18 am	Aries
May 3	4:54 pm	Taurus
May 18	1:53 am	Gemini
Jun 1	10:54 pm	Cancer
Aug 10	12:51 am	Leo
Aug 26	2:06 am	Virgo
Sep 11	6:18 am	Libra
Sep 30	9:09 am	Scorpio
Dec 6	8:04 pm	Sagittarius
Dec 26	7:47 am	Capricorn

1994

Jan 13	7:25 pm	Aquarius
Feb 1	5:28 am	Pisces
Feb 21	10:15 am	Aquarius
Mar 18	7:04 am	Pisces
Apr 9	11:30 am	Aries
Apr 25	1:27 pm	Taurus
May 9	4:08 pm	Gemini
May 28	9:52 am	Cancer
Jul 2	6:18 pm	Gemini
Jul 10	7:41 am	Cancer
Aug 3	1:09 am	Leo
Aug 17	7:44 am	Virgo
Sep 3	11:55 pm	Libra
Sep 27	3:51 am	Scorpio
Oct 19	1:19 am	Libra
Nov 10	7:46 am	Scorpio
Nov 29	11:38 pm	Sagittarius

Dec 19	1:26 am	Capricorn

1995

Jan 6	5:17 pm	Aquarius
Mar 14	4:35 pm	Pisces
Apr 2	2:29 am	Aries
Apr 17	2:54 am	Taurus
May 2	10:18 am	Gemini
Jul 10	11:58 am	Cancer
Jul 25	5:19 pm	Leo
Aug 9	7:13 pm	Virgo
Aug 28	9:07 pm	Libra
Nov 4	3:50 am	Scorpio
Nov 22	5:46 pm	Sagittarius
Dec 11	9:57 pm	Capricorn

1996

Jan 1	1:06 pm	Aquarius
Jan 17	4:37 am	Capricorn
Feb 14	9:44 pm	Aquarius
Mar 7	6:53 am	Pisces
Mar 24	3:03 am	Aries
Apr 7	10:16 pm	Taurus
Jun 13	4:45 pm	Gemini
Jul 2	2:37 am	Cancer
Jul 16	4:56 am	Leo
Aug 1	11:17 am	Virgo
Aug 26	12:17 am	Libra
Sep 12	4:32 am	Virgo
Oct 8	10:13 pm	Libra
Oct 26	8:01 pm	Scorpio
Nov 14	11:36 am	Sagittarius
Dec 4	8:48 am	Capricorn

1997

Feb 9	12:53 am	Aquarius
Feb 27	10:54 pm	Pisces
Mar 15	11:13 am	Aries
Apr 1	8:45 am	Taurus
May 4	8:48 pm	Aries
May 12	5:25 am	Taurus
Jun 8	6:25 pm	Gemini
Jun 23	3:41 pm	Cancer
Jul 8	12:28 am	Leo
Jul 26	7:42 pm	Virgo
Oct 2	12:38 am	Libra
Oct 19	7:08 am	Scorpio
Nov 7	12:42 pm	Sagittarius
Nov 30	2:11 pm	Capricorn
Dec 13	1:06 pm	Sagittarius

1998

Jan 12	11:20 am	Capricorn
Feb 2	10:15 am	Aquarius
Feb 20	5:22 am	Pisces
Mar 8	3:28 am	Aries
May 14	9:10 pm	Taurus
Jun 1	3:07 am	Gemini
Jun 15	12:33 am	Cancer
Jun 30	6:52 pm	Leo
Sep 7	8:58 pm	Virgo
Sep 24	5:13 am	Libra
Oct 11	9:45 pm	Scorpio
Nov 1	11:03 am	Sagittarius

1999

Jan 6	9:04 pm	Capricorn
Jan 26	4:32 am	Aquarius
Feb 12	10:28 am	Pisces
Mar 2	5:50 pm	Aries
Mar 18	4:23 am	Pisces
Apr 17	5:09 pm	Aries
May 8	4:22 pm	Taurus
May 23	4:22 pm	Gemini
Jun 6	7:18 pm	Cancer
Jun 26	10:39 am	Leo
Jul 31	1:44 pm	Cancer
Aug 10	11:25 pm	Leo
Aug 31	10:15 am	Virgo
Sep 16	7:53 am	Libra
Oct 5	12:12 am	Scorpio
Oct 30	3:08 pm	Sagittarius
Nov 9	3:13 pm	Scorpio
Dec 10	9:09 pm	Sagittarius
Dec 31	1:48 am	Capricorn

2000

Jan 18	5:20 pm	Aquarius
Feb 5	3:09 am	Pisces
Apr 12	7:17 pm	Aries
Apr 29	10:53 pm	Taurus
May 14	2:10 am	Gemini
May 29	11:27 pm	Cancer
Aug 7	12:42 am	Leo
Aug 22	5:11 am	Virgo
Sep 7	5:22 pm	Libra
Sep 28	8:28 am	Scorpio
Nov 7	2:28 am	Libra
Nov 8	2:54 pm	Scorpio
Dec 3	3:26 pm	Sagittarius
Dec 22	9:03 pm	Capricorn

Venus Positions 1930 – 2000

1930
Jan 23	7:22 pm	Aquarius
Feb 16	5:11 pm	Pisces
Mar 12	5:34 pm	Aries
Apr 5	9:57 pm	Taurus
Apr 30	7:37 am	Gemini
May 24	11:36 pm	Cancer
Jun 18	11:39 pm	Leo
Jul 14	11:34 am	Virgo
Aug 9	7:54 pm	Libra
Sep 6	11:05 pm	Scorpio
Oct 11	9:45 pm	Sagittarius
Nov 22	2:44 am	Scorpio

1931
Jan 3	3:03 pm	Sagittarius
Feb 6	7:25 am	Capricorn
Mar 5	4:46 pm	Aquarius
Mar 31	2:04 pm	Pisces
Apr 25	9:10 am	Aries
May 20	9:38 pm	Taurus
Jun 14	6:04 pm	Gemini
Jul 9	10:35 am	Cancer
Aug 2	10:29 pm	Leo
Aug 27	5:42 am	Virgo
Sep 20	9:15 am	Libra
Oct 14	10:45 am	Scorpio
Nov 7	11:32 am	Sagittarius
Dec 1	12:29 pm	Capricorn
Dec 25	2:44 pm	Aquarius

1932
Jan 18	8:52 pm	Pisces
Feb 12	11:58 am	Aries
Mar 8	9:07 pm	Taurus
Apr 4	7:19 pm	Gemini
May 6	4:04 am	Cancer
Jul 13	5:33 am	Gemini
Jul 28	7:36 am	Cancer
Sep 8	2:45 pm	Leo
Oct 7	12:46 pm	Virgo
Nov 1	11:01 pm	Libra
Nov 26	7:06 pm	Scorpio
Dec 21	2:43 am	Sagittarius

1933
Jan 14	4:56 am	Capricorn
Feb 7	5:30 am	Aquarius
Mar 3	6:24 am	Pisces
Mar 27	8:58 am	Aries
Apr 20	2:00 pm	Taurus
May 14	9:47 pm	Gemini
Jun 8	8:01 am	Cancer
Jul 2	8:29 pm	Leo
Jul 27	11:45 am	Virgo
Aug 21	7:23 am	Libra
Sep 15	9:54 am	Scorpio
Oct 10	11:32 am	Sagittarius

| Nov 6 | 11:02 am | Capricorn |
| Dec 5 | 1:00 pm | Aquarius |

1934
Apr 6	4:23 am	Pisces
May 6	3:54 am	Aries
Jun 2	5:11 am	Taurus
Jun 28	4:38 am	Gemini
Jul 23	1:22 pm	Cancer
Aug 17	10:45 am	Leo
Sep 10	10:32 pm	Virgo
Oct 5	2:56 am	Libra
Oct 29	2:37 am	Scorpio
Nov 21	11:59 pm	Sagittarius
Dec 15	8:39 pm	Capricorn

1935
Jan 8	5:44 pm	Aquarius
Feb 1	4:36 pm	Pisces
Feb 25	7:30 am	Aries
Mar 22	5:29 am	Taurus
Apr 16	2:37 am	Gemini
May 11	5:01 pm	Cancer
Jun 7	2:11 pm	Leo
Jul 7	3:33 pm	Virgo
Nov 9	11:34 am	Libra
Dec 8	9:36 am	Scorpio

1936
Jan 3	9:16 am	Sagittarius
Jan 28	9:00 am	Capricorn
Feb 21	11:14 am	Aquarius
Mar 17	9:53 am	Pisces
Apr 10	7:41 pm	Aries
May 5	5:53 am	Taurus
May 29	4:39 pm	Gemini
Jun 23	3:16 am	Cancer
Jul 17	12:51 pm	Leo
Aug 10	9:11 pm	Virgo
Sep 4	5:02 am	Libra
Sep 28	1:36 pm	Scorpio
Oct 23	12:00 am	Sagittarius
Nov 16	1:36 pm	Capricorn
Dec 11	9:51 am	Aquarius

1937
Jan 5	10:18 pm	Pisces
Feb 2	5:39 am	Aries
Mar 9	8:19 am	Taurus
Apr 13	11:19 pm	Aries
Jun 4	1:41 am	Taurus
Jul 7	4:13 pm	Gemini
Aug 4	3:14 am	Cancer
Aug 30	7:08 pm	Leo
Sep 24	11:03 pm	Virgo
Oct 19	11:33 am	Libra
Nov 12	2:43 pm	Scorpio
Dec 6	1:06 pm	Sagittarius

| Dec 30 | 9:42 am | Capricorn |

1938
Jan 23	6:16 am	Aquarius
Feb 16	4:00 am	Pisces
Mar 12	4:20 am	Aries
Apr 5	8:46 am	Taurus
Apr 29	6:35 pm	Gemini
May 24	10:56 am	Cancer
Jun 18	12:44 am	Virgo
Jul 14	12:44 am	Virgo
Aug 9	11:26 am	Libra
Sep 6	8:36 pm	Scorpio
Oct 13	1:49 pm	Sagittarius
Nov 15	11:07 am	Scorpio

1939
Jan 4	4:48 pm	Sagittarius
Feb 6	4:20 am	Capricorn
Mar 5	8:29 am	Aquarius
Mar 31	3:34 am	Pisces
Apr 25	9:28 am	Aries
May 20	9:13 am	Taurus
Jun 14	5:11 am	Gemini
Jul 8	9:25 pm	Cancer
Aug 2	9:11 am	Leo
Aug 26	4:24 pm	Virgo
Sep 19	8:02 pm	Libra
Oct 13	9:41 pm	Scorpio
Nov 6	10:41 pm	Sagittarius
Nov 30	11:52 pm	Capricorn
Dec 25	2:25 am	Aquarius

1940
Jan 18	9:00 am	Pisces
Feb 12	12:51 am	Aries
Mar 8	11:25 am	Taurus
Apr 4	1:10 pm	Gemini
May 6	1:47 pm	Cancer
Jul 5	11:17 am	Gemini
Jul 31	9:20 pm	Cancer
Sep 8	11:59 am	Leo
Oct 6	4:10 pm	Virgo
Nov 1	12:24 pm	Libra
Nov 26	7:32 pm	Scorpio
Dec 20	2:36 pm	Sagittarius

1941
Jan 13	4:29 pm	Capricorn
Feb 6	4:49 pm	Aquarius
Mar 2	5:33 pm	Pisces
Mar 26	7:58 pm	Aries
Apr 20	12:53 am	Taurus
May 14	8:36 am	Gemini
Jun 7	6:53 pm	Cancer
Jul 2	7:33 am	Leo
Jul 26	11:12 pm	Virgo
Aug 20	7:29 pm	Libra

Venus Positions 1930 – 2000

Sep 14	11:01 pm	Scorpio	Nov 12	2:05 am	Scorpio	Jul 26	10:43 am	Virgo
Oct 10	2:21 pm	Sagittarius	Dec 6	12:22 am	Sagittarius	Aug 20	7:39 am	Libra
Nov 6	5:17 am	Capricorn	Dec 29	8:56 pm	Capricorn	Sep 14	12:12 pm	Scorpio
Dec 5	6:04 pm	Aquarius				Oct 10	5:18 am	Sagittarius

1942 · **1946** · Nov 5 11:53 pm Capricorn · Dec 6 1:06 am Aquarius

Apr 6	8:14 am	Pisces	Jan 22	5:28 am	Aquarius			
May 5	9:26 pm	Aries	Feb 15	3:11 pm	Pisces		**1950**	
Jun 1	7:26 pm	Taurus	Mar 11	3:32 pm	Aries	Apr 6	10:13 am	Pisces
Jun 27	5:18 pm	Gemini	Apr 4	8:01 pm	Taurus	May 5	2:19 pm	Aries
Jul 23	1:10 am	Cancer	Apr 29	5:59 am	Gemini	Jun 1	9:19 am	Taurus
Aug 16	10:04 pm	Leo	May 23	10:39 pm	Cancer	Jun 27	5:45 am	Gemini
Sep 10	9:38 am	Virgo	Jun 18	12:00 am	Leo	Jul 22	12:50 pm	Cancer
Oct 4	1:58 am	Libra	Jul 13	2:22 pm	Virgo	Aug 16	9:18 am	Leo
Oct 28	1:40 pm	Scorpio	Aug 9	3:34 am	Libra	Sep 9	8:37 pm	Virgo
Nov 21	11:07 am	Sagittarius	Sep 6	7:16 pm	Scorpio	Oct 4	12:51 am	Libra
Dec 15	7:53 am	Capricorn	Oct 16	5:45 am	Sagittarius	Oct 28	12:33 am	Scorpio
			Nov 8	3:56 am	Scorpio	Nov 20	10:03 pm	Sagittarius
						Dec 14	6:54 pm	Capricorn

1943 · **1947**

Jan 8	5:03 am	Aquarius	Jan 5	11:45 pm	Sagittarius		**1951**	
Feb 1	4:02 am	Pisces	Feb 6	12:41 am	Capricorn	Jan 7	4:10 pm	Aquarius
Feb 25	7:04 am	Aries	Mar 5	12:09 am	Aquarius	Jan 31	3:14 pm	Pisces
Mar 21	5:24 pm	Taurus	Mar 30	5:14 pm	Pisces	Feb 24	6:26 pm	Aries
Apr 15	3:12 pm	Gemini	Apr 24	10:03 pm	Aries	Mar 21	5:05 am	Taurus
May 11	6:56 am	Cancer	May 19	9:06 pm	Taurus	Apr 15	3:33 am	Gemini
Jun 7	7:09 am	Leo	Jun 13	4:35 pm	Gemini	May 10	8:41 pm	Cancer
Jul 7	6:56 pm	Virgo	Jul 8	8:30 am	Cancer	Jun 7	12:10 am	Leo
Nov 9	1:25 am	Libra	Aug 1	8:06 pm	Leo	Jul 7	11:54 pm	Virgo
Dec 8	2:45 am	Scorpio	Aug 26	3:17 am	Virgo	Nov 9	1:48 pm	Libra
			Sep 19	7:01 am	Libra	Dec 7	7:19 pm	Scorpio
			Oct 13	8:49 am	Scorpio			

1944 · Nov 6 9:59 am Sagittarius · Nov 30 11:23 am Capricorn · Dec 24 2:13 pm Aquarius

Jan 2	11:43 pm	Sagittarius					**1952**	
Jan 27	10:11 pm	Capricorn		**1948**		Jan 2	1:44 pm	Sagittarius
Feb 21	11:40 am	Aquarius	Jan 17	9:14 pm	Pisces	Jan 27	10:58 am	Capricorn
Mar 16	9:46 pm	Pisces	Feb 11	1:51 pm	Aries	Feb 20	11:42 am	Aquarius
Apr 10	7:09 am	Aries	Mar 8	1:59 am	Taurus	Mar 16	9:18 am	Pisces
May 4	5:04 pm	Taurus	Apr 4	7:40 am	Gemini	Apr 9	6:17 pm	Aries
May 29	3:39 am	Gemini	May 7	3:27 am	Cancer	May 4	3:55 am	Taurus
Jun 22	2:12 pm	Cancer	Jun 29	2:58 am	Gemini	May 28	2:19 pm	Gemini
Jul 16	11:47 pm	Leo	Aug 2	9:15 pm	Cancer	Jun 22	12:46 am	Cancer
Aug 10	8:13 am	Virgo	Sep 8	8:40 am	Leo	Jul 16	10:23 am	Leo
Sep 3	4:16 pm	Libra	Oct 6	7:25 am	Virgo	Aug 9	6:58 pm	Virgo
Sep 28	1:12 am	Scorpio	Nov 1	1:42 am	Libra	Sep 3	3:17 am	Libra
Oct 22	12:07 pm	Sagittarius	Nov 25	7:55 pm	Scorpio	Sep 27	12:36 pm	Scorpio
Nov 16	2:26 am	Capricorn	Dec 20	2:28 am	Sagittarius	Oct 22	12:02 am	Sagittarius
Dec 10	11:47 pm	Aquarius				Nov 15	3:03 pm	Capricorn
						Dec 10	1:30 pm	Aquarius

1945 · **1949**

Jan 5	2:18 pm	Pisces	Jan 13	4:01 am	Capricorn		**1953**	
Feb 2	3:07 am	Aries	Feb 6	4:05 am	Aquarius	Jan 5	6:10 am	Pisces
Mar 11	6:17 am	Taurus	Mar 2	4:38 am	Pisces	Feb 2	12:54 am	Aries
Apr 7	2:15 pm	Aries	Mar 26	6:54 am	Aries	Mar 14	1:58 pm	Taurus
Jun 4	5:58 am	Taurus	Apr 19	11:44 am	Taurus	Mar 31	12:17 am	Aries
Jul 7	11:20 am	Gemini	May 13	7:25 pm	Gemini	Jun 5	5:34 am	Taurus
Aug 4	5:59 am	Cancer	Jun 7	5:47 am	Cancer	Jul 7	5:30 am	Gemini
Aug 30	8:05 am	Leo	Jul 1	6:40 pm	Leo	Aug 3	8:08 pm	Cancer
Sep 24	11:06 am	Virgo				Aug 29	8:35 pm	Leo
Oct 18	11:09 pm	Libra						

Venus Positions 1930 – 2000

Sep 23	10:48 pm	Virgo
Oct 18	10:27 am	Libra
Nov 11	1:12 pm	Scorpio
Dec 5	11:24 am	Sagittarius
Dec 29	7:53 am	Capricorn

1954

Jan 22	4:20 am	Aquarius
Feb 15	2:01 am	Pisces
Mar 11	2:22 am	Aries
Apr 4	6:55 am	Taurus
Apr 28	5:03 pm	Gemini
May 23	10:04 am	Cancer
Jun 17	12:04 pm	Leo
Jul 13	3:43 am	Virgo
Aug 8	7:34 pm	Libra
Sep 6	6:29 pm	Scorpio
Oct 23	5:07 pm	Sagittarius
Oct 27	5:42 am	Scorpio

1955

Jan 6	1:48 am	Sagittarius
Feb 5	8:15 pm	Capricorn
Mar 4	3:22 am	Aquarius
Mar 30	6:30 am	Pisces
Apr 24	10:13 am	Aries
May 19	8:35 am	Taurus
Jun 13	3:38 am	Gemini
Jul 7	7:15 pm	Cancer
Aug 1	6:43 am	Leo
Aug 25	1:52 pm	Virgo
Sep 18	5:41 pm	Libra
Oct 12	7:39 pm	Scorpio
Nov 5	9:02 pm	Sagittarius
Nov 29	10:42 pm	Capricorn
Dec 24	1:52 am	Aquarius

1956

Jan 17	9:22 am	Pisces
Feb 11	2:46 am	Aries
Mar 7	4:31 pm	Taurus
Apr 4	2:23 am	Gemini
May 7	9:17 pm	Cancer
Jun 23	7:10 am	Gemini
Aug 4	4:49 am	Cancer
Sep 8	4:23 am	Leo
Oct 5	10:12 pm	Virgo
Oct 31	2:40 pm	Libra
Nov 25	8:01 pm	Scorpio
Dec 19	2:07 pm	Sagittarius

1957

Jan 12	3:23 pm	Capricorn
Feb 5	3:16 pm	Aquarius
Mar 1	3:39 pm	Pisces
Mar 25	5:46 pm	Aries
Apr 18	10:28 pm	Taurus
May 13	6:08 am	Gemini

Jun 6	4:35 pm	Cancer
Jul 1	5:42 am	Leo
Jul 25	10:10 pm	Virgo
Aug 19	7:44 pm	Libra
Sep 14	1:20 am	Scorpio
Oct 9	8:16 pm	Sagittarius
Nov 5	6:46 pm	Capricorn
Dec 6	10:26 am	Aquarius

1958

Apr 6	11:00 am	Pisces
May 5	6:59 am	Aries
May 31	11:07 pm	Taurus
Jun 26	6:08 pm	Gemini
Jul 22	12:26 am	Cancer
Aug 15	8:28 pm	Leo
Sep 9	7:35 am	Virgo
Oct 3	11:44 am	Libra
Oct 27	11:26 am	Scorpio
Nov 20	8:59 am	Sagittarius
Dec 14	5:55 am	Capricorn

1959

Jan 7	3:16 am	Aquarius
Jan 31	2:28 am	Pisces
Feb 24	5:53 am	Aries
Mar 20	4:55 am	Taurus
Apr 14	4:08 pm	Gemini
May 10	10:45 am	Cancer
Jun 6	5:43 pm	Leo
Jul 8	7:08 am	Virgo
Sep 19	10:01 pm	Leo
Sep 25	3:15 pm	Virgo
Nov 9	1:11 pm	Libra
Dec 7	11:41 am	Scorpio

1960

Jan 2	3:43 am	Sagittarius
Jan 26	11:46 pm	Capricorn
Feb 20	11:47 am	Aquarius
Mar 15	8:53 pm	Pisces
Apr 9	5:32 am	Aries
May 3	2:56 pm	Taurus
May 28	1:11 am	Gemini
Jun 21	11:34 am	Cancer
Jul 15	9:11 pm	Leo
Aug 9	5:54 am	Virgo
Sep 2	2:29 pm	Libra
Sep 27	12:13 am	Scorpio
Oct 21	12:12 pm	Sagittarius
Nov 15	3:57 am	Capricorn
Dec 10	3:34 am	Aquarius

1961

Jan 4	10:31 pm	Pisces
Feb 1	11:46 pm	Aries
Jun 5	2:25 pm	Taurus
Jul 6	11:32 pm	Gemini

Aug 3	10:28 am	Cancer
Aug 29	9:18 am	Leo
Sep 23	10:43 am	Virgo
Oct 17	9:58 pm	Libra
Nov 11	12:33 am	Scorpio
Dec 4	10:40 pm	Sagittarius
Dec 28	7:07 pm	Capricorn

1962

Jan 21	3:31 pm	Aquarius
Feb 14	1:09 pm	Pisces
Mar 10	1:28 pm	Aries
Apr 3	6:05 pm	Taurus
Apr 28	4:23 am	Gemini
May 22	9:46 pm	Cancer
Jun 17	12:31 am	Leo
Jul 12	5:32 pm	Virgo
Aug 8	12:13 pm	Libra
Sep 6	7:11 pm	Scorpio

1963

Jan 6	12:35 pm	Sagittarius
Feb 5	3:36 pm	Capricorn
Mar 4	6:41 am	Aquarius
Mar 29	8:00 pm	Pisces
Apr 23	10:39 pm	Aries
May 18	8:21 pm	Taurus
Jun 12	2:57 pm	Gemini
Jul 7	6:18 am	Cancer
Jul 31	5:38 pm	Leo
Aug 25	12:49 am	Virgo
Sep 18	4:43 am	Libra
Oct 12	6:50 am	Scorpio
Nov 5	8:25 am	Sagittarius
Nov 29	10:21 am	Capricorn
Dec 23	1:53 pm	Aquarius

1964

Jan 16	9:54 pm	Pisces
Feb 10	4:09 am	Aries
Mar 7	7:38 am	Taurus
Apr 3	10:03 pm	Gemini
May 8	10:16 pm	Cancer
Jun 17	1:17 pm	Gemini
Aug 5	3:53 am	Cancer
Sep 7	11:53 pm	Leo
Oct 5	1:10 pm	Virgo
Oct 31	3:54 am	Libra
Nov 24	8:25 pm	Scorpio
Dec 19	2:02 am	Sagittarius

1965

Jan 12	3:00 am	Capricorn
Feb 5	2:41 am	Aquarius
Mar 1	2:55 am	Pisces
Mar 25	4:54 am	Aries
Apr 18	9:31 am	Taurus
May 12	5:08 pm	Gemini

Venus Positions 1930 – 2000

Jun 6	3:39 am	Cancer
Jun 30	4:59 pm	Leo
Jul 25	9:51 am	Virgo
Aug 19	8:06 am	Libra
Sep 13	2:50 pm	Scorpio
Oct 9	11:46 am	Sagittarius
Nov 5	2:36 pm	Capricorn
Dec 6	11:37 pm	Aquarius

1966

Feb 6	7:46 am	Capricorn
Feb 25	5:55 am	Aquarius
Apr 6	10:53 am	Pisces
May 4	11:33 pm	Aries
May 31	1:00 pm	Taurus
Jun 26	6:40 am	Gemini
Jul 21	12:11 pm	Cancer
Aug 15	7:47 am	Leo
Sep 8	6:40 pm	Virgo
Oct 2	10:44 pm	Libra
Oct 26	10:28 pm	Scorpio
Nov 19	8:06 pm	Sagittarius
Dec 13	5:09 pm	Capricorn

1967

Jan 6	2:36 pm	Aquarius
Jan 30	1:53 pm	Pisces
Feb 23	5:30 pm	Aries
Mar 20	4:56 am	Taurus
Apr 14	4:54 am	Gemini
May 10	1:05 am	Cancer
Jun 6	11:48 am	Leo
Jul 8	5:11 pm	Virgo
Sep 9	6:58 am	Leo
Oct 1	1:07 pm	Virgo
Nov 9	11:32 am	Libra
Dec 7	3:48 am	Scorpio

1968

Jan 1	5:37 pm	Sagittarius
Jan 26	12:35 pm	Capricorn
Feb 19	11:55 am	Aquarius
Mar 15	8:32 am	Pisces
Apr 8	4:49 pm	Aries
May 3	1:56 am	Taurus
May 27	12:02 pm	Gemini
Jun 20	10:20 pm	Cancer
Jul 15	7:59 am	Leo
Aug 8	4:49 pm	Virgo
Sep 2	1:39 am	Libra
Sep 26	11:45 am	Scorpio
Oct 21	12:16 am	Sagittarius
Nov 14	4:48 pm	Capricorn
Dec 9	5:40 pm	Aquarius

1969

Jan 4	3:07 pm	Pisces
Feb 1	11:45 pm	Aries
Jun 5	8:48 pm	Taurus

Jul 6	5:04 pm	Gemini
Aug 3	12:30 am	Cancer
Aug 28	9:48 pm	Leo
Sep 22	10:26 pm	Virgo
Oct 17	9:17 am	Libra
Nov 10	11:40 am	Scorpio
Dec 4	9:41 am	Sagittarius
Dec 28	6:04 am	Capricorn

1970

Jan 21	2:26 am	Aquarius
Feb 14	12:04 am	Pisces
Mar 10	12:25 am	Aries
Apr 3	5:05 am	Taurus
Apr 27	3:33 pm	Gemini
May 22	9:19 am	Cancer
Jun 16	12:49 pm	Leo
Jul 12	7:16 am	Virgo
Aug 8	4:59 am	Libra
Sep 6	8:54 pm	Scorpio

1971

Jan 6	8:00 pm	Sagittarius
Feb 5	9:57 am	Capricorn
Mar 3	9:24 pm	Aquarius
Mar 29	9:02 am	Pisces
Apr 23	10:44 am	Aries
May 18	7:48 am	Taurus
Jun 12	1:58 am	Gemini
Jul 6	5:02 pm	Cancer
Jul 31	4:15 am	Leo
Aug 24	11:25 am	Virgo
Sep 17	3:25 pm	Libra
Oct 11	5:43 pm	Scorpio
Nov 4	7:30 pm	Sagittarius
Nov 28	9:41 pm	Capricorn
Dec 23	1:32 am	Aquarius

1972

Jan 16	10:01 am	Pisces
Feb 10	5:08 am	Aries
Mar 6	10:25 pm	Taurus
Apr 3	5:48 pm	Gemini
May 10	8:51 am	Cancer
Jun 11	3:08 pm	Gemini
Aug 5	8:26 pm	Cancer
Sep 7	6:27 pm	Leo
Oct 5	3:33 am	Virgo
Oct 30	4:40 pm	Libra
Nov 24	8:23 am	Scorpio
Dec 18	1:34 pm	Sagittarius

1973

Jan 11	2:15 pm	Capricorn
Feb 4	1:43 pm	Aquarius
Feb 28	1:45 pm	Pisces
Mar 24	3:34 pm	Aries
Apr 17	8:05 pm	Taurus
May 12	3:42 am	Gemini

Jun 5	2:20 pm	Cancer
Jun 30	3:55 am	Leo
Jul 24	9:13 pm	Virgo
Aug 18	8:10 pm	Libra
Sep 13	4:05 am	Scorpio
Oct 9	3:08 am	Sagittarius
Nov 5	10:39 am	Capricorn
Dec 7	4:37 pm	Aquarius

1974

Jan 29	2:51 pm	Capricorn
Feb 28	9:25 am	Aquarius
Apr 6	9:17 am	Pisces
May 4	3:21 pm	Aries
May 31	2:19 am	Taurus
Jun 25	6:44 pm	Gemini
Jul 20	11:34 pm	Cancer
Aug 14	6:47 pm	Leo
Sep 8	5:28 am	Virgo
Oct 2	9:27 am	Libra
Oct 26	9:12 am	Scorpio
Nov 19	6:56 am	Sagittarius
Dec 13	4:06 am	Capricorn

1975

Jan 6	1:39 am	Aquarius
Jan 30	1:05 am	Pisces
Feb 23	4:53 am	Aries
Mar 19	4:42 pm	Taurus
Apr 13	5:26 pm	Gemini
May 9	3:11 pm	Cancer
Jun 6	5:54 am	Leo
Jul 9	6:06 am	Virgo
Sep 2	10:34 am	Leo
Oct 4	12:19 am	Virgo
Nov 9	8:52 am	Libra
Dec 6	7:29 pm	Scorpio

1976

Jan 1	7:14 am	Sagittarius
Jan 26	1:09 am	Capricorn
Feb 19	11:50 am	Aquarius
Mar 14	7:59 pm	Pisces
Apr 8	3:56 am	Aries
May 2	12:49 pm	Taurus
May 26	10:43 pm	Gemini
Jun 20	8:56 am	Cancer
Jul 14	6:36 pm	Leo
Aug 8	3:36 am	Virgo
Sep 1	12:44 pm	Libra
Sep 25	11:17 pm	Scorpio
Oct 20	12:22 pm	Sagittarius
Nov 14	5:42 am	Capricorn
Dec 9	7:53 am	Aquarius

1977

Jan 4	8:01 am	Pisces
Feb 2	12:54 am	Aries
Jun 6	1:10 am	Taurus

Venus Positions 1930 – 2000

Jul 6	10:09 am	Gemini
Aug 2	2:19 pm	Cancer
Aug 28	10:09 am	Leo
Sep 22	10:05 am	Virgo
Oct 16	8:37 pm	Libra
Nov 9	10:52 pm	Scorpio
Dec 3	8:49 pm	Sagittarius
Dec 27	5:09 pm	Capricorn

1978

Jan 20	1:29 pm	Aquarius
Feb 13	11:07 am	Pisces
Mar 9	11:29 am	Aries
Apr 2	4:14 pm	Taurus
Apr 27	2:53 pm	Gemini
May 21	9:03 pm	Cancer
Jun 16	1:19 pm	Leo
Jul 11	9:14 pm	Virgo
Aug 7	10:08 pm	Libra
Sep 7	12:07 am	Scorpio

1979

Jan 7	1:38 am	Sagittarius
Feb 5	4:16 am	Capricorn
Mar 3	12:18 am	Aquarius
Mar 28	10:18 pm	Pisces
Apr 22	11:02 pm	Aries
May 17	7:29 pm	Taurus
Jun 11	1:13 pm	Gemini
Jul 6	4:02 am	Cancer
Jul 30	3:07 pm	Leo
Aug 23	10:16 pm	Virgo
Sep 17	2:21 am	Libra
Oct 11	4:48 am	Scorpio
Nov 4	6:50 am	Sagittarius
Nov 28	9:20 am	Capricorn
Dec 22	1:35 pm	Aquarius

1980

Jan 15	10:37 pm	Pisces
Feb 9	6:39 pm	Aries
Mar 6	1:54 pm	Taurus
Apr 3	2:46 pm	Gemini
May 12	3:53 pm	Cancer
Jun 5	12:44 am	Gemini
Aug 6	9:25 am	Cancer
Sep 7	12:57 pm	Leo
Oct 4	6:07 pm	Virgo
Oct 30	5:38 am	Libra
Nov 23	8:35 pm	Scorpio
Dec 18	1:21 am	Sagittarius

1981

Jan 11	1:48 am	Capricorn
Feb 4	1:07 am	Aquarius
Feb 28	1:01 am	Pisces
Mar 24	2:43 am	Aries
Apr 17	7:08 am	Taurus

May 11	2:45 pm	Gemini
Jun 5	1:29 am	Cancer
Jun 29	3:20 pm	Leo
Jul 24	9:04 am	Virgo
Aug 18	8:44 am	Libra
Sep 12	5:51 pm	Scorpio
Oct 8	7:04 pm	Sagittarius
Nov 5	7:39 am	Capricorn
Dec 8	3:52 pm	Aquarius

1982

Jan 22	9:56 pm	Capricorn
Mar 2	6:25 am	Aquarius
Apr 6	7:20 am	Pisces
May 4	7:27 am	Aries
May 30	4:02 pm	Taurus
Jun 25	7:13 am	Gemini
Jul 20	11:21 am	Cancer
Aug 14	6:09 am	Leo
Sep 7	4:38 pm	Virgo
Oct 1	8:32 pm	Libra
Oct 25	8:19 pm	Scorpio
Nov 18	6:07 pm	Sagittarius
Dec 12	3:20 pm	Capricorn

1983

Jan 5	12:58 pm	Aquarius
Jan 29	12:31 pm	Pisces
Feb 22	4:35 pm	Aries
Mar 19	4:51 am	Taurus
Apr 13	6:26 am	Gemini
May 9	5:56 am	Cancer
Jun 6	1:04 am	Leo
Jul 10	12:25 pm	Virgo
Aug 27	6:43 am	Leo
Oct 5	2:35 pm	Virgo
Nov 9	5:52 am	Libra
Dec 6	11:15 am	Scorpio
Dec 31	9:00 pm	Sagittarius

1984

Jan 25	1:51 pm	Capricorn
Feb 18	11:53 pm	Aquarius
Mar 14	7:35 am	Pisces
Apr 7	3:13 pm	Aries
May 1	11:53 pm	Taurus
May 26	9:40 am	Gemini
Jun 19	7:48 pm	Cancer
Jul 14	5:30 am	Leo
Aug 7	2:40 pm	Virgo
Sep 1	12:07 am	Libra
Sep 25	11:05 am	Scorpio
Oct 20	12:45 am	Sagittarius
Nov 13	6:54 pm	Capricorn
Dec 8	10:26 am	Aquarius

1985

Jan 4	1:23 am	Pisces

Feb 2	3:29 am	Aries
Jun 6	3:53 am	Taurus
Jul 6	3:01 am	Gemini
Aug 2	4:10 am	Cancer
Aug 27	10:39 pm	Leo
Sep 21	9:53 pm	Virgo
Oct 16	8:04 am	Libra
Nov 9	10:08 pm	Scorpio
Dec 3	8:00 am	Sagittarius
Dec 27	4:17 am	Capricorn

1986

Jan 20	12:36 am	Aquarius
Feb 12	10:11 pm	Pisces
Mar 8	10:32 pm	Aries
Apr 2	3:19 am	Taurus
Apr 26	2:10 pm	Gemini
May 21	8:46 am	Cancer
Jun 15	1:52 pm	Leo
Jul 11	11:23 am	Virgo
Aug 7	3:46 pm	Libra
Sep 7	5:15 am	Scorpio

1987

Jan 7	5:20 am	Sagittarius
Feb 4	10:03 pm	Capricorn
Mar 3	2:55 am	Aquarius
Mar 28	11:20 am	Pisces
Apr 22	11:07 am	Aries
May 17	6:56 am	Taurus
Jun 11	12:15 am	Gemini
Jul 5	2:50 pm	Cancer
Jul 30	1:49 am	Leo
Aug 23	9:00 am	Virgo
Sep 16	1:12 pm	Libra
Oct 10	3:49 pm	Scorpio
Nov 3	6:04 pm	Sagittarius
Nov 27	8:51 pm	Capricorn
Dec 22	1:29 am	Aquarius

1988

Jan 15	11:04 am	Pisces
Feb 9	8:04 am	Aries
Mar 6	5:21 am	Taurus
Apr 3	12:07 pm	Gemini
May 17	11:26 am	Cancer
May 27	2:36 am	Gemini
Aug 6	6:24 am	Cancer
Sep 7	6:37 am	Leo
Oct 4	8:15 am	Virgo
Oct 29	6:20 pm	Libra
Nov 23	8:34 am	Scorpio
Dec 17	12:56 pm	Sagittarius

1989

Jan 10	1:08 pm	Capricorn
Feb 3	12:15 pm	Aquarius
Feb 27	11:59 am	Pisces

Venus Positions 1930 – 2000

Mar 23	1:32 pm	Aries
Apr 16	5:52 pm	Taurus
May 11	1:28 am	Gemini
Jun 4	12:17 pm	Cancer
Jun 29	2:21 am	Leo
Jul 23	8:31 pm	Virgo
Aug 17	8:58 pm	Libra
Sep 12	7:22 am	Scorpio
Oct 8	11:00 am	Sagittarius
Nov 5	5:13 am	Capricorn
Dec 9	11:54 pm	Aquarius

1990

Jan 16	10:23 am	Capricorn
Mar 3	12:52 pm	Aquarius
Apr 6	4:13 am	Pisces
May 3	10:52 pm	Aries
May 30	5:13 am	Taurus
Jun 24	7:14 pm	Gemini
Jul 19	10:41 pm	Cancer
Aug 13	5:05 pm	Leo
Sep 7	3:21 am	Virgo
Oct 1	7:13 am	Libra
Oct 25	7:03 am	Scorpio
Nov 18	4:58 am	Sagittarius
Dec 12	2:18 am	Capricorn

1991

Jan 5	12:03 am	Aquarius
Jan 28	11:44 pm	Pisces
Feb 22	4:02 am	Aries
Mar 18	4:45 pm	Taurus
Apr 12	7:10 pm	Gemini
May 8	8:28 pm	Cancer
Jun 5	8:16 pm	Leo
Jul 11	12:06 am	Virgo
Aug 21	10:06 am	Leo
Oct 6	4:15 pm	Virgo
Nov 9	1:37 am	Libra
Dec 6	2:21 am	Scorpio
Dec 31	10:19 am	Sagittarius

1992

Jan 25	2:14 am	Capricorn
Feb 18	11:40 am	Aquarius
Mar 13	6:57 pm	Pisces
Apr 7	2:16 am	Aries
May 1	10:41 am	Taurus
May 25	8:18 pm	Gemini
Jun 19	6:22 am	Cancer
Jul 13	4:07 pm	Leo
Aug 7	1:26 am	Virgo
Aug 31	11:09 am	Libra
Sep 24	10:31 pm	Scorpio
Oct 19	12:47 pm	Sagittarius
Nov 13	7:48 am	Capricorn
Dec 8	12:49 pm	Aquarius

1993

Jan 3	6:54 pm	Pisces
Feb 2	7:37 am	Aries
Jun 6	5:03 am	Taurus
Jul 5	7:21 pm	Gemini
Aug 1	5:38 pm	Cancer
Aug 27	10:48 am	Leo
Sep 21	9:22 am	Virgo
Oct 15	7:13 pm	Libra
Nov 8	9:07 pm	Scorpio
Dec 2	6:54 pm	Sagittarius
Dec 26	3:09 pm	Capricorn

1994

Jan 19	11:28 am	Aquarius
Feb 12	9:04 am	Pisces
Mar 8	9:28 am	Aries
Apr 1	2:20 pm	Taurus
Apr 26	1:24 am	Gemini
May 20	8:26 pm	Cancer
Jun 15	2:23 am	Leo
Jul 11	1:33 am	Virgo
Aug 7	9:36 am	Libra
Sep 7	12:12 pm	Scorpio

1995

Jan 7	7:07 am	Sagittarius
Feb 4	3:12 pm	Capricorn
Mar 2	5:11 pm	Aquarius
Mar 28	12:10 pm	Pisces
Apr 21	11:07 pm	Aries
May 16	6:22 pm	Taurus
Jun 10	11:19 am	Gemini
Jul 5	1:39 am	Cancer
Jul 29	12:32 pm	Leo
Aug 22	7:43 pm	Virgo
Sep 16	12:01 am	Libra
Oct 10	2:48 am	Scorpio
Nov 3	5:18 am	Sagittarius
Nov 27	8:23 am	Capricorn
Dec 21	1:23 pm	Aquarius

1996

Jan 14	11:30 pm	Pisces
Feb 8	9:30 pm	Aries
Mar 5	9:01 pm	Taurus
Apr 3	10:26 pm	Gemini
Aug 7	1:15 am	Cancer
Sep 7	12:07 am	Leo
Oct 3	10:22 pm	Virgo
Oct 29	7:02 am	Libra
Nov 22	8:34 pm	Scorpio
Dec 17	12:34 am	Sagittarius

1997

Jan 10	12:32 am	Capricorn
Feb 2	11:28 pm	Aquarius
Feb 26	11:01 pm	Pisces

1998

Mar 23	12:26 am	Aries
Apr 16	4:43 am	Taurus
May 10	12:20 pm	Gemini
Jun 3	11:18 pm	Cancer
Jun 28	1:38 pm	Leo
Jul 23	8:16 pm	Virgo
Aug 17	9:31 am	Libra
Sep 11	9:17 pm	Scorpio
Oct 8	3:25 am	Sagittarius
Nov 5	3:50 am	Capricorn
Dec 11	11:39 pm	Aquarius

1998

Jan 9	4:03 pm	Capricorn
Mar 4	11:14 am	Aquarius
Apr 6	12:38 am	Pisces
May 3	2:16 pm	Aries
May 29	6:32 pm	Taurus
Jun 24	7:27 am	Gemini
Jul 19	10:17 am	Cancer
Aug 13	4:20 am	Leo
Sep 6	2:24 pm	Virgo
Sep 30	6:13 pm	Libra
Oct 24	6:06 pm	Scorpio
Nov 17	4:06 pm	Sagittarius
Dec 11	1:33 pm	Capricorn

1999

Jan 4	11:25 am	Aquarius
Jan 28	11:17 am	Pisces
Feb 21	3:49 pm	Aries
Mar 18	4:59 am	Taurus
Apr 12	8:17 am	Gemini
May 8	11:29 am	Cancer
Jun 5	4:25 pm	Leo
Jul 12	10:18 am	Virgo
Aug 15	9:12 am	Leo
Oct 7	11:51 am	Virgo
Nov 8	9:19 pm	Libra
Dec 5	5:41 pm	Scorpio
Dec 30	11:54 pm	Sagittarius

2000

Jan 24	2:52 pm	Capricorn
Feb 17	11:43 pm	Aquarius
Mar 13	6:36 am	Pisces
Apr 6	1:37 pm	Aries
Apr 30	9:49 pm	Taurus
May 25	7:15 am	Gemini
Jun 18	5:15 pm	Cancer
Jul 13	3:02 am	Leo
Aug 6	12:32 pm	Virgo
Aug 30	10:35 pm	Libra
Sep 24	10:26 am	Scorpio
Oct 19	1:18 pm	Sagittarius
Nov 12	9:14 pm	Capricorn
Dec 8	3:48 am	Aquarius

Mars Positions 1930 – 2000

1930
Feb 6	1:21 pm	Aquarius
Mar 17	12:55 am	Pisces
Apr 24	12:27 pm	Aries
Jun 2	10:15 pm	Taurus
Jul 14	7:54 am	Gemini
Aug 28	6:27 am	Cancer
Oct 20	9:43 am	Leo

1931
Feb 16	9:27 am	Cancer
Mar 29	10:48 pm	Leo
Jun 10	9:58 am	Virgo
Aug 1	11:38 am	Libra
Sep 17	3:43 am	Scorpio
Oct 30	7:46 am	Sagittarius
Dec 9	10:11 pm	Capricorn

1932
Jan 17	7:35 pm	Aquarius
Feb 24	9:36 pm	Pisces
Apr 3	2:02 am	Aries
May 12	5:53 am	Taurus
Jun 22	4:19 am	Gemini
Aug 4	2:52 pm	Cancer
Sep 20	2:43 pm	Leo
Nov 13	4:25 pm	Virgo

1933
Jul 6	5:03 pm	Libra
Aug 26	1:34 am	Scorpio
Oct 9	6:35 am	Sagittarius
Nov 19	2:18 am	Capricorn
Dec 27	10:43 pm	Aquarius

1934
Feb 3	11:13 pm	Pisces
Mar 14	4:09 am	Aries
Apr 22	10:40 am	Taurus
Jun 2	11:21 am	Gemini
Jul 15	4:33 pm	Cancer
Aug 30	8:43 am	Leo
Oct 17	11:59 pm	Virgo
Dec 11	4:32 am	Libra

1935
Jul 29	12:32 pm	Scorpio
Sep 16	7:59 am	Sagittarius
Oct 28	1:22 pm	Capricorn
Dec 6	11:34 pm	Aquarius

1936
Jan 14	8:59 am	Pisces
Feb 21	11:09 pm	Aries
Apr 1	4:30 pm	Taurus
May 13	4:17 am	Gemini
Jun 25	4:53 pm	Cancer
Aug 10	4:43 am	Leo
Sep 26	9:51 am	Virgo
Nov 14	9:52 am	Libra

1937
Jan 5	3:39 pm	Scorpio
Mar 12	10:16 pm	Sagittarius
May 14	5:52 pm	Scorpio
Aug 8	5:14 pm	Sagittarius
Sep 30	4:08 am	Capricorn
Nov 11	1:31 pm	Aquarius
Dec 21	12:46 pm	Pisces

1938
Jan 30	7:44 am	Aries
Mar 12	2:48 am	Taurus
Apr 23	1:39 pm	Gemini
Jun 6	8:28 pm	Cancer
Jul 22	5:26 pm	Leo
Sep 7	3:22 pm	Virgo
Oct 25	1:20 am	Libra
Dec 11	6:25 pm	Scorpio

1939
Jan 29	4:49 am	Sagittarius
Mar 21	2:25 am	Capricorn
May 24	7:19 pm	Aquarius
Jul 21	2:31 pm	Capricorn
Sep 23	8:13 pm	Aquarius
Nov 19	10:56 am	Pisces

1940
Jan 3	7:05 pm	Aries
Feb 16	8:54 pm	Taurus
Apr 1	1:41 pm	Gemini
May 17	9:45 am	Cancer
Jul 3	5:32 am	Leo
Aug 19	10:58 am	Virgo
Oct 5	9:21 am	Libra
Nov 20	12:16 pm	Scorpio

1941
Jan 4	2:42 pm	Sagittarius
Feb 17	6:32 pm	Capricorn
Apr 2	6:46 am	Aquarius
May 16	12:05 am	Pisces
Jul 2	12:17 am	Aries

1942
Jan 11	5:21 pm	Taurus
Mar 7	3:04 am	Gemini
Apr 26	1:18 am	Cancer
Jun 13	10:56 pm	Leo
Aug 1	3:27 am	Virgo
Sep 17	5:11 am	Libra
Nov 1	5:36 pm	Scorpio
Dec 15	11:51 am	Sagittarius

1943
Jan 26	2:10 pm	Capricorn
Mar 8	7:42 am	Aquarius
Apr 17	5:25 am	Pisces
May 27	4:25 am	Aries
Jul 7	6:05 pm	Taurus
Aug 23	6:58 pm	Gemini

1944
Mar 28	4:54 am	Cancer
May 22	9:16 am	Leo
Jul 11	9:54 pm	Virgo
Aug 28	7:23 pm	Libra
Oct 13	7:09 am	Scorpio
Nov 25	11:11 am	Sagittarius

1945
Jan 5	2:31 pm	Capricorn
Feb 14	4:58 am	Aquarius
Mar 24	10:43 pm	Pisces
May 2	3:29 pm	Aries
Jun 11	6:52 am	Taurus
Jul 23	3:59 am	Gemini
Sep 7	3:56 pm	Cancer
Nov 11	4:05 pm	Leo
Dec 26	10:04 am	Cancer

1946
Apr 22	2:31 pm	Leo
Jun 20	3:31 am	Virgo
Aug 9	8:17 am	Libra
Sep 24	11:35 am	Scorpio
Nov 6	1:22 pm	Sagittarius
Dec 17	5:56 am	Capricorn

1947
Jan 25	6:44 am	Aquarius
Mar 4	11:46 am	Pisces
Apr 11	6:03 pm	Aries
May 20	10:40 pm	Taurus
Jun 30	10:34 pm	Gemini
Aug 13	4:26 pm	Cancer
Sep 30	9:31 pm	Leo
Dec 1	6:44 am	Virgo

1948
Feb 12	5:28 am	Leo
May 18	3:54 pm	Virgo
Jul 17	12:25 am	Libra
Sep 3	8:58 am	Scorpio
Oct 17	12:43 am	Sagittarius
Nov 26	4:59 pm	Capricorn

1949
Jan 4	12:50 pm	Aquarius
Feb 11	1:05 pm	Pisces
Mar 21	5:02 pm	Aries
Apr 29	9:33 pm	Taurus

Mars Positions 1930 – 2000

Jun 9	7:57 pm	Gemini
Jul 23	12:54 am	Cancer
Sep 6	11:51 pm	Leo
Oct 26	7:58 pm	Virgo
Dec 26	12:23 am	Libra

1950

Mar 28	6:05 am	Virgo
Jun 11	3:27 pm	Libra
Aug 10	11:48 am	Scorpio
Sep 25	2:48 pm	Sagittarius
Nov 6	1:40 am	Capricorn
Dec 15	3:59 am	Aquarius

1951

Jan 22	8:05 am	Pisces
Mar 1	5:03 pm	Aries
Apr 10	4:37 am	Taurus
May 21	10:32 am	Gemini
Jul 3	6:42 pm	Cancer
Aug 18	5:55 am	Leo
Oct 4	7:20 pm	Virgo
Nov 24	1:11 am	Libra

1952

Jan 19	8:33 pm	Scorpio
Aug 27	1:53 pm	Sagittarius
Oct 11	11:45 pm	Capricorn
Nov 21	2:39 pm	Aquarius
Dec 30	4:35 pm	Pisces

1953

Feb 7	8:07 pm	Aries
Mar 20	1:54 am	Taurus
May 1	1:08 am	Gemini
Jun 13	10:49 pm	Cancer
Jul 29	2:25 pm	Leo
Sep 14	12:59 pm	Virgo
Nov 1	9:19 am	Libra
Dec 20	6:22 am	Scorpio

1954

Feb 9	2:18 pm	Sagittarius
Apr 12	11:28 am	Capricorn
Jul 3	2:23 am	Sagittarius
Aug 24	8:22 am	Capricorn
Oct 21	7:03 am	Aquarius
Dec 4	2:41 am	Pisces

1955

Jan 14	11:33 pm	Aries
Feb 26	5:22 am	Taurus
Apr 10	6:09 pm	Gemini
May 25	7:50 pm	Cancer
Jul 11	4:22 am	Leo
Aug 27	5:13 am	Virgo
Oct 13	6:20 am	Libra
Nov 28	8:33 pm	Scorpio

1956

Jan 13	9:28 pm	Sagittarius
Feb 28	3:05 pm	Capricorn
Apr 14	6:40 pm	Aquarius
Jun 3	2:51 am	Pisces
Dec 6	6:24 am	Aries

1957

Jan 28	9:19 am	Taurus
Mar 17	4:34 pm	Gemini
May 4	10:22 am	Cancer
Jun 21	7:18 am	Leo
Aug 8	12:27 am	Virgo
Sep 23	11:31 pm	Libra
Nov 8	4:04 pm	Scorpio
Dec 22	8:29 pm	Sagittarius

1958

Feb 3	1:57 pm	Capricorn
Mar 17	2:11 am	Aquarius
Apr 26	9:31 pm	Pisces
Jun 7	1:21 am	Aries
Jul 21	2:03 am	Taurus
Sep 21	12:26 am	Gemini
Oct 28	7:00 pm	Taurus

1959

Feb 10	8:57 pm	Gemini
Apr 10	4:46 am	Cancer
May 31	9:26 pm	Leo
Jul 20	6:03 am	Virgo
Sep 5	5:46 pm	Libra
Oct 21	4:40 am	Scorpio
Dec 3	1:09 pm	Sagittarius

1960

Jan 13	11:59 pm	Capricorn
Feb 22	11:11 pm	Aquarius
Apr 2	1:24 am	Pisces
May 11	2:19 am	Aries
Jun 20	4:05 am	Taurus
Aug 1	11:32 pm	Gemini
Sep 20	11:06 pm	Cancer

1961

Feb 4	7:23 pm	Gemini
Feb 7	12:25 am	Cancer
May 5	8:13 pm	Leo
Jun 28	6:47 pm	Virgo
Aug 16	7:41 pm	Libra
Oct 1	3:02 pm	Scorpio
Nov 13	4:50 pm	Sagittarius
Dec 24	12:50 pm	Capricorn

1962

Feb 1	6:06 pm	Aquarius
Mar 12	2:58 am	Pisces
Apr 19	11:58 am	Aries

May 28	6:47 pm	Taurus
Jul 8	10:50 pm	Gemini
Aug 22	6:37 am	Cancer
Oct 11	6:54 pm	Leo

1963

Jun 3	1:30 am	Virgo
Jul 26	11:14 pm	Libra
Sep 12	4:11 am	Scorpio
Oct 25	12:31 pm	Sagittarius
Dec 5	4:03 am	Capricorn

1964

Jan 13	1:13 am	Aquarius
Feb 20	2:33 am	Pisces
Mar 29	6:24 am	Aries
May 7	9:41 am	Taurus
Jun 17	6:43 am	Gemini
Jul 30	1:23 pm	Cancer
Sep 15	12:22 am	Leo
Nov 5	10:20 pm	Virgo

1965

Jun 28	8:12 pm	Libra
Aug 20	7:16 am	Scorpio
Oct 4	1:46 am	Sagittarius
Nov 14	2:19 am	Capricorn
Dec 23	12:36 am	Aquarius

1966

Jan 30	2:01 am	Pisces
Mar 9	7:55 am	Aries
Apr 17	3:35 pm	Taurus
May 28	5:07 pm	Gemini
Jul 10	10:15 pm	Cancer
Aug 25	10:52 am	Leo
Oct 12	1:37 pm	Virgo
Dec 3	7:55 pm	Libra

1967

Feb 12	7:20 am	Scorpio
Mar 31	1:10 am	Libra
Jul 19	5:56 pm	Scorpio
Sep 9	8:44 pm	Sagittarius
Oct 22	9:14 pm	Capricorn
Dec 1	3:12 pm	Aquarius

1968

Jan 9	4:49 am	Pisces
Feb 16	10:18 pm	Aries
Mar 27	6:43 pm	Taurus
May 8	9:14 pm	Gemini
Jun 21	12:03 am	Cancer
Aug 5	12:07 pm	Leo
Sep 21	1:39 pm	Virgo
Nov 9	1:10 am	Libra
Dec 29	5:07 pm	Scorpio

Mars Positions 1930 – 2000

1969
Feb 25	1:21 am	Sagittarius
Sep 21	1:35 am	Capricorn
Nov 4	1:51 pm	Aquarius
Dec 15	9:22 am	Pisces

1970
Jan 24	4:29 pm	Aries
Mar 6	8:28 pm	Taurus
Apr 18	1:59 pm	Gemini
Jun 2	1:50 am	Cancer
Jul 18	1:43 am	Leo
Sep 2	11:57 pm	Virgo
Oct 20	5:57 am	Libra
Dec 6	11:34 am	Scorpio

1971
Jan 22	8:34 pm	Sagittarius
Mar 12	5:11 am	Capricorn
May 3	3:57 pm	Aquarius
Nov 6	7:31 am	Pisces
Dec 26	1:04 pm	Aries

1972
Feb 10	9:04 am	Taurus
Mar 26	11:30 pm	Gemini
May 12	8:14 am	Cancer
Jun 28	11:09 am	Leo
Aug 14	7:59 pm	Virgo
Sep 30	6:23 pm	Libra
Nov 15	5:17 pm	Scorpio
Dec 30	11:12 am	Sagittarius

1973
Feb 12	12:51 am	Capricorn
Mar 26	3:59 pm	Aquarius
May 7	11:09 pm	Pisces
Jun 20	3:54 pm	Aries
Aug 12	9:56 am	Taurus
Oct 29	5:56 pm	Aries
Dec 24	3:09 am	Taurus

1974
Feb 27	5:11 am	Gemini
Apr 20	3:18 am	Cancer
Jun 8	7:54 pm	Leo
Jul 27	9:04 am	Virgo
Sep 12	2:08 pm	Libra
Oct 28	2:05 am	Scorpio
Dec 10	5:05 pm	Sagittarius

1975
Jan 21	1:49 pm	Capricorn
Mar 3	12:32 am	Aquarius
Apr 11	2:15 pm	Pisces
May 21	3:14 am	Aries
Jun 30	10:53 pm	Taurus
Aug 14	3:47 pm	Gemini

Oct 17	3:44 am	Cancer
Nov 25	1:30 pm	Gemini

1976
Mar 18	8:15 am	Cancer
May 16	6:10 am	Leo
Jul 6	6:27 pm	Virgo
Aug 24	12:55 am	Libra
Oct 8	3:23 pm	Scorpio
Nov 20	6:53 pm	Sagittarius
Dec 31	7:42 pm	Capricorn

1977
Feb 9	6:57 am	Aquarius
Mar 19	9:19 pm	Pisces
Apr 27	10:46 am	Aries
Jun 5	10:00 pm	Taurus
Jul 17	10:13 am	Gemini
Aug 31	7:20 pm	Cancer
Oct 26	1:56 pm	Leo

1978
Jan 25	8:59 pm	Cancer
Apr 10	1:50 pm	Leo
Jun 13	9:38 pm	Virgo
Aug 4	4:07 am	Libra
Sep 19	3:57 pm	Scorpio
Nov 1	8:20 pm	Sagittarius
Dec 12	12:39 pm	Capricorn

1979
Jan 20	12:07 pm	Aquarius
Feb 27	3:25 pm	Pisces
Apr 6	8:08 pm	Aries
May 15	11:25 pm	Taurus
Jun 25	8:55 pm	Gemini
Aug 8	8:28 am	Cancer
Sep 24	4:21 pm	Leo
Nov 19	4:36 pm	Virgo

1980
Mar 11	3:46 pm	Leo
May 3	9:26 pm	Virgo
Jul 10	12:59 pm	Libra
Aug 29	12:50 am	Scorpio
Oct 12	1:27 am	Sagittarius
Nov 21	8:42 pm	Capricorn
Dec 30	5:30 pm	Aquarius

1981
Feb 6	5:48 pm	Pisces
Mar 16	9:40 pm	Aries
Apr 25	2:17 am	Taurus
Jun 5	12:26 am	Gemini
Jul 18	3:54 am	Cancer
Sep 1	8:52 pm	Leo
Oct 20	8:56 pm	Virgo
Dec 15	7:14 pm	Libra

1982
Aug 3	6:45 am	Scorpio
Sep 19	8:20 pm	Sagittarius
Oct 31	6:05 pm	Capricorn
Dec 10	1:17 am	Aquarius

1983
Jan 17	8:10 am	Pisces
Feb 24	7:19 pm	Aries
Apr 5	9:03 am	Taurus
May 16	4:43 pm	Gemini
Jun 29	1:54 am	Cancer
Aug 13	11:54 am	Leo
Sep 29	7:12 pm	Virgo
Nov 18	5:26 am	Libra

1984
Jan 10	10:20 pm	Scorpio
Aug 17	2:51 pm	Sagittarius
Oct 5	1:02 am	Capricorn
Nov 15	1:09 am	Aquarius
Dec 25	1:38 am	Pisces

1985
Feb 2	12:19 pm	Aries
Mar 15	12:06 am	Taurus
Apr 26	4:13 am	Gemini
Jun 9	5:40 am	Cancer
Jul 24	11:04 pm	Leo
Sep 9	8:31 pm	Virgo
Oct 27	10:16 am	Libra
Dec 14	1:59 pm	Scorpio

1986
Feb 2	1:27 am	Sagittarius
Mar 27	10:47 pm	Capricorn
Oct 8	8:01 pm	Aquarius
Nov 25	9:35 pm	Pisces

1987
Jan 8	7:20 am	Aries
Feb 20	9:44 am	Taurus
Apr 5	11:37 am	Gemini
May 20	10:01 pm	Cancer
Jul 6	11:46 am	Leo
Aug 22	2:51 pm	Virgo
Oct 8	2:27 pm	Libra
Nov 23	10:19 pm	Scorpio

1988
Jan 8	10:24 am	Sagittarius
Feb 22	5:15 am	Capricorn
Apr 6	4:44 pm	Aquarius
May 22	2:42 pm	Pisces
Jul 13	3:00 pm	Aries
Oct 23	5:02 pm	Pisces
Nov 1	7:57 am	Aries

Mars Positions 1930 – 2000

1989
Jan 19	3:11 am	Taurus
Mar 11	3:51 am	Gemini
Apr 28	11:37 pm	Cancer
Jun 16	9:10 am	Leo
Aug 3	8:35 am	Virgo
Sep 19	9:38 am	Libra
Nov 4	12:29 am	Scorpio
Dec 17	11:57 pm	Sagittarius

1990
Jan 29	9:10 am	Capricorn
Mar 11	10:54 am	Aquarius
Apr 20	5:09 pm	Pisces
May 31	2:11 am	Aries
Jul 12	9:44 am	Taurus
Aug 31	6:40 am	Gemini
Dec 14	2:46 am	Taurus

1991
Jan 20	8:15 pm	Gemini
Apr 2	7:49 pm	Cancer
May 26	7:19 am	Leo
Jul 15	7:36 am	Virgo
Sep 1	1:38 am	Libra
Oct 16	2:05 pm	Scorpio
Nov 28	9:19 pm	Sagittarius

1992
Jan 9	4:47 am	Capricorn
Feb 17	11:38 pm	Aquarius
Mar 27	9:04 pm	Pisces
May 5	4:36 pm	Aries
Jun 14	10:56 am	Taurus
Jul 26	1:59 am	Gemini
Sep 12	1:05 am	Cancer

1993
Apr 27	6:40 pm	Leo
Jun 23	2:42 am	Virgo
Aug 11	8:10 pm	Libra
Sep 26	9:15 pm	Scorpio
Nov 9	12:29 am	Sagittarius
Dec 19	7:34 pm	Capricorn

1994
Jan 27	11:05 pm	Aquarius
Mar 7	6:01 am	Pisces
Apr 14	1:02 pm	Aries
May 23	5:37 pm	Taurus
Jul 3	5:30 pm	Gemini
Aug 16	2:15 pm	Cancer
Oct 4	10:48 am	Leo
Dec 12	6:32 am	Virgo

1995
Jan 22	6:48 pm	Leo
May 25	11:09 am	Virgo
Jul 21	4:21 pm	Libra
Sep 7	2:00 am	Scorpio
Oct 20	4:02 pm	Sagittarius
Nov 30	8:58 am	Capricorn

1996
Jan 8	6:02 am	Aquarius
Feb 15	6:50 am	Pisces
Mar 24	10:12 am	Aries
May 2	1:16 pm	Taurus
Jun 12	9:42 am	Gemini
Jul 25	1:32 pm	Cancer
Sep 9	3:02 pm	Leo
Oct 30	2:13 am	Virgo

1997
Jan 3	3:10 am	Libra
Mar 8	2:50 pm	Virgo
Jun 19	3:30 am	Libra
Aug 14	3:42 am	Scorpio
Sep 28	5:22 pm	Sagittarius
Nov 9	12:33 am	Capricorn
Dec 18	1:37 am	Aquarius

1998
Jan 25	4:26 am	Pisces
Mar 4	11:18 am	Aries
Apr 12	8:05 pm	Taurus
May 23	10:42 pm	Gemini
Jul 6	4:00 am	Cancer
Aug 20	2:16 pm	Leo
Oct 7	7:28 am	Virgo
Nov 27	5:10 am	Libra

1999
Jan 26	6:59 am	Scorpio
May 5	4:32 pm	Libra
Jul 4	10:59 pm	Scorpio
Sep 2	2:29 pm	Sagittarius
Oct 16	8:35 pm	Capricorn
Nov 26	1:56 am	Aquarius

2000
Jan 3	10:01 pm	Pisces
Feb 11	8:04 pm	Aries
Mar 22	8:25 pm	Taurus
May 3	2:18 pm	Gemini
Jun 16	7:30 am	Cancer
Jul 31	8:21 pm	Leo
Sep 16	7:19 pm	Virgo
Nov 3	9:00 pm	Libra
Dec 23	9:37 am	Scorpio

Also by ACS Publications

All About Astrology Series of booklets
The American Atlas, Expanded 5th Edition (Shanks)
The American Ephemeris Series 2001-2010
The American Ephemeris for the 20th Century [Noon or Midnight] 1900 to 2000, Rev. 5th Ed.
The American Ephemeris for the 21st Century [Noon or Midnight] 2000-2050, Rev. 2nd Ed.
The American Heliocentric Ephemeris 1901-2000
The American Heliocentric Ephemeris 2001-2050
The American Sidereal Ephemeris 1976-2000, 2nd Edition
The American Sidereal Ephemeris 2001-2025
Asteroid Goddesses (George & Bloch)
Astro-Alchemy (Negus)
Astrological Insights into Personality (Lundsted)
Astrology for the Light Side of the Brain (Rogers-Gallagher)
Basic Astrology: A Guide for Teachers & Students (Negus)
Basic Astrology: A Workbook for Students (Negus)
The Book of Jupiter (Waram)
The Book of Neptune (Waram)
The Book of Pluto (Forrest)
The Book of Saturn (Dobyns)
The Book of Uranus (Negus)
The Changing Sky (Forrest)
Complete Horoscope Interpretation (Pottenger)
Cosmic Combinations (Negus)
Dial Detective (Simms)
Easy Astrology Guide (Pottenger)
Easy Tarot Guide (Masino)
Expanding Astrology's Universe (Dobyns)
Finding our Way Through the Dark (George)
Future Signs (Simms)
The International Atlas, Revised 4th Edition
Hands That Heal (Bodine)
Healing with the Horoscope (Pottenger)
The Inner Sky (Forrest)
The Michelsen Book of Tables (Michelsen)
New Insights into Astrology (Press)
The Night Speaks (Forrest)
The Only Way to... Learn Astrology, Vols. I-VI (March & McEvers)
        Volume I - Basic Principles
        Volume II - Math & Interpretation Techniques
        Volume III - Horoscope Analysis
        Volume IV- Learn About Tomorrow: Current Patterns
        Volume V - Learn About Relationships: Synastry Techniques
        Volume VI - Learn About Horary and Electional Astrology
Planetary Heredity (M. Gauquelin)
Planets on the Move (Dobyns/Pottenger)
Psychology of the Planets (F. Gauquelin)
Spirit Guides (Belhayes)
Tables of Planetary Phenomena (Michelsen)
Twelve Wings of the Eagle (Simms)
Your Magical Child (Simms)
Your Starway to Love (Pottenger), 2nd Edition

Personalized Readings from Maritha Pottenger...

Get your own personalized reading from the author of this book. Maritha has designed a series of customized reports based on your personal astrological data.

Take advantage of this opportunity to understand yourself better using the tools of this well-respected astrologer/ counselor.

Here are some of her most popular readings:

Planetary Profile
Find out what makes you special! Wisdom is power, use this wisdom to transform your life.
Planetary Profile   (PP-BPLFC) $29.95

Your Astro Analysis
Learn astrology using *your horoscope* as your guide!
Your Astro Analysis   (YAA-BPLFC) $29.95

Relocation Profile
Relocation astrology is a valuable tool for making choices and understanding the changes you experience as you move from place to place.
Relocation Profile   (RP-BPLFC) $24.95

Compatibility Profiles
These reports analyze you and another person separately; identifies what each of you requires/desires from the relationship.
Romantic Partners   (CPL-BPLFC) $24.95
Friends   (CPF-BPLFC) $24.95
Business Colleagues   (CPC-BPLFC) $24.95

PAST LIVES
CUSTOM READING

Maritha Pottenger, the astrologer who wrote **Past Lives, Future Choices** has also developed customized readings that compliment the book. These personalized readings use your birth data and are written *just for you.*

Your custom reading will include information from the book **Past Lives, Future Choices**—*and more*! Don't worry about doing any of the calculations or work involved, just order **Your Past Lives** custom reading today!

Your Past Lives will explain so many mysteries: irrational fears, destructive relationships, flashbacks, feeling of familiarity, deeply rooted habit patterns, and skills that seem to come so naturally.

Order your 15-25 page custom reading today! Find out what the stars have to say about **Your Past Lives**!

Your Past Lives Reading YPL-BPLFC $24.95

Prices subject to change. Shipping and handling will be added.

♈ ♉ ♊ ♋ ♌ ♍ ♎ ♏ ♐ ♑ ♒ ♓

Astro Communications Services, Inc.
5521 Ruffin Road, San Diego, CA 92123

1-800-888-9983

Operators available Mon-Fri 8am to 5pm Pacific Time

NOTES

NOTES

NOTES

NOTES

NOTES